Alchemy of Bones

ALCHEMY OF BONES

Chicago's Luetgert Murder Case of 1897

Robert Loerzel

University of Illinois Press
Urbana and Chicago

Library of Congress Cataloging-in-Publication Data
Loerzel, Robert, 1966–
Alchemy of bones : Chicago's Luetgert Murder Case
of 1897 / Robert Loerzel.
p.   cm.
Includes bibliographical references and index.
ISBN 0-252-02858-9 (cloth : alk. paper)
1. Luetgert, Adolph Louis, 1845–1899.
2. Murder—Illinois—Chicago.
3. Murder—Investigation—Illinois—Chicago.
4. Trials (Murder)—Illinois—Chicago.
I. Title.
HV6534.C4L64   2003
364.15'23'092—dc21   2002154447

CONTENTS

ILLUSTRATIONS FOLLOW PAGES 56, 114, 170, AND 226

Alchemy of Bones

INTRODUCTION

WHILE FLIPPING THROUGH a scrapbook at the Palatine Historical Society one day in 1995, I came across the following article clipped from the October 23, 1897, *Palatine Independent:* "Fred A. Smith of this place and another reporter, of the *Chicago Journal,* caused a sensation among the other Chicago dailies by reporting the actions and discussions of the Luetgert jury while in their room. It is the first time that such a thing has been accomplished during the progress of such an important trial. They obtained the news by means of the air shaft running through the room, one of them being lowered in a chair, suspended by a rope from the room above, and watched the proceedings through the air register."

What was this important trial that these correspondents took such pains to cover? I had never heard of the Luetgert case, but this brief glimpse of it piqued my curiosity. I visited Chicago's Harold Washington Library and looked at some city newspapers from the week of the *Independent* story. I discovered the Luetgert trial filled page after page in the dailies. Eventually I learned that newspapers in Chicago and some other cities had covered the story of Louise Luetgert's disappearance in great detail for more than a year.

This book is the story of Adolph Luetgert and his trial on charges of murdering his wife, presented in narrative form. Wherever people are quoted, their words are taken from newspaper articles, courtroom testimony, and other historical documents. The sources of the quotations are listed in the notes at the end of this book rather than in the main narrative.

It's impossible to know whether these people were quoted correctly. In some cases the quotations were almost certainly cleaned up by reporters or editors. For instance, when a newpaper publishes a comment from an interview that runs for several paragraphs with no ellipses to indicate gaps, it strains credibility to suggest that the reporter was able to capture every word. One person's style of speech may also vary over the course of many newspaper articles, indicating that the journalists probably took different approaches in the ways they conveyed dialect and slang and the extent to which they fixed grammatical errors. Whenever possible, I have checked articles for accuracy by comparing them to stories in rival publications. I believe the resulting narrative closely approximates what these people said more than a century ago—about as closely as possible, given the available records. It also accurately represents how these incidents were reported to the public in the newspapers of the time. In addition, it shows how the people of Chicago spoke and wrote in the 1890s. They were not always articulate—especially when English was not their native language—but their diction was colorful.

◆◆◆

The Luetgert story offers us a glimpse of a moment in Chicago history, showing how a sensational trial was conducted at the end of the nineteenth century and how the public reacted. The criminal cases that get the biggest newspaper headlines rarely reflect the typical functioning of the criminal justice system. They do offer, however, the most detailed record available of the way the courts determine guilt or innocence. Moreover, they are a form of public theater and spectacle, nearly universally discussed, that shapes a community's views of right and wrong and the best ways to mete out justice.

In his book *Crime and Punishment in American History*, Lawrence M. Friedman describes the role that major trials assumed in American society as the country's criminal justice system evolved in the late nineteenth century. "Major courtroom trials, even though they are posed, hypocritical, stage-managed, even though they sift and twist facts, and distort evidence for the sake of making points, are nonetheless extremely telling," Friedman writes. "At times they can lay bare the soul of a given society. . . . These shows were messengers, preachers; they carried tales of conventional morality, stories of evil and good, to the audience inside and outside of the courtroom."

The Luetgert case was hardly the first trial to generate a public sensation and intense press coverage. Many such cases occurred in the nineteenth century, including a few in Chicago. The booming city had a reputation for sin and lawlessness, inspiring books with lurid titles such as *Chicago, Satan's Sanctum,* and major crimes in Chicago often drew national attention. The city's most famous trials before Luetgert were the Haymarket Square bombing case in 1886 and the murder of Dr. Patrick Henry Cronin in 1889.

Both those cases involved two of the key police officials who later worked on the Luetgert case, Michael Schaack and Herman Schuettler. The controversies surrounding those cases suggest that the Chicago police of that era could not be trusted to conduct any major investigation in an entirely professional manner. Although newspapers would salute particular police officers for their bravery or ingenuity, the department as a whole was infamous for graft, brutality, and political cronyism. Several years after the Luetgert trial, a civic commission summed up the department's reputation by saying, "The police of Chicago are piano movers, bums, cripples, janitors, ward heelers—anything but policemen! They have no respect for the law and they depend on the aldermen to get them out of trouble."

One of the most striking aspects of the Luetgert case is the press coverage. That first clipping I found at the Palatine Historical Society reminded me of the great play and film *The Front Page* and its portrayal of the antics of Chicago newspaper reporters. In the late nineteenth and early twentieth centuries, Chicago's reporters were highly competitive and famous for playing practical jokes on one another—or on the city's political windbags. Newspapermen (and the few female reporters) resorted to unethical and even criminal shenanigans, all in the quest of an exclusive story. They were known to ransack homes and offices. They often impersonated police officers, coroners, and other officials to get an inside word. Some eavesdropped on meetings that were supposed to be closed to the public. And when officials refused to release documents, some reporters simply stole them.

"There has always been a special quality, an extra dimension to the Chicago news-gathering rivalry," the longtime Chicago reporter John J. McPhaul wrote in *Deadlines and Monkeyshines.* "Chicagoans added the extra fillip, the broad brush of slapstick and derring-do." McPhaul notes that the authors of *The Front Page,* Ben Hecht and Charlie MacArthur, had to dilute the truth in their play because the real stories seemed too outlandish. They had "misgivings about how far they dared go with the truth lest it be rejected as fantasy."

Despite the breathtaking ethical lapses of Chicago reporters and their tendencies toward sensationalism, I found some excellent journalism on the Luetgert case. The reporters who covered the case, most of whom wrote without bylines, deserve great credit for chronicling history on a deadline. The newspapers published trial coverage far more detailed than anything in today's publications. Even in a recent blockbuster case such as the O. J. Simpson trial, newspapers and magazines did not publish entire transcripts of a day's court proceedings (although watching the case on CNN or Court TV provided a similarly detailed experience).

Although one may question the ethics of the reporters who surreptitiously listened in on the deliberations of the Luetgert jury, they left us a detailed record of the jurors' debates.

The newspapers also reflected 1890s prejudices toward Chicago's immigrant population and an uneasiness about a newly assertive generation of women. People of German or Polish descent were sometimes ridiculed as simpleminded because they lacked fluency in English, while the newspapers questioned the morality of women who dared to attend a macabre public spectacle such as the Luetgert trial.

Lauren Rabinovitz provides some context for this attitude toward women in her book *For the Love of Pleasure: Women, Movies, and Culture in Turn-of-the-Century Chicago*. Before 1880 women in American cities rarely appeared in public unless they were accompanied. "If loitering and alone, a woman risked being regarded as a prostitute," Rabinovitz writes. But the 1880s and 1890s saw a huge increase in the number of women with jobs in cities. Chicago attracted women workers at a rate three times higher than the national average.

The dramatic result was that unaccompanied women suddenly filled the sidewalks. It was still considered improper for a woman to wander about the city casually, looking around at her surroundings in the same fashion as a man might. Rabinovitz argues that Chicago's department stores and the 1893 Columbian Exposition provided venues where women could become spectators. Although Rabinovitz does not make the connection, the women who attended the Luetgert trial also fit into this pattern. As women began to "erode the male's exclusive right to the city," not everyone was sure how to react. Many people referred to single women living apart from their families as "women adrift," who were "understood as lost and, therefore, requiring saving."

The Luetgert case offers one of the earliest examples of testimony by scientific experts. At the time the science of identifying fingerprints was still being developed and had not yet been tested in the criminal courts. Only a couple of weeks after Luetgert's arrest, a Cook County judge handling a civil lawsuit refused to allow the use of X-ray pictures in the courtroom because the science supporting these mysterious images of the human body's interior hadn't been sufficiently well established. Meanwhile, one of the era's most famous criminologists was the Italian physician Cesare Lombroso, who believed certain physical stigmata—such as enormous jaws or handle-shaped ears—mark someone as a born criminal.

The Luetgert case was the first trial featuring testimony by an anthropologist, making it a precursor of the field now known as forensic anthropology. Even as the scientists took the witness stand, however, the other news of the day included alternately superstitious and skeptical stories about palm readers, hypnotists, ghosts, and alchemists.

Luetgert's trial probably wouldn't have become famous had it not featured one unusual circumstance: it was a murder case in which no corpse—or at least, very few remnants of a corpse—had been found. Until Adolph Luetgert was arrested in 1897, few people had been indicted on murder charges unless authorities had a corpse to prove that a murder had taken place.

No doubt many murderers over the ages have escaped prosecution by disposing of the corpse. One person who may have succeeded at this gruesome tactic was Herman Mudgett, alias Dr. Henry H. Holmes. In a sensational trial only a year before the Luetgert case, the former Chicagoan was convicted of one murder in Philadelphia. A corpse was found in that case, but other victims may have vanished at Mudgett's hands. Before he was hanged, Mudgett confessed to killing twenty-seven people, and he was suspected of murdering even more. Inside the castlelike home Mudgett had built on Chicago's South Side, police found evil-smelling odors, human bones, torture chambers, trapdoors, a crematory, vats of acid and quicklime (which he had apparently used to dissolve the flesh from his victims' bones), and an apparatus for articulating skeletons so that they would be suitable for sale to medical schools. Many Chicago residents probably recalled Mudgett's chamber of horrors when they heard about the Luetgert case in 1897.

The Luetgert case had at least a couple of precedents in the world of fiction. As they were covering the Luetgert trial, some newspapers pointed out parallels to Melville Davisson Post's 1896 short story "The Corpus Delicti." The tale graphically describes a murderer dismembering his victim's body and dissolving it with sulfuric acid. Although the evidence against the killer seems overwhelming, he is acquitted because the prosecutors have no corpse to prove that a murder had occurred. In Oscar Wilde's 1891 novel *The Picture of Dorian Gray,* the title character murders one man and then blackmails another into destroying the corpse. Wilde describes the devices necessary to dissolve a human body as "a large mahogany chest of chemicals, with a long coil of steel and platinum wire and two rather curiously-shaped iron clamps."

The most important legal precedent for the Luetgert case was a widely publicized murder trial in 1850. Dr. John White Webster was convicted in Boston of murdering and dismembering Dr. George Parkman, one of his colleagues on the faculty of Harvard Medical College, leaving behind some 150 charred bones and a set of dentures. An anatomy professor testified that all the bones had come from one person's skeleton and that they indicated a violent death. A dentist identified the dentures as a set he had once made for Parkman.

The key question of Webster's trial was whether the state had enough evidence to prove corpus delicti. Despite the use of the Latin word *corpus,* this legal phrase does not refer solely to the corpse in a murder case. Rather, it signifies the body of evidence showing that a crime has been committed. In most murder cases, however, the victim's body constitutes the key piece of evidence that a murder has taken place.

Until the Parkman case legal authorities in the English and American courts insisted that corpus delicti in a murder case be proven by direct rather than circumstantial evidence, and the courts did not allow room for even a reasonable doubt. As Robert Sullivan wrote in his history of the Parkman case, the fact of the murder had to be proved "to an absolute certainty, or beyond the least doubt. After this had been established absolutely, then the burden of proof was on the prosecution to show that the defendant had committed the crime beyond a reasonable doubt."

Nevertheless, the judge in Webster's trial, Chief Justice Lemuel Shaw, did not follow this theory when he instructed the jury. "It is sometimes said by judges that a jury ought never to convict in a capital case unless the dead body is found," Shaw said. "That as a general proposition is true. It sometimes happens, however, that the dead body cannot be found, even though proof of death is clear—for example, a murder at sea when the body is thrown overboard." If the jurors decided the false teeth and bones had belonged to Dr. Parkman, then that was good enough to establish corpus delicti, Justice Shaw said. This circumstantial evidence was sufficient to prove the murder had happened.

Even before the jury came back with its verdict of guilty, some legal observers condemned Shaw's legal logic. A respected attorney watching the case,

Rufus Choate, remarked: "Well, Judge Shaw made law tonight. Beginning tonight all that's required to establish the *corpus delicti* is a reasonable certainty. No longer is it necessary to prove by direct evidence or actual inspection of the body. That's a major change, I must say." Later someone identifying himself only as a "member of the legal profession" published a pamphlet criticizing Shaw for issuing a decision with no legal precedent. "Proof of homicide requires positive evidence of the perpetration of the crime or the actual production of the body," the anonymous critic wrote.

Despite such attacks, Shaw's instructions to the jury became a groundbreaking legal precedent. "Virtually every student of criminal law has been taught . . . Shaw's charge to the jury in the Webster trial," Sullivan wrote in 1971. "Perhaps no other case is more often cited and quoted today on the criminal side of the American courts."

The Webster trial set the stage for the Luetgert case almost five decades later. Once again, the mystery was not simply who had committed a murder but whether a murder had taken place at all.

1 Omens

THE OMENS were against him. First came the sparrow, somehow gaining entrance to the jail's waiting room. It flitted against the walls and windows all afternoon, looking for a way out—a bad sign for Luetgert, one of the guards said. A bird had flown into the jail few years earlier, the guard remembered, the day before a prisoner named George Painter was found guilty of murder. Was it just coincidence that a bird had come into this cage again, the day before the Luetgert jury began deliberations?

John Whitman scoffed at the supposed omen. The jailer didn't know about any bird foretelling Painter's guilt, and he doubted that this bird had anything to do with Adolph Louis Luetgert. As far as he knew, the fluttering of a sparrow in a jail signified nothing.

Even if Luetgert knew about the sparrow, it did not appear to disturb him. He talked about what he would do after the jury set him free. He would exhibit himself in one of those dime museums, alongside the skeletons and freaks, demanding a daily fee of $5,000. Once he had saved enough money to go back into business, he would open a downtown saloon, with a sideshow of curios from his trial, including the notorious "middle vat."

A second sign came with the dawn, when a screech owl pierced the quiet outside the Cook County Jail. Some people on the street caught sight of the bird beating its wings against the windows of the towering gray courthouse. The owl fell to the ground, and they captured it, taking it into a saloon. The *Chicago Journal* called it the "Bird of Evil Omen."

A thousand men and women fought their way into the elevators and up the three flights of stairs to Judge Richard Tuthill's courtroom, hoping to hear the trial's final words. Only a few hundred made it past the blue-coated bailiffs. Some found places to sit on the long oaken benches, but most were content to stand by the windows or on the railings. The crowd included the usual quota of females, the ones the papers derisively labeled "morbid women." Many of the same women who had been coming day after day vied for seats behind the clerk's desk, where they would have the best view. When the trial began in late August 1897, they had worn summer hats with brilliant flowers. Now it was October, and autumn's nodding plumes adorned their hats.

At the courtroom door the bailiff Edward Cool stopped a little woman who wore an old straw hat over her gray locks. He inquired what business she had in court.

"I am Mrs. Luetgert," she said.

Her statement caused a brief stir. Someone in the sheriff's office dashed hatless down the stairs to catch a glimpse of the lady who claimed to be Luetgert's missing wife, Louise. The mob struggled to get closer to her, but it quickly became obvious that this was just another hoax.

Now the woman said she was a teacher. One of Judge Tuthill's daughters was in her class, she said, and she had a letter from the judge requesting the bailiffs to admit her. They looked at the letter and allowed her into the court, which was noisy with the hum of voices.

The room hushed when the judge came in and the prosecutor, Charles Deneen, began to speak. Pale and tired, he addressed the jury at first in low tones. The audiences had often been boisterous during the trial, but no one even whispered now. The messenger boys ceased their vigorous gum chewing. The spectators in the back rows strained to hear another variation of the story they had been hearing for months: what had happened on May 1, 1897, the day Luetgert's wife disappeared; what had happened that night in Luetgert's sausage factory; and what the police had found inside the vat.

Luetgert appeared to be the least-concerned person in the tense courtroom. He occasionally rocked his chair on its hind legs or closed his eyes as if drifting off to sleep. Luetgert's face was florid and ruddy, and his expression often seemed to show a man quite satisfied with himself. He was five feet, ten inches tall, broad-shouldered, and heavy. Writers used the adjective *thick* to describe his hair, his hands, his neck, and the fat on his cheeks.

Deneen's voice gained strength as he went on. "Is the law so weak that it cannot cope with skillful, fiendish, inhuman crimes?" he asked. "Can the skill of a criminal cover up all traces of guilt? And the more fiendish the guilt, the less chance the law has to cope with it? Not at all. She will not reappear. You have her bones and her rings. You have her tooth and her hairpin. You have her corset steels. . . . She will not reappear. She is dead. He has treated her so. He has treated her memory so."

As Deneen spoke, a couple of *Chicago Journal* reporters were looking for a way to sneak some rope, boards, speaking-tube pipe, and pulleys into the courthouse's attic. The newspapermen, Fred A. Smith and W. H. Stuart, decided that the only way to carry out their secret mission was to advance straight through the multitude of spectators and sheriff's deputies in and around the courthouse and hope for the best. They packed their gear into a dry-goods box, covering it with coarse brown paper and nailing a board across the top for a handle. They carried it up to the courthouse entrance, where the deputies demanded to know its contents.

"Refreshments for the all-night newspaper crowd," one of the reporters mumbled.

Satisfied, the officers waved them through. As the reporters pushed into the horde, their box drew many curious glances. They made their way through the halls and up the stairs, repeating their ruse to the guards on each floor. They got as far as the fourth story, where the men and women stood so close together that Smith and Stuart had to stop. They set down their heavy box on a landing and rested a few moments, only to be startled by two deputy sheriffs running down the stairs. "It's all off. They have had a tip," Stuart whispered. But the deputies didn't betray the slightest suspicion about the box; instead they offered to clear a path through the crowd.

At last the pair reached an empty corner of the sixth floor and climbed an iron stairway up to the roof. From there they opened a set of folding doors and lowered the box eight feet into the attic. Reentering the building, they sent word to the *Journal* office that the apparatus was ready.

In the courtroom Deneen had finished his speech. One of the few female journalists covering the trial, a *Chicago Chronicle* reporter who wrote under the byline "Katharine," noticed how calm Luetgert seemed. Sitting in the front row, she leaned over the railing and whispered to him, "I am terribly nervous, ain't you?"

"No, not a bit," Luetgert said, laughing. "Here, give me your hand." Katharine reached out her right hand to him, and he said, "Take courage. That will give you some of mine. Don't you feel it?" Luetgert pointed to her left hand and she gave him that one as well. "I am not nervous," he said. "You should not be. I am brave."

It was about four o'clock when Judge Tuthill began reading his instructions to the jury. As the shadows lengthened, the electric lights came on. The judge had come to the trickiest part of the entire case: how to prove a murder when no corpse has been found. "To prove the *corpus delicti* in a case of murder," he said, "does not require the state or prosecution to produce the body of the alleged deceased, or any part thereof, or the testimony of any witness who has seen the same since the commission of the alleged crime."

As the judge droned out the words on the verdict form—the words the jurors were supposed to use if they found Luetgert guilty—the defendant displayed his first visible reaction to the day's proceedings. A *Chicago Record* reporter wrote that he "winced like a wounded animal."

"Now, gentlemen," the judge said, "you may retire and consider your verdict."

A sigh of relief swept over the courtroom. Judge Tuthill looked around sharply at the noise and ordered the room cleared. Luetgert tensed, his fingers flattening out on the arms of his chair. He cast his eyes across the faces of the twelve men filing into the jury room. Their expressions offered no hints regarding how they would vote, but the reporter Katharine, who clearly hoped they would be merciful, thought their choice of attire indicated they were unsympathetic toward Luetgert.

"How I wished that one of those jurymen had worn a scarlet tie," she would write. "The strength of flaming red on one of those twelve men would have helped me to have believed that one of them at least realized what a perilous thing is life. . . . But there was not a gay tie or cravat among those twelve men. Nothing but black and white ones were worn, and I trembled for fear the men who had donned dark-colored ones valued life as little as did Charles Deneen, who pled long and seriously for a brother's life."

The crowd moved out slowly, for the curious hoped to catch one more glance of the sausage maker. Young women gathered around Luetgert and tried to draw him into conversation, but he did not waste much time with them. The bailiff Isaac Reed told Luetgert he would have to go back to the jail, and the pack of court watchers opened a path for the prisoner. Luetgert saw his youngest son come through the crowd, arms outstretched. Luetgert bent forward, murmuring, "Elmer, Elmer," as the five-year-old clasped his hands around his father's neck. Elmer's lips brushed against Luetgert's mustache in a kiss.

"My boy, my boy," Luetgert said, as Reed touched his sleeve. "Yes, in a minute, in a minute," Luetgert told the bailiff. "I must see my son."

"Is it all over, Papa?" the boy asked.

"Not yet, baby, but it will be so today." Luetgert handed the boy back to Mary Charles, a family friend who had been holding the boy during court that day. Luetgert marched over to the jail with tears in his eyes.

By now the *Journal* had dispatched nine reporters to the courthouse. Stuart and William Etten were the decoys. As the newspaper would later report, the two "were stationed in the courtroom to leave the impression that the *Journal* was using the same old-fashioned, plodding means of obtaining news as the representatives of other Chicago dailies." Meanwhile, three *Journal* reporters went to various parts of the courthouse to act as lookouts. Smith took three colleagues—Charles Mitchell, Edwin F. Payne, and Cornelious Rourke—to the attic.

The four men lit their lanterns and unpacked the rope and pulleys that had been deposited into the attic earlier. They entered a tunnel that was four feet wide and barely as high. As soon as they pressed down on the tunnel's sheet-iron floor, the metal gave out a loud groan. Fearing the noise would be heard throughout the building, the men set down some boards along the tunnel's lining, which quieted the creaks.

After crawling fifteen feet they came to the building's west air shaft, a sheer drop of 150 feet. The shaft was walled with smooth, solid stone, but it was not completely black. Beams of light shone into the darkness from vents in the eight jury rooms—including the chamber on the third floor that the Luetgert jury would soon be entering.

The four men crouched at the shaft's edge, where they had planned to set up a pulley. Three of them would use the rope to lower the other man down the shaft. But a large water pipe near the edge didn't give them enough space to set up the pulley, so instead they looped the rope twice around the pipe. One end of the rope was fastened to a strong plank seat. They slipped the seat over the tunnel's sheet-iron edge.

The reporters hesitated. Since they had nothing to use as a brace, they could be pulled into the shaft by a sudden jerk of the rope. The sharp metal edge might cut the rope before the man in the shaft had descended even five feet, dropping him far down to the basement—and almost certainly to his death. The *Journal* reporters would later claim they gained some courage when they looked out through narrow chinks in the attic wall and caught a glimpse of rival newspapermen on the roof of an adjoining building, vying for the best vantage points to peer into the jury room with their spyglasses.

And a sound drifted up into the attic from four stories below: reporters for the other papers were rushing about and discussing the case. The *Journal* men decided to go on with their mission.

They laid some strong burlap across the edge of the shaft, hoping it would prevent the rope from fraying. They lowered the sixty feet of speaking tube down the shaft. They chose Smith, the lightest man, to make the descent. They tied one end of a string to a nail in the metal floor, and Smith put the ball of string in his pocket. He got onto the plank seat, clinging to the rope until he was a few feet below the tunnel. He ordered the others to pay out the rope. As the rope made its first turn around the pipe, a wailing sound echoed through the building's dark corners. Mitchell, Payne, and Rourke paused to moisten the pipe with oil from one of their lanterns. That reduced the din as they continued lowering Smith.

He swung back and forth in the six-by-four-foot airshaft, using his knees as cushions to keep the wooden seat from striking the walls. He had thought of this in advance and worn an extra pair of trousers for padding. As he neared the third floor, he heard a confused noise below him, sounding unmistakably like the Luetgert jurors retiring to their room. Smith yanked on the twine—the signal to stop—and the creaking rope became silent. After a momentary lull in the jury room, the voices became louder, and Smith decided it was safe to go down a bit farther. He tugged twice on the twine. The rope lowered him to the third floor. Brushing cobwebs from his face with one hand and holding the rope with the other, Smith came to rest within two feet of the Luetgert jury.

As the sound of the jurors, arguing over bones and rings, came through the register, Smith repeated their words, whispering into a funnel on the end of the speaking tube. One of the reporters in the attic listened to the earpiece on the other end of the tube and jotted down the jurors' words.

It soon became clear the jurors weren't going to have an easy time reaching a decision. At times it sounded as if they might break out into a brawl. After a while Smith heard one of the jurors suggest a compromise: find Luetgert guilty but sentence him to prison rather than death. "If Mrs. Luetgert should turn up," he said, "we would feel pretty badly after giving this man the extreme penalty."

Several jurors protested. "This man is either innocent or guilty," said a juror Smith recognized as William Harlev. "If guilty, he is a monster, and there is not a scaffold in the country high enough for him. If innocent, he should go free."

Smith whispered it all into the tube. A cold draft blew on him steadily, and as the hours wore on, his arms and legs grew numb.

Outside two thousand people had gathered, waiting for news. Entire families lingered in the street, some of the women holding infants. Businessmen in high hats and patent-leathers stood among dusty, grimy laborers, unattended women, chattering urchins, and bicyclers trundling their wheels.

Lacking any news, the spectators talked about the trial and guessed what the jurors would decide. The crowd quickly surrounded and questioned anyone coming out of the courthouse, and the police repeatedly ordered the sidewalks cleared. It had been one of the hottest autumns in the history of Chicago, but tonight was cold, and the chill wind sent shivering women into the shelter of window embrasures and doorways. Men lacking overcoats ducked into nearby saloons.

The people watched the lighted windows on the third and fourth stories of the courthouse, searching for signs of action in the prosecutor's office or the courtroom. Others looked toward the jail, gazing up at the window of Luetgert's cell. They could see the barred door and occasionally thought they had caught a glimpse of the prisoner.

A rumor that the jury had sent for blankets crept through the crowd. Hundreds of tired people took this as their signal to set out for home, but scores remained, sitting on the curbs. Some of them walked around the block, returning from time to time to inquire for news. Hotel waiting rooms, saloons, and cigar and drug stores were thronged for two blocks around the jail. At midnight a hundred men and a dozen women were still on the sidewalks.

"Through all the long, chilly hours of waiting no loud talking or any kind of disturbance occurred," the *Chicago Daily Tribune* noted. "It was simply an eagerly curious crowd watching for the curtain to descend on the most remarkable murder case of this generation."

2 Legends

STREAKS OF SMOKE trailed behind the steamboats on Lake Michigan, where the azure water was speckled with the white sails of schooners. It resembled an ocean more than a lake, extending past the horizon. Near the breakwater and the lighthouse, however, the blue gave way to brown and gray.

A nauseating reek rose from the Chicago River as it emptied its black, oily contents into the lake. Bloated carcasses of beasts floated in the water, which was so thick with sludge that some people claimed they had seen rats scurry across the river.

The land around the river's mouth had been a patch of swamp only sixty years before, but now a city stood there, one that thrilled American entrepreneurs while frightening some European visitors, who called it perplexing, excessive, barbarous, frowning, and satanic, "a gigantic peepshow of utter horror." Iron-cored, masonry-clad skyscrapers rose fourteen, fifteen, or even twenty stories in the city's center, clustered close together. The architecture was blunt, the scale of these immense, rectangular blocks overwhelming the ornamental details. The gridlike pattern of windows resembled the steel skeletons underneath.

The walls of the buildings were black or gray; if they hadn't been that color when first constructed, the heavy air-borne soot had dulled their hue since then, etching dark designs on the brick and terra cotta. A foul stench clung in every throat. In the downtown alone, twelve hundred chimneys connected to two thousand boilers spewed out bituminous smoke, burning millions of tons of the dirty "coal of the West" each year. On some days the smoke kept the city in continuous twilight. Inside the offices and along the streets, the gas jets and electric lights burned all day. Countless columns of white, gray, and black rose to merge into a murky dome above the endless avenues. The smoke hung there, but it did not merely hover. The sooty air periodically swooped down in gusts, swirling about in the streets and choking pedestrians' lungs. "The smoke of Chicago has a peculiar and aggressive individuality," an observer noted.

The muddy, littered sidewalks and streets were a motley patchwork of flagstones, asphalt, and planks, all somehow balanced atop what once had been a marsh. The people scurried down these thoroughfares, dodging streetcars. The city's mighty din—the rustle of people rushing about; the clacking of horses pulling hansom cabs, wagons, and carriages; the cracking of whips; and the constant hammering and riveting of construction—was punctuated with the ringing of locomotive bells. Grip cars, trolleys, elevated trains, and steam locomotives blocked streets everywhere, crisscrossing one another's tracks.

Crowds poured in and out of the skyscrapers' ground-floor arches. Beggar and baron; immigrant and native; laborer, clerk, businessman, and shopper—all brushed against one another in the chaos. The men wore black, while the women wore lighter and more colorful hues, but they all wore hats. Impatient deliverymen clutching telegrams surged forward. People stretched out their arms to catch their hats, blown off their heads by sudden gusts. Yells came from policemen, pedestrians, and drivers: "Out of the way! Look out!" And above the sidewalks, additional multitudes went about their day's work. The pedestrians at ground level could catch only glimpses of the workers moving from office to office.

Chicago was twenty-six miles from its northernmost point to its southernmost and more than fourteen miles across. Cottages, flats, tenements, churches, mills, and warehouses filled the flat land surrounding the downtown skyscrapers. North, along Lake Shore Drive, the castles of the business magnates, made from great blocks of rough-hewn granite with wide, round arches for doors and windows, stood on tree-shaded avenues. In some places the homes of the rich stood not far from shanties with broken windows and peeling paint or empty patches of scrubby waste, choked with rubble and weeds.

Farther north was Lake View, a neighborhood that had been a separate municipality known for its celery farms until Chicago annexed it in 1889. Shops sprang up in clusters around the main intersections there and along the cable-car lines. The "best families" dwelt in beautiful, spacious houses toward the east along the lake shore, havens from the bustle of downtown. West of Clark Street, however, lived "a different class of people," as one of the well-to-do residents put it. These were the Germans and Poles, along with some Swedes and Irish—immigrant laborers in the Deering Harvester Works, the iron foundry, and the Luetgert sausage factory. Several brickyards operated in the area, and when their clay pits filled with water, the neighborhood children used them as swimming holes. In Lake View the Germans had their own city within the city, their own businesses, schools, churches, hospitals, newspapers, gymnastic halls, and beer gardens. Many had barely any need to speak English.

In southwest Lake View the A. L. Luetgert Sausage and Packing Company, a five-story brick-and-stone building on the south side of Diversey Street, towered over the saloons and workmen's frame homes on the street's north side. Adolph Louis Luetgert and his family lived in an ornate, two-story wooden house just south of the factory, facing east toward Hermitage Avenue, surrounded by shrubs and fruit trees.

The Germans and Poles in Lake View called Luetgert a king, giving the brawny, bearded man a wide berth when he came down the sidewalk with his fearsome great Danes. When he spoke to his neighbors, they pulled off their hats in respect. Millions of pounds of sausage, including a popular sort of German salami known as *Dauerwurst*, were carted away from the huge brick building and sent all over the country. By some estimates, it was the nation's largest sausage-manufacturing concern. Luetgert's neighbors had inflated ideas about his wealth, believing he was a millionaire. There were many stories going around the neighborhood about Louis Luetgert—that was what his friends and family called him, Louis. Only strangers used his first name.

On his arrest in 1897, facts from Luetgert's life that had previously seemed unremarkable took on sinister meanings. It was said he had once committed arson to further his business career. There may have been nothing unusual about the death of his first wife twenty years before—records show she died from peritonitis—but now the *Tribune* said she had "died very suddenly during confinement. There were some rumors going around at the time, and it never has been properly understood how the woman came to her death." A German newspaper said it was rumored Luetgert had poisoned her.

Three of Luetgert's children had died when they were very young. For a century the Bickneses, Luetgert's second wife's family, would repeat the story that Luetgert had gassed one of his young daughters to death.

The rumors extended to Luetgert's ancestry. Germans in his neighborhood said that, in the old country, his grandfather had been executed by the sword for robbery and murder. Neighbors claimed that Luetgert's father was always getting into trouble with the law. According to the stories, Luetgert had been born in Holland because his mother had been forced to flee from the police in Prussia. A similar legend was passed down years later in the Bicknese family: it was said that Luetgert's father had been notorious in his business dealing, forcing him to keep moving. As a result, according to the legend, Luetgert and his fifteen siblings (at least three of whom died as infants) were all born in different places. At least that part of the rumors was false, however: Luetgert and his siblings had all been born in the small town of Gütersloh.

Telling his own version of his life story, Luetgert omitted any mention of scandal involving his grandfather and father, saying only that his father, Christian Heinrich Lütgert, a tanner by profession, was also a dabbler in real estate and "money matters."

Luetgert—who was born Adolph Ludwig Lütgert—was from Gütersloh, a backwater in the German region of Westphalia. Most of the townspeople were conservative, worshipful toward God and king. When Luetgert and his twin, Heinrich Friedrich ("Fritz"), were born two days after Christmas in 1845, Gütersloh had three thousand people; two-thirds of them made their living by spinning yarn. One of the oldest businesses in town was the Kornbrennerei Lütgert whiskey distillery, which their great-great-great-great-grandfather, Conrad Lütgert, had built in 1689. In the mid-eighteenth century another branch of the family had taken over the distillery. By the time Luetgert was born, his side of the family had been selling hides, tallow, and wool for four generations.

Luetgert studied for seven years at a Lutheran school in Gütersloh and then spent a couple of years as a tanner's apprentice. He left home at about seventeen and walked from town to town in the German countryside for three years, working in many places. Then Luetgert went to London.

"I did anything I could get hold of. The best work I could find was scrubbing in a restaurant nights," he later remembered. "I concluded like thousands of my countrymen to come to America. I came to this country when I was twenty-four years of age, ignorant of the ways of the world, allured from my peaceful German village by tales of the riches to be acquired, reputations established and happiness to be secured in this 'land of the free and home of the brave.' I landed in the United States in 1865 or 1866. I found myself in New York with thirty dollars in my pocket, in a strange land, among strange people and dazed by the sights of a great city."

He spent a few months in Quincy, Illinois, where some family friends lived, and then went to Chicago. Twenty years earlier, when Luetgert was born, Chicago hadn't been much bigger than Gütersloh. By the time he got to Chicago, the city's population was approaching 400,000.

"I knew not a soul," Luetgert said. "I had three cents then. A stranger handed me a quarter that same morning. I bought my breakfast and then went out to hustle for my job."

Luetgert went to some leather stores and asked where he could find a tannery. He soon found a job with the Union Hide and Leather Company. The tannery shut down a month or so later, and Luetgert spent the summer looking for work. While the weather was warm, he helped move houses. When the weather turned cold, he worked at a meatpacking plant. He spent the next few years working in tanneries around Goose Island and along the North Branch of the Chicago River. "I worked early and late," he later wrote. "I saved my money. I was ambitious to be a man among men, to accumulate property and to give my children a better start in life than I had had; and I hoped to leave behind me not only riches but a reputation in which my children would all take pride."

Luetgert was still something of a newcomer to Chicago on October 8, 1871, when the Great Chicago Fire nearly leveled the city, destroying most of the downtown area. When the fire finally ceased its northward march at Lincoln Park, it had claimed a few hundred lives, but it had stopped short of the neighborhood where Luetgert lived. Then, in what seemed like a matter of days, Chicago began to rebuild.

Having saved $4,000 from his jobs at the tanneries, Luetgert went into business for himself in 1872 and married Caroline Roepke. They bought a lot on Chicago's North Side and had a cottage moved there. Luetgert began selling liquor out of the basement. The couple had a boy named Max, who died before he was two. Another boy, Arnold, was born, and then Caroline died in November 1877. Luetgert sent his son to live with Caroline's family until he could find a new wife.

The search lasted only two months. In January 1878 he married Louise Bicknese, who had sailed from Germany five years earlier. Louise (whose name was pronounced "Louisa," in German fashion, and often printed that way) stood five feet tall and weighed 115 pounds, with light hair and a light complexion. A pretty German domestic servant, she knew scarcely a word of English. At the time Luetgert was thirty-two years old, and Louise was twenty-three. In 1879 they sold their property for $10,000, moved to Clybourn and Webster in Lake View, and opened a saloon and liquor store.

One morning that September the corpse of a sixty-four-year-old millwright named Hugh McGowan was found in a barn on Luetgert's property. McGowan's head had been cut open, and an immense plug of tobacco had been shoved down his throat.

McGowan had been missing since September 9, two nights earlier, when he was drinking at Luetgert's saloon. Around ten o'clock a man named Fred Butler was supposed to take him home but left him in the barn instead. The *Chicago Times* said McGowan had been on a "tear" and was put in the barn to get sober. Hugh's seventeen-year-old son, James, went searching for his father that night. He visited Hugh's haunts, including Luetgert's saloon, but the bar had already closed for the night by the time James got there at eleven o'clock.

Luetgert reported discovering the body on September 11. He said the door to the barn had been locked on the inside when he found McGowan. The newspapers reported that an overdose of whiskey had killed the millwright, whom they described as "a hard-drinking man." Years later, however, McGowan's son would recall that although his father was sometimes given to drink, it was unusual for him to stay out an entire night.

Luetgert said McGowan had gone to his barn to sleep because he had been afraid to return home in an intoxicated state. But McGowan's family said they had never given him any trouble over his drinking. So why would he have feared coming home this time? James McGowan thought his father had met a violent end, and he suspected Luetgert might have had something to do with it.

The coroner held an inquest, calling Luetgert as a witness. The panel ruled McGowan had died "from asphyixia caused by a large quid of tobacco lodging in his throat and bronchial tubes while he was in a state of intoxication." James McGowan, however, said his father never used plug tobacco. The wad in his throat had weighed almost two ounces. The son believed someone had rammed it down his father's throat. The tobacco had choked his father senseless, and the attacker had then struck a fatal blow, splitting open the skull.

The son also thought it unusual that little blood had been discovered in the barn, even though his father's head was cracked almost from its crown to the nape of the neck. Moreover, Hugh McGowan was found in an unusual posture for a dead man. The body had been propped up in a sitting position on a low pile of boards. James McGowan believed the coroner's jury had been biased; the jurors were Luetgert's neighbors and friends, he said. The son demanded a postmortem examination. He chose a physician to represent him at the examination and went with him to the morgue. When they arrived, however, they discovered that the examination already had taken place. The son protested, but the coroner would investigate no further.

◆◆◆

Louis and Louise Luetgert had three children in the 1880s: Louise, who died of cholera infantum when she was ten months old; then a boy named Louis, who would have a long life; and then Elsa, who died when she was fourteen months old, another cholera victim.

Luetgert's saloon was profitable, and he and his wife were thrifty, living in small rooms above the tavern. Soon he sold the business for $10,000 and bought a meat route and a butcher shop on North Avenue. He began by peddling meat at the back doors of his friends' homes and then started making sausage in a back room of his store. After a while the sausage sales outstripped the regular meat business. Luetgert hadn't yet figured out how to make and store sausage during the warm months, though. He shut down the business each year on April 1 and sold whatever sausage remained. Still, it was hard work, requiring his constant attention, and his health was poor. Luetgert suffered from indigestion, and sometimes he vomited blood, which his physician attributed to liver congestion. His only relief came from drinking Hunyadi mineral water.*

After a few years he decided to quit the business and buy a sixty-acre farm near Elgin, a town northwest of Chicago. "I was almost worked down," he said. Louise hated living on the farm, however, perhaps in part because of a frightening encounter with a patient who had escaped from a nearby state mental hospital. "After that, my wife would not stay on the farm for any money," Luetgert said.

After a year on the farm, Luetgert built a sausage plant at North and Sheffield Avenues in Chicago, employing more than fifty men. "I succeeded in devising processes by which I could manufacture sausages in summer as well as in winter—something that all other sausage manufacturers in the

---

* An advertisement boasted: "The World's Cure for Constipation is Hunyadi János Natural Laxative Mineral Water. It is the Best and Safest remedy for disordered stomach, biliousness and liver trouble, and it cures Constipation. Drink one-half glassful on arising in the morning and you will feel the remarkable and agreeable effects in a short time. Hunyadi János (FULL NAME.) If you simply ask for Hunyadi water you may be IMPOSED UPON. Bottle has blue label with red center."

world are unable to do," Luetgert later boasted. "This gave me prestige and brought me wealth." He was not just the owner but also the manager and overseer of the factory, watching every detail of the business. Soon he was selling $100,000 worth of sausage a year.

The Luetgerts lived in a flat above the factory, but Louise did not care for the odors. "We was living on the third floor," Luetgert recalled, "and whenever people used to call, they used to smell the smoke of the sausage . . . and it was kind of disagreeable to them."

And so the couple moved out of the factory flat, living in a couple of different homes over the next few years. In 1892 Louise gave birth to their final child, Elmer. The same year Luetgert bought about five acres at Hermitage and Diversey for $30,000 and spent $140,000 building a house and a bigger factory there. Some claimed that Mrs. Luetgert was reluctant to see so much of their money spent on the new factory, but Luetgert had his way. He subdivided part of the land into eighteen smaller lots where homes could be built. Cook County's property records called the area "Luetgert's Subdivision."

Luetgert was aware of his reputation around the neighborhood. He wrote: "It was said that I was proud, haughty and arrogant because I did not associate much with my neighbors and because I did not hang around beer saloons and put in my time as many others of my nationality do; but the truth is, I was so hard at work building up my business that I had no time for such diversions. If I had my life to do over again, I think I would pay more attention to the social side of life and make an attempt to cultivate more friends." Luetgert may have been exaggerating his lack of social activity, however. Many people said they often saw him in the saloons.

Louise did not care much for socializing, either. According to Dr. J. Sanderson Christison, a criminologist who apparently worked for Luetgert's defense lawyers, "she was a servant girl when married and seems never to have risen above that social level, and thus with an elegantly appointed home and a liberal supply of money and dress she always appeared an over-dressed woman."

In 1893 Chicago hosted the Columbian Exposition, or World's Fair, but it was of little interest to Luetgert. "My head is always so full of business affairs, that I haven't had time for anything else," he said. "Do you know I didn't even attend the World's Fair? I told the members of my family to go and have a good time and I worked away as hard as ever. I've been in Chicago for almost thirty years and I think during that time I have attended but two picnics. During my whole life I think I have attended but ten parties."

Luetgert may not have cared to visit the fair, but his sausage was on sale there, in a German restaurant inside the Manufactures Building. The restaurateurs disguised Luetgert's sausage as an import from Europe. Four years later a reporter remembered that "'imported' frankfurters of surpassing juiciness and flavor had been served with sauerkraut. No man who had eaten those frankfurters could fail to remember them—and they were of Luetgert's make."

When the exposition closed that fall, the financial troubles that had been looming over the economy during the whole fair became a full-blown panic and depression. Mills and factories shut down, and a fifth of Chicago's workers lost their jobs. A tenth of the people came close to starving each day. Families sent out their children to steal food or went scouring for it in garbage dumps. An army of beggars tried to earn change by sweeping sidewalks or opening carriage doors for businessmen. At night men sleeping on newspapers with wet shoes for pillows occupied the floors of City Hall's corridors, a fetid stench rising from their unwashed bodies.

Up until the time of the Columbian Exposition, Luetgert had been making great profits in the sausage business, but now many of the people who had ordered large shipments from him were unable to sell the product. Luetgert said he had to compromise with his clients and "make allowances," taking less money than they owed him. According to newspaper accounts, Louise never ceased to chide him for having sunk all their savings into the factory. The laborers in Lake View still imagined that Luetgert was rich, but his employees noticed how Frau Luetgert toiled day and night, despite having a servant. And she did not appear to spend much of her husband's earnings.

Luetgert had taken out a $50,000 loan from the E. S. Dreyer and Company bank to pay for building the factory. He still owed the entire $50,000 in 1896 and was paying 6 percent interest on it. In addition, he often found himself a couple of thousand dollars short, and he would go to the bank for another loan, paying it back a week later.

One morning a friend named William Charles visited Luetgert and offered to sell him some goods. Luetgert was angry about the state of his business. According to Luetgert, he told Charles, "Don't talk to me about business just now. I won't buy anything. I won't hear anything at all."

"What is the matter?" Charles asked.

"I am sick of the whole thing."

"I wouldn't be. You have a nice business. You mustn't be sick of it."

"You ought to be in my shoes once in a while. You would get sick, too."

"I will buy you out," Charles said. "What do you want for it?"

Luetgert offered to sell the "whole caboodle" for $300,000, and Charles said he would take him up on the offer. Charles drew up the papers, but the sale was never closed. Luetgert later claimed the deal fell through because he couldn't clear the property of its $50,000 mortgage. Just as Charles's option on the factory was about to expire in the fall of 1896, Charles introduced Luetgert to an Englishman named Robert Davey, who said he wanted to invest in the Luetgert sausage works.

"Davey told me that he came here from England with a capital of about $37 million back of him, and he was looking for some good securities," Luetgert said. "He spoke of Amsterdam banks and Amsterdam capitalists and Rotterdam capitalists. In fact, he spoke of all high-standing people, banks, et cetera, from all over England and Europe, Hanover, Rhine. . . . He had a bunch of letters from different countries and banking firms. And I, as a damned fool, took it for granted they were all right."

A reporter showed Luetgert a sketch of Davey that the *Inter Ocean* had published in 1893, along with an exposé of the con man. Luetgert confirmed it was the same man. "That's the rascal who is responsible for all my trouble and for the misfortunes of my wife," he said. "If I could lay my hands on him, I would make mush of him. That scoundrel should be hanged. He has ruined me, and I may thank him for being where I am today."

3 The Englishman

CHICAGO'S POPULATION of criminals was estimated at ten thousand, but four times as many were expected on May 1, 1893, the opening day of the Columbian Exposition. The *Chicago Inter Ocean* newspaper called it a veritable "Crooks' Congress," predicting the imminent arrival of shell men, shortchange men, penny-weighters, bank sneaks, and pickpockets.

They even came from across the Atlantic. A man calling himself Dr. Davey checked into the fashionable Lexington Hotel on January 9 and showed up three days later at a charity ball. Davey was said to be an Englishman of some wealth, traveling in America for pleasure. He charmed wealthy Chicagoans by recounting his exploits with dukes, marquises, princes, and capitalists. Davey hinted he was in Chicago for a philanthropic purpose—he wanted to help "a certain enterprise" connected with the exposition. Davey introduced Colonel Fitzhugh Dibbell, a capitalist from Massachusetts, and began asking for "financial considerations" to support Dibbell's enterprise. Davey and Dibbell dressed almost alike, wearing tall silk hats by day, when they might be taken for prosperous city men, and affecting soft fedoras by night. Something in their manner aroused suspicion.

A Chicagoan who had been approached by Davey and Dibbell cabled a firm of London lawyers on January 21, asking whether they knew anything about Davey. The lawyers responded that *London Truth* had recently denounced a Robert W. Davey as a swindler and "a most dangerous man." The newspaper reported that Davey had blackmailed a member of Parliament.

Dethlef C. Hansen, a young lawyer from Tacoma, Washington, who was staying at the Lexington, later described Davey as "the tallest talker I ever encountered." Hansen said Davey and Dibbell wanted to learn as much as they could about any California millionaires Hansen might know. "I could never make out what the two were driving at," Hansen said, noting that Davey showed disdain toward Chicago's society ladies. "It seemed to be his purpose to lessen everybody he spoke of, with the view, it appeared to me, of exalting himself."

The *Inter Ocean* dispatched a reporter to the Lexington the night of February 1 to find Davey. The reporter expected Davey to be dashing, but he was disappointed to find a stout man of medium stature, about forty years old and rather "clumsily built." Davey dressed plainly, and his shoes were out of fashion. His head was almost a perfect sphere, reminding the reporter of a billiard ball. Davey's eyes were small, bright, and close together. His hair was sparse, and he wore a closely cropped, sand-colored beard and mustache.

The reporter told Davey he merely wanted to know his views on things in general, since he was a traveled and educated Englishman. The flattery worked, and Davey talked volubly for more than half an hour about the fair, British politics, and the certainty of a European war. The reporter let Davey chatter on, but then he showed him the *London Truth* article on the blackmail scandal. After reading several minutes, Davey coolly said, "The matter is a complete surprise to me."

"You are not the person denounced in that article?"

"Certainly not."

"The similarity of the names is rather curious."

"Very curious. I'll tell you what I'll do. I'll cable to London tomorrow and find out who the member of Parliament is."

"It is not of material importance who the member of Parliament is. The identity of the blackmailer is the matter demanding settlement. You are not the person denounced by *Truth*? A simple answer, yes or no."

"Now, your question is surprising. There are thousands of R. W. Daveys in the London directory. It is unfair to spring such a question on one at this hour and demand an answer in a matter so momentous to me."

"Surely it is an easy matter to prove that you are not the 'R. W. Davey' referred to. Have you any of your cards about you?"

"No, and I haven't exchanged a card with any person in Chicago. I am here on private business." Davey said the only friend in Chicago who could vouch for his identity was visiting Wisconsin and wouldn't be back until the next day.

The once-talkative Davey refused to answer questions unless the reporter would write them down and give him a night to think over the replies. Davey pleaded with the reporter not to publish anything the following day. "I will make a full explanation tomorrow," he said.

No explanation was forthcoming, however. At nine o'clock the next night Davey stepped up to the cashier's window at the Lexington and paid his bill. He exited the hotel, bag in hand, leaving no forwarding address.

The *Inter Ocean* delayed publication for a day, but when Davey failed to show up for a scheduled interview, the newspaper printed its exposé on the front page beneath the headline:

WHO IS DAVEY?
Visiting Britisher in an Embarrassing Position.
IS HIS NAME ROB W.?
Sensational Story of Life on Two Continents.
IT COMMENCED IN LONDON
And Was Printed in Henry Labouchere's Paper, Truth.
Incidents Which Make the Narrative
Interesting for Chicago Society.

Not long after that headline hit the newsstands, the *Inter Ocean*'s editors received a letter from Davey's lawyers informing them they were being sued. When a reporter for the *Inter Ocean* called on the law firm and saw Davey entering the offices, the Englishman refused to come out and speak. Davey was also seen with Colonel Dibbell at the post office, checking for letters.

"And you tell me 'Dr.' Davey is still in Chicago," Hansen, the Tacoma lawyer, told the *Inter Ocean*. "Well, that's queer. When he was leaving here Thursday night he told me he was going to New York to meet some friends that were coming from England, and that it was not unlikely he would return to London. Colonel Dibbell was with him at the time."

"Taken all in all, what do you think of him?"

"I think him an untruthful man, and no person that is untruthful is safe."

As the *Inter Ocean*'s reporters continued pursuing Robert Davey in 1893, he moved from hotel to hotel and finally fled Chicago altogether. Information about Davey's whereabouts over the next few years is sketchy. He became engaged to a wealthy widow in New York but was arrested on the eve of the marriage. Facing a charge of swindling, Davey put up $1,200 for his appearance in court and was released. He never showed up for court.

Sometime around late 1895 or early 1896, Davey turned up in Berlin, where he made the acquaintance of Oliver J. Thatcher, a professor of medieval history from the University of Chicago who was on leave in Germany. "He seemed to me to be a pleasant, unassuming fellow, and was one of the most delightful companions I had ever met," Thatcher said. "He had been everywhere, and was well read and well educated."

Davey returned to Chicago in the fall of 1896, checking into the Great Northern Hotel. He used the same name as before, apparently unconcerned that anyone would remember the *Inter Ocean*'s stories from 1893. He did avoid banks and financial centers, where he feared he would be recognized. Davey placed an advertisement in a Sunday paper, stating that an English gentleman representing large capitalists would be glad to meet with people who had manufacturing property to sell. The advertisement drew the attention of Luetgert and William Charles.

Luetgert met Davey at the Great Northern, where the Englishman charmed the sausage maker with stories about his old chum, the prince of Wales. Davey claimed to be a millionaire, freely pouring champagne as he boasted.

"He was a man who would make a very good appearance and good impression. At least he did to me," Luetgert later said. "The more I became acquainted with the man the more I liked him, and, in fact, he visited me as often as twice a week. . . . At my house, we had coffee together when he came. Once I had a nestful of great Dane puppies. He picked one and I picked another one, and I says, 'This is a better one than the one you picked,' so I kept that puppy for him, and he called him John Bull. . . . I trusted Davey in all things."

On October 29 Davey worked out a deal with Charles, who agreed to drop his option to buy the A. L. Luetgert Sausage and Packing Company. Luetgert met Davey at his hotel to sign papers to incorporate the company and issue $225,000 in bonds. Davey claimed he had already lined up buyers for the bonds in Antwerp and other distant cities. Luetgert would get $200,000 in cash and $100,000 in stock while continuing to run the business at an annual salary of $5,000.

Davey wanted to take the bonds to New York himself, and Luetgert was willing to trust him, but Luetgert's lawyers, the former judges Adams Goodrich and William Vincent, were suspicious. They insisted on sending the bonds through a banker, holding them in escrow until Luetgert had received the money from investors.

Davey spent a long time negotiating with Luetgert's lawyers, hoping to get possession of the bonds, but he could never produce the money he promised to get from his supposed financial backers. Davey represented himself as a lawyer and addressed Vincent and Goodrich as his "learned friends," but they weren't convinced by his anecdotes about the English aristocracy. In December they asked him if he knew anyone in Chicago who could vouch for his reliability.

Davey had recently run into Professor Thatcher, who had returned from Berlin. Davey invited Thatcher to dinner, and they reminisced about Germany. Davey wouldn't tell the professor why he was in Chicago, saying he "never talked business to friends," but he suggested he was planning to invest his considerable wealth in some local enterprise. One day in late December, as the two were on their way to dinner again, Davey asked Thatcher to step into a lawyer's office with him. He said he had to transact a little business that would scarcely detain them a moment. Thatcher agreed and accompanied Davey into the law offices of Goodrich and Vincent in the downtown office building known as the Rookery. Davey introduced him as a friend.

"That was the first time I had ever met any of them, and [I] knew nothing of what the business connection between the men was," Thatcher later said. "Davey never mentioned business to me, and I had no idea that he was not what he represented himself to be—a wealthy English gentleman. I did not, on any occasion, introduce him to anyone, nor was I, in the least degree, sponsor for any of his actions. On one occasion Judge Goodrich asked me if he had any money, and I told him I knew nothing about it, but supposed so. I am naturally exceedingly sorry that such a thing has happened. . . . I had no idea he was a swindler, and was making a fool of me."

By bringing the professor into the law office, Davey nearly convinced the attorneys that his social pretensions had some basis in fact, but they still refused to give him any financial credit. Luetgert felt that his lawyers had treated Davey rather shabbily. He proved to be a soft mark when Davey approached him for loans.

"He would come to me for a thousand or two thousand dollars," Luetgert said. "He always had a plausible story. He would say that he had been disappointed in receiving cash from England, and had bought some securities which should be paid for at once. He always insisted on getting currency, saying that he could not use my check. He got away with about $16,000 altogether."

Luetgert had told Davey to do his banking at E. S. Dreyer and Company, the same firm where Luetgert had financed the construction of his sausage factory. On December 21, 1896, the National Bank of Illinois failed, setting off a rapid chain reaction of failures at other banks, including Dreyer's. Luetgert visited Davey that day in his room in the Great Northern. According to Luetgert, Davey chided him, saying, "You recommended this bank so highly." Davey pulled out his pocketbook and showed Luetgert that he had only three cents with him in Chicago now that his money in Dreyer's bank was gone. "That is all the money I have at present and I can't pay my board."

"Don't you worry," Luetgert replied, writing him a check for $400.

At noon the stairs outside E. S. Dreyer and Company were crowded with German and Scandinavian immigrants in shaggy overcoats, their faces sullen and their voices filled with anger and despair. The husky guards inside the bank opened the doors from time to time and offered a few pleasant words to the crowd, but they would admit no one. A big bearded man wearing a checked gingham roundabout got out of a wagon and ran up the steps, where he saw the sign on the window and the despairing expressions in the crowd. Mocking his accent, the *Daily News* reported that he cried out, "Mein Gott! Id is all gone—all gone—und now I haf got not so much as I gome ofer mit!"

4 Everything Is Gone

THE BUSINESS PROPERTY that had been Luetgert's—including the "buildings, boilers, engines, shaftings fixed, and other machinery . . . , together with all appurtenances [and] all certain formulas, special mixtures, trade secrets"—now belonged to the newly incorporated A. L. Luetgert Sausage and Packing Company.

The expenses of incorporating the sausage company needed to be met, and Davey expected Luetgert to cover them. Luetgert said he gave Davey between $3,000 and $4,000. Increasingly strapped for cash, Luetgert mortgaged his eighteen residential lots for $3,006 on February 25, 1897, with his friend the widow Christine Feld as lien holder, even though he had already sold some of the lots to other buyers. The following day Luetgert borrowed $30,000 from the Foreman Brothers Bank using the factory as collateral. The loan was due in six months. On March 5 he again used the factory as collateral when he borrowed $7,019 from Bechstein and Company.

In late February Davey had taken a trip to New York to line up investors, using a $500 check from Luetgert to cover travel expenses. Soon afterward Luetgert received a telegram from a Dr. John Phillips of New Haven, Connecticut, saying Davey was threatened with rheumatic fever. Luetgert went to New York in search of Davey, but the Englishman was not at the hotel he had given as his address. Luetgert traveled to New Haven and discovered that Dr. Phillips was an old man who had not practiced for fifteen years. The doctor had never heard of Davey and said he'd sent no telegram. Luetgert checked all the hospitals around New Haven, but it was no use. Luetgert returned to Chicago without Davey or the money.

A month passed before Luetgert told his wife what had happened. Trying to explain later why he had kept Davey's disappearance a secret from her for so long, Luetgert said, "She wasn't satisfied with the location of our home—she liked the neighbors and everything all right and the building, but she said the location isn't all right on account of the smoke. At the time the deal was in progress, Mr. Davey was with us every day and had made arrangements she would get $50,000, and could do with the $50,000 whatever she pleased." According to Luetgert, his wife had "felt all glorious" at the possibility of a better home and financial security.

He claimed he just couldn't break the bad news to her. "I told her . . . everything would be all right," he said. "She became worse and worried more than ever. I quieted her down and told her things would come out all right. She wanted to know how, and I told her we would get the debts settled up some way. I didn't tell her everything, because I was afraid it would make her worse."

Luetgert shut down the factory and laid off most of the workers. The butchers and market men who were in Luetgert's debt were unable to help him. Notes were coming due, and without any income, it seemed almost certain that the factory would fall into the hands of Luetgert's creditors. All Mrs. Luetgert's predictions were coming true. She continued to worry, scolding him for allowing their debts to run up as they had.

Luetgert insisted that he still provided for his wife, even in their precarious financial state. "She got all the money she asked for," he said. "I gave her money right along whenever she asked for it, and once in a while when I lie on the lounge she picked my pockets, et cetera, for fun. On one occasion I can recollect, I guess there was three gold pieces I had in my pocket and she liked that and I let her have them. . . . One day she intended to go downtown and she asked me for money and I gave her fifteen or twenty dollars, something like that, but she didn't go downtown, I recollect. . . .

"She always had a washerwoman and she had a hired girl as long as I am married to her, and during the time the boy was sick there was a nurse there right along. . . . [Louise] never needed to do hard work, because she had all the help she wanted."

The people in the neighborhood heard stories about arguments, or "family jars," at the Luetgert house. Mrs. Luetgert scolded her husband for his ways with other women. He was known to flirt with Christine Feld and Agatha Tosch, who with her husband ran the saloon across the street from the factory. While the newspapers described Tosch as an attractive woman with a fetching neckline, they said Feld was "a large, well-developed German woman" whose "strong chin" gave her "a somewhat masculine look." Luetgert also seemed overly fond of the family servant, Mary Siemering. Luetgert's sleep habits were odd. He spent every night in the factory office, saying he had to keep an eye on the plant or giving the unlikely excuse that he slept there to improve his health. Mary made Luetgert's bed in the office, and Mrs. Luetgert suspected she did more than tuck in his sheets.

Mrs. Luetgert's brother, Diedrich Bicknese, later said, "Mary Siemering is a cousin of ours, and we hated to believe what had been said about her going to Luetgert's office. But my sister knew about it some time. . . . One day she came out in the country to see us, and told me she had offered to do the work herself and save the money which they had been paying Mary every week. She said Luetgert was mad when she offered to do the work, and told her to keep still about Mary, or he would let [Mary] work in the factory all the time."

Mary Siemering, who was then twenty-two, had known Luetgert since she had moved to Chicago four years earlier. Mrs. Luetgert had been friendly toward her, often giving her an extra $1.20 or $2 a week. Mary later testified that she had been thinking about leaving in January and that Mrs. Luetgert had asked her to stay.

On February 13, concerned that Luetgert's business might not be worth as much as his debts, Foreman Brothers took an inventory of the factory. Mrs. Luetgert's nephew Fred Mueller—who worked as a treasurer for the Luetgert business and was known by the nickname "Professor" because of his education—said Luetgert had approached him on the day before the inventory and told him, "I have fixed up a scheme so that the same sausage will be weighed a couple of times."

When the inspector from the bank had finished his work on the fifth floor, he asked for light on the fourth floor. Allegedly, Luetgert told one of his workers, "We will fix that. We will stop the gas from going in the pipes, and we will take two brushes out of the dynamo." That stopped the lights from coming on, so the inspector left for the day. The lights came on within five minutes, and Luetgert is said to have ordered his employees to move the sausage that had already been counted on the fifth floor down to the fourth and third floors of the factory. Luetgert later denied he had deceived the bank. "I was sick at the time," he said. "I do not recollect any such thing."

Mueller also said Luetgert had ordered him to fill out a false set of accounting books, making the business appear to be turning a profit of $30,000 or $40,000 a year when it was losing money. He added that Luetgert took the books and smeared them with Bismarck brown, a coloring ingredient used in sausages, and rubbed a brick against the pages to make them look old.

"That won't do," Mueller told Luetgert. "They will get onto it."

"No, they won't," Luetgert is alleged to have replied. "I have done it before."

Luetgert eventually decided that Mueller was right, however, and according to the latter man, he destroyed the fraudulent records in a furnace inside the factory. Luetgert would deny all these allegations, as well as an accusation that he had told his bookkeeper to stuff the payrolls by about $1,000 a month so that Luetgert could take money from the payroll using fictitious names.

Sometime in February Luetgert told Diedrich Bicknese that Davey's disappearance had left him in a bad fix. He said the "damned Jews" at Foreman Brothers were going to close him down, and he wanted to take some horses to Bicknese's farm to hide them from the creditors. Louise was eavesdropping on their conversation and interjected, "It's a shame to start such a humbugging game."

Bicknese later remembered Luetgert's reaction: "Luetgert jumped up and looked as if he meant to strike her and then began walking up and down the room. I went out to the stable and directly Luetgert came out and said: 'I guess we'll drop that. The old woman is liable to go and report me.'"

On April 3 Luetgert told Bicknese he had given up all hope of saving his business. He wanted only to salvage something from the wreck. He said he had already managed to get $8,000 out of the business and he would get more if he were given the time. He asked Bicknese about the price of farms, mentioning one that he had once tried to buy for $9,000. Luetgert said he wanted to go into the chicken business.

In mid-April Foreman Brothers called Luetgert to their offices and demanded money. Luetgert told Oscar Foreman* that he thought he didn't have to make any payments for another six months. Foreman demanded Luetgert pay at least $5,000 by May. Luetgert reluctantly agreed to try to come up with the money.

---

* Foreman's nephew, Nathan Leopold Jr. (b. 1904), and Richard Loeb joined the ranks of Chicago's most notorious murderers when they killed Bobby Franks in 1924.

"All right," Foreman said. "By the fifth of May you must have $5,000, and then you have to pay us after that every five days." Luetgert signed an agreement, and the banker asked him once again, "Can you do that?"

"I will try, but hardly believe I can."

When Luetgert returned home and told Louise what had happened, she said, "You'd better look out. What can they do to us?"

"Well," Luetgert replied, "they won't do anything. They only tried to hustle me a little bit, that's all."

But Louise insisted on knowing more, according to Luetgert's later account. When she demanded details, Luetgert reassured her: "Never mind. Everything is all right. Don't you worry yourself."

"Yes," she retorted, "that's the same thing you told me when you came back from New York and you said everything is all right and I found afterward everything was all wrong."

According to Luetgert, he still resisted telling her, but when she kept teasing him for details, he at last divulged the sorry state of his business, including the money he had lost when Davey disappeared. Instead of getting $200,000 out of the deal with Davey, they wouldn't get five cents. Louise asked whether they were going to lose everything, and Luetgert replied, "No, I don't really believe that Foreman Brothers would take any act."

Luetgert said he also told his wife that it wouldn't do them much good to pay Foreman Brothers the $5,000 they wanted, because he owed another $3,000 to Swift and Company. "I see the conduct of these big packers," Luetgert said. "So I was more afraid of Swift and Company than I was of Foreman Brothers." Luetgert sent 170 forty-two-gallon casks of sausage casings to Swift as security, hoping for more time to pay off that loan. Prosecutors would later claim that those casings were worthless.

In the spring of 1897 Elmer was ill; Mrs. Luetgert "hardly ever came downstairs at all, especially when the boy was sick, and after the boy was sick was generally upstairs," Luetgert said. "Her body health was all right, but her mind health was not all right. . . . Her general condition was not good. . . . She had all kinds of medicine in the house."

When the Luetgert family physician, Clarendon Rutherford, came to treat Elmer, he noticed that Mrs. Luetgert was less tidy than usual and appeared to be worried. She wore a vacant stare, with her mouth and lower jaw drooping, and sometimes she seemed unaware of her surroundings. Rutherford surmised that she was going through "the change of life." Luetgert, Christine Feld, and Mary Siemering all said later that Mrs. Luetgert had been having prolonged and irregular menstrual flows.

Rutherford said Mrs. Luetgert didn't follow his instructions about giving Elmer medicine, so he insisted that the family hire a nurse. According to Rutherford, Mrs. Luetgert showed little sympathy for Elmer while acting suspicious toward the nurse.

This wasn't the first time Mrs. Luetgert had exhibited odd behavior. She had recently purchased a pair of expensive russet-colored satin slippers. They were much too small for her feet, but she refused to return them, instead keeping them by her side as she sat on the front porch, admiring the pretty shoes. Around that time Luetgert purchased a pet canary, but his wife ordered it to be taken away the minute she saw it.

Mary Siemering usually straightened up Mrs. Luetgert's room each day, but around the beginning of April, Mrs. Luetgert began spending more time there, making it difficult for Mary to do her work. "She always tried to keep the door shut," Mary testified. "She would not let me go into her room."

In mid-April Mrs. Luetgert gave her nephew, "Professor" Mueller, a watch and chain. "She gave me the watch and she says I should take care of it for her, as she was afraid Mr. Luetgert would take it away from her," he later recalled. "He had been scolding about her having a gold watch."

One of Mrs. Luetgert's in-laws, Louis Balgamann, a farmer who lived in Union Hill, south of Chicago, visited her the last week of April. He noticed nothing unusual about her mental condition and said she had not mentioned planning to leave home. When Diedrich Bicknese talked with her in April, he saw nothing unusual about her state of mind. But others said she had acted in a peculiar manner.

On April 27 or 28 Adolph Elandt, an delivery man who formerly worked at the sausage factory, stopped by the house and talked with Mrs. Luetgert. He later testified: "She said everything was gone and she didn't think she could stand it any longer. If she would go to the outside they would be pointing with their fingers at her. . . . She would not stay in the house, but would leave the house and go away somewhere. . . . I asked her then where would she go to, and she said she thought of going out in the country somewhere and working as a hired girl, and then nobody would know her."

On April 28 another former Luetgert employee, Charles Bahanke, also spoke with Mrs. Luetgert. He later testified: "We was talking . . . about this hard time in town. And then she told, she says, 'Better we go out in the country.' I says, I told her, 'That is just as worse in the country than in here. Everywhere is bad, worse, everywhere. Where you go to?' I was talking about this breaking in the banks, different banks here in Chicago."

Frank Dettler, who had known her since she married Luetgert, talked with her on April 28. He testified: "She was crying and laughing, kind of shaking all over. . . . I said to her, 'Mrs. Luetgert, what is the matter? You look kind of worried.' She said, 'Yes, there is no wonder, Mr. Dettler, look at my child, couldn't walk, five years old. Now all the business trouble I got. Oh, Mr. Dettler, everything is gone now, everything is gone now, everything is lost now, I will not stay here anymore, I will go. I will go.'"

Dettler tried to comfort Mrs. Luetgert, but she seemed inconsolable. "I asked her to stay a week in my house, but she did not say anything," he recalled.

The same week Marcus Heineman, a Milwaukee resident who had once been a salesman for the sausage company, came to the house looking for Luetgert. "Is he asleep?" Heineman asked.

"No, he is upstairs," Mrs. Luetgert replied. "He wants to be alone. He has got so much business trouble. I am going away."

"Well, come to Milwaukee and stay with us a little while."

"No," she said, "I am going away."

Mary Charles, the wife of William Charles, also spoke with Mrs. Luetgert during the last week of April. She testified: "Her whole conversation was— every time I saw her—that she intended to go away if her husband did not succeed in his business. If his business failed she would not live with him. She couldn't stand it. . . . She wouldn't be seen going out. . . . Everyone would point their finger at her and say, 'There is Mrs. Luetgert. Her husband was a rich man once, and now she is as poor as we are.' And she said, 'I couldn't stand it and I won't stay here.'"

According to later testimony by Mary Siemering (which should be viewed with a certain amount of skepticism, because she may have been trying to protect Luetgert), at one point she stood in the doorway of Mrs. Luetgert's bedroom on April 29. Mrs. Luetgert called her into the room, which was in the house's northeast corner, with a door opening onto the main hall. "She showed me her coat. She said, 'Look here, the moths are in my coat. See how they eat that.' . . . She was dusting her clothes. . . . I noticed that she had all the clothes out. She had some wrapped up in a paper there, lying on the bed. . . . It was a bundle of some common white paper."

Mrs. Luetgert did not sleep much that week. Three or four times she got up in the middle of the night and went to Mary's bedroom. "She would come to the door and tell me she was not feeling well, to make her a whisky punch," the maid said.

According to Mary, Mrs. Luetgert passed hours sitting in front of the window or walking from one room to another. She spent much of her time reading newspapers and books. "She always says, 'Everything is gone.' She kept rubbing her hands. 'Everything is gone. The old man lost his business. I ain't going to stay. I shan't stand it,' she says. 'I must leave.'

"I told her, 'Mrs. Luetgert, . . . as long as you have got a chair to sit on and something to eat . . . , don't worry yourself.'

"'Well,' she says, 'I can't stay no more. I am going to leave.'"

Mary thought Mrs. Luetgert might be joking, because over the years she had often talked about leaving her husband without ever doing it. Mrs. Luetgert usually laughed at the idea, and it became a recurring joke. "She always talked that way," Mary said. "She says she wouldn't live with him. She was going to look for a millionaire. She wanted to have another man—a millionaire, she says."

Twice that week Mary saw Mrs. Luetgert crying. She claimed Mrs. Luetgert often spoke dreamily of living in a castle on a lake shore and wearing extravagant clothes and draped trains, with a colored servant at her disposal. At other times Mrs. Luetgert talked about going out into the country, changing her name, and working as a hired girl.

One day Mrs. Luetgert helped Mary gather up the dirty dishes after a meal. Mrs. Luetgert carelessly threw the dishes into the sink, breaking a cup. Mary said, "You want to be a little bit careful—you will break all of our new cups."

"Oh, I don't care," replied Mrs. Luetgert.

April 30 was a Friday, a cleaning day in the Luetgert household, but Mrs. Luetgert said not to worry about the housework. According to Mary, Mrs. Luetgert said, "Well, never mind the cleaning. I won't stay here long anymore."

5 Moving Day

IT HAD BEEN unusually cold in Chicago the last week of April 1897. A forty-five-mile-per-hour gale stirred up Lake Michigan, and few vessels ventured out. On the morning of Saturday, May 1, a heavy frost covered the ground. The temperature hovered in the low forties all day, and the skies remained cloudy.

For many of Chicago's residents, May 1 was moving day. In late April and early May 1897 some 30,0000 households loaded their possessions into wagons and vans and moved. The city had rarely been so crowded with vans, trunks, drays, and wheelbarrows. The men who piled the things into vans shivered from the cold blasts of lake air as they juggled oil paintings and bric-a-brac. Mattresses, bedsteads, and children's red wagons stood in heaps under the leaden sky. Women stood nearby, fearing it would rain and waiting fretfully for the vans to arrive. Maids walked nervously down the streets carrying rugs, parlor lamps, sofa pillows, coffee pots, flatirons, and bags of onions. The rumble of heavy drays was heard long into the night, along with the clatter of people carrying boxes and furniture up the stairs into their new apartments.

The entertainment in Chicago that evening included a performance by the champion swimmer Cora Beckwith and "Her Swimming School of Funny, Fat, Female Floaters" in a 10,0000-gallon tank at the Clark Street Dime Museum, which urged the public to "see the big girls." Another diversion was the exhibition of mind reading, rope tying, and illusions performed at the Hopkins Theater by "Houdini, the Mysterious Conjurer," who was billed below equilibrists, a "dashing and vivacious soubrette," and "travesty artists."

Luetgert had purchased two tickets from Christine Feld for a ball on May 1—one for himself and one for Mary Siemering—but he told Feld they wouldn't be able to attend. "He said to me that he could not go to the dance," Feld said. "He had too much trouble in the factory, his head was full of business."

That morning Mary noticed something peculiar about the way Mrs. Luetgert was wearing her dress. "She had it on kind of funny. She had it pushed up and . . . buttoned every other button. I says, 'Fix your dress a little decent.'

"'Oh, I don't care,' she says. 'Let it go the way it is.'"

Mary said Mrs. Luetgert continued to wear the dress that way all day. "There was something wrong in her mind," she said.

Mary said she talked with Mrs. Luetgert after lunch. "That Saturday noon at the dinner table after Mr. Luetgert had gone out she told me, she says— she kept wringing her hands and she said, 'Everything is gone, and I am going, too, where nobody can find me.'"

A couple of Luetgert's employees—a teamster named William Follbach and a butcher named Anton Schuster—said they saw Mrs. Luetgert on May 1. Follbach observed her knitting as she sat at a window around eight in the morning. He said she appeared to be working around the house the rest of the day. As Schuster was filling some barrels with tallow and bones for the drayman to carry off, he observed Mrs. Luetgert washing windows in the house. Follbach and Schuster noticed nothing unusual about her.

That evening, around seven o'clock, Mrs. Luetgert sent for one of her neighbors, Amelia Kaiser. The woman brought along a bowl of the cheese spread known as *Schmierkäse,* which pleased Mrs. Luetgert. Mary Siemering, who said she witnessed no quarrels in the Luetgert house that night, went to bed around eight o'clock, as Mrs. Luetgert and Mrs. Kaiser were talking. Mrs. Luetgert walked her neighbor home at half past eight.

"She gave me four oranges and said I should take them to the children," Kaiser later recalled. Kaiser found something peculiar about Mrs. Luetgert's demeanor, although she had difficulty saying exactly what.

Around nine Mrs. Luetgert stopped at the home of William Charles to see whether he had been able to get some money he had been trying to raise from a broker to help save the factory. Charles's wife told her that no money had been found.

"She said, 'I am going,'" Mary Charles later recounted. "She said she couldn't stand it any longer. She said, 'I will go,' in her German way of speaking." Mrs. Luetgert walked back out into the night, a little shawl wrapped around her shoulders.

One of the Luetgert children, eleven-year-old Louis, had gone to the circus that evening with a friend, Willie Esau. Mary Siemering heard Louis ask his mother for permission to go. "She told the little boy he better stay at home and save the ten cents, because money was scarce," Mary said. "Well, the little boy asked his father for ten cents, and he gave him ten cents and he went to the circus."

Howe's London Circus had set up its tents six or seven blocks away, at the corner of Diversey and Herndon. The traveling troupe featured Professor Stuart Young, who made nightly ascensions in his hot-air balloon, a certain "Monsieur Goliath," and Charles Drayton, "the Herculean Cannon Ball performer, who throws high in the air his 100 pound Cannon Balls, as if they were made of India Rubber." The Davenport family performed equestrian acts in the sawdust ring. The riders stood on the backs of their steeds, which then rose up on their hind legs, as still as statues.

"It was about ten o'clock when I got home," young Louis later recalled. "I went into the house by the rear door. My mother let me into the kitchen door." Louis said his mother was wearing a loose brown wrapper with red and blue figures and had slippers on her feet. "She then went back to her chair. She sat down under the gas jet by the sink on the east side of the kitchen, and started reading the newspaper again. The gas was lighted. There was no other light in the kitchen. She asked me if the show was worth ten cents. I said it was worth more than ten cents.

"I went into the pantry and hung up my overcoat, and I came out and started talking about the circus. Then I saw my father come out. He carried a lantern, a thing which he always did when he intended to go to the office. He said it was getting rather late, and I should go to bed and talk about the circus in the morning. I went to my room and undressed. This took me four or five minutes. I talked with brother Elmer when I got to bed.

"I never saw my mother after seeing her with the newspaper."

6 Missing

ON SUNDAY, MAY 2, 1897, Mary Siemering arose at her normal time, about half past five. She ate breakfast with Mr. Luetgert between six and seven, while the children were still in bed. Around nine or ten o'clock Mary realized Mrs. Luetgert was not in the house. She went into her room and noticed the bed was "all upset." The small banks for the two children, which were usually kept in the dining room, were on the bureau in Mrs. Luetgert's bedroom, with all the money taken out. Mary said she had counted the $1.75 in pennies in Elmer's bank only three days before, when she gave Elmer a cent. Louis said his bank had held four dollars.

According to Mary, Luetgert came back to the house between ten and eleven. They and the two children ate together around noon. William Charles and another business associate arrived shortly after that, and Luetgert went out with them.

Agatha Tosch said Luetgert came into her saloon between two and four in the afternoon. "He asked me for a glass of beer. . . . He didn't say anything, and I asked him what was the matter with him, he looked so strange and excited in his face. He didn't answer me. He just told me he was going home to his house to change clothes. . . . He looked very pale, as if he had not slept."

Luetgert came home alone around four or five o'clock, Mary Siemering recalled. After drinking a cup of coffee, he returned to the factory for the evening.

On Monday morning Luetgert went to the offices of his lawyer, Adams Goodrich, to talk about his business troubles. Goodrich called Foreman Brothers on the telephone and talked to them about the money Luetgert owed. When Goodrich hung up, Luetgert said, "Judge, that is not the greatest trouble that I have."

"What else has happened to you? I thought you was in trouble enough," Goodrich said.

"My wife left me Saturday night," Luetgert replied. Goodrich would later recall that Luetgert broke down in tears, although there was some question as to whether Luetgert was crying about his wife's departure or his financial difficulties.

"What was the trouble?" Goodrich asked.

"Well, she has been mad at me on account of my losing my money, and she thinks I am going to lose the business, and she said she was going away and she did go away Saturday night. I don't know where she is."

"Where do you think she has gone?"

"I think she has gone to her brother's or her sister's."

"Hadn't you better get the police to look her up?"

"Oh, no, she is with her brothers and sisters, and if it gets in the newspapers, she won't come back to me at all."

Goodrich thought for a moment and then said, "There is a better reason than that why you should not get it in the newspapers. If it gets in the papers, it will not help you in your trouble between you and your wife, and you will not be able to raise the money that you need, and you better look quietly around yourself and see where she is and try and get her to come back to you."

"Judge, I will do that."

William Follbach, the former hostler for the factory, said he talked with Mary Siemering that morning at the Luetgert house. "She said Mrs. Luetgert was upstairs asleep," he said.

On Tuesday Luetgert went back to his lawyers' office. Goodrich was absent, so Luetgert talked with a junior partner, Ralph R. Bradley. Luetgert urged Bradley to do something to protect the factory. He said he feared Foreman Brothers was about to seize it under the chattel mortgage he had taken out on it. Bradley noticed tears in Luetgert's eyes.

"Don't break down, old man," Bradley said. "Maybe you will pull through it all."

"That is not all the trouble I have got," Luetgert said.

"What is the matter now? What else is there? It seems to me there is enough as it is."

"My wife has gone away, and I don't know where she is."

Bradley asked Luetgert what he had done about his wife's disappearance, and Luetgert said Goodrich had counseled him not to let it get in the newspapers. Bradley said he thought that was good advice.

Later that day Foreman Brothers seized ownership of Luetgert's factory. Frank Moan, an employee of the Cook County Sheriff's Office, served a writ on Luetgert and began guarding the factory. He inspected the entire building and found it to be "very clean." He noticed at least fifty boxes of soap in the grocery that Luetgert ran at the front of his factory, the same type Moan had seen used for scrubbing at the courthouse.

Around one o'clock Diedrich Bicknese came to the house looking for his sister. He saw Mary Siemering, but Luetgert wasn't around. Mary told him Mrs. Luetgert had been missing since Sunday morning. "The first thing I asked was whether there had been any quarrels lately," Bicknese later recounted. "Mary Siemering told me there had not, that there had been no words between them for ten days."

Bicknese went to the home of his other sister, Wilhemina Mueller, at 158 Cleveland Avenue, and learned that Louise wasn't there, either. Bicknese returned to the Luetgert house around four o'clock and saw Luetgert at the rear entrance of the home.

Luetgert and two or three employees were putting some sort of incubator, a device of Luetgert's own design, into the basement of the house. Bicknese greeted Luetgert and watched for a while. He then motioned Luetgert toward him, and they went over to the gate of the property. Luetgert seemed anxious to tell Bicknese how they could make lots of money with the incubator, but Bicknese had more important things to discuss. They spoke in a mixture of High and Low German and English, according to Bicknese's later account.

"What is the matter? Where is Louise?" Bicknese asked.

Luetgert said he didn't know. "Hain't she out to your place?"

"No. If she was out to my place I wouldn't have to look for her here," Bicknese said. He asked Luetgert where he supposed Louise had gone.

"Well, I can't tell. She might have gone away or wandered away, something like that," Luetgert said, betraying no emotion.

"Where could she go? Is there any of her clothes gone, or has she got any money to go with?"

Luetgert said he hadn't looked to see whether any of her clothes were gone. He guessed she'd had about eighty dollars on Saturday. He said he had recently given her three twenty-dollar gold pieces. He had also given her fifteen dollars in paper money, when she wanted to go downtown and buy some clothes for her and the boys, but she hadn't made the shopping trip. And she had the change from Louis and Elmer's banks, Luetgert said.

"Well, you know she would not go very far alone in the night," Bicknese pointed out. "She was awful scared. Do you suppose she could have gone off in her mind, or did she show anything before?"

"No," answered Luetgert. "She didn't show me anything."

Luetgert said Louise had returned from Amelia Kaiser's home around ten Saturday night, and then he had taken his key and gone to the factory. That was the last he had seen of her.

"Well, what do you suppose now?" asked Bicknese.

"Well, that she had gone with another man."

Bicknese said he couldn't believe that, because Louise didn't care about men. "Have you done anything or tried to find out where she is?" he asked. "Or ain't you going to do something?"

"I gave a couple of detectives five dollars apiece." Luetgert said the private eyes would accomplish more than all the Chicago police. He said it was no use having anything published, since Louise would probably be coming back.

Bicknese didn't know what to think of Luetgert's words and manner. "Well, Louis," he said, "I think that woman is not alive. If she was, she wouldn't leave the children three days. You know that."

Luetgert said he thought Louise didn't really care about the smaller boy, Elmer. Louis, the older boy, was the only one for whom she really cared, he said.

Bicknese took out his watch and said, "Well, I have got to make the train."

"Well, all right," Luetgert said. "If I find out anything in a week or two, I will let you know." Bicknese told Luetgert that wouldn't do. He promised to return in the morning.

"All right," Luetgert said, as Bicknese walked toward the Milwaukee and Saint Paul Railroad station to catch a train back to his farm in Wood Dale.

Bicknese returned to the city on Wednesday, first going to Wilhemina Mueller's house to see whether anything had turned up. There was no news about Louise. Bicknese went to the Luetgert house and found it locked and the curtains closed. He waited ten minutes and then saw Luetgert coming from across the street. Bicknese greeted him and asked whether he had learned anything.

"No, I don't know anything new," said Luetgert, who then asked about a man in Elgin who was selling a farm. Bicknese gave him the man's address. Luetgert wanted to talk some more about the farm, but Bicknese impatiently tried to change the subject. They went into the house, and Luetgert lay down on the lounge as if he were going asleep.

Bicknese talked with Mary, asking her where her parents lived in Kankakee County, south of Chicago, and which train he should take to go there. He asked Mary whether any clothes were missing from Louise's room. Mary said she had not gone into the room, because she was afraid Mrs. Luetgert would return and would be angry at her for having meddled with her things. Bicknese told Mary he would stand that risk, and they went into the room together. They found a lot of clothes, including a black jacket, several dresses, and two or three pairs of shoes.

Bicknese visited Amelia Kaiser and his cousins Sophia and Carl Tews.

None of them knew anything about Louise's whereabouts.

On Thursday Luetgert went to his lawyers' office and said he wanted to go to Wheaton, a town west of Chicago, to see whether he could find any trace of his wife. Bradley told him not to leave the city, because he might be needed in court to answer questions about his debts. If he went out of town, his creditors might think he was trying to evade examination.

That same day Bicknese took a train to Kankakee to visit Louis Balgamann, the relative who had a farm nearby in Union Hills. Bicknese then called on Mary Siemering's parents, who lived in the same neighborhood. Louise hadn't been seen in the area. Bicknese looked for his sister in Elgin as well but found no trace.

On Friday Bicknese took a train into Chicago and went to the home of his sister, Wilhemina. Together they went to the Luetgert house around noon. Luetgert wasn't home, and they sat there, waiting for him to return from downtown. While they waited, one of the boys, Louis, asked his uncle, "Is Mama at your house?"

"No," Bicknese said.

"Well, I know where she is. She is at Mrs. Tews's, on the West Side," Louis announced.

"How do you know that?"

"Because Mary told me so. Papa took her there in a buggy."

"How do you know that?"

"Mary told me that, too." Louis added that "Mama and Papa went downstairs together" after he had gone to bed on the night of May 1.

Bicknese was sitting outside in a garden chair around five o'clock when Luetgert finally walked up. Bicknese stood and met Luetgert on the sidewalk, greeting him.

"Well," Luetgert said. "Did you find out anything?"

"No. Ain't you either?"

Luetgert started to sit down in the garden chair, but Bicknese said they'd better go in the house, because his sister was waiting inside. They went into the kitchen. Wilhemina got up and walked over to Luetgert. Staring him in the face, she said, "Now, Louis, what is the matter here? Don't you know where Louise is? If you do, why, say so and save my brother from spending time and money."

Luetgert said they wouldn't believe him if he told the truth.

Wilhemina asked, "How can you be so still, act so like nothing happened? You have been sitting that afternoon in the yard drinking [with] some of the boys."

Bicknese said, "It don't look so like a woman was missing. It looks more like a wedding going on than anything else."

Luetgert said he had so much business to worry about that he would not bother himself much about his wife's disappearance or he might have a doctor's bill to pay afterward.

Bicknese retorted, "Louie, you know if one of your big dogs would go away, you would get the police to go after him, and now your wife is gone, you act as though nothing happened. Now, there is got to be something done. I have been all over. I can find nothing. If you don't report this matter to the police, I will. I want it cleared up."

Luetgert told Bicknese to go ahead and notify the police. He said it was no disgrace to him. It was their sister, and the disgrace would fall on their side of the family. Bicknese said he didn't care; he just wanted to see her or at least know where she was.

Bicknese and Wilhemina left. After eating supper, Bicknese went to the home of Wilhemina's son, Fred. At about eight o'clock they went to the Sheffield Avenue police station and told Captain Herman Schuettler about the disappearance.

The next morning, May 8, Luetgert visited the home of Mrs. Luetgert's cousins Carl and Sophia Tews. He told them that he had hired some private detectives to find his wife. "He said he gave them $30 and told them if they needed more to come to him and they would get it," Sophia Tewes recalled. Luetgert told her that Diedrich and Wilhemina were angry at him for not reporting the matter to police, but he felt that they were being unfair to him.

The same morning Captain Schuettler sent two of his officers, Walter Dean and Martin Qualey, to the sausage factory to interview Luetgert. Luetgert was away, and the officers spent two hours waiting for him. At noon they gave up and went back to the station. At about five Schuettler went to the Luetgert home with Inspector Michael Schaack and Lieutenant George Hutchinson. Schuettler saw Luetgert pulling up in a buggy, just behind the police buggy. They went into the house with him and talked to him in the kitchen, along with Luetgert's son Louis and Mary Siemering.

"I understand, Mr. Luetgert, that your wife is missing, and we came up here to see what we could do for you in regard to the matter," Schuettler said.

"Yes, she is gone since last Saturday."

"How do you account for it?"

"Well, she has been acting strange, and I think she got crazy—one of her crazy spells."

"Why didn't you report this matter to the police before, Mr. Luetgert?"

"Well, I didn't want to have anybody know my wife was away."

Luetgert said he wanted to avoid the notoriety that would come with the news of his wife's disappearance. Schuettler told Luetgert it had been his positive duty to report his wife's disappearance, adding that he didn't see why it would bring any disgrace on Luetgert. If Mrs. Luetgert had gone insane, Luetgert had to take care of her, and the police would do whatever they could to help him. "Don't you know we would assist you in getting her?" Schuettler asked. "You know me a long time. We have been acquainted. Why didn't you come and tell me about it?"

"Well, I watched the papers very close."

"The papers don't have all these cases of people being picked up. She may have been injured and taken to a hospital, and may be dead and buried. You certainly don't want to have your wife buried unless you knew her grave." Schuettler told Luetgert the body of an unidentified woman had been found the week before and sent to the morgue. No one knew who she was.

"I didn't think about that," Luetgert said.

"Did you notify anybody?" asked Schuettler.

"No, but I watched the papers and made inquiries myself."

"Did you notify any private detectives?"

"No."

"You are positive of that?"

Luetgert said he was.

"Did you tell anybody?" Schuettler asked.

"No, I did not tell anybody outside of my family circle."

"You told Bicknese and mentioned Mueller's name."

"Yes." Schuettler then told Luetgert that it seemed odd that he had suggested his wife might be at the Muellers' home.

"How do you make out that she was insane?" Schuettler asked.

"She acted strange ever since the failure, and didn't want to be here."

Luetgert added that she had recently been making odd mistakes when she cooked—for example, using onions when a recipe called for potatoes.

Schuettler questioned the boy, who told the detective he hadn't seen his mother since she was reading the newspaper that night. Schuettler asked him whether he had noticed anything strange about his mother, and the boy said no, she had just read the newspaper and taken off her slippers.

"What made you think of that?" Schuettler asked.

"As if she wanted more ease and more comfort," Louis said.

"That is the last you saw of your mother?"

"Yes, that is the last I saw of her."

Schuettler, who remembered that Luetgert had come to the police station some time earlier to report the disappearance of two dogs, thought Luetgert's behavior now seemed suspicious. "It seemed strange to me that Luetgert, who had a short time previously insisted on a vigilant search for two great Dane dogs, should fail to report the disappearance of his wife," Schuettler later remembered.

7 Case Histories

FEW PEOPLE in Chicago had as many enemies as did Inspector Michael Schaack, but somehow he always clung to power. For more than a decade his name had been connected to the city's most sensational criminal cases. He was self-assured, defiant, ambitious, methodical, and untiring. He was also described as a vain, pompous, blustery, rotund, and corpulent ego- and megalomaniac. One observer called him a man "of restless and unregulated energy and, let us say, of small discretion." Another noted that he "hugely enjoyed being in the limelight."

With broad shoulders and a sturdy torso, he stood nearly six feet tall and weighed about 220 pounds, but he was quick on his feet. While sitting he looked as if he would prefer to be in motion. His cheeks were ruddy, and a dark brown mustache partly concealed his mouth. His face was often compared to that of a bulldog or an Egyptian sphinx.

After observing Schaack in court, the *New York Journal* correspondent

Julian Hawthorne decided the inspector's eyes were his most remarkable feature:

> They are dark gray, very bright and quick, of good size; in spite of their quickness there is at times great steadiness in their regard. They are expressive eyes; they would be of great use to the inspector had destiny made him an actor instead of a police officer. He can say things with them; not only question and reply, but menace, command, disbelieve, defy, comprehend. There is a magnetism in them; the inspector, that is, is a man of immense vitality and individuality, and there is a sort of contagion in him, inclining you to oppose him or agree with him vehemently, as the case may be. All this shows in his eyes.

Schaack ran the East Chicago Avenue police station like a military unit, and he was to reputed to know every corner and crooked alley north of the Chicago River. Schaack had a good memory for faces and facts, but he seldom trusted himself without a pen when interrogating a suspect in the "sweat box." He was also notorious for paying witnesses to testify or helping them to find jobs.

The son of a locksmith, Schaack was born in Luxembourg in 1843 and came to the United States as a child. After working as a night watchman in a brewery and a sailor on the Great Lakes, he joined the Chicago Police Department as a patrolman in 1869. Schaack earned a reputation for happening on crimes in progress, always arriving just as a safe exploded or a wagon loaded with stolen goods pulled out of an alley. Schaack became a detective, and within five years he had made 865 arrests. Nevertheless, while Schaack's detective work inspired adulation in certain quarters, some judges criticized his rough methods.

Schaack was most famous for his role in the investigation of the deadly bombing at Haymarket Square on May 4, 1886. The police marched on a labor demonstration near the square, and someone in the crowd threw a bomb, killing one officer instantly. The police fired into the crowd, killing at least one and wounding many. Six officers who were injured during the riot died from their wounds over the next few weeks.

Schaack felt contempt toward Police Superintendent Frederick Ebersold and the officers running the Haymarket investigation. When Schaack wrote a book about the case three years later, he described a department "rent and paralyzed with the feuds and jealousies." In Schaack's eyes, Ebersold and "his pet gang of ignorant detectives . . . made a fine mess of it." Schaack watched as other officers questioned suspects and then let them go, saying they had no evidence to press charges. Schaack was furious. He would later write, "I saw some of those red-handed murderers come out of that office smiling and laughing instead of being made to feel that they were about to have a rope around their necks."

Schaack claimed that a frightened man stopped him as he walked home May 6. The stranger gave him a tip about the Haymarket case, and Schaack stayed out until four in the morning, tracking down leads on the bombing. He went to Ebersold the next day and received permission to investigate. He sent a crew of detectives from the East Chicago Avenue police station—which some called "Schaack's Bastille"—searching every house, barn, and shed that might be connected somehow with the anarchists. They seldom bothered to obtain search warrants. Schaack's plainclothesmen rounded up dozens of individuals they suspected to be socialist and anarchist sympathizers. (Luetgert's friend Christine Feld was rumored to be a spy for Schaack, although she later denied it.)

Schaack's officers and spies claimed to find bombs everywhere. They carted away subversive literature and put 160 suspects under surveillance. They raided more than fifty gathering places, including meeting halls, newspaper offices, and homes. All the while the newspapers printed tales of outlandish plots that Schaack had supposedly unraveled. If the public had not been in such a panic, the stories might have been laughable, but many residents accepted them. It was widely believed the radicals were plotting Chicago's destruction.

In his book *Anarchy and Anarchists* Schaack tells a cloak-and-dagger tale of women in black veils slipping into the police station with clues. Schaack almost seems to be bragging as he tells of the "very savage and gory letters" and death threats he received. Schaack's enemies twice attempted to burn down his house, and one saloonkeeper often toasted Schaack by proclaiming, "I hope that that damned Luxembourger, Schaack, will be killed before I go to bed tonight!"

Ebersold later recalled that he had been trying to calm down the public until Schaack took over. "Captain Schaack wanted to keep things stirring," Ebersold said. "He wanted bombs to be found here, there, all around, everywhere. I thought people would lie down to sleep better if they were not afraid their homes would be blown to pieces any minute. But this man, Schaack, . . . wanted none of that policy. . . . After we got the anarchist societies broken up, Schaack wanted to send out men to organize new societies right away. You see what this would do. He wanted to keep the thing boiling, keep himself prominent before the public."

Many saw Schaack's book as the product of a warped mind. One observer at the time said, "I have often wondered whether his delusions resulted from a kind of self-hypnotism or from mere mania; but certainly he saw more anarchists than vast hell could hold. Bombs, dynamite, daggers, and pistols seemed ever before him; in the end, there was no society, however innocent or even laudable, among the foreign born population that was not to his mind an object of grave suspicion."

One of Schaack's men, a twenty-six-year-old former streetcar conductor named Herman Schuettler, became a hero when he tracked down Louis Lingg, a suspect in the Haymarket case. The fugitive tried to pull a revolver on Schuettler, but the tall officer grappled with Lingg. As they rolled on the floor, Lingg tried to choke Schuettler, so Schuettler bit Lingg's thumb, nearly severing it. Officer Jacob Loewenstein rushed in and clubbed Lingg on the head.

Schaack's detective work resulted in the arrest of eight anarchists. No evidence tied them to the Haymarket bomb, but this did not bother the prosecutor Julius Grinnell or Judge Joseph Gary. Gary told the jurors that the prosecutors did not need to establish the identity of the bomber. All they had to prove, he said, was that the defendants had called on labor activists to commit killings. The jury followed his instructions and convicted them all.

Before being sentenced one of the anarchists, Oscar Neebe, told the court that Schaack's officers were among the city's worst gangs, ransacking houses and stealing money and watches. Schaack laughed, and Neebe retorted, "You need not laugh about it, Captain Schaack. You are one of them. You are an anarchist, as you understand it. You are all anarchists, in this sense of the word, I must say."

Seven of the anarchists were sentenced to death, and the eighth, Neebe, was given fifteen years in prison. Before the state could hang one of the condemned men, Lingg, he died in a bomb explosion in his jail cell. Governor Richard J. Oglesby commuted two of the death sentences to life imprisonment. Four of the men died at the gallows outside Cook County Jail on November 11, 1887.

In 1889 Schaack and Schuettler were in the news again when they investigated the murder of Dr. Patrick Henry Cronin, but this time the two policemen were at odds. Police looked for Cronin after he disappeared on May 4, but the search lost momentum following reports that the doctor had been seen in Canada. His body was finally discovered in a Lake View sewer catchment on May 22. Cronin, a member of the underground Irish revolutionary organization Clan-Na-Gael, had been assassinated by other members of the group. One of those accused of taking part in the killing was a detective under Schaack's command, Dan Coughlin. Another close Schaack associate, Michael Whalen, was believed to have covered up information. Schaack didn't pursue the investigation with his usual vigor, prompting the new police chief, George Hubbard, to remark, "It has bothered me a great deal—his negligence in this business. . . . Previous to that, he had always been a thorough officer who was conscientious in his duties."

Schuettler took the case more seriously, though, investigating without much support from Schaack. His efforts helped to win the convictions of four men, although Coughlin was later acquitted in a retrial. Schuettler made enemies in the Irish community, and shortly after the Cronin trial, he found himself in a skirmish at a saloon with some prominent Irishmen, including an alderman. Schuettler shot and killed one of the men in self-defense. He remained an object of hatred for the Irish political clan known as "the Market Street Crowd."

In 1889, the same year the Cronin case was under way, a stash of stolen goods was discovered in Officer Loewenstein's home, including watches, dresses, and jewelry belonging to Lingg's fiancée. Loewenstein and Schaack were accused of trafficking in stolen goods. Meanwhile, the former police chief Ebersold went public with his charge that Schaack had manufactured evidence in the Haymarket case. Schaack was suspended from the force. Nevertheless, when the city government fell back into Republican hands a few years later, Schaack returned to the department, and the record of his misconduct was "corrected." The force created a new position for Schaack, inspector of the North Side, and gave him almost total control over the police north of the Chicago River.

In 1893 the new governor, John Peter Altgeld, pardoned the three anarchists still in prison. He roundly criticized Gary for allowing a miscarriage of justice, and he had scathing words for Schaack's crew as well: "Some of the prominent police officials, in their zeal, not only terrorized ignorant men by throwing them into prison and threatening them with torture if they refused to swear to anything desired, but . . . they offered money and employment to those who would consent to do this."

◆◆◆

One of the most challenging cases in Schaack's career stemmed from the events of the election held on November 5, 1894. A saloonkeeper named Gus Colliander was shot and killed by a gang of thugs while counting ballots at a polling place. In April 1896 Schaack interviewed a witness who told him that the Democratic committeeman Thomas J. O'Malley was the gunman. Schaack, however, could not persuade State's Attorney Jacob Kern to charge O'Malley, who had since been elected as a Chicago alderman.

Later in the year Kern lost his bid for reelection. In December 1896 a thirty-three-year-old Republican with a reputation for honesty, Charles Deneen, took office as the new state's attorney. Schaack convinced Deneen to charge O'Malley, but the prosecution case fell apart during the trial when witnesses gave conflicting accounts of the crime. The jury acquitted O'Malley, and Schaack and Deneen faced criticism for their handling of the case.

After the Democrat Carter Harrison II was elected mayor in April 1897, supporters of Alderman O'Malley visited City Hall and demanded Schaack be fired, but Harrison refused to take any action. An anonymous source at City Hall told the *Daily News* that Cyrus McCormick Jr. and other members of the conservative North Side aristocracy had pressured the mayor to keep Schaack on the police force. Harrison was reluctant to fire Schaack, because the only way to please the anti-Schaack crowd was to replace the inspector with someone in cahoots with the Irish-dominated Market Street Crowd. "This does not suit the wealthy folk of the North Side," the anonymous source said. "They know Schaack and are satisfied with him."

Two days later Louise Luetgert disappeared. Schaack and Schuettler would soon have another sensation on their hands.

8 The Search

MANUFACTURING PLANTS with grimy walls and tall chimneys lined the crooked stream of the Chicago River's North Branch. Here and there piles of yellow pine added a little color to the dingy surroundings and the fragrant scent of freshly cut lumber to the air. At one spot the blackened timbers of an old grain elevator stood against the eastern sky. Although it had burned months earlier, the piles of debris surrounding the ruined building were still smoking.

The haunts of river men—weather-beaten yachts and disabled boats transformed into roughly constructed homes—were half-concealed beneath bridges. A sign on a boathouse designated it as a chapel, but it was hardly big enough to hold a dozen worshipers. Disabled ships and partially constructed boats sat in dry docks, where dams shut out the slow-moving brown water.

Steam-propelled buckets descended into the holds of vessels moored at docks and came out loaded with glistening anthracite. They rose sixty or eighty feet, swung away from the water, and then plunged abruptly, disappearing among the rafters of the coal yards. A rumble could be heard a few seconds later, and then the buckets reappeared, ready for another load.

North of Goose Island the river turns abruptly west and then moves back north a few hundred feet later. Not far from that bend stood the cupolas and smokestacks of the North Chicago Rolling Mills. At night sheets of flame shot up from the enormous metal works, as great masses of molten iron and steel poured into the furnaces.

Around Diversey, where the river ran just a short distance west of the Luetgert factory, the scenery along the North Branch became more rural. The low banks were covered with trees that surrounded the low, flat-roofed homes of laborers, mostly devoid of paint. White rock was heaped high in a nearby stone yard. Brickyards could be seen in the distance. The banks were yellow, the color of clay, and the land along the river was pockmarked with many deep pits, dug by the operators of brick kilns.

After the police had interviewed Luetgert about his wife's disappearance, Schaack told Schuettler to drag the river for her body and to search the clay pits, many of which were filled with water. They also looked for her in the large piles of terra cotta at the Northwestern Terra Cotta Factory down the street from the Luetgert home. The search came up empty.

Schuettler sent Officer Bernard Preuss to find out where Luetgert dumped the ashes from his factory. Preuss found piles of cinders and ashes, enough to fill many wagons, along Hermitage Avenue, the entire distance from the Luetgert house to Diversey. Sifting through the ashes with his hands, he fished out some rusted, half-burned strips of steel that looked as if they might have once been part of a woman's corset. Preuss returned the following morning, May 9, with another two officers and a garden rake. They raked the cinders and found more pieces of steel. Officer Fred Tallowse found a hairpin.

The Luetgert factory was actually two connected buildings, with the shorter south wing hidden from Diversey behind the main structure. The south building, where most of the sausage manufacturing took place, had an open cupola on each of its corners to admit fresh air. "The odor during the time of putting meat through the sausage process is said to be overpowering to all but men with trained olfactory organs," the *Tribune* reported. This building was filled with scraping machines, choppers that reduced animal flesh to mincemeat, steam-operated propeller cleaners, vats, boilers, engines, racks, and machines that shot meat stuffing into skin casings. The police officers went into the factory and searched a cinder pile in the corner of the engine room, but there was little evidence in the south wing of the plant of what had happened to Mrs. Luetgert.

The officers also checked the north wing, which was primarily a warehouse where the sausage was stored. The front part of the first floor, facing Diversey, included Luetgert's office and a large retail salesroom where Luetgert sold groceries and meat. The front part of his office contained several desks. A massive old-fashioned fireproof safe stood in the rear. Behind that was a nine-by-five-foot windowless area, formed with wooden partitions, where Luetgert usually slept. The dark area was equipped with a cot, mattress, sheets, and a blanket and was connected to a narrow space with a washstand and toilet. The door leading into this dingy apartment bore a placard marked with rough black letters: "THIS ROOM FOR MR. LUETGERT ONLY." A doorway led from the back of Luetgert's office into the shipping room.

Not far from that doorway a staircase led down into the north wing's basement, where six large furnaces used for smoking sausages occupied the

Adolph Louis Luetgert, photographed in 1898.

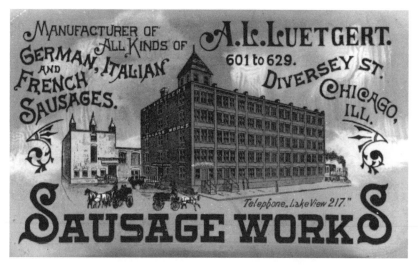

The Luetgert sausage factory, on Diversey Street west of Hermitage Avenue. (Courtesy of Jim Luetgert)

Louise Luetgert. (Courtesy of Jim Luetgert)

The Luetgert home, just south of the factory. (*Chicago Tribune*, May 17, 1897)

Robert Davey, the English con man alleged to have swindled money from Luetgert. (*Chicago Inter Ocean*, May 19, 1897)

Diedrich Bicknese, Louise Luetgert's brother. (*Chicago Tribune*, Aug. 31, 1897)

Chicago Police Captain
Herman Schuettler, who led
the Luetgert investigation,
in a 1906 *Chicago Daily
News* photo. (Chicago
Historical Society, DN-
0003937)

Chicago Police Inspector
Michael J. Schaack, posing
for a *Chicago Inter Ocean*
photo in 1886, the time of
his most famous case, the
Haymarket Square bomb-
ing. (Chicago Historical
Society, ICHi-12391)

Frank Odorofsky, a laborer in the Luetgert factory. (*Chicago Daily News,* Sept. 2, 1897)

Frank Bialk, the night watchman at the Luetgert factory. (*Chicago Daily News,* Sept. 18, 1897)

Some of the Most Prominent Personages in the Great Luetgert Trial.

A newspaper illustration showing some of the key players in the Luetgert case. (*Chicago Journal,* Oct. 19, 1897)

Judge Richard S. Tuthill, who presided over the first Luetgert trial, depicted in a drawing by John Francis Holme, one of the most highly regarded newspaper illustrators of the era. (Courtesy of Special Collections, University of Arizona Library, Collection of John Francis Holme, MS 001 no. 9)

State's Attorney Charles S. Deneen, the lead prosecutor for the Luetgert murder trial. (Courtesy of Special Collections, University of Arizona Library, Collection of John Francis Holme, MS 001 no. 9)

west end. Their flues extended the entire five stories of the building, and on each floor the flues opened onto chambers where the sausages could be placed for smoking. The basement also had three square wooden tanks, each about twelve feet long and divided into two sections. Luetgert's employees used these vats for dipping the sausage into a solution made with salt from alum.

The officers discovered that the middle vat was filled with a brownish fluid. They put some of liquid in a bottle. They also found a false tooth, which they turned over to Schaack.

That same day Christine Feld went to the Luetgert home and found Mary Siemering alone, ironing. She asked, "Where is Mrs. Luetgert?" According to Feld, Siemering said Mrs. Luetgert had gone downtown to make some purchases. When Luetgert returned home a while later and sat down to coffee with Feld, she asked him, "Why is Mary telling lies that your wife is gone downtown?" Luetgert said he didn't want everybody to know his wife's absence. He claimed that she had disappeared for a few days on several previous occasions and then returned. Feld told him, "That is not nice of Mary to tell a lie to me."

By then it was too late for Luetgert to keep his wife's disappearance a secret. That morning's *Tribune* had announced the information on page 1. The article gave no indication that Luetgert was suspected of killing her. In fact, the *Tribune* incorrectly reported that Luetgert had notified the police. Furthermore, without citing any sources, the newspaper claimed that Mrs. Luetgert had abandoned her family:

> Mrs. Luetgert left home one week ago last night. It is believed that the failure of her husband's business so preyed upon her mind that she sought relief in suicide somewhere near her comfortable home at No. 1501 Hermitage Avenue. . . . Mrs. Luetgert left home at ten o'clock at night. She took no clothing save the hat which she wore. Over her head and shoulders she threw a light shawl. A young son had spent the evening at a circus showing on a vacant lot a few blocks distant, and Mrs. Luetgert talked cheerfully to him about the show.
>
> While mother and son were thus engaged the former suddenly reached for a shawl which lay on a chair near by, and, throwing it carelessly over her head and shoulder, she stepped out of the front door.

The *Tribune* changed its tone the next day, however, when it suggested Mrs. Luetgert had met with foul play:

Mr. Luetgert, when seen yesterday at his home, . . . did not appear much concerned about his wife's absence of nearly ten days. The children, too, played around the house and lawn as contentedly as if nothing unusual had taken place in their home. The sausage man did not advance any theory concerning the mystery and pooh-poohed the suicide notion.

"Oh, I think she'll come back some day—maybe when I get out of my financial troubles," he said. "Then if she has jumped in the river and the police find her, they will let me know. I have offered a reward of $200 for her, or any information that will lead to her whereabouts."

When asked why he failed to notify Capt. Schuettler of his wife's sudden disappearance from her home at ten o'clock on a cold and rainy night he dismissed the matter with a shrug and the statement that he believed she was safely housed with some of her relatives.

Mrs. Luetgert's relatives know nothing about her. . . . Mrs. Wilhelmina Mueller, No. 158 Cleveland Avenue, is a sister of Mrs. Luetgert. When seen last night she could advance no theory. Her daughter, who formerly lived with the Luetgerts, spoke freely of the quarrels of the couple.

"Mr. and Mrs. Luetgert frequently quarreled," said the young woman. "Mrs. Luetgert was not the sort of person to run off and commit suicide, even though her husband failed, or they quarreled. Their quarrels have been frequent and extended over a long time."

Luetgert was furious when he read the story. He visited the Sheffield Avenue police station with a copy of the newspaper in hand. Schuettler asked, "What is the matter?"

According to Schuettler, Luetgert replied, "There is something in the paper that my wife didn't die a natural death, and I want it understood that she was sick for two weeks. I don't want anything of this kind."

"I can't control the newspapers," Schuettler said. "You will have to go to the editor of the newspaper."

Schuettler asked him whether he had meant what he said in the article about offering a two-hundred-dollar reward. Luetgert said he did, and Schuettler replied, "You better put that in writing and I will let it go to the public that you offer that, and someone might turn up that we know nothing about at the present time." Luetgert wrote down a two-hundred-dollar-reward offer for any information leading to the discovery of his wife, dead or alive. Luetgert also sent a couple of men to the *Tribune*'s offices to "demand the authority" for the statements the newspaper had made.

Schuettler had compiled a list of Mrs. Luetgert's relatives and sent officers to various corners of the city and the surrounding country, seeking clues of her whereabouts. After four days they had learned nothing.

An officer dragging the river found a few strands of hair. Then, on May 12, a fisherman named John Eldin was casting his line into the river at the Diversey Street bridge when his hook snared on something under the surface. Thinking the line had caught on a log, he pulled hard and it broke loose. When he pulled it out of the water, he discovered that he had caught a coil of human hair, which looked as if it had belonged to a blonde woman. Eldin went to Schuettler and showed him the hair, and police searched again at the site, but they still found nothing of note. After hearing about the discovery of the hair, Luetgert returned to the police station and asked to see it. He said it didn't look like his wife's hair, but he asked to take the hair with him, so he could show it to someone. Schuettler insisted on keeping the hair in police custody.

Detectives were swarming over the neighborhood, but after a week of investigating, they still didn't know what had happened to Mrs. Luetgert. Then, on the morning of Saturday, May 15, Officers Walter E. Dean and Martin Qualey were walking toward the Luetgert factory when they saw Frank Bialk, Luetgert's night watchman. Bialk said he wanted to tell them something, but they couldn't understand his German, so they told him to go to the police station on Sheffield Avenue. Around noon Dean and Qualey returned to the station and found Bialk telling his story to Schaack and Schuettler.

9 Strong Stuff

IT SEEMED AS IF all the workers in Luetgert's factory were named Frank, including the night watchman, Frank Bialk. After most of the manufacturing work ceased in February, Luetgert had kept on Bialk and a skeleton crew of employees. Bialk's tasks included running a boiler that powered a brine pump used to keep the carcasses in cold storage from spoiling. As he went about his work, Bialk habitually reached into his pocket with his calloused fingers, removed a horn-shaped snuff box, and took a big sniff.

Frank Odorofsky's main job was smoking meat, but he did whatever

Luetgert told him to do. Known as Smokehouse Frank (or "Pökelhaus Frank" in German, literally "Pickle-House Frank"), he would put sawdust in the smokehouses, add kerosene, and light it with a match. Odorofsky, a Polish immigrant, dipped the meat into curing vats and swept floors, and he was also something of a foreman. If the men didn't follow Luetgert's orders, Odorofsky would report them.

Another Polish worker, Frank Lavandowski, was known as Ham Frank ("der Schinkenfranz" in German) or sometimes little Ham Frank to avoid confusion with yet another worker nicknamed big Ham Frank. As Lavandowski's moniker indicated, he was a small man, no more than 110 pounds. His job was cooking and wrapping hams.

Bialk told the police a barrel had been delivered to the factory in March. He didn't know what was in the cask. One morning around seven, after the barrel had been standing several days in the shipping-room office, Luetgert called out for "Frank" to clean out the middle vat in the north-wing basement and to take the barrel down there.

"Who do you mean by 'Frank'?" Lavandowski said.

"Smoke Frank," Luetgert said.

And so Odorofsky cleaned the old sausage residue out of the vat with a broom and a scraper. Then he began moving the four-hundred-pound barrel. When he touched the substance inside it, Luetgert told him, "Take care. That is very strong stuff."

The barrel was too heavy for Odorofsky to carry by himself, so he had Lavandowski help him down the steps with it. When they spilled some of the barrel's contents, Luetgert said, "Now you clean up that very good." Once they had moved the barrel into the basement, they rolled it over to the middle vat. Luetgert told Odorofsky to break the stuff in the barrel into small pieces and put it in the vat. Luetgert warned him to be careful about his hands. Odorofsky wrapped his hands with rags to prevent burns. He tried breaking up the block with a hammer. When that didn't work, he used a hatchet, but the hatchet broke. Odorofsky complained to Luetgert that the stuff was burning his skin.

"I told him that stuff was eating so, burning," Odorofsky later recounted. "Then I told him whenever I knocked on it, it was flying around, like fire all over. If it touched somewhere, it burned like fire, and I took a rag and wiped it."

Luetgert suggested using an iron rod to break up the stuff in the barrel, but the rusty piece of metal broke when Odorofsky tried that. Odorofsky went back to his hammer. He kept working until he could stand the burning no longer. Around eleven he went to see Lavandowski and showed him his hands. "Damn the luck," Odorofsky said. "My hands are all burnt up with this stuff. Come and help me with the work." When Lavandowski asked him what the stuff was, he replied, "The devil knows what it is."

The two Franks went into the basement. Lavandowski, in his usual working clothes, simply covered his hands with some rags and began breaking up the material with a big hammer normally used for fixing barrels. He wore nothing over his face, and when bits flew up onto his sweaty skin, it made him jump. He took a piece of rag, tied it around his neck and over his head, and then put his hat on over the rag. The two men spent nearly the entire day breaking up the mysterious stuff, finally using it to fill three smaller barrels near the middle vat.

Luetgert had intended to help Odorofsky dissolve the substance in water that day, but it was already four o'clock, so Luetgert said he would get the night watchman to help him later.

In the last week of April Bialk and Luetgert filled the middle vat—which was three feet wide, eleven feet long, and three feet deep—about a quarter full with water, Bialk said. They poured the three barrels of the "strong stuff" into the vat, and Luetgert opened a steam pipe. He told Bialk to let the steam enter the vat until the solid was thoroughly dissolved. Bialk checked on the vat every fifteen minutes that night, until all the pieces had dissolved. He turned off the steam at 2 A.M.

Meanwhile Odorofsky had cleaned out the factory's six smokehouses. Luetgert put sawdust in the third smokehouse, about twelve inches deep. Sometime during the last two days of April, Odorofsky asked him, "Shall I smoke in the third smokehouse?"

"There is a little too much sawdust," Luetgert said. "You have to take some off. Do it as you always do."

Odorofsky put some bacon and hams in the smokehouse and started a fire. He took them out the morning of May 1.

Bialk remembered well what had happened May 1, the night Mrs. Luetgert had disappeared. The watchman said that he entered the factory's south wing at 6 P.M. and noticed a fire burning under the boiler, generating sixty pounds per square inch of pressure. Five or six men were working in the factory, and Luetgert was in his office.

Luetgert came into the shop and told Bialk, "Frank, go and get the big stepladder." The first ladder Bialk fetched was too short, so he retrieved a larger one. Bialk set it up so that Luetgert could reach the valve that let steam generated by the boiler run into the north-wing basement. At about 8:45 Luetgert told Bialk to keep the steam running so that he could use it in the vat. Bialk was not surprised to see Luetgert prowling about the factory at night. It was Luetgert's custom to visit the boiler room in the middle of the night. He watched his factory closely. But this business with the steam was a bit odd. "It was suspicious to me," Bialk said. "When he let in the steam at nine o'clock, those in the store asked me what he was going to do with the steam that night."

At about 9:15 Luetgert gave Bialk a dollar and an empty square white bottle. "Frank, you have to go to the drug store and if you will just show that bottle, you will get one like it," Luetgert said. Bialk walked to a drug store at Fullerton and Clybourn, about fifteen minutes away, and bought a bottle of Stanley's Celery Kola Compound from H. F. Krueger.* It was similar to the beverage Luetgert had requested, but not the same brand. Bialk came back into the boiler room in the factory's south wing. He intended to pass through the small door that led into the north wing, but something on the other side of the door was blocking it, so he tried to get in through the elevator.

The two wings of the factory had been constructed at different levels, so Luetgert and his employees used the elevator shaft at their juncture as a kind of passageway. They usually left the elevator car halfway between the ground floors of the two buildings. By placing a box on the floor in front of the elevator and another box inside the elevator, they created a makeshift stairway. Luetgert had always scolded Bialk when he used the elevator to go back and forth, but this time, with the other door blocked, Bialk didn't have any choice. When Bialk reached the elevator, Luetgert stepped into it from the other side.

---

* A 1902 advertisement for another brand of celery water explained its supposed benefits: "Thousands of people in whose blood lurk the seeds of disease, decline mentally and physically when the hot weather comes on. They become weak, languid, morose, have loss of memory, loss of appetite with wasting of flesh. For all such Paine's Celery Compound is an absolute necessity at this time. It is the only remedy approved of by able physicians for purifying and enriching the blood, for feeding and nourishing the nerves, for maintaining digestive vigor, for the building of flesh, tissue and muscle, and for promoting refreshing and healthful sleep."

Bialk handed him the bottle. "Frank, it is all right," Luetgert said. "Now go back to your fires. It is all right." Luetgert returned to the basement.

A while later Luetgert came to Bialk again and handed him a blue bottle. "Frank, you have to hurry again to the drug store and have to get me like there was in this bottle," he said. Bialk said he left on his second errand shortly after 10 P.M., which was about the time when little Louis Luetgert said his father came into the house and sent him to bed.

Bialk took the bottle to the drug store, which he found locked up. Bialk knocked on the door and the proprietor came out and gave him a bottle of Hunyadi water. When Bialk returned to the factory, the door leading into the north wing was still blocked, so he went again to the elevator. Luetgert stepped into the elevator from the other side and took the bottle. "That's all right, Frank," Luetgert said. "Now return to your fire." Bialk went back to the brine pump in the south wing. From where he worked, Bialk could see through some windows into the north wing's basement. He noticed Luetgert was moving about with a lantern.

Bialk was awake the whole night, tending the fire in the boiler room. He did not go into the basement because Luetgert had blocked the door. Shortly before three in the morning, Bialk heard the steam in the basement being shut off. Luetgert came upstairs and went into his office between three and four o'clock.

Bialk finished his night's work at 7 A.M. He went into the office to clean the stove and saw Luetgert sitting in his chair with his feet on the table. At first he wasn't sure whether Luetgert was asleep or awake. Bialk asked, "Mr. Luetgert, should I let the fires go down? Or shall I let the steam go in the box?" Luetgert turned pale and shook his head. He told Bialk to let the fire run at fifty pounds.

When Bialk came back to work that evening, he went to the engine room. He saw that the fires were out and was astonished to realize Luetgert had raked out the ashes—a task Luetgert usually left for his workers. The watchman next went to the office and cleaned the stove. He went into the north-wing basement for some coal and noticed that the water was running over the top of the vat. He turned it off. He observed a shovel leaning against the vat. Six or seven old sacks were hanging on the other vats. A loose door covered the first vat, and a door was lying in the first box. A chair from Luetgert's office sat near the middle vat. Brown water ran over the vat's top and into the sewer drain on the floor, leaving a trail of pale red slime, two to three inches deep in places.

"It was red-brown and it smelled bad," Bialk said. "I stepped into it and it was slimy. It smelt moist, like as if meat was boiled or something like it."

Bialk looked at the door he had been unable to use the night before. Apparently it had been blocked with a barrel and some boxes, but these obstacles were now moved to the side.

Luetgert came into the factory office around nine o'clock. "Mr. Luetgert, the water was running over in the box and I turned the water off," Bialk said.

"Frank, that's all right," Luetgert said.

Bialk told him he had brought the chair from the basement and put it in the office.

"That's all right, Frank," replied Luetgert.

When Smokehouse Frank Odorofsky came to work the next day, Monday, May 3, Luetgert told him to clean out the basement. "As I stepped downstairs, Mr. Luetgert followed me, and as I got to the middle vat he was rubbing his hands and stood back of me," Odorofsky recalled. "I never noticed him, as long as I had knew the man, that he looked so wild as he did on that morning."

Luetgert told him, "Frank, now you hear that water? With this water, you sweep and clean out the whole basement."

"What shall I do with the dirt at the middle box?" Odorofsky asked. "Are we going to do anything with the stuff, or has it been done already?"

Odorofsky remembered Luetgert responded, "Frank, that is all right. Only clean everything up, and then you take the whole stuff and take it to the yard and throw it all over the yard. Frank, you worked a long time. Don't tell about it, and you have your work with me as long as you live."

Odorofsky saw that the vat was full of brown slime and dirt. A nearby shovel, which Odorofsky remembered seeing there on Saturday, was also covered with slime. He picked up a piece of a bag lying nearby and discovered that it, too, was slimy. Luetgert knocked the stopper out of the vat, and its contents began running into a large gutter that ran the length of the room, ending in a sewer drain near the stairway.

A steamhouse door leaned against the middle vat, and eight or nine wet sacks were hanging from it. Odorofsky remembered that the door had been clean on Saturday, but now it was spattered with bits of slime. A couple of other doors were lying nearby. Odorofsky suspected that the doors had been on top of the vat when it was boiling with the red stuff. They all bore spatter marks but were clean for about a foot on either end, as if the ends of the doors had extended past the edge of the vat. Odorofsky had worked in the factory since it opened, and he had never seen a door laid across a vat like that.

As Odorofsky began scraping up the residue, he remembered how much the substance had stung him that day in March when he was breaking it up. He told Luetgert, "This stuff is not so powerful now. It does not hurt my hands any more."

"Why, I reduced it, rinsed it out with clean water, let clean water into the vat," Luetgert said.

Lavandowski, who helped Odorofsky clean the basement, later said, "I observed that there was some material, some peculiar material, smeared over the floor. . . . It was a reddish color, about the color of a brick. It was soft and slimy."

Odorofsky took half a shovelful of the stuff from the vat, including a piece of a red handkerchief or rag, and then turned on a hose and began filling the vat with water. The substance in the vat began to clear, but a reddish foam formed on the surface. "I observed when the water turned hot, on top the surface was foamy like on beer, only it was different color," Lavandowski said. "It was reddish, it was pale-reddish. Smokehouse Frank took a piece of board and shoveled all this scum in one corner."

"It was slimy and it was greasy," Odorofsky recalled. "The stuff was brown and slimy, and so I put some of it on the shovel and took it to the window and took a spoon and spread it. It was small pieces of flesh and it was small pieces of bone. It was slimy and sticky and if you stepped in it with your shoes, your shoes stuck to it."

Odorofsky scraped out the vat with a shovel and put the slime into a barrel. Luetgert told him, "Frank, take it to the yard and dump it out and spread it all over the yard. Throw it all over the yard." Odorofsky followed his instructions, scattering the stuff in the yard near the railroad tracks and kicking dirt on top of it. He scraped up the residue on the floor near the two doors and dumped that in the yard as well. He burned some of the rags in the boiler room and threw some into the yard. At one point Odorofsky told Lavandowski to come outside, because he thought the stuff from the vat smelled odd. "Come here, Frank, and just take a nose to this," he said. Lavandowski thought it was "a very unhealthful smell."

Odorofsky left the vat half-full of water and went into the third smoke-house. He saw sawdust was strewn across the floor, about three inches deep. Some matches were lying there, too, indicating that someone had tried to light the sawdust. Odorofsky examined the sawdust, which had footprints in it, and noticed that some slimy stuff similar to the fluid in the vat had been mixed in with it. He got some of it on his hands and felt a burning sensation. Odorofsky poured a line of kerosene in the center of the smokehouse floor and lit it with a match. When the fire had burned out, a smooth layer of ashes about an inch high was left inside the smokehouse.

10 Grewsome Clews

ON THE AFTERNOON OF MAY 15 Luetgert walked into the Tosch sa-loon. Agatha Tosch had noticed police were constantly hanging around the Luetgert house and factory, and she had heard rumors that he was suspected in his wife's disappearance. She asked him where he believed his wife was.

According to Tosch, Luetgert said, "I do not know where my wife is. I am as innocent as the sun in the sky. And all the trouble I have, my brother-in-law caused. We had made up a plan that Mary and the children should go to the country and I was going to board until all the trouble was over."

Tosch asked him whether he was going to live with Mrs. Feld. Luetgert told Tosch she was crazy to suggest such an idea. She replied, "Mr. Luetgert, I myself believe you guilty."

Luetgert had been resting his hand on a post, but now he dropped it excit-edly. "Child, did you see anything?" he asked. "Or do you know of anybody that saw anything? Then tell me. We always have been friends, and your hus-band is a friend of mine, and I am now in trouble, and now help me as much as you possibly can. I did, so far as business is concerned, all for you I could."

"What was the matter with the smoke Sunday forenoon, Sunday?" Tosch asked. "What was the matter with the smoke Sunday?"

Luetgert asked Tosch if she had seen any smoke at the factory. She said, "No. The engineer saw the smoke." Charlie Maeder, who worked as an engineer at the factory, boarded at the Tosch house, and he had told her he had seen smoke coming from the Luetgert factory in the early morning hours of May 2.

Luetgert asked Tosch to tell Maeder not to say anything about the smoke. He then added, "I just feel like taking a revolver and shooting myself, if it would not be for the children." He asked Tosch to let him know if she heard the detectives say anything at her saloon.

Luetgert noticed Frank Bialk's son John sitting in the saloon. Luetgert asked him what the police were doing with his father. John Bialk said he didn't know. According to Bialk, Luetgert responded, "Well, you stay here and wait until your father comes out and call him on one side and tell him I want to see him, and send him over to my house. And don't let the police know about it." As Bialk walked out of the bar, Luetgert followed him. "Don't forget," he said.

Around the same time Frank Bialk was leading Schaack and Schuettler in through the front door of the Luetgert factory, along with Officers Dean, Qualey, and Anton Klinger. Bialk took the police into the basement and pointed out the middle vat. Although Odorofsky and Lavandowski had cleaned it two weeks earlier, it was still half-filled with fluid. Holding candles and a lantern, the detectives peered into the vat.

Schaack took some of the liquid into his hand and saw that it was brown. He asked for a stick, and one of the officers handed him a scraper. Feeling around for a place to let out the water, Schaack discovered a plug. He knocked it out and watched the water shoot out onto the floor. He told an officer to grab one of the bags hanging on the next vat, and then he shoved the bag under the bunghole to catch the substance. They also got bottles and a pitcher to catch the fluid, which was fairly thick. The officers lifted the vat about three inches on the other side to help it drain, and they used a broom to empty it as well as they could.

Dean jumped into the vat, but Schaack told him to get out, warning, "You will burn your shoes." He stepped out of the vat, but a few minutes later Schaack told him to go back in and look around. Dean later testified that the substance in the vat had a "very sickening smell," as if there were "something dead around it." When he felt around in the muck, his fingers began to burn.

Schaack found a light-colored hair about a foot long on the top edge of the vat. Then, as the officers searched for clues by candlelight, Schaack took one of the bags to a window to get a better look at its contents. The window was so dirty that it admitted barely any sunlight, so Schaack opened it. Examining the sack, he found several fragments of something that appeared to be bone, including one that he thought looked like a piece of skull. The shards felt like sandstone, and they came in many shapes, some only half the size of a fingernail and others thin and a quarter-inch long. As Schaack was examining these, he heard Dean call out, "Wait, what is that?" Dean bent over and picked up something from the bottom of the vat. "Here are some rings," he said.

Dean handed Schaack two gold rings, a plain wedding band with a smaller ring stuck inside it. Schaack took out his handkerchief to clean the slime from the gold bands. As he wiped off the bigger of the two rings, he noticed the words "18 karat" inscribed in the metal, along with two initials in German Gothic script: "L. L."

◆◆◆

The police brought in Mary Siemering for questioning and placed her in a basement cell for the night.

John Bialk told his father that Luetgert wanted to see him that Saturday night or Sunday morning, but Frank Bialk didn't feel well, so he stayed in bed. Around 5:30 in the morning Schuettler and Klinger came to the Bialk house. Schuettler told John Bialk to go to Luetgert's house. Schuettler left, but Klinger stayed there as the son went off to see Luetgert. Around 6:15 John Bialk told Luetgert his father was ill and wanted Luetgert to come see him.

"All right," Luetgert said. "I will come right away."

A short distance from the Luetgert house, three police officers in civilian attire sat in a boxcar and peered through the mist at the big buildings. They did not venture onto the Luetgert premises, looking as if they might be afraid of the great Danes chained behind the house. The detectives themselves were being watched by a newspaper reporter.

Around seven Klinger was standing in Frank Bialk's bedroom when he noticed Luetgert coming down the alley toward the house. He hid under Bialk's bed. As Klinger listened, Luetgert came into the bedroom, sat down in a chair, and spoke with Bialk in German, with a few words of Polish thrown in.

"Frank, are you sick," Luetgert said.

"Yes."

"Them, was them in here—them police yesterday?" Luetgert asked. Bialk gave no answer. Luetgert asked, "You was with him by the Sheffield Avenue station, by Captain Schuettler?"

"Yes, sir."

"What did those men want from you? You should not have gone with them [unless] they had papers. Did they have any papers?"

"I don't know."

"You was with them. Bialk, you was with them in the factory, looking all over the factory."

"Yes, I was there."

"Did they find anything?"

"No."

"That's good. Now, did they ask you whether I had a bed or slept in the office?"

"Yes."

"What did you say?"

"Yes, I told them you had a bed and was sleeping there."

"Hmmm . . . so you said they didn't find anything?"

"No, they didn't find anything."

Luetgert asked whether the police had found bones in the smokehouse, and Bialk, whom the police had instructed to say nothing, again replied that the detectives didn't find anything.

Luetgert said, "In a week or two you and your son can start to work for me again. I will open the factory, and you can start to work for me." He promised Bialk he could work for the sausage company as long as he lived. Then Luetgert got up, put on his overcoat, and walked out.

One of the plainclothes men working on the case, Officer Charles Griebenow, walked into the Tosch saloon that afternoon around two and saw Luetgert speaking with the Tosches. Griebenow thought Luetgert appeared "very much excited, pale-looking."

"Charley, have you got a warrant for my arrest?" Luetgert said.

"No, sir," said Griebenow, who had known Luetgert for twenty-five years. "Louis, I have not got a warrant for your arrest."

"Come here a moment," Luetgert said. "I want to speak to you." He motioned for Griebenow to follow him into a side room where the Tosches ran a bowling alley. Luetgert took his hand and squeezed it. "Charley, you are my friend, are you not?"

"Why, yes, Louis, I am your friend."

"Tell me, what have they found?"

"Why, I couldn't tell you that."

"Tell me, what can I expect?"

"Well, you can expect to be arrested at most any time."

"Well, now, you are my friend, Charley, do what you can for me, and I will see you later." Luetgert walked out of the saloon and rode away in his buggy.

All day witnesses came in and out of the police station on Chicago Avenue, refusing to answer reporters' questions. Mrs. Luetgert's niece, Frieda Mueller, left the station under police escort. A short time later a reporter visited Mueller at her home. She appeared to be "deeply agitated," with traces of tears in her eyes. "I am sorry, but I cannot talk any tonight," she said. "I am almost ill. Please excuse me." Her friends said she had broken down sobbing again and again as Inspector Schaack interviewed her inside the station.

All the next morning Luetgert complained of feeling ill, and he seemed half-hearted and dispirited. When Schuettler, Qualey, and Dean walked up to the house around 1:30 in the afternoon, a pair of Luetgert's dogs leaped to their feet and growled, showing their teeth. They might have sprung at the officers, but Elmer, who was playing in the yard, threw his chubby arms around the necks of first one dog and then another. "Be good, Duke," he said to one, petting it. "You mustn't bark at the gentlemen." The detectives continued up the steps and rang the bell. Christine Feld answered the door, and they told her they had to see Luetgert at once on important business. She led them back to the sitting room, where Luetgert lay on a sofa, talking with his wife's nephew, Fred Mueller, and a reporter from the *Chicago Journal*.

"What do you want?" Luetgert asked the policemen. "I am not feeling well today."

"We have come to arrest you, Mr. Luetgert," Qualey said, "on the charge of murdering your wife."

Luetgert's face turned white, and he jumped up from the sofa. "Take me if you want, but I am innocent," he said. "God knows I am innocent."

"Yes, of course he is," Feld said. "Mrs. Luetgert told me lots of times that if ever her husband was bankrupt, she would go away."

The detectives interrupted Feld's outburst and read the arrest warrant to Luetgert, who listened quietly until they were through. He asked permission to go upstairs and change some of his clothing. They allowed him to do this, and while he changed, Feld continued telling the police about the many times Mrs. Luetgert had said she never could remain with her husband if he lost his fortune. "But I said, 'Mrs. Luetgert, a woman's place is always by her husband, no matter what happens.'"

Luetgert came down and said he was ready to go. He put on his hat and, drawing on a light overcoat, stepped out on the porch with Mueller and the detectives. "Good-bye, Papa," Elmer shouted. "Good-bye! Bring Mama back with you."

"I think we had better go," said Luetgert hurriedly, and they went out the gate and around to the front of the factory, where a police buggy was waiting. The officers took Luetgert into the buggy and drove off.

Feld remained standing at the gate outside the Luetgert house. "It was a shame," she told everyone who came along. "It was a shame. Mrs. Luetgert told me herself, right on that porch, time and time again, that she would leave if her husband ever lost his money. But I said, 'No.' I said, 'No, Mrs. Luetgert, a woman's place is by her husband, whatever happens to him.' It's all the fault of the English press. It's all their fault. A-stirring up all this trouble, and she's a-making for her folks. And him such a nice man, too. Why, all the men in the factory thought everything of him. One of them told something to a German newspaper two years ago that made trouble for Mr. Luetgert, and I went right over to the factory and I said, 'You tell such things again and I'll settle you,' and I had him a-beggin' in no time."

As she talked, Elmer played with the great Danes in the big yard under the newly budded trees. Curious neighbors stood on the sidewalk and stared at the house. Little groups gathered in front of the saloons, looking at the deserted, gloomy sausage works and then at the residence behind it. Newsboys swarmed around the neighborhood, selling extra editions of the afternoon papers with the news that Luetgert had been arrested. The papers reported that the police were accusing Luetgert of having used a solution made with crude potash* to dissolve his wife's body. The papers quickly sold out, even though the price had been raised from two cents to a nickel.

---

* Crude potash is made by burning hardwood trees. The ashes are dissolved in water, then the liquid is drained off and boiled. When the water evaporates, a white alkaline residue is left in the bottom of the pot, containing potassium carbonate. Potash is used for fertilizing plants, dyeing fabric, and making soap, glass, and saltpeter (a component of gunpowder). Beginning in the mid-nineteenth century, potash began to be mined from salt deposits formed during the natural evaporation of ancient oceans and lakes.

11 The Sweating

THE MISCELLANY of arrests in Chicago in 1897 included 253 for being "inmates of opium dens," 62 for prizefighting, 56 for mayhem, 55 for fast driving, 45 for rioting, 33 for violating the ordinance concerning bathing, 14 for bigamy, 10 for "crimes against nature," 9 for stealing horses, 9 for abortion, 5 for illegal voting, and 4 for distributing obscene literature. The most serious crimes, however, were the 21 abductions, 17 kidnappings, 4 manslaughters, 7 attempted murders, and 33 murders.

In 1897 the Forty-first Precinct in Lake View delivered twenty-one corpses to the morgue for the coroner to examine. In addition, the police in that precinct charged one man, Adolph Louis Luetgert, with killing someone whose body was never found.

Schuettler's police buggy carried Luetgert to the Sheffield Avenue police station, and then the prisoner was taken to "Schaack's Bastille," the station on East Chicago Avenue. "Though a man of powerful physique and reputed to be 'nervy' to desperation, after the arrest was made, Luetgert collapsed and was almost carried into the police station," the *Tribune* reported. Policemen remained on constant watch outside Luetgert's cell, saying they feared he might commit suicide. Around the same time the police finally released Mary Siemering from custody.

Officers at the police station would not admit William Vincent, an attorney whom one of Luetgert's friends had called for help. After persistent pleas Vincent gave up and went to the courthouse to file a writ of habeas corpus alleging Schaack was putting Luetgert through the "sweating" process. "This thing is an outrage," Vincent said. "There is no situation or circumstance which justifies the police in refusing to allow a prisoner the right to see his attorney." He said Schaack had a personal reason for being uncooperative. Vincent had organized a protest against Schaack over the investigation of Alderman O'Malley on murder charges. And now, Vincent said, "He is trying to whip me over poor Luetgert's shoulders."

"I have nothing to say about the case," Schaack told a reporter, "except that we found what we considered good evidence of Luetgert's guilt at the sausage mill. . . . We have all along felt that there was nothing in the theory of suicide, and have not done this thing without careful deliberation."

Although Schaack wouldn't let Vincent see Luetgert, a reporter for the *Chicago Inter Ocean* gained admittance and interviewed the prisoner through the bars of his cell. The reporter thought Luetgert appeared rather unconcerned, with an "air of martyrdom" about him.

"I don't know where my wife has gone to," Luetgert said, adding: "She has been in the habit of telling me that she would go away to her people, as she said she was not satisfied with this country, and wanted to go back to her home. I feel sure that is where she has gone, and as soon as she arrives, all of these charges against me will be cleared up. We have lived happily together until recently, when I have had financial trouble, and then she became dissatisfied. This statement, that we had quarrels, and that I had threatened her life, is not true. I do not feel very much worried over the outcome, as I am innocent. My wife has not had time to arrive in Germany yet, but she will surely clear me when she does."

Reporters made their own examinations of the crime scene inside the Luetgert factory. They claimed to find "clews" the police had overlooked. An *Inter Ocean* reporter discovered several red stains on the door of the makeshift bedroom in Luetgert's office, noting, "It is so removed from all the operations of the factory that it could not come from any of the meat handled there. The stain is still fresh and has been made by a drop. It is deep red and has run down slightly." In a closet next to the room, the reporter found a rusted iron chisel with blood stains on it. And the knob of the door leading out of the office into the factory was also bloody. A deep stain marked one of the supporting upright timbers on the stairway leading into the basement. It appeared someone had washed the wood, trying to remove the stain.

Eugene B. Palmer, a reporter for the *Journal,* went into the factory May 18 with a bottle he had procured at a neighborhood saloon. "We went to the middle vat there, and there was some number of workmen there cleaning out the sewers and things and several police officers," Palmer later remembered. "I secured a tin pail from them that was lying there and had that washed out very carefully and went to the middle vat, and one of the men . . . got a broom and swept some of the solution from the vat to the bunghole and into the pail. It was poured immediately into the bottle and I took the bottle with me." Palmer sent his bottle to a chemist for analysis.

The next day the *Inter Ocean* reporter returned to the building and found more blood, this time on the two trapdoors covering the basement stairway. If Luetgert had carried a body down the stairs, the *Inter Ocean* theorized, blood might have dripped onto the doors. Indeed, three drops and a large daub several inches long stained the door on the right side. The reporter also found a four-foot-long stick soaked with the same dark reddish-brown stuff that had been in the vat. The reporter placed the stick on top of a timber in the basement, carefully noting its location in the next day's newspaper in case the police wanted to retrieve it.

12 The Woman in Black

LATE IN THE AFTERNOON of May 3, a woman in black got off a train in Kenosha, a town of about 6,500 just across the Wisconsin border. No one in town had ever seen her before. She stopped into the saloon at the Hotel Maple.

"There was a strange woman there at a quarter to five on the evening of May 3," the hotel's bartender, Matthew Scholey, later recalled. "She was a very thin, slim woman, black hair and black eyes, light-complected. She wore a black slouch hat with a little veil tied around it, a dark dress, and she had on a cape, a black cape. She seemed to be very excited and nervous when she came in there, and she didn't hardly give us a chance to tell her when the next train was going where she wanted to go. . . . She went over to the depot."

The following day Frank Scheve, a farm laborer in Pleasant Prairie, several miles south of Kenosha, saw a woman in a black hat and cape walking along a country road.

"I was on horseback going home to dinner, it was twenty minutes to twelve, I met this woman," Scheve said. "I saw her coming from far. I thought it something strange to see a woman around there. This woman, as quick as I seen her face, why, it struck me that I knew her. Of course, I was riding in the same path that she was a-walking. I turned out and gave her the path, and I stopped the horse and looked at her and I thought, yes, you know that woman, but couldn't place her. I didn't know who it was, and I went home for dinner and told my wife."

The bartender Scholey had visited Chicago and was returning on the 8 P.M. train, due to arrive in Kenosha at 9:25. The train came to an unscheduled stop a half-mile south of Spring Bluff.

"The train never stops there, and I was sitting in the south end of the smoking car as the train was going north, and as it stopped so sudden, I stepped right outside the door to see what was wrong," Scholey said. "It was a pretty good jar, and I looked down the east side of the train, and there was a lady standing on the bank in the dusk. And she mumbled something that I could not understand. She was reaching for the side of the handles of the steps of the train as you get on. I helped the lady on the train. She walked across the platform and stepped off on the west side of the train. There was some other gentleman helped her off. When I was there with the crowd, this lady walked around the car and got up in the front end of the smoking car, and finally in a few minutes we all got on the train and started off, and this lady kept sitting in the smoking car until we struck Kenosha, with her head down." Scholey said it was the same woman he had seen the day before at the Hotel Maple. She was wearing the same clothes.

Henry Feldshaw, a policeman who walked the beat around Kenosha's Chicago and North Western depot from seven at night until five in the morning, noticed the woman in the depot around 9:30. "I went in there and said, 'Good evening.' She didn't answer me, and I said, 'Good evening,' again, and she said, 'Good evening,' and I asked her if I could do anything. She was dressed in black and had a dark brown jacket. She had a black sailor felt hat, and an old string slipper. . . . I remained there about five minutes. I took her over to the hotel, and the bartender came outside and talked to her in my presence."

Feldshaw tried to get a room at the hotel for the woman, but she refused to pay for one and went back to the station. After the last train left Kenosha, all the lights in the station had been turned out except for one in the large waiting area. The woman sat down in the dimly lit room. "I saw her in the depot about half past ten that same night, dressed the same as before," Feldshaw said. "She was sitting down and leaning over, with a handkerchief over her face."

Sometime after eleven Leonard Brunner, a barber, saw the woman in the depot, crying into her handkerchief. He asked if she needed help. At first she refused any assistance, but then she allowed him to take her to the Hotel Grand. William Gunster, a clerk there, told them he had no vacancies.

"I asked her where she came from," Gunster later remembered. "She said she wanted a room. She didn't take a room. She stayed about ten minutes and went out—went down Main Street with the barber. She went in the direction of the station. I never saw her after that." Something about the woman's manner and appearance caused Gunster to doubt her moral character.

Feldshaw returned to the train station a little after two in the morning, accompanied by Officer William Smith. The woman was still there. "She was sitting down in the station, and I sat alongside of her and I talked with her," Smith said. "She looked as though she had been traveling around considerable and was worn out, and looked tired. I asked her where she was from and where she was going. She said she was going in the country about a mile and a half or two miles to her sister by the name of Miller. She expected to go out in the morning. And I asked her if she knew whereabouts [the sister] lived, and she said she thought she lived south of the town. I asked her where she came from and how long she was in this country. She told me she came from Joliet, Illinois."

A few minutes later the woman walked out of the station, leaving behind her shoes and her black hat. She returned to retrieve them around five in the morning.

The woman was never seen in Kenosha again. A couple of weeks later, however, people in town read about the disappearance of Louise Luetgert in Chicago and began to wonder whether it had been the same woman. The morning after Luetgert's arrest, Vincent received a call from a lawyer in Kenosha named Louis Bohmrich, who said he had seen the woman at the depot around 4:30 A.M. on May 5. Vincent thought it sounded like Mrs. Luetgert.

Vincent dispatched two men to Kenosha and one to Racine with photographs of Mrs. Luetgert. The people who had seen the woman in black on May 4 and 5 looked at the picture and said it was her. Scheve, the farm laborer, said he now recalled the person of whom the woman walking down the road had reminded him—Mrs. Luetgert, whom he claimed to have known for several years.

William Charles went to Kenosha in the hope of finding Mrs. Luetgert. He accompanied Kenosha police chief Charles Stemm and a detective as they drove to every farm within fifteen miles occupied by a family named Miller, Mueller, or Muller. They visited seventeen homes in all but found no one who had seen the woman, no one related to Mrs. Luetgert, and no one who had a sister coming to see them. Mrs. Luetgert's sister in Chicago, Wilhelmina Mueller, said they had no relatives near Kenosha.

Charles, certain that his friend was innocent and that the easiest way to prove it would be to find Mrs. Luetgert, did not give up his search. "I have men on bicycles scouring the country around Kenosha in every direction," he said. "I am satisfied the demented woman did not go to the home of any Mueller within twenty miles of Kenosha. . . . I am inclined to think she was taken into some private house and is there now, sick. One circumstance more than anything else convinces me that the woman seen in Kenosha was Mrs. Luetgert. When she went to the Maple House and asked for a room, she was told it would cost fifty cents. 'What, fifty cents! I'll not pay it,' she said, turning abruptly to go. 'Have you no money?' the clerk asked. 'Oh, yes, I've got the geld,' she answered immediately. 'I've got the geld.' That was a characteristic expression with Mrs. Luetgert—one she used continually. I can bring half a dozen witnesses into court who have heard her use just these words scores of times. Mrs. Luetgert would as soon have paid five dollars for a car ride as fifty cents for a night's lodging. She was a very stingy woman."

Vincent and his assistant on the Luetgert case, Arnold Tripp, issued a public statement insisting that Luetgert was innocent. "Mrs. Luetgert has been suffering for almost a year from an affliction peculiar to women of her age, and which has, at times, caused her to be temporarily deranged, and has made her nervous, despondent, and excitable," they wrote. "These misfortunes were aggravated by a full knowledge of her husband's financial embarrassment."

Vincent and Tripp said they were convinced the woman seen in Kenosha had been Mrs. Luetgert, but they added, "We candidly confess that we do not know where she is now. She may have committed suicide, she may be confined in jail, poorhouse or asylum. She may be working on some distant farm, remote from the metropolitan press." They then remarked that the conduct of the police in the prosecution of Alderman O'Malley indicated another innocent man was about to be railroaded, and they promised a $200 reward for any information on Mrs. Luetgert's whereabouts.

Vincent visited Mayor Harrison's office May 20, asking him to investigate Schaack for the way he had run the Luetgert case. Harrison referred the matter to Superintendent Joseph Kipley. A few days later Kipley said he saw no reason to question the credibility of Schaack and Assistant State's Attorney Willard McEwen. "I believe they have made out a strong case and I shall leave the entire matter in their hands," he said.

Schaack brushed off the Kenosha story, saying he had already received a dozen letters from people in various places who claimed to have seen Mrs. Luetgert since May 1.

"I take no stock in such communications," he said. "None would be better pleased than I if that poor, abused woman could be restored to her children and her home. Mrs. Luetgert disappeared May 1. Is it reasonable to suppose that she is roaming unnoticed through Wisconsin? She was in good mental condition on the evening of her disappearance and was as cheerful as usual. She did not get to Wisconsin in a night. Let the public understand that I am doing police duty and not issuing statements about the case. The O'Malley case is dragged forth, because, it is thought, people are prejudiced against me on its account. I pay absolutely no attention to this."

A detective working on the Luetgert case told a newspaper that the defense attorneys' plea to the public was an act of desperation. "The O'Malley case is also being worked for all it is worth that a sentiment may be created against Inspector Schaack," he said. "What has the O'Malley case in common with this one? We ask nothing difficult of Mr. Luetgert. We only ask that he explain the presence in his sausage factory of a vat of a concentrated solution of caustic soda in which are pieces of bone. He replies that it is a 'secret process of making sausage.' Surely never before was such a way of manufacturing sausage! It certainly would not be fit to eat if the meat were saturated with lye."

13 Cell 21

LUETGERT WAS SENT to the Cook County Jail, just north of the Chicago River and across an alley from the courthouse. It was unusual for a man of Luetgert's social standing to be in the county lockup, but not unprecedented. He was one of only 22 manufacturers arrested on various charges by the Chicago police in 1897. Other arrestees that year included 14,663 laborers and 32,158 people with no occupation. In addition, police arrested thousands of housekeepers, teamsters, clerks, peddlers, prostitutes, saloonkeepers, and carpenters. Criminal charges were also filed against 1,177 building painters, 37 artistic painters, 179 musicians, 24 piano makers, 52 actors, 6 actresses, 666 agents, 2 organ grinders, and 1 showman. One publisher, 127 newsboys, 35 reporters, and 10 editors were arrested, as well as 205 firemen, 100 constables, 147 attorneys, 29 stenographers, 1 stereotyper, 34 undertakers, 5 "capitalists," 6 clergymen, and 2 state fish wardens.

Unlike many new prisoners, Luetgert showed no reluctance in eating the jail food. However, he seemed to be receiving better fare than did the average prisoner. On Luetgert's first morning his breakfast consisted of a porterhouse steak, two eggs, a quantity of fried potatoes, and a generous bottle of coffee. The coffee served to the ordinary prisoners was a clay-colored mixture to which milk and sugar were added while the beverage was still in a big pot. Knowing that Luetgert was accustomed to better things, the jail included a little pitcher of cream on his tray, with four lumps of sugar in a china receptacle.

On May 20 Luetgert's eldest son, twenty-two-year-old Arnold, came from Indianapolis, where he worked as a traveling representative for an engine and refrigerator manufacturer. Arnold was tall and athletic, and it was often said he closely resembled his father. They had the same hair, the same moustache, and the same high forehead. The son had ordinary eyes, however, whereas some reporters commented that the father's eyes were "abnormally small," which some theories of the day considered to be a predictor of criminal behavior. The father and son conversed through the bars of the visitors' cage.

"Ich glaube nicht, daß meine Mutter todt ist," the son told reporters: "I don't believe my mother is dead. If she is, I am sure my father had nothing to do with her death. Some of the newspaper publications in reference to my father have been simply scandalous. But after a while, our turn will come. Wait. Inspector Schaack and several newspapers will hear from us. I will now look after the interests of my father, who has been defenseless as far as blood relations are concerned. If Mother is dead, she died while in a demented condition while wandering and not by any violence of my father. But I do not care to talk any more about this case at present." Describing the anger he felt about police department's "shameless" handling of his father, Arnold Luetgert used a German idiom—"(es) hat mein Blut in Wallung gebracht"— literally meaning, "(it) makes my blood surge through my veins."

On May 22 Judge George Kersten began a preliminary hearing to determine whether the police had amassed enough evidence to prosecute Luetgert. Crowds got an early preview of the testimony that would be heard later, when Luetgert went on trial. Luetgert's son Louis talked about the last time he saw his mother. Diedrich Bicknese and Frank Bialk told their stories. But Charlie

Maeder, the engineer who had seen smoke coming from the factory, disappeared, apparently leaving for Germany without notifying the prosecutors.

Judge Kersten ruled that the prosecution of Luetgert should go forward. On June 4 the grand jury subpoenaed Christine Feld to testify. Her attitude toward Luetgert seemed to have changed. She was indignant at a newspaper report that she had given Luetgert $1,400 the day before. "The money I sent to Luetgert yesterday," she said, "is money he gave me to keep for him the day on which he was arrested. I received word from attorney Vincent to give the money to Luetgert, and I sent it, by Mary Siemering, so that I would not have to go to the jail. Luetgert is no friend of mine. He borrowed $3,000 of me and gave me as security fourteen lots. I have since found that these lots are already mortgaged."

The next day, June 5, the grand jury indicted Luetgert. Unsure exactly how Luetgert had killed his wife before apparently dissolving her body in the vat, the grand jury offered a whole menu of possible methods, listing them all in a stream of words with barely any punctuation. It accused Luetgert of striking, pushing, shoving, and thrusting a certain knife in and on the head and belly of his wife. The jury said he gave her diverse mortal wounds, each being three inches long. It further claimed that he pulled, pushed, cast, and threw her down "unto and upon" the ground with great force and violence. Then, while she was lying on the ground, he had struck, beat, pushed, pressed, and kicked her, using both his hands and feet on her head, stomach, breast, belly, back, and sides.

The indictment went on to say that Luetgert had used a blunt instrument to push, shove, thrust, and strike his wife, giving her various mortal wounds, bruises, fractures, contusions, and concussions, each of which was two inches wide and one inch deep. And finally, he had choked, suffocated, and drowned her. In conclusion, the grand jury accused Luetgert of having done all this unlawfully, feloniously, willfully, and with malice aforethought.

On the day of his indictment, Luetgert gave an interview in German to the *Chicago Abendpost*. "Most of what the newspapers have published about my case gets every fact wrong, and it is truly no miracle if one flies into a flaming wrath over it," he said. "I am entirely certain that the rings found in the vat were not truly my wife's. It is a riddle to me, how the rings came to be found in the vat. Maybe the police put them there later, although I wouldn't want to put that down as fact. I myself am ever more firmly convinced that my wife is alive, and I would not be surprised if one day she would appear before my cell door. . . . I don't believe that twelve citizens of this city can ever be brought together, who would say—based on the body of evidence collected by the police after such hard work—that I am guilty."

14 Spring and Summer

WHILE ALL CHICAGO read about the gruesome discoveries in the Luetgert factory, rumors were going around another neighborhood about the experiments taking place inside the long, low building of the Chicago Chemical Company, where the blinds were closely drawn all day, bright fires burned at night, volumes of smoke poured from the chimney, and silent black figures came and went. A newspaper reported the firm's business was not so much chemistry as alchemy.

"Here, rumor whispers, E. C. Brice, the manager of the transmutation concern, was wont to dabble in weird mysteries and try occult operations with alembic, crucible and retort in the hope of discovering the long-sought philosopher's stone, which is supposed to possess the property of turning base metals into fine gold," the newspaper reported. "Mr. Brice claims he has unearthed the hitherto elusive secret and is now in Washington, where he is trying to sell it to the government and thus in a trice make necessary an entirely new set of financial theories."

A reporter knocking at the door found himself facing a man with a stubby black pipe between his lips. Puffing clouds of smoke, the man said, "It's none of my business and it's none of nobody else's, and I don't know nothing about it, anyhow."

"Mr. Brice conducted his investigation here, did he?"

"Well, I don't know what you'd call it. But I do know there's been a pile of chemical business going on here."

The man refused to let the reporter inside, abruptly bidding him good-bye and bolting the door.

A crowd of children prowled the grounds of the chemical company looking for gold. They triumphantly scooped up ashes from a pile inside a deserted and forlorn-looking barn nearby, imagining they had found something precious.

◆◆◆

The banking crisis at the end of 1896 quickly faded, and the U.S. and Euro-pean economies began to prosper. By the middle of 1897 deposits rapidly in-creased at Chicago banks. The city's financial institutions, which had been on the verge of collapse a year ago, began loaning money to people on the East Coast and in Europe at rates of 4 to 5 percent. Chicago had emerged from financial chaos to become one of the world's chief creditor cities. If Luetgert had not been in jail, he might have finally been able to turn around his business.

◆◆◆

Many of Chicago's police officers wondered whether they would keep their jobs under the new superintendent, Joseph Kipley, who had been among the eight hundred officers with ties to the Democratic Party who were ousted from the department when the Republicans took over City Hall. Now, with the Democrat Carter Harrison II as mayor, Kipley was back. The Democrats who had been let go under the previous administration had formed a group called the Star League, and now they all expected to get their jobs back. Re-publican officers feared they would lose their positions. The question was how Kipley would manage to do this under the state's new civil-service law, which was supposed to prevent political hiring and firing.

All those already on the force and anyone hoping to become an officer went through a battery of tests to determine their physical and mental fitness for police work. Then, in June, Kipley issued an order discharging, retiring, demoting, or promoting 158 members of the police department. "Superin-tendent Kipley last evening gave the Police department the greatest shaking up it ever received in the history of Chicago," the *Tribune* reported. "When he got through there was not a Republican holding a place higher than desk sergeant. . . . The civil service law was ignored as a thing of no conse-quence. . . . The discharged or reduced men, with hardly an exception, show by their names they are of American or English birth, while with as few ex-ceptions, the officers put in their places are Irish."

Kipley soon decided to let all the members of the Star League take the examination for reinstatement. The Star Leaguers were growing impatient as they waited to get back on the force. Although some of the Star Leaguers were undoubtedly good officers who had been dismissed for political reasons, many of them had lost their jobs for intoxication, disobedience of police rules, or willful maltreatment of citizens. As the department braced for the return of these officers, Kipley showed up for roll call at the detective headquarters and read the riot act to the men. He warned "a cyclone would sweep over headquarters and carry all before it" if he didn't see improvements.

◆◆◆

On July 11 Cook County opened a new wing of the jail. "Colored" waiters served salads, dainty dishes, and wine to county commissioners and other politicians for the grand opening. For two hours hundreds of Chicagoans were allowed to inspect the new jail. Everything down to the big handle of the grim-looking front door on Dearborn Avenue had been polished until it shone. Murderers' row, containing the four cells of those condemned to die, was the popular attraction among the visitors, many of whom were women.

Over the next week most of Cook County's prisoners, including Luetgert, would be transferred to the new building, which had four tiers, each containing 110 cells. Each department of the jail had an exercising corridor, and iron bridges connected each tier with the old jail.

"Four cells are called dungeons, compared with which the blackness of the hole of Calcutta is snowy white," the *Tribune* reported. "They are for prisoners who do not behave according to the rules."

◆◆◆

Luetgert's new cellmate was an old acquaintance, a North Side butcher and saloonkeeper named Nic Marzen, who had been charged in 1895 with killing Fritz Holzhueter, a butcher and cattle buyer. Holzhueter had disappeared on January 30, 1895, after being seen in Marzen's saloon. Almost a month later his corpse was found, partly cremated, in the south suburb of Evergreen Park. Prosecutors theorized Marzen had kept Holzhueter's body in his barn for three weeks before taking it to Evergreen Park and attempting to burn it. The evidence against Marzen was circumstantial, and his trial, lasting six and a half weeks, was at the time the longest that had taken place in the new Criminal Court Building.

The jury found Marzen guilty and sentenced him to death, but Governor Altgeld gave Marzen a reprieve from execution so that he could appeal his case to the Illinois Supreme Court. The state's highest court then reversed the conviction, because one of the jurors had been separated from the rest of the jury for two and a half hours one day when they were taking a walk in Lincoln Park.

Marzen was given the chance at having another trial, and now he waited in a jail cell with Luetgert. The two of them were allowed to fry ham and eggs on an oil stove in their cell, and the aroma filled the jail corridors. Luetgert often talked with Marzen about his case.

"Luetgert is surely innocent," Marzen told a reporter one day. "He will surprise them all when it comes to a trial. He will knock the props from under Schaack and the rest of them. . . . That woman is alive today, and she will show up."

"It is peculiar how Marzen and I have come together here," Luetgert said. "I have known him for six years. We used to do business together. We never supposed then that we would be thrown together in the same cell here in the jail, charged with murder. Nic is a good fellow and I am glad of his company."

15 Fixed Opinions

A STEADY STREAM of reporters visited the jail in late August 1897 as the Luetgert trial approached. Luetgert's only condition for granting an interview was payment in the form of cigars. He puffed away at one in the visitors' cage on the eve of the trial, chatting with a reporter for the *Tribune*. Since entering jail Luetgert had shaved off his chin whiskers and put on some weight. The reporter thought the effects of confinement were beginning to show, but Luetgert still acted as if he was the happiest inmate in the place.

"They will have to put a plaster over my mouth if they want to keep me still when witnesses get to lying about me," he said.

"But how about following your attorneys' advice?"

"I will respect my attorneys' advice when I can consistently do so, but how is a man going to keep still when his enemies swear falsely?"

"You expect to be acquitted?"

"Acquitted? Why, of course, I expect to be acquitted. They can't convict me because I'm not guilty."

Asked about the evidence in the case, Luetgert changed the subject, saying, "Smoking and walking and eating and sleeping take up my time, and I feel the necessity of getting some manual exercise to keep my weight from increasing. I have gained twenty-two pounds since May 16, the date of my incarceration. Does that look as if I was worrying to death, and that my conscience hurts me?" Laughing, he slapped his sides and surveyed his increased girth with a satisfied look.

Referring to the jail, Luetgert said, "There are some pretty good fellows in here, and this would be a good place to run a German *Weinstube,* or beer tunnel. The boys, if they all had five dollars apiece, would spend it like princes. Wouldn't you, boys?" Luetgert looked toward some prisoners who stood peeking through the screen separating the visitors' cage from the jail's inner section. "But I guess there are enough bars here already."

Luetgert laughed heartily at his joke. As he puffed eagerly at his cigar, he noticed he needed a fresh one. Lighting up, he said, "I expect to take the stand and they'll get the whole truth from me. All those little circumstances can and will be explained by me. I'll tell everything I know, and when the jury gets the facts, they won't think I am such a bad fellow."

Luetgert noticed a black guard staring at him, apparently shocked at Luetgert's lighthearted attitude. Luetgert made another joke, calling out, "Guard. I'm going to have all colored men on the jury, and you can be the foreman." Luetgert then returned to the exercising corridor, exhibiting what the *Tribune* reporter thought to be forced jocularity.

The next morning, August 23, Luetgert paced nervously in the exercise space on the jail's third floor. Now he refused to see any reporters or even acquaintances. When one journalist came, Luetgert said, "You fellows get out of here. I am sick and tired of talking for the newspapers. I shall do all my talking from now on in the courtroom."

By 9:30 A.M. the corridor outside the courtroom was crowded with men and women. They stood on tiptoe to catch a glimpse of Luetgert as a deputy jailer named Isaac Reed escorted him into court at 9:50. They begged and pleaded with the deputies guarding the door, but the deputies allowed only two hundred into the room. Those nearest the door got in first.

As he entered, Luetgert was smoking a cigar and making a strong effort to appear unconcerned, but his hand trembled when he held out his cigar to shake off the ashes. He had made sure he was carefully groomed for court. He was closely shaved, and his light hair, which had just been trimmed, shone with oil. His slate-colored suit had been brushed, but he wore his vest unbuttoned because it was too tight. A low collar with an old-fashioned ready-made black tie tucked under it encircled his thick neck. Reporters watching Luetgert thought he looked paler than before, and they noticed perspiration on his brow. His eyes avoided the crowd. He took his seat without a word, sliding low into the chair. As the attorneys talked, Luetgert took a pair of spectacles from his pocket and began reading an account of himself in a morning newspaper.

Judge Richard Tuthill was a fifty-six-year-old Civil War veteran who had served as the Tennessee attorney general, Chicago city attorney, and U.S. attorney for the Northern District of Illinois. His ten years on the bench had earned him a reputation for intelligence and diligence.

Charles S. Deneen, the Cook County state's attorney, handled the prosecution of the case. Deneen was a thirty-four-year-old lawyer from downstate Illinois, the son of a Latin professor, the grandson of a Methodist minister, and the great-grandson of an abolitionist politician. His honesty was unquestioned, and the press praised him for bringing a new sense of integrity to the state's attorney's office as he prosecuted criminals ranging from lowly thieves to powerful politicians. He seemed oblivious to any attempts to influence him. "He is a rank heretic so far as respect for so-called society is concerned or faith in the outwardness of things," the *Times-Herald* wrote. "He knows that the worst temptations offered a state's attorney come not from the lowest strata of society, but from the highest."

Although Deneen had charge of the case, he delegated much of the examination of witnesses to Assistant State's Attorney Willard McEwen. After being elected in 1896, Deneen had chosen McEwen, his former partner and law-school classmate, as his first assistant. The newspapers sometimes referred to the broad-shouldered Scotsman as "wily."

William Vincent was Luetgert's defense attorney. He had been the chief justice of the New Mexico Supreme Court, and most people still called him "Judge Vincent." He had also been a founding officer of the Ferris Wheel

Company and had been one of the passengers on the ceremonial first spin of the wheel at the 1893 Columbian Exposition. Vincent was a man of striking appearance, with a massive head and broad shoulders. Every day he appeared in court he wore his trademark pink shirt—he apparently had a stock of them—and pink tie, which the *Daily News* called "cute."

Although Vincent had been assisted by the lawyer Arnold Tripp at the time of Luetgert's arrest, Tripp had dropped out of the case, and Albert Phalen was now the second defense counsel. Phalen said he wouldn't wear pink shirts because they too closely matched the complexion of his cheeks, but on one occasion he wore a shirt decorated with "marvelously shaped flowers."

After listening to the attorneys argue about the constitutionality of the state's new jury law, Tuthill ordered the sheriff's deputies to bring a hundred potential jurors, also known as veniremen or talesmen, to the court the next day. Luetgert was taken back to the jail, and the women ran ahead of him to the stairs, lining up for a good view. As he crossed the jail yard, women leaned out the courthouse windows, their eyes following him until he had disappeared into the lockup.

The next morning Diedrich Bicknese went into the jail and walked up to his brother-in-law's cell. He pointed at Luetgert through the bars and said, "There is the man who murdered my sister. This is the best place for him. He ought to be hanged." Luetgert glared back but made no sign that he recognized Bicknese. A *Journal* reporter standing nearby suggested to Bicknese that he speak with Luetgert, but Bicknese drew away, saying, "No, he killed my sister, and I don't want to say a word to him. I have never spoken to him since the day I notified the police of Mrs. Luetgert's disappearance, and I never want to speak to him again."

Luetgert seemed less nervous in court the second day. Asked about his health, he said, "I feel splendid. Why shouldn't I? I had four whiskies before I came over."

Luetgert's young sons, twelve-year-old Louis and five-year-old Elmer, were often in court. The *Daily News* noted that they appeared to be bright, with "traces of refinement in their features," adding, "Neither of them resembles the father in the least." The boys attracted admiring looks from many of the women in attendance. Elmer laughed and chatted. When the trial was not in session, Luetgert would often take Elmer into his arms and kiss him. The boy showed a deep regard for his father, wrapping his arms around Luetgert's neck. One day Elmer brought a big bouquet of red roses into the courtroom, which he said a woman had given him in the hallway. "The pretty lady said the flowers were for you, Papa," he said.

Over the next four days the lawyers and the judge questioned the veniremen. The *Daily News* noted the list of potential jurors "did not seem to be made up from citizens who could demonstrate ordinary intelligence. In as many as fifteen cases, out of the hundred names called by the clerk, the owners of the names did not seem to understand they were the ones spoken to. The clerk frequently had to call a venireman's name four times before he would respond, and in six or seven cases the man did not answer until his address was called out."

Some tried to get out of serving on the jury with excuses about their jobs, but Judge Tuthill was seldom sympathetic. When A. L. Kuhn's name was called, Special Bailiff Frank Fucik told the judge that Kuhn had tried to avoid jury duty. The previous day the bailiff had gone to see Kuhn at the warerooms of the Union Steamboat Company, where Kuhn worked as a clerk. Kuhn ran off and hid behind a pile of merchandise. The bailiff told him, "Come out of there. I have a paper from the court to serve upon you." Kuhn replied, "I don't give a ———— for the court or anybody else. I will not serve on a jury." Fucik got close enough to push the court summons into Kuhn's pocket. When Kuhn came to court the next day and Tuthill heard about his behavior, the judge fined him ten dollars for contempt of court and dismissed him.

The main difficulty during jury selection was finding people who hadn't read the extensive newspaper coverage of the Luetgert case. Most of those questioned had already made up their minds about the case. One venireman, John Erickson, told the court he believed Mrs. Luetgert was dead. When one of the lawyers asked him whether that was a fixed opinion, Erickson said he didn't know what that meant.

"Would you change your mind after hearing evidence regarding Mrs. Luetgert's death?"

"Well, after reading the newspapers, I think I—"

"Excused," interrupted the judge.

Another potential juror, Louis Bauer, said, "I don't think Luetgert killed her."

"I'll take him," Vincent said, laughing.

"Excused for cause," ruled the judge.

One man, a machinist, claimed he had never read about the case, despite the fact that he subscribed to three Chicago dailies. The defense attorneys excused him.

Some veniremen said they would never convict someone based merely on circumstantial evidence, despite Tuthill's explanation that it was a normal legal practice to do so. Cases with solid direct evidence, such as eyewitness testimony, weren't as common as cases built on a set of circumstances.

John H. Krozer said he wouldn't hang a man unless he heard direct evidence proving him guilty.

"You don't mean that," Judge Tuthill said.

"Yes, I do."

"Then you are not sufficiently intelligent to be on a jury. Excused for cause."

The court questioned 175 veniremen and excused 114 of them for cause. The prosecutors used seventeen peremptory challenges—dismissing jurors without stating a reason—and the defense used fifteen. By Saturday, August 28, the court had selected twelve men. The jurors included two clerks, a butcher, a manager, a building contractor, a salesman, a soap maker, a railroad watchman, a collector, a sewing-machine maker, an unemployed printer, and an unemployed locomotive engineer. The oldest man was seventy-one; the youngest, twenty-one. The judge told the jurors the trial would begin Monday morning, and then the bailiffs escorted them over to the Le Grand Hotel, where they would be sequestered for the entire trial, cut off from almost all contact with their families. The judge had said they were in for a long ordeal, but no one had any idea just how long. It would be another two months before they were allowed to return to their normal lives.

16 The Rustling Noise

McEWEN LEANED his hands on the rail in front of the jury box and began his opening speech. "One hundred and twenty-one days ago," he said, "Louise Luetgert, the wife of the prisoner of the bar, disappeared from the face of this earth. She passed away as absolutely as though the earth had opened and swallowed her. . . .

"It was known that Luetgert was not living happily with his wife, and he was asked by acquaintances why he did not get a divorce. We will show by witnesses that he said he would find another way to get rid of his wife after his factory was closed by creditors. . . . It is the theory of the state that Luetgert left the house about 10 P.M. May 1, and went direct to the engine-room door of the factory. We will prove by direct testimony that Mrs. Luetgert was with her husband at the time, and we will prove that he took the woman into the building. That is the last time anyone saw Louise Luetgert outside the factory. She never did come out. She went in there to her death. . . .

"Luetgert hated and despised his wife. He had no affection for her and referred to her on one occasion as a 'low Dutch wooden shoe.'* We will show that his treatment of her was cruel and brutal, that at one time he was seen to choke her. . . . We will show that Luetgert not only despised his wife but that he violated his marriage vows and that numerous women visited Luetgert at the factory, where he had a bed and where he spent most of his nights for some time before Mrs. Luetgert disappeared. . . .

"From these things—from his indifference, attempts at concealment, and many other matters which cannot be accounted for on any other hypothesis than that on which the state is acting—we expect to prove that Adolph L. Luetgert murdered his wife and destroyed the remains in the middle vat."

After McEwen had concluded his address to the jury, Vincent made the surprise announcement that he would not make his opening statement until after the prosecution had presented its case. With that, McEwen and Deneen began calling witnesses.

One of the first witnesses was Diedrich Bicknese. Speaking in a German drawl, Bicknese related how he had discovered that his sister was missing. He impressed observers as being honest and straightforward. Once or twice it appeared he had ruffled Luetgert's temper. Nevertheless, Luetgert did not interrupt the witness, as he had promised to do whenever he disapproved of any testimony.

On cross-examination Vincent asked Bicknese, "Do you know what her physical condition was on May 1 and some months prior?"

---

* When Chicagoans of the 1890s are quoted using the phrase "Low Dutch," they may have been referring to Plattdeutsch, a German dialect spoken in northern Germany. The author Rudolf Hofmeister noted that "damned Dutch" was a common insult against German Americans in Chicago during the nineteenth century. The term "wooden shoe" was apparently another idiomatic insult of the era.

"I didn't know but what it was all right," Bicknese said. "She never complained."

"Did you notice any difference in her mental condition?"

"No difference."

"Did you ever observe any indication of mental trouble or insanity in members of the family?"

"No, sir."

"Don't you know that your sister was cross and irritable to the children and punished them a good deal?"

"No, sir."

"You say your sister was a hard-working woman. Don't you know she didn't get up until nine in the morning?"

"No."

"She always had a servant girl, didn't she?"

"Most always, I guess."

"You don't feel very kindly toward Mr. Luetgert, Mr. Bicknese?"

"I can't say that now, but before I did not feel bad toward him, but I don't suppose anybody can blame me now."

Vincent tried to ask Bicknese about one of his cousins, Louisa Law, who had died at a mental institution in Kankakee. Vincent also wanted to ask Bicknese about his brother, Henry, who had mysteriously disappeared in 1873. It was Vincent's theory that the stories of these relatives proved the Bicknese family had a history of mental illness and disappearances, which made it more likely that Louise had gone crazy and fled her home. Before Vincent got far with this line of questioning, however, the prosecutors objected. Vincent walked up to the bench and told Tuthill, "Your Honor, I want to show that mysterious disappearances have followed this family the same as suicides follow families." Tuthill refused to let him go on.

The next witness was young Louis Luetgert, who told of going to the circus on May 1 and of talking with his mother that night. At first Louis's story was the same as it had been when he talked to police and when he testified in earlier court hearings. After Louis described hearing his father walk out of the house, however, McEwen asked him whether anything had happened after he fell asleep. "That was the last that you paid attention to that night?" McEwen asked.

"About two in the morning I heard some rustling around in the dining room," the boy said. "I don't know if it was in the kitchen, and I said, 'Is that you, Pa?' and it sounded like my mother's voice, and said, 'It's me.'"

McEwen looked startled, his face flushed. "You never told me that before," he said.

"I never was asked."

"You remember, I asked you before Judge Gibbons—just to refresh your recollection—whether you heard anything after your father went out, whether you heard anything that night, and you remember that you told me that you did not?" Vincent objected, arguing that in the earlier hearing, McEwen had asked Louis whether he had seen anything, not whether he had heard anything.

"I understood you asked me if I saw anything," Louis said.

As McEwen continued his questioning, the boy never flinched, looking steadily at McEwen with his wide blue eyes. As Louis testified, his father watched him closely. Luetgert seemed to be breathing deeply with anxiety and anticipation. He scribbled notes with the stub of a pencil.

"Now," McEwen went on, "you woke up in the night just to hear that, did you?"

"I just turned myself around and I heard some rustling and . . . I heard something like my mother's voice say, 'No, it's me.'"

"What time was that?"

"I don't know. I know it was around in the middle of the night."

McEwen changed the subject, asking Louis about his mother's rings. The boy said she had worn a wedding ring and a smaller ring, both on the second-to-smallest finger of her left hand. The wedding ring had been a plain gold band without any stone.

"Did she always wear it?" asked McEwen.

"Yes, sir, she couldn't get it off," Louis said.

After discussing the rings for a minute, McEwen went back to the testimony that had startled him earlier. "Now, coming back to that rustling noise you heard, Louis, have you talked about that with anybody?"

"Well, Judge Vincent asked me about if I heard anything afterward and I told him."

"Did you ever tell anybody besides Judge Vincent?"

"No, sir."

"You didn't tell us before the grand jury?"

"I wasn't asked there, either."

"Now, when was it, what was the date, if you can give it us, when you first told Judge Vincent about that rustling?"

"I don't know the date. I don't know the date."

McEwen sat down and turned the witness over to the defense for cross-examination. "I don't believe we will cross-examine him at all," Vincent said. The boy stepped down from the witness stand.

◆◆◆

A couple of days after Louis testified, J. Sanderson Christison, a physician and criminologist who had previously worked at the New York City Asylums for the Insane, visited the Luetgert home. Christison was covering the trial for the *New York Herald* and was also "connected with the defense as an expert of some kind," according to the *Chicago Inter Ocean.* Christison later recounted talking with little Elmer that day:

> Gently stroking his head and speaking in a sympathetic tone of voice, I said to him: "Elmer, don't you want your mamma back?" His reply was an immediate shake of the head. Again I put the same question but in a tone of surprise, and again he shook his head. Then with an expression of astonishment I said to him: "Why! Elmer! Why! Don't you want your mamma back?" The prompt and emphatic response came as if in a subdued tone of injury: "Because she hurt me too much." If this is not unquestionable evidence of an abnormal mother, what is it? . . . A child of his age cannot be coached against his inherent feelings.

17 The Morbid Women

LONG BEFORE the doors of the courtroom opened each morning, nearly a thousand people crowded into the hall. On September 3 the *Daily News* called it an unruly mob, noting, "It cannot be called a crowd." The people struggled to get closer to the doors, yelling, wrestling, pulling, and pushing with a complete disregard for safety. It was as if, the *News* reported, "they wanted to crush the life out of somebody." And it was not just men but also women who clawed their way toward the entrance. More people kept arriving from the elevator and stairs.

Hearing the din, Inspector Schaack arrived in the hallway and saw there would be no space to bring in the prisoner and jury. He called in a score of officers, but when the reinforcements showed up, they discovered that simply ordering the crowd to disperse wasn't sufficient. The police pushed many of the curiosity seekers tumbling down the stairs to the second floor, provoking cries of disapproval. Women who hoped they would be given special treatment because they were members of "the gentler sex" found themselves led away just like the men.

The deputies grew more careful in examining the passes visitors presented to get into court. One woman extracted a folded paper from a richly garnished case and presented it with a look of innocent assurance. A deputy looked at it and realized it was a gas bill. He told the woman where the bill should be paid and escorted her to the elevator.

A well-dressed young man despairingly said, "It's no use. I came here from Batavia, Illinois, expecting to see Luetgert and hear the testimony. . . . I've tried about every way of getting in, but they know me now and I can't work any dodge. . . . I guess I'll trek back to Batavia. The bailiffs are too much for me."

Other visitors who failed to get in remained outside. "This is a public building and you have no right to stop me from going into it," one said. "I am an American citizen and as such I should have the privilege of going into any public building."

"But you are not an employee," a bailiff said.

"That doesn't make any difference," the man replied angrily. "You have no right to stop me whether I am or not. I tell you this Criminal Court Building is open to the public. The first come should be the first served." About three hundred people standing nearby applauded.

The courtroom had barely enough room for all the reporters and sketch artists, so the court clerk hired a carpenter to build three rows of long pine-board tables, each of them about a foot wide, for the press near the front of the chamber. Chicago had ten English-language dailies at the time—the *Daily Tribune, Daily News, Record, Evening Post, Inter Ocean, Chronicle, Journal, Times-Herald, Dispatch,* and *Daily Sun*—and each of them sent at least one reporter to the Luetgert trial, usually accompanied by a sketch artist (also known as "sketchists" and "chalk talkers"). On some days a given newspaper would fill more than two entire broadsheet pages with accounts of the trial, including transcripts taken down by additional reporters. Chicago's German-language newspapers, the *Abendpost* and *Staats-Zeitung,* covered the trial, too, as did reporters working for newspapers in New York and Saint Louis and for wire services. Stories about the case also appeared in newspapers ranging from the *Los Angeles Times* and *Atlanta Journal* to the *Salem (Mass.) Gazette* and *Brattleboro (Vt.) Reformer.* The intensive press coverage fed the public's interest in the Luetgert case, and large crowds continued turning out each day.

Lawyers, judges, and ministers got special treatment when they showed up to observe the trial. Some women got in on the recommendation of friends connected with the case. Many men were shut out because they lacked this needed "pull." Some people came day after day, but each session drew newcomers, usually women who had begged their husbands or fathers for "just a half a day at the trial" so they could see Luetgert.

Throughout the trial the crowd was predominantly female. These court watchers came from all grades of society; they were old and young, pretty and homely, rich and poor. Many were stylishly dressed, resplendent in new September millinery and modish gowns. A bevy of "matinee girls"—women who typically spent their afternoons at the theater—filled the front rows, watching the trial through opera glasses.

The women outside the railing were mostly immigrants. Many were Germans from Luetgert's neighborhood who whispered gossip to other women who had never seen Luetgert before. They were poorer than the opera-glass crowd, but most of them wore their Sunday best. The working-class women were willing to stand throughout the sessions, if the bailiffs would let them. One reporter noted nearly all the women of this class chewed gum. "They have as many different ways of chewing it as they have hats and bonnets, but they all chew, and it is to be doubted if the biggest bailiff in the room could stop them."

Judge Tuthill appeared to be astonished at the size of the crowd and its "matinee make-up," but he would occasionally invite a maid or matron to sit on the bench with him for a few moments during recesses. The other women in the audience would look on in envy.

"I could think of nothing in looking at them but a great colored, angry sea," wrote Katharine, reporting for the *Chronicle.* "The audience was not for one moment quiet. Throughout the entire day it was one billowy wave of pink, lavender, white and red. Gay roses nodded at somber plumes on the hats of women who bobbed up and down, endeavoring by stretching of necks this way and that to get a view of the stolid German."

Although the women followed Luetgert's every movement with an almost obsessive fascination, many of them said they believed he was guilty. "And all the women present yesterday in that close-smelling courtroom were ready and willing to say so," Katharine wrote. "At least the married women were, for each and every one of them felt that such a fate as is charged might await her, and so, while making every effort to see the prisoner, they still expressed their contempt for him."

When the women weren't staring at Luetgert, they were looking at Schaack, another tall and stocky man of Germanic heritage. With his impressive blue uniform and brightly shining yellow buttons, he had become a center of "feminine interest."

Although other newspapers described the "high society" portion of the courthouse crowd, the *Journal* reporter H. Gilson Gardner was skeptical. He looked around for any carriages dropping off rich people in handsome costumes but saw nothing other than "fat, red-faced individuals, who sign bail bonds for a living, and a few tough-looking constables and loafers." As for the women in the front row, Gardner doubted they were truly upper class, although they might be figures of prominence at dances in the German neighborhood around the sausage factory.

As Gardner observed one day's court proceedings, a uniformed officer repeatedly yelled at the crowd, "Siddown! Siddown! You're worse than children!" The officer waved his mallet at the craning women and men in the audience and motioned them to return to their seats. When the officer turned his back on the court watchers, they began edging slowly forward. Gardner himself found little startling in the day's evidence, and he wondered why the audience was so interested. "There seems to be a fascination in this Luetgert trial, and a large part of the audience acts as if it were perpetually impelled upward by invisible strings," he wrote. To find out what was driving the crowd's curiosity, Gardner left the area reserved for reporters and sat out in the audience. He recounted his experience:

I walked back and took my seat next to three pitched-faced little old women in black, who seemed to be having a most exciting time. It was Luetgert they were watching. His back was toward them, and all they could see was a patch of slate-colored coat, and the oily black hair swaying back and forth with the rocking of his chair.

But this was enough to interest them. They doubtless believed they were looking upon a monster—a freak worth coming miles to see, a great murderer with a world-wide reputation: a fiend in the guise of a man, who went about committing frightful deeds of darkness.

These little old ladies had heard that Luetgert had an evil eye, and they believed it. It appeared from their talk that he could make one crazy by merely looking at one. There was the monster's back! That was his hand there, fingering a pencil; a look, now he was turning around and the evil eye was looking in their direction. The three little ladies sank into their seats, and with heads in a bunch discussed the event in awed whispers.

"See! Now he speaks!" cried one, and all three were immediately on their feet to see Luetgert talk into the ear of the man at his side. . . .

I looked around and tried to estimate the general character of the audience; but I found that no generalization would do. In a way it seemed much the sort of a crowd that might be attracted to a continental hanging. It was mixed—so mixed in fact that it was difficult to pick out the component parts. . . .

There was a bullet-headed man earnestly chewing tobacco and pointing out the celebrities to a frowsy-looking girl. Distributed about the back of the room were a dozen men of the sort that may be seen sitting on the courthouse steps of a sunny afternoon. One was dozing with his mouth open and his head describing short arcs of a circle with its center at his Adam's apple. Most of the men looked decidedly "unemployed," although there were among them a number of bronzed and lean-looking fellows who might from their appearance have put in fourteen hours a day cultivating cabbages.

The younger women are evidently morbid sensation lovers—or lovers of morbid sensation. In general they are either dowds or slatterns. In the front row was a female particularly conspicuous in widow's weeds. It was plain that she gloried in her affliction, and a murder trial was but another symptom of the same complaint.

There were girls there of a very common appearance. Luetgert's reputation as a lady-killer appears to have enveloped him with a particular interest for women of a certain sort. . . .

It is not so much what is happening as what might at any moment take place that keeps these people sitting and standing hour after hour during these hot September days.

"Suppose Mrs. Luetgert should walk into the courtroom," I heard one woman say.

Women received similar treatment from the most famous correspondent covering the trial, Julian Hawthorne. The son of Nathaniel Hawthorne, he had written twenty-six novels, including mysteries and supernatural tales. He abandoned novel writing in 1896, however, when William Randolph Hearst hired him as a star reporter for the *New York Journal,* where his assignments including covering the presidential campaign of William Jennings Bryan. Hawthorne was often mentioned in the same breath as the *Journal's* other famous roving correspondent, Stephen Crane. When Hawthorne came to Chicago for the Luetgert trial, he had recently covered an outbreak of the black plague in India for *Cosmopolitan.*

"The seats assigned to the spectators looked like a flower garden, such was the array of feminine hats," Hawthorne wrote, adding that the audience included "fantastic women, all nerves and oglings, and nondescript creatures who seemed to have been created especially for this trial."

Ironically, Hawthorne, whose own melodramatic and often fantastic reports on the trial (which were reprinted in the *Tribune*) surely fueled feminine interest in it, mused about the women's motives: "What did all these women come here for? To admire Luetgert and sympathize with him? To see him condemned? Or merely to gaze at a man who has the reputation not only of having murdered his wives but of being a Don Juan of low life, a fellow with whom no woman was safe? I need not give my own opinion, but I will say that I think their presence and manner here are not to their credit. They penetrated even to the judge's bench today; and there is no telling what they may do tomorrow. . . . I have seen many trials, but I never saw anything like these women."

A day after publishing Hawthorne's comments, the *Tribune* received a letter that was signed by "A Woman":

> It seems unfair even to narrowness that women should be criticised in a sweeping, wholesale manner for visiting a courtroom where a man is being tried for the murder of a woman—his wife. What do women go for? Well, what do men go for? For various reasons; certainly not necessarily to sympathize with the accused nor to see him condemned.
>
> Society has been, is now, and doubtless always will be infested with an uncertain number of morbid men and women who love nothing so much as the excitement of blood-seasoned sensation. The majority of the visitors in the courtroom where the Luetgert case is now being tried are no doubt in

this class, but it must be admitted by all fair-minded persons that some of them are prompted by higher motives—that of the love of justice and an intelligent interest in the wonderful technicalities of the law, strained to its utmost tension, as shown by contending attorneys—a veritable battle of law and language.

Women being subject, equally with men, to the laws of our country, should know something of it. From an educational point there is no better school of law—and we might add morals—than the law courts during great trials.

Ignorance is not innocence. . . . The day when it was considered "proper" for women to do nothing in particular but to sit behind closed boudoir doors and [pore] over in worshipful silence what men do and think is numbered with the past, and only a few men . . . carry any flowers to its tomb.

18 Trained Beasts

THE MORNING OF AUGUST 31 Agatha Tosch took the witness stand dressed in a black satin skirt with a waist of brown-figured silk trimmed with lace. Her toque was stylish, trimmed with violets, and a white veil obscured her face. She impressed the reporters as an attractive woman. Luetgert was nervous as she entered the room. Noticing that everyone was closely observing his own reaction, Luetgert remarked to someone sitting near him, "Mrs. Tosch looks gay today. The newspapermen ought to get her picture in the papers just as she looks now."

Tosch did not speak English well, so she testified in German, with Rudolph Liebrecht, a reporter for the *Staats-Zeitung,* interpreting. Tosch testified about the conversations she'd had with Luetgert in the first two weeks of May. In addition, she talked about things he had said earlier, as when, sometime in April, Luetgert had come into the saloon.

"He was mad and I asked him what was the matter. He was very mad," Tosch said. "He said he had lots of trouble in the business and when he came home he had troubles at home. He said he did not want to live any longer with her. He could not and would not live any longer with her. And I said, 'You would not get a divorce from her as long as you have children with her?' . . . And then he did not answer."

Another time, Tosch testified, Luetgert had told her that Mary Siemering was the only reason he could stand to remain in his home. He said he couldn't eat Mrs. Luetgert's cooking. He had thrown the food at her feet several times. "And Mrs. Luetgert wanted Mary to leave the house," Tosch testified. "And he said if she did not like to have Mary in the house, he would take Mary to the factory. Mary could stay with him as long as he lived. He thought sometimes he could take Mrs. Luetgert and crush her. . . . Then he clinched his fist. And then I told him not to say anything like that—it would be like if I took my baby and crushed it."

Years earlier, when the Tosches had a saloon on Roscoe Street, Luetgert had told Agatha Tosch about his wife's having fallen ill. "He told me," she testified, "that Mrs. Luetgert was very sick. . . . She had trouble with her throat and if he waited one minute longer with the doctor, then the 'dead, rotten beast would have croaked.'"

Tosch said she had often quarreled with her husband, Otto. Luetgert gave her advice concerning how to deal with these arguments. "He told me not to quarrel," Tosch said. "I should do it like he does. He punished his wife with contempt. He did not look at her certain times for three or four weeks, and he told me to do it the same way. That would worry and anger my husband more than if I raised the dickens with him or if I made trouble with him."

On cross-examination Tosch acknowledged feeling bitter toward Luetgert. She said she had been his good friend until the time Mrs. Luetgert disappeared. Vincent suggested that Tosch hadn't been quite as friendly toward Luetgert in the six months leading up to the disappearance as she had been previously.

"You did not go to the factory as often in the last six months or a year as you did before that, did you?" Vincent asked, alluding to the rumors that Tosch used to visit Luetgert's bed. McEwen objected, and Judge Tuthill refused to let Tosch answer. Vincent tried to show that Tosch felt envy toward the other women vying for Luetgert's attention, but she didn't show any signs of jealousy on the witness stand.

The next witness was Frank Bialk, who hobbled up to the stand and, taking occasional pinches of snuff from his horn, told about the delivery of the potash barrel to the factory, Luetgert's actions on May 1, the events afterward, and the conversation that had taken place as the police officer eavesdropped from beneath Bialk's bed.

As Tosch and Bialk testified Luetgert abandoned all pretense of being uninterested. Continually twiddling a pencil, he anxiously listened to the interpreter and sprang up from his chair whenever the translation did not suit him.

When Luetgert came to court the next morning, he was not dressed as tidily as before. He shook hands with one or two acquaintances as he entered the room, but not in his old cheerful manner. He mechanically took his seat. Despite his dejected appearance, Luetgert agreed to answer reporters' questions. "I am not made of cast iron, and I did not like some of the things Mrs. Tosch and Frank Bialk said," he admitted. "That woman told lies about both me and my wife. . . . It was rather hard for me to sit here and listen to the lies she told, but I consider the source. My wife never associated with her or people like her, and all I can say about her is that she had been so influenced by the police that she lies to please them—otherwise, her business might be interfered with. Frank Bialk is an honest man, and he does not intend to tell any wrong stories, but he is like an elephant or a bear—you can train him. Too, he is like a dumb beast that can be trained, and he has been in the training of the police so long he tells according to his training."

When cross-examined by Vincent that morning, Bialk admitted he had been under constant police watch for the past three months. He said he had no money, having spent all his savings soon after losing his job at the sausage factory. When he said he didn't know who was paying his living expenses at the present time, Vincent suggested that it was the police.

Bialk acknowledged it had been necessary to keep the engine fires burning the night of May 1 to keep the meat cool, but Vincent failed to get Bialk to change his story. Bialk seemed uninterested in Luetgert's guilt or innocence. He said he admired Mrs. Luetgert's gentle and ladylike manners, but he didn't know whether she was dead and wasn't prepared to say she had been murdered.

Vincent told Luetgert to stand near the witness so that Bialk could get a good look at him. "Is that not the same suit of clothes Mr. Luetgert had on the night of May 1?" Vincent asked.

As Bialk scrutinized Luetgert's suit, Luetgert smiled at him, and Bialk smiled back. Bialk said he believed it to be the same suit that Luetgert had worn on May 1. Bialk closely looked at Luetgert's feet and added, "And the boots he now has on are the same he had on that night."

"Did you see any burns on his clothing or on his hands?" Vincent asked. Bialk said he hadn't, and Luetgert went back to his chair.

Bialk was followed on the witness stand by Frank Odorofsky, who wore a blue flannel shirt. He showed signs of nervous strain as he began testifying, in German and through an interpreter, on the afternoon of September 1. Once the guileless-looking Odorofsky got started answering a question, it was hard to head him off. As he answered Deneen's questions about breaking up the potash in the middle vat and cleaning up the mess in early May, he often got far ahead of the interpreter. Odorofsky told his tale with wild gestures and grimaces. At times he became so wrapped up in his story that he rose from the chair and stood in front of the jury, trying to show with his hands and arms what his tongue had trouble explaining. Over and over he said the stuff he had found in the basement was "*schleimig.*" He emphasized the word with long hisses, as if he'd been impressed by the ghostly character of the slime. The women in the audience who did not understand German shivered at Odorofsky's ghastly descriptions even before they heard the translations.

When Odorofsky came back to court the next morning, he laughed like a child at the pictures of him in the papers. He said the sketchists had made him look like a monkey. Deneen asked him to show his hands to the jury. Each of the twelve men carefully examined Odorofsky's hands as he pointed out the scars left by the potash. He said his wrists had been badly swollen after Luetgert made him break up the potash in the middle vat.

On his second day Odorofsky testified in Polish, and he found it easier to relate the details of the events. When Vincent asked him why he had never before mentioned these details, Odorofsky blamed his difficulty in speaking German. He also said he had thought a great deal about the events of the spring, and his memory of the incidents had improved. Vincent suggested that the police had told Odorofsky what to say, but he replied, "I am not working for no money. My testimony is from my conscience."

Frank Lavandowski took the stand next, his face as pallid as if he were the one on trial, but he never allowed himself to get confused. He, too, testified in Polish, and his answers became clearer and more emphatic as the day went on.

Vincent failed to shake the testimony of the two Polish laborers. Writing about Odorofsky and Lavandowski, Julian Hawthorne observed: "These men are as simple as children and their aim is to deliver the truth that is in them, whether by voluble speech or exhaustive gesture. It is vain to attempt to discredit their testimony by asking them whether they have been coached by the police, and it even proved vain to confuse them as to matters of fact. Though simple, they are very observant and see in their minds living pictures of what occurred during the momentous pounding of the potash and the cleaning of the vat."

A lawyer watching the trial noted that the necessity of an interpreter was making it difficult for Vincent to attack the witnesses as vigorously as he would have liked. "An attorney can look fiercely at the witness, put one hand behind his coat and shake the other threateningly while propounding some question, but what is the good of it?" the observer asked, speaking anonymously to a newspaper. "The witness appreciates the character of the pantomime, but does not understand the words until the calm, impassive interpreter has repeated them. By that time the witness has forgotten the shaking hand and the red, incredulous face of his real interrogator in grasping the question and formulating an answer. It's a good thing, for the witness can seldom be frightened so that he does not know whether he is in court or catching a trolley car in the middle of the block."

Although Odorofsky and Lavandowski did not know the proper name for the "strong stuff" that had burned their hands, another witness did. Corydon Clark, a salesman at the wholesale drug house of Lord, Owen and Company, testified he had sold Luetgert 50 pounds of arsenic and 375 pounds of potash on March 12. Clark said crude potash is similar to concentrated lye and was typically used for making soap and cleaning. "I told him the crude potash was dangerous stuff to handle, and he said he knew that," Clark testified. "I told him of an experience one of our men had with potash some time before that; he was struck in the eye with a piece of the material and badly burned."

19 Trial by Newspaper

THE NEWSPAPER SCRIBBLERS reveled in their depictions of Luetgert, noting every nuance of his posture, every tiny gesture, every change in expression. At times Luetgert seemed oblivious to the seriousness of the proceedings, walking jauntily into court, smoking a cigar, and smiling with a satisfied expression. He joked with his attorneys and acquaintances he recognized in the audience. "He was waggish, satirical, genial and affectionate by turns," one newspaper reported. He acted as if he was flattered by all the attention showered on him by the "morbid women."

During some of the testimony Luetgert demonstrated indifference, reading newspapers as witnesses were examined. At times, however, reporters watching Luetgert thought he was actually listening to the testimony as he read.

The *Chronicle* reporter Katharine thought Luetgert did not look like a wife killer. "The prisoner is not at all like the stage murderer," she wrote. "He is not a man to be noticed anywhere, except perhaps for his size. He is a big man; true, in size he follows out the theatrical idea of a lifetaker, but he has not the least bit of a bloodthirsty look about him. If he were not constantly pointed out from the group of men sitting at the attorneys' table as the prisoner, I doubt very much if any woman would ever pick him out for Luetgert."

H. Gilson Gardner of the *Journal,* however, called Luetgert an "evil-visaged man." Gardner wrote, "His look breathes hate and reflects the malice in his soul. It shows the dullness of all the sensibilities which might arouse in another mind feelings of interest, horror, regret, or wonder at the events which had become so vital to his welfare. That sneer tells of a mind strongly entrenched in stupid self-content."

The newspaper sketch artists also found a fruitful subject in Luetgert. The *Inter Ocean* critiqued the artwork in rival newspapers, saying one of the *Tribune*'s pictures looked "like a composite map of twenty emotions of the soul, executed with a whisk broom. . . . They may be summed up off-hand as a cross between a look of fright and a frown of agony arising from green apples." The *Times-Herald*'s sketch of Luetgert was "the nearest to an expression of peace that the pig grinder has yet assumed," the *Inter Ocean* said, and the *New York World*'s artist drew Luetgert with his whiskers standing erect. "It looks more like the trade mark of a patent hair vigor," the *Inter Ocean* remarked. (As for the sketches of the women testifying in the case, the *St. Paul Dispatch* editorialized, "If their pictures in the Chicago newspapers are good likenesses, the female witnesses in the Luetgert trial are all characterized with that superlative lack of beauty which is proverbially said to exercise a paralyzing influence upon the machinery of time pieces. As the courtroom clock probably stopped, the extraordinary duration of the trial may be thus accounted for.")

Whenever the case was looking bad for Luetgert, he found it hard to smile. Julian Hawthorne wrote that Luetgert "felt something unpleasant round his fat neck; his condition was, as Emerson says, that of 'lust in the chill of the grave.'" It was said Luetgert slept soundly and ate heartily at the jail, but Hawthorne reported Luetgert had required poppy and mandrake to medicate him to sleep one night.

When Luetgert's attorneys argued with each other, Luetgert became discouraged and staggered out of court, looking haggard, as if he had aged ten years in a day. "His hands were clutched convulsively, and his head, when he stopped for a moment, nodded like a man with palsy," the *Tribune* reported.

When Luetgert became nervous, he would rock in his chair and fidget with his newspaper or a pencil. Beads of sweat stood out on his forehead. His face would turn a darker shade of red than its typical florid hue, or else it would go white. One reporter even wrote that he turned a curious shade of yellow on hearing a particularly damning statement. Luetgert often looked over at the jurors to see what effect the testimony was having, and they looked at him for the same reason. When the testimony was going badly for him, he would hiss whispers into his lawyers' ears or stare at the witness with such a stunned look that his attorneys could not break him out of his reverie.

The reporters had a field day describing Luetgert's reactions on September 3, when Captain Schuettler took the stand. After Schuettler described his conversations with Luetgert and the initial police probe into Mrs. Luetgert's disappearance, he recounted how the detectives had found the two gold rings inside the vat. McEwen asked him, "Have you the rings now in your possession?"

"I have."

"Will you produce them?"

"Yes, sir."

Schuettler fumbled in his pocket, drew out the rings, and handed them to McEwen. After McEwen had held them in his right palm for a moment, he laid them on the rail in front of the jury box. One by one, each of the jurors examined the golden circlets. Luetgert riveted his attention on the rings. No one described it in more dramatic terms than did Hawthorne:

JULIAN HAWTHORNE SEES
TERROR TRANSFIX ADOLPH L. LUETGERT

There was an indescribable movement throughout the crowded courtroom. But I fixed my eyes on Luetgert. He had some time before ceased to rock his chair backwards and forwards; now he sat as still as an image. He sat huddled low down in his chair, as if he wished to disappear through it. He had been gazing at the witness as if fascinated; now he looked at him no longer; he looked at nothing. He knew what was coming and he dreaded it as he dreaded death, and with much reason. . . .

He presented an unpleasant spectacle. All the stiffening had gone out of his body; his head settled down on his shoulders as if the bone were gone from his neck, and the head had a constant vibration precisely like that of the palsy. His pallor was extraordinary, as if his pendulous cheeks had been smeared with chalk. Shakespeare must have seen a man in this condition when he wrote, "Distilled almost to a jelly [with] the act of fear." I had always recognized the power of that description, but I had never happened to meet with so complete an illustration of it. If Luetgert goes to the gallows there will be a ghastly scene on the scaffold. . . .

A man beside him leaned over and spoke to him, forcing a smile. Luetgert had no smile in him; he could not even change his position to lean, as his habit is, close to his interlocutor. His mouth was dry, and he swallowed, and swallowed, but no moisture would come. Presently he made a desperate effort to sit erect and recover himself, but he could not do it; the next moment he sank back again in a loose mass. The deadly faintness would not be shaken off. There he sat, alone with his terror, for even his counsel did not think to say consoling words to him just then; they looked distraught, too.

Hawthorne's vivid accounts of the Luetgert trial began drawing criticism on the editorial pages of rival newspapers. The *Daily News* ridiculed his contention that Luetgert had been "transfixed in terror" by the sight of the rings, noting that Luetgert had known for quite a while that police had some rings in their custody. "Herr Luetgert knew all about the ring business two months ago, but Mr. Hawthorne has recently arrived from New York—where the journalists come from—and he cannot be expected to know any too much about the ins and outs of sausage making."

The *Daily News* also questioned how the various depictions of Luetgert could be reconciled. "From the several newspaper reports of the Luetgert murder trial we learn that the prisoner changed color twenty-six times, smiled scornfully eighteen times, moved nervously seventeen times, was impassive at all times, took deep interest in everything, spent all his time watching his youngest son and blinked his 'evil eye' as often as convenient."

Some of the papers criticized their competitors for acting as if they were the prosecutors. "One would suppose from the way some of our contemporaries, especially the *Tribune,* report the Luetgert case, that the latest thing in criminal law is trial by newspaper, with an amateur journalist and professional novelist in charge of the case with instructions to convict," the *Inter Ocean* editorialized, alluding to Hawthorne. "Such abuse of the liberty of the press is not journalism, and it is worthy of remark that the press of the country is beginning to show unmistakable signs of dissatisfaction with the dangerous innovation."

The *Waukegan Gazette* condemned the "pernicious side of journalism" that was destroying the credibility of newspapers while creating "an intoxication of the mind." The yellow journalists were denying Luetgert his constitutional right to a fair trial, the *Gazette* asserted. "The author of 'The Scarlet Letter' must rest uneasily in his grave at the spectacle of his less skillful son's lapse from the ways of grace."

Even the *Tribune,* which was getting much of the blame for sensational coverage, jokingly noted, "If this Luetgert trial doesn't tone down somewhat, it will provoke the presence of Stephen Crane, and then the poor man will be a goner."

The *Kansas City Times* editorialized, "Julian Hawthorne has been sent to Chicago to paint the Luetgert trial in language gory for a New York paper. . . . Steve Crane is not in it with Jule when mur-r-der-r most hor-r-ible is to be painted, although he is ahead of him when it comes to viewing a battle through cigarette smoke and adopting stray bull pups."

When Hawthorne expressed some dissatisfaction at the way the Luetgert trial was being conducted, the *Rochester Port and Express* editorialized, "The only thing possible under the circumstances is for Julian to run the thing himself."

The press coverage created nationwide interest in the Luetgert case. Jacob Kern, who had been the Cook County state's attorney before Deneen, visited New York that fall and was surprised to find the people there talking about Luetgert as if they lived in Chicago. He was even more taken aback when he met a friend arriving on a steamer from London. "The first thing he said to me when he stopped from the gangplank," Kern said, "was to ask about the Luetgert trial, and he said, 'From what I read of the case in the London papers, this man Luetgert must be a smart fellow to have killed that woman and not left any more evidence than he did.'"

20 The Throwing Mania

ON MAY 1, 1897, the last day Louise Luetgert was seen alive, the *Chicago Daily News* published an article under the headline "Love Killed by Toast," detailing the typical goings-on in divorce court. In about half the cases one spouse accused the other of violently throwing household objects: dishes, wine bottles, and coal scuttles, to name a few. One woman secured a divorce because her husband had thrown hot buttered toast at her. One man stated his wife had pelted him with "a glass, a bottle and a razor, causing great physical pain and mental anguish."

"The men who have thrown plates at their objecting spouses are legion," the article noted. "This is explained by the fact that nine-tenths of family quarrels occur at the breakfast table. The man or woman who is blessed with a sweet, cheery temper and good will toward humanity at seven o'clock A.M. is rare enough to be enshrined in pearls and diamonds. Many persons pretend they feel this way but in reality down deep in their hearts they are gritting their teeth and yearning for revenge on something or somebody."

The *Daily News* claimed that people were getting divorced for increasingly trivial reasons. The article concluded: "Perhaps our monkey ancestors threw too many cocoanuts at one another and cracked too many heads in jungle differences of opinion for the throwing mania to be entirely wiped out in these few thousand years, and, if so, there is a striking reversion to primal traits shown forth in the columns of divorce news."

Some four months after the publication of that article, the jury in branch 2 of the Cook County Criminal Court heard similar stories about the Luetgerts' marriage.

Elvina Stanger, who had been a domestic in the Luetgert household in 1890, testified, "They did not get along very nicely. Often, he scolded her. . . . I don't remember the words, but he often quarreled. . . . I never saw him abuse her. . . . I mean that he never struck her. . . . He often kicked the chairs and pushed them about when he was mad."

Luetgert once turned livid because his wife had cooked some pancakes improperly, Stanger said. Luetgert complained the hotcakes were too hot, so he threw them out the window into the backyard. Vincent objected to this testimony, telling Tuthill, "It is possible that they were pancakes which ought to have been thrown out into the yard." Tuthill sustained the objection, but the jury had heard the testimony nevertheless.

The pancake story prompted a sarcastic editorial in the *Chronicle:* "The prosecution returns to the charge with this *tour de force:* 'What did LUET-GERT throw the pancakes out of the window for?' 'Because,' said the witness, understanding that the whole point of the trial rested upon her answer, 'he said they were too hot and he wanted to eat them cold.' Can there be any doubt now of the defendant's guilt? A man who would prefer cold pancakes to hot ones is just the person to reduce his wife to a fluid state by means of a potash bath."

Carl Voelcker, a clerk and chemist who had worked for Luetgert in 1894 and had since become an opera singer, testified he had often seen Mrs. Luetgert in her husband's factory office. Voelcker was asked: "Do you remember one day when Mrs. Luetgert and another woman went to Luetgert's office?"

"Yes, Mrs. Luetgert wanted some money, but her husband said he was sick and did not want to talk to them. They insisted on having the money, and Luetgert became angry and struck his wife. He pushed the other woman so that she fell on the floor outside the door. The woman ran into the factory, crying out that Luetgert was going to kill them, that he had a revolver in his hand. . . . They cried out: 'Hilfe! Hilfe! Er tödtet uns. Er hat einen Revolver in der Hand [Help! He is going to kill us. He has a revolver].' I saw a revolver."

Luetgert, rocking back and forth in his chair, did not even look at Voelcker. He seemed to be studying the effect of the words on the jurors, who were exchanging glances.

Voelcker also testified he had once mentioned potash to Luetgert. "I told him what powerful stuff potash was, and he appeared interested," the witness said.

Anna Grieser of Chicago Heights, who worked for Luetgert as a domestic in 1888 and 1889, also told of Luetgert's cruelty to his wife. "Mr. Luetgert once had bad sausage on his hands and many complaints came from downtown," she said. "Mr. Luetgert came up the steps and Mrs. Luetgert said, 'Louis, what is the matter?' and Mr. Luetgert got mad and told Mrs. Luetgert to go upstairs and stick her nose in her cooking-pots, she had nothing to do with his business. Then Mr. Luetgert went to the front room and he picked up the marble plate from the table and threw it against the ceiling and it broke in three pieces, and then Mr. Luetgert said she was no wife for him."

"Did he say anything else?"

"She had been raised in a pig-sty and was a Low Dutch wooden shoes."

Frederick A. Schultz, who had known Luetgert for twenty-five years, recalled an incident he witnessed as he passed by the Luetgert factory in September 1896. Schultz said he was standing at the wooden fence along Diversey when he heard a sound coming from the other side of the fence. "I heard somebody whimper," he said. Schultz peered over the top of the fence, which was five or six feet high, and saw Luetgert and his wife standing in a chicken coop, located about twenty-five or thirty feet south of the fence. "He had his wife by the throat. . . . Then I called to [a] policeman, and Luetgert looked around, and the wife looked, too, but nobody saw me. I was behind the fence. Then the woman ran away from him and she said, 'You want to choke me like you choked that man, but I don't have $2,000.' And then he said, 'Wait, you shall not tell anybody about me. You shall not give me away.' . . . He went to the factory and she went to her house."

Schultz, who was seventy-one, acknowledged under cross-examination that he was hard of hearing. He added, "Sometimes I hear quite well."

"Were the cries very loud that you heard from Mrs. Luetgert?" asked Phalen.

"The woman didn't yell very loud. If I choke you, you won't be able to yell very loud."

As the witnesses told how Luetgert had treated his wife, the court was interrupted several times by noises from the street. The judge sent bailiffs out to quell a musical band, an energetic street piano, a boilermaker, and the hammering of a laborer. Tuthill remarked, "Between carpenters and German bands, it looks as though the court might have to quit business."

The defense lawyers insisted Mrs. Luetgert's rings had been different from the rings that the police said they had found in the vat. A photograph of Mrs. Luetgert showed her wearing two rings of the same size. Her son Louis said she had been unable to remove the rings at the time when the photo was taken. "The rings produced by the state are dissimilar in almost every respect and could not possibly be the rings shown in the photograph," the *Times-Herald* reported. The prosecution claimed Mrs. Luetgert had worn the smaller ring, a thin circlet of gold that originally had a milled edge, as a "guard ring" or "friendship ring" to keep the larger one from falling off her finger.

"Both rings show plainly in the picture, and they are exactly of the same size and shape," Vincent said. "It is a fact that Mrs. Luetgert never wore such a ring as the little one produced by the state. . . . We have always maintained that the rings were manufactured for the purposes of this case. Someone put them in that vat for the purpose of making evidence against Luetgert."

Nonetheless, several witnesses identified the rings Schuettler had brought into the court as the same ones Mrs. Luetgert had worn. Stanger and Grieser recognized the golden circlets when they examined them on the witness stand. Ida Harris, who had known Mrs. Luetgert for seven years, said the missing woman had worn two rings on the ring finger of the left hand. She identified the prosecutors' rings as the same ones Mrs. Luetgert had worn. Under cross-examination, Harris acknowledged she had read a news story about the rings before she went to the police to identify them.

Mrs. Luetgert's cousin, Sophia Tews, testified Louise had indeed worn a "guard ring" to fix the larger ring on her finger. Mrs. Luetgert's niece, Frieda Mueller, also identified the rings.

After Mueller had looked at the rings, Luetgert stood up and, with his face wrinkled by a smile, asked to see them. He examined them carefully, closely scrutinizing the inscription on the larger ring. The *Daily News* reporter wrote that Luetgert looked at the rings "with an air of amused contempt, turning them this way and that, thinking, perhaps, that the Chicago police were certainly quite clever in preparing fakes of this sort." Luetgert quietly handed the rings back to Deneen and nodded his head approvingly to his attorneys. If Luetgert had ever truly felt any terror at the sight of the rings, he had gotten over it by now, but his eyes were bloodshot.

21 The Widow

CHRISTINE FELD entered the courtroom dressed in black. Feld had been the subject of earlier rumors that she was preparing to flee to Germany to avoid testifying, and there had been much speculation concerning whether she would remain loyal to Luetgert. Luetgert seemed stunned to see her walking in as a prosecution witness. In its lurid account the *Tribune* described how Luetgert's "eyes bulged out with terror and thick drops of greasy sweat formed on his flabby cheeks and neck" as Feld trembled on her way to the stand. When she sat, "Luetgert bowed his head as though to shut out the whole horrible nightmare of the courtroom."

Feld testified at first in a feeble voice, with Rudolph Liebrecht translating her German. Luetgert stared at her, but she met his eyes only once; her face reddened then, and she quickly looked away. Luetgert once shook a folded newspaper at the interpreter and hissed out a correction. His attorneys quieted him. Luetgert sat with legs crossed, swinging his raised foot nervously.

"Mrs. Feld went on unfalteringly then," the *Tribune* reported. "Every sentence, uttered in vigorous Hanoverian dialect, had on Luetgert the effect of a thumb screw given a fresh twist. He pounded the arms of his chair with such fury that it was heard all over the courtroom. It was his sweetheart, the woman to whom he had made love while his wife was living."

Despite rumors that Luetgert "used to make hot love" to Feld, reporters covering the trial had difficulty believing that he found her attractive. Hawthorne observed, "It must be admitted that Mrs. Feld is not exactly a pretty girl. She has the appearance of not having been one for a good many years past. She is dressed in black, has a dark, heavily lined countenance, and wears spectacles and (on this occasion) a veil. But Luetgert, as we all know, is a fascinating if not an irresistible man. And it is to be feared that Mrs. Feld may once in a while have been so indiscreet as to stop into the factory and have a chat with him."

Deneen asked Feld about conversations she'd had with Luetgert in February, March, and April. "He said he could not live any longer with his wife," Feld testified. "Then I said, 'You must lead a nice life. Why don't you separate, why don't you get a divorce?' Well, then he said he had too much trouble in the factory. 'When the trouble in the factory is over, then I will settle with her.' . . . He said if he had trouble in the factory and he came home, she started to scold, and said with 'that carcass' he could not live any longer."

Feld also testified Luetgert had said he preferred Mary to his wife. Moreover, he had told Feld that he could make his wife angry simply by mentioning Feld's name. "I told him he should not do that again," Feld testified. "I didn't like anything like that. I believe it is probably that the woman was mad or got excited on account of my name."

Deneen asked Feld whether she had visited Luetgert at the jail. She said she had gone to the jail after Vincent wrote her a letter asking her to visit Luetgert. "I went there and he asked me to get him money, and I had to take a mortgage on my house, so he could pay the lawyers," Feld testified. "And I said, 'It is sorry—it is bad if you have no friends than me. It is time that you looked for your friends to pay the lawyers.' He said to me then, if I go back on him, he would rather take his life. Then I said he should be ashamed on account of his children, and then he said even then he didn't care for his life."

Deneen showed Feld some papers, and she identified them as letters Luetgert had written while he was in jail. Luetgert's son, Arnold, had delivered them to her house, she said.

When Luetgert saw the packet of letters in the prosecutor's hand, he became livid for an instant, and then all the color drained from his face. He whispered something to his attorneys, who apparently had been unaware of the letters' existence until now. The state's attorney handed one of the soiled letters, scrawled in German, to Vincent. Luetgert grabbed it. He saw the greeting "Innigst geliebt Christine!" at the top and his own name signed at the bottom.

On Monday, September 8, following a break for Sunday, McEwen read English translations of Luetgert's six letters to the jury. Luetgert appeared surprisingly calm as he listened to his own words being read aloud. He smiled at the jabs he had made at the police.

"Beloved, dear Christine," the first began. "For a long time I have been waiting with an ardent desire to see you, but unfortunately, I would not enjoy this pleasure. . . . Quite often I speak to you, then you are not there. Quite often, I speak to you at night, and when I wake up then, I am alone in my prison cell. . . . Now, my dear Christine, the war is beginning. The police under Schaack all must work against me, as they have no proof against me and know that I am innocent. But the gang have commenced this and they do not know how to retreat because it would be bad for the gang."

In the letter Luetgert accused his former attorney, Arnold Tripp, of taking his money. Luetgert implored Feld to give him $2,000 to help pay the fees for a new lawyer. "You have no idea, my beloved Christine, how I must suffer here as an innocent man. You can imagine a man like me must lay in shackles in a prison cell like a criminal, and here I find out who my friend is. . . . I know positive, my beloved Christine, if it were not for you, I would have taken my life long ago. Then again, I think of your being so true and kind and so sincere to me, and I think so much of you. If I only could see you now and then. As soon as my trial begins, I will be a free man. Then we will not be short of anything."

In his second letter, Luetgert again asked Feld for money. "Lawyers are like bloodsuckers," he wrote.

By the time Luetgert wrote the third letter, he had heard through his lawyers that Feld "would not give up another cent."

"Now, Christine, is it not awful bad to run one down like that," Luetgert wrote, "while I am sitting here in the lockup, and the rogues know that I cannot defend myself? But just wait, beloved friend, as soon as I am free I will show you by everything clear and plain that I have treated you as an honest and upright man and dealt with you as such."

By now Luetgert was asking her for only $250. He challenged her: "If you think that I at any time done a wrong to you, or at any time betrayed your confidence, then inform me what way, or if you have only the slightest proof that I cannot set myself right and show that I am innocent, then say to me, 'Louis, I do not want to have anything to do with you anymore.'"

In the fourth letter the salutation had changed to "Honored Mrs. Feld." He suggested she give him a mortgage she owned on a property in the neighborhood. "My life and death is now in your hands," he wrote. By the fifth letter Luetgert was beseeching Feld to give him even ten dollars.

The *Daily News* took a look at Luetgert's original German letters and concluded that the translators had corrected many grammatical errors. "Luetgert is not an educated man," the paper reported. "He cannot write English well and his German is also of a kind that is not picked up at any of the average places of learning. . . . In his letters to Mrs. Feld he did not use any punctuation marks from the beginning of his epistles to the end of them, all of his sentences being strung along together. Even capital letters were found to be unnecessary in his construction of a letter. . . . The accused wife murderer does not know as much about the proper construction of a letter as does his twelve-year-old boy."

After McEwen had read the letters aloud, Vincent got his turn to cross-examine Feld. He did his best to fluster the widow, rapidly firing questions. Her already florid face turned dark red at times.

Feld said Luetgert had given her $4,000 for safekeeping before he went to jail, but she denied that she had refused to give it back to him. She said

A crowd listening to testimony at the Luetgert trial. (Courtesy of Special Collections, University of Arizona Library, Collection of John Francis Holme, MS 001 no. 9)

A crowd outside the court-house entrance. (*Chicago Daily News*, Sept. 9, 1897)

Luetgert holding his son Elmer while in court. (*Chicago Journal*, Aug. 28, 1897)

Assistant State's Attorney Willard McEwen pointing to a diagram of the factory while making his opening argument. (*Chicago Daily News*, Aug. 30, 1897)

Louis Luetgert swearing to tell the truth. (*Chicago Tribune,* Aug. 31, 1897)

Women and men struggling for admission to the trial. (*Chicago Journal,* Sept. 3, 1897)

Newspaper reporters sitting at improvised desks in the courtroom. (*Chicago Daily News*, Aug. 26, 1897)

Agatha Tosch, the keeper of a saloon near the Luetgert factory, testifying. (*Chicago Journal*, Aug. 31, 1897)

Newspaper artists sketching scenes from the trial. (*Chicago Journal*, Sept. 1, 1897)

The journalist and novelist Julian Hawthorne, son of Nathaniel Hawthorne, who covered the first Luetgert trial for the *New York Journal*. (Chicago Historical Society, ICHi-35430)

Anna Grieser, a neighbor of the Luetgert family, trying on the gold rings that were supposed to have been Mrs. Luetgert's. (*Chicago Daily News*, Sept. 7, 1897)

Christine Feld, the widow who received love letters from Luetgert. (*Chicago Inter Ocean*, May 21, 1897)

Gottliebe Schimke, who claimed to have seen Adolph and Louise Luetgert on the night of the disappearance. (*Chicago Daily News*, Sept. 4, 1897)

she returned all of it. She also conceded that she had stayed at the Luetgert house a few times following the disappearance of Mrs. Luetgert, taking care of the children when Mary Siemering was in police custody.

"You asked Mr. Luetgert to send Mary away, did you not?" Vincent asked.

"It is a lie."

"Didn't you ever tell Mr. Luetgert if he would send Mary away, that you would keep house for him and take care of the children?"

"No, I do not have to be a housekeeper."

Feld said she had taken Luetgert's letters to the police. She had become worried when Luetgert asked her to put a new mortgage on her house to help pay his attorneys, she said, fearing that she might lose her property.

"You were mad, then, at Luetgert when you went to see Inspector Schaack, were you?" Vincent asked.

"Well, if a woman is alone and they fix it so she loses everything she had, well, that is not to laugh about," Feld replied.

"Did not the police say they would cause your arrest as an accessory to the murder of Mrs. Luetgert if you did not turn against him? . . . Did not the inspector say to you that . . . he would put a rope around your neck, too?" Annoyed, Feld said it was a lie to suggest such a thing. As Feld testified, Luetgert smiled whenever his attorney's inquiries perturbed her.

In court the next morning, Vincent playfully held up a sketch of Feld in one of the newspapers and joked, "Any man who would write love letters to a face like that ought to be hanged on general principles."

Feld returned to the witness stand that morning to disclose one final detail of her story. She said Luetgert had given her a knife just before his arrest. In July, she said, she had given the knife to her nephew for safekeeping. The nephew corroborated Feld's account, adding that he had noticed a rust-colored stain on the blade. The nephew turned over the knife to police in August, and the prosecution's experts had concluded the stain was blood but were unable to determine whether the blood came from a human or some other mammal.

One morning at jail a reporter asked Luetgert about the knife and he laughed, calling it "a bit of by-play" concocted by the prosecutors to make him angry. "That knife. Oh, ho—that was just to make Luetgert wild," he said. "I gave that knife to Charles when I was arrested. I used it to cut up sausages. The blade was long so that it would make a clean cut." Luetgert demonstrated how to cut a sausage by drawing one finger across another. Asked about the stain, he laughed again. "Oh, that's all right. If there were any blood-stains the police put them there. I know their tricks—they can't fool Luetgert any longer."

22 The Experiments

AN ENTERPRISING newspaperman climbed the fence along the Chicago and North Western Railroad tracks west of the Luetgert factory on August 28. As the reporter jumped over the fence, William Charles dashed into the boiler room and bolted the door. August Riehman, the watchman, came running up with three large dogs. He drew a revolver and placed it to the reporter's head.

Attracted by the commotion, Arnold Luetgert and several assistants rushed out of the factory, where they were preparing to conduct an experiment. They had planned to put a cadaver obtained from the Northwestern University medical school into the basement vat, hoping to prove Luetgert couldn't have dissolved his wife's body in the manner charged by the prosecutors. The men coming from the factory were in their shirtsleeves, with long aprons reaching from their chins to their feet. They threatened to replace the cadaver with the reporter.

Prosecution experts were conducting similar tests at other sites, including Rush Medical College. The press heard that the defense attorneys planned to bring the jury to the factory to witness a corpse boiled in potash. Luetgert's lawyers characterized the rumors as "bosh." The defense, however, did conduct two tests with bodies and pieces of human flesh in the vat, trying to reproduce the conditions described by the prosecution.

On several occasions people in the Luetgert neighborhood noticed smoke pouring from the factory's chimneys, prompting speculation that the defense was at its experiments again. Carriages would stop at the factory, letting out professional-looking men whom the neighbors assumed to be scientists.

The *Chicago Chronicle* claimed that the people going into the factory were in the "Sausage Society," although no other paper reported on this seemingly far-fetched story. The *Chronicle* wrote: "This queerly named organization is composed of some two or three dozen medical and chemical experts and newspapermen who have eaten sausage in the Luetgert factory. Their sessions have been held when the experiments were carried on by the defense . . . , and on each occasion it has been a merry party that partook of the sausage. No man had any doubts that the sausages served were of the best materials and made in the cleanest way."

On Friday night, September 3, Schaack took a coupe with Hutchinson and Griebenow to the factory. It was quiet and calm when they arrived at 8:30. The moon shone and the bare walls of the factory rose cold and forbidding. No one was on the streets. Many people in the neighboring houses were said to be afraid of going near the factory. The detectives found the factory gate locked. Griebenow and Hutchinson boosted Schaack, who grasped the gate's top. Grunting, Schaack swung one leg over, but then the voice of Arnold Luetgert came from inside: "Hold. Who goes there?" He refused to let the officers enter.

The following Monday a reporter noticed Schaack stopping at a bootblack stand to scrape yellow clay—of the sticky, sandy sort common in Luetgert's neighborhood—from his heels. Schaack acknowledged that he had attempted an expedition into the factory. Griebenow explained, "We went up to take some measurements in the yard."

"But they didn't get in," Arnold Luetgert told the reporter, "and they will not while I'm watching matters."

Six great Danes ranged about the factory day and night. Luetgert had trained them well; a tap on a factory window at night would be rewarded a minute later by a pair of gleaming eyes appearing in the inner darkness. The dogs quietly approached at the slightest noise and leaped at intruders' throats. Another three dogs patrolled the yard around the factory and the Luetgert home. Some claimed that Luetgert had originally used the watchdogs because he feared someone would steal the secrets of his sausage-making processes.

One day near the start of September, the curious began prying around the Luetgert factory as early as five in the morning. Many of these early visitors rode their bicycles to the site. "Agatha Tosch . . . was astir that early and was ready to draw small or large ones for those who were thirsty or who had simply dropped into the bar to get a look at her," the *Chronicle* reported. "Mrs. Tosch is a thrifty soul as well as a dashing witness. She wore a low-necked dress while she drew beer and everybody who dropped into the place was fortunate enough to get a glimpse of her alabaster neck, which has become one of the noted features of the celebrated case." The newspaper noted that Tosch's saloon was prospering from all the new business created by her "whilom friend" Luetgert's misfortunes.

Two young women and two young men rode up to the factory on bicycles. They knocked on the window until Riehman came out. They offered him ten dollars to let them enter the basement, but he refused. Ten minutes later, while Riehman was in the engine room, he heard one of the dogs baying. He ran out and saw one of the young women had her wheel in front of her to ward off the dog, which was lunging at her furiously. Riehman called off the dogs, which were well trained to obey his voice. The surly hounds drew off at his call, leaving the bicyclists trembling with fright.

It was rumored that a "syndicate" had offered Luetgert $100,000 for the plant. The group of investors planned to convert it into a museum, charging an admission fee to allow visitors into the famous crime scene. Arnold Luetgert said his father had refused the offer and wouldn't take less than $150,000 for the property. "We are not anxious to sell it for museum purposes anyway," Arnold said. "We do not care to have morbid people thronging the place. But if my father is offered what it is worth, he will sell it, of course. People today have been offering as much as five dollars for a look into the basement, and I have been fearful that some of the women who have been venturing into the factory yard will be attacked by the dogs. Twice this morning I happened into the yard just in time to call the dogs off. The watchman is instructed to warn people away, and if any of them are torn by the dogs, they will be themselves to blame."

23 Cries and Whispers

FOUR PROSECUTION witnesses claimed to have heard or seen things around the factory the night of May 1. Charles Hengst, who had been working in the city sewer department at the time, said he had visited the same circus as had young Louis Luetgert. During an earlier court hearing Hengst had testified he had heard someone crying out as he walked past the sausage factory around 9:30 that night. Hengst now repeated the story for the jury.

"What kind of a cry was it you heard?"

"I cannot tell. I know I heard it and I looked around for a few minutes."

In a series of questions about Hengt's drinking habits, the defense attorney Phalen suggested he was an unreliable witness. "Did you drink anything the afternoon of May 1?"

"I drank something in the morning."

"Did you drink pretty heavy that afternoon?"

"I don't think so."

"Did you not go to Turner Hall* when on your way to the circus?"

"Yes, sir."

"Did you drink two glasses of beer when in there?"

"Yes, sir."

"Did you not visit several other saloons in the neighborhood?"

"No, sir, I don't think so."

"Were you not in Tom Hetchinger's saloon six weeks after May 1?"

"Yes, I think so."

"Do you remember of telling Hetchinger that you heard some sort of a cry that night and that you would have to stick to the story you have told here today or you would lose your job?"

"No, sir."

"You say you think the cry was the cry of a human being?"

"Yes, sir."

"Do you remember of saying in Justice Kersten's court that you could not tell whether it was the cry of an animal or the cry of a human being?"

"No, sir, the cry was from a human being."

"Is it not a fact you were drunk May 1?"

"No, sir."

The judge interjected, "Do you drink beer?"

"Yes," Hengst said. "I drink my beer when I am thirsty."

Another witness, Nicholas Faber, said he had been walking around the

---

* This was the hall of the Turnverein Nordwest on Clybourn Avenue, one of several German athletic clubs and social organizations in Chicago, each of which was commonly called "Turner Hall."

Luetgert neighborhood the evening of May 1, hoping to find a job. "I was sitting alone at home. I had nothing to do and I was thinking by myself to go to this man and ask him if he has any work," Faber said. "A friend of mine that used to work with me together at Luetgert's . . . his name is Otto Schiller, or Otto Schriller. I cannot exactly say what his name is."

Faber arrived at his friend's home near Clybourn and Fullerton—several blocks from the Luetgert factory—around ten o'clock. "He lives in a small cottage and there was no light, and I thought that he was asleep, so I turned around and went home," Faber said. "I went along on Clybourn Avenue, as far as the terra cotta works . . . on Hermitage Avenue. . . . When I passed the Luetgert residence, I saw him between the stable and the garden and her in the alley—Mr. and Mrs. Luetgert. . . . They were near the icehouse, near the first window in the alley. . . .

"They were speaking together, or else I would not have noticed him, probably . . . They walked around like a person went out for a walk. . . . I didn't hear anything. They spoke Low German, Low Dutch," said Faber, who was testifying in High German. "I can't understand a word."

Faber said he stopped for a minute, watching as Luetgert and his wife walked toward the factory's west end. Explaining his reason for pausing, Faber said, "I thought Mrs. Luetgert would go to bed, and when Mr. Luetgert goes to his office to go to bed, he might come out and I could speak with him. . . . I could not be so impertinent as to walk up to the man and ask him in the presence of his wife. Mr. Luetgert is not a man to fool with."

Faber used the prosecution's diagram of the factory grounds to point out the place where he had seen Luetgert and his wife. As he did so, Luetgert stepped forward to take a look at the map himself, but Isaac Reed, the deputy jailer, grabbed his sleeve and held him back. Luetgert turned white with rage, showing his first outburst of anger in front of the jury. According to one newspaper, he shook off the jailer's hand and said, "Yes, I can go up and look." Another newspaper reported he exclaimed, "You dirty dog, let me along. You are not on trial for your life." The jurors took notice of his behavior, and many in the audience stood up to get a better view of the scene. Vincent intervened, and the deputy allowed Luetgert to examine the map. Luetgert's hands shook. When he sat down, he still hadn't regained his composure, and Vincent had to whisper caution into his ear.

During cross-examination Phalen tried to cast doubt on Faber's truthfulness. He asked Faber whether he had told Luetgert and William Charles he could produce some witnesses who had seen Mrs. Luetgert in Chicago on May 2. With an emphatic shake of his head, Faber loudly replied, "That is a dirty, infamous lie."

After watching Faber's testimony, Julian Hawthorne concluded, "He was a man whose face and manner were entirely trustworthy."

A fourteen-year-old girl from the Luetgert neighborhood named Gottliebe Schimke had signed a police statement in July alleging that she had seen Luetgert and his wife the night of May 1. She said she had gone with her twenty-year-old sister, Emma, that afternoon to see their older sister, Mrs. John William Freund.

"We remained there until about 9:30 P.M., when we started home," Gottliebe said in her statement, "and when about to open the gate leading to our house, my sister said: 'There goes Mr. Luetgert and his wife.' I looked across the street, and saw Mr. and Mrs. Luetgert near Hermitage Avenue and Diversey Street, going west. They went as far as the railroad tracks, or about 350 feet from Hermitage Avenue, and then they came back and went south on Hermitage Avenue and into a gate near what is called the hencoop north of the alley and on the factory property. On going into [our] house the same evening, which was about ten o'clock or after, my sister, Emma Schimke, stated to my mother, 'We saw Mr. Luetgert and his wife.'"

On the witness stand Gottliebe was timid and frightened. The reporters thought she wore a vacant expression on her pale face. Luetgert sat reading a German newspaper, as if to show contempt for the girl's testimony. In halting answers the girl repeated her story, but the tale was not entirely the same. Gottliebe no longer said she and Emma had visited their sister's home. Now Gottliebe testified she had gone along with Emma to a dance at a local ballroom on May 1. She said she waited outside while Emma went in to dance, and then they had walked home together. She said she saw Luetgert and his wife coming out from a street, but she did not know the name of the street. The Luetgerts had walked around a corner and into the factory office, and then they came back out and turned into the alley; that was the last she had seen of them. Gottliebe said all this happened a little after eleven o'clock, but she acknowledged she was guessing about the time.

On cross-examination Phalen questioned how she knew these events happened on May 1. Gottliebe said she had looked at the calendar that day and seen it was May 1. She said she always looked at a calendar on the first day of the month. "You never look at any other day except the first of the month?" Phalen asked.

"No," she replied.

Under Phalen's questioning Gottliebe admitted she hadn't written the statement she had signed for the police in July.

"Did Inspector Schaack write a lot of questions to you and ask you a lot of questions and have you sign that statement?"

"Yes," she said, barely whispering and casting a scared glance around the courtroom.

"You don't know what was in the writing that you signed, do you?"

"No."

"You have no knowledge of what was in there?"

"No."

"Had it been read over to you?"

"No," she said, and began crying. Tuthill ordered Phalen to wait a few moments. Gottliebe normally spoke German and was having difficulty understanding the questions in English. Tuthill allowed Gottliebe's mother to take the girl into the jury room for a minute to calm her down. When she came back to the stand, Phalen reminded her of the oath she had taken to tell the truth. "You don't know anything about this case, do you?" he asked.

"No," she said.

"You tell this because the officers want you to, don't you?"

"Yes."

"They made the whole story for you, didn't they?"

"Yes," she said. But Tuthill asked a question of his own, trying to clarify what she meant, and the girl insisted she really had seen Luetgert and his wife the night of May 1.

"I seen him," she said.

McEwen asked, "Did any police officer tell you to come here and say anything that was not true?"

"No," she replied.

The prosecution later brought Emma Schimke into court to corroborate her sister's testimony. The slender, yellow-haired woman's voice was just as faint as her sister's, prompting jurors to protest they couldn't hear her.

Emma said she had worked at Deering's twine works on May 1 until about half past five. She had eaten supper at home and then gone out with Gottliebe.

The two of them had returned home between ten and eleven. "When we got toward the gate, I just happened to look across and I seen Mr. Luetgert and Mrs. Luetgert walking toward the track, and then they went toward the alley and I didn't see them any more," Emma testified. She said she had told Gottliebe, "Look, there comes Mr. Luetgert and his wife." Emma added that she knew what time this had happened because her mother had scolded them for coming home so late.

Under cross-examination by Luetgert's attorneys, Emma said she didn't recall talking about the incident with any police.

"Can you recollect who called at your home yesterday to talk with you about this case, if anybody?" Phalen asked.

"Well, there was nothing said, only that they were going to ask me if I seen Mr. Luetgert or not. Nothing else was to be asked but that."

"Who said that?"

"I said that myself."

"You said it yourself?"

"Yes, sir."

"To whom did you say it?"

"To myself."

"Now, after you got through talking to yourself, did you talk to anybody else?"

"Who shall I speak to? There is nobody else here to be spoken to but you."

"Who was at your house yesterday concerning this case?"

Emma refused to answer, insisting she had been told she wouldn't be asked any questions like this. Tuthill interrupted and told her she had to answer Phalen's questions. She blurted out, "I am not on Luetgert's side, am I?" The courtroom broke out into laughter, with even Luetgert joining in.

"It don't make any difference whether you are or not," Tuthill said.

Emma finally acknowledged that Officer Griebenow had visited her home the evening before, and she admitted she had previously told a police officer that she hadn't seen anything on May 1. "I first said that I didn't know about it," Emma testified. "Of course, I did not want to get into Luetgert's case, that was the reason."

As Emma testified, the voice of a strong-lunged boy on the street below could be heard through the courtroom windows. "All about Luetgert! All about Luetgert!"

Luetgert laughed again.

24 The Experts

AS MARK DELAFONTAINE, a chemistry teacher at South Division High School, walked into court, he remarked, "There are many happy boys and girls on the South Side today. They are glad there is a Luetgert case. While I am here, there are no chemistry classes in my school and the young people make merry holiday."

Delafontaine was about sixty, with a dark complexion, a bald pate, a strong, "salient" chin, and keen eyes behind his spectacles. He made graceful gestures, chiefly with his left hand, as he spoke in a French accent. The teacher said the police had asked him to examine some samples from the Luetgert factory on May 19. They gave him liquid taken from the middle vat. It came in a green bottle and a white bottle that still bore the label "Sweet Pickles," showing its previous use. Over the past few months Delafontaine had kept some of the evidence hidden behind books in his bookcase.

Delafontaine said he had studied the liquid inside these bottles and used a spectroscope to determine that it contained bits of potash and sodium, chloric acid, sulfuric acid, carbonic acid gas, fatty acid, the coloring compound known as Bismarck brown, some solid matter, and hematin, a compound that forms when the hemoglobin protein in blood breaks down.

The police had also given Delafontaine other evidence from the factory: two gunnysacks, some coarse powder of a reddish color from the gunnysacks that had caught the runoff from the vat, and some charred bone fragments.

"How can you be sure they were bones?" Tuthill asked.

"From their composition and from their structure."

"Are you sure that that was bone?"

"No doubt in my mind, because bones are a peculiar structure," Delafontaine said. "If you take, for instance, the ends of the long bones and break them, you find inside the tissue of the bone is spongy, I would say."

He said he had found a small fragment of a tooth in one of the gunnysacks. It was flat, slightly concave, about three-sixteenths of an inch wide and a quarter of an inch long. It had some enamel on it, and Delafontaine conducted an experiment that showed it was likely a tooth. Unfortunately, his experiment had also caused the fragment to crumble into even smaller pieces, he said.

In late June Schaack had brought more evidence to Delafontaine. According to police, this was the stuff that Odorofsky had thrown out into the yard when Luetgert told him to clean up the basement. Schaack gave Delafontaine a tin tobacco box containing putrefied animal matter and two boxes containing pieces of bone, leather, cheesecloth, cotton tablecloth, string, and fiber.

"I received them at the time of the hottest days of the season and it was so putrid that I had to dry it as quickly as I could in the sun, with the exception of a few lumps which I quickly put into alcohol for my analytical work," he said.

As he testified, the bailiffs hauled a large dry-goods box into court, prompting a murmur from the crowd. Delafontaine pulled a series of gruesome objects from the box as he described his experiments. Prosecutors took the gunnysacks and laid them in front of the jury. A couple of the other expert witnesses sitting in court became excited at the sight of these objects, rushing up to the jury box and beginning to paw the evidence. Tuthill angrily ordered them back into their seats. A fruit jar filled with dusty stuff was passed around. Luetgert was calm and even jovial as all this evidence was brought out. He seized the jar with a laugh and turned to joke with the reporters. Delafontaine lifted up the can containing lumps of what he said were putrid and disintegrated flesh. McEwen took the can and stirred its contents with his pencil. Some people in the courtroom noticed an "indescribable sickening stench." The can was handed around, and when Luetgert got hold of it, he stuck his hand into the can and rolled bits of the stuff between his fingers as a farmer might examine a sample of wheat.

The bone fragments were passed around, too. Luetgert didn't flinch as he turned them over in his hands, sniffing at them and laughing heartily until his big cheeks shook. He turned to the reporters' table, holding a fragment of what the prosecution claimed was once his wife's shoulder blade. "This is a bit of a cow's shoulder bone," he said to the newspapermen.

The spectators were on tiptoe with excitement as they tried to get a clear view of the evidence and Luetgert's reactions to it. The bailiffs brought their hammers down a dozen times and yelled out, "Be seated!" The jurors had puzzled expressions as they watched Luetgert handling the bones.

"Luetgert took the least possible opportunity to smile," the *Daily News* reported. "His whole bearing was that of a man witnessing a farce comedy and fearful lest something amusing might escape him. Either the man is playing a remarkably clever game before the jury, or he is utterly oblivious to the serious side of what is being enacted around him."

McEwen asked Delafontaine, "What would be the effect on a human body weighing 110 pounds placed in a solution of 378 pounds of caustic potash and boiled for two and one-half hours?"

Vincent objected, but Tuthill allowed Delafontaine to answer. "The soft tissues of the flesh would be completely dissolved," he said. "Some of the bones would be so disintegrated that they would crumble under the slightest pressure."

Without any doubt in his voice, Delafontaine declared that the fragments found in the Luetgert factory were human bones. Under cross-examination by Vincent, however, he acknowledged that he was no expert on anatomy. Vincent posed a series of mathematical problems to Delafontaine, asking him to calculate the cubic volume of the vat, the weight of that amount of water, and the percentage of the human body composed of water.

The professor reluctantly agreed that Vincent's arithmetic seemed accurate. Based on the amount of organic matter found in the vat by police, it must have come from a human body much larger than that of Mrs. Luetgert, Vincent argued. "The human body . . . placed in that vat must have weighed about 750 pounds, must it not?" Vincent asked.

"I don't know," Delafontaine said.

Vincent asked numerous technical questions that had been suggested by the apparently amused scientists at the defense table. When Delafontaine again replied, "I don't know," Vincent gloated, saying, "Oh, you don't know, don't you?"

After sitting quietly a long while, Judge Tuthill finally interrupted. "It seems to me that no one could answer the questions you are asking this witness," he said.

Another prosecution expert, Dr. Walter S. Haines, said he had used a microscope to examine the knife that Luetgert had given Feld on his arrest. "I found muscular fiber, or in other words, minute particles of flesh, and I also found a little blood," Haines testified. "The blood was that of some mammal of the higher animals, but I couldn't say anything further about it."

As Delafontaine and Haines were testifying, an osteologist and paleontologist named George Vincent Bailey was busy at the Field Columbian Museum of Chicago (popularly known as the Field Museum) assembling the skeleton of a zeuglodon from fossil bones. On September 9 Bailey's bosses asked him to interrupt his work on the prehistoric whale to pay a visit to the state's attorney's office. Bailey, who hadn't been following the stories about the Luetgert case, didn't know why law-enforcement officials would need his expertise. When he arrived at the office, Deneen, McEwen, Schaack, and two of the expert witnesses showed Bailey the bone fragments from the sausage factory. Bailey, who had mounted many hundred skeletons over the previous fifteen years, couldn't immediately identify the fragments, but he spent a night studying them and returned the next morning with his findings. On Saturday, September 11, Bailey testified.

Despite McEwen's public warning that the day's testimony was likely to be tedious and technical, a large crowd turned out. The audience rose at the sight of McEwen carrying the bones of a human arm and head toward the witness stand. He handed them to Bailey, who used them to demonstrate the similarity between these definitively human bones and the fragments found in the factory.

McEwen gave Bailey one of the fragments, and the scientist unhesitatingly identified it as a piece of the third human rib. The experts at the defense table tittered. One of them muttered, "A piece as small as that, and identified as a third rib! We'll soon settle that."

McEwen startled the courtroom by stretching out the bones of a leg and foot on the railing before the jury. The jurors stopped fanning themselves. Tuthill left the bench to get a closer view himself. He nodded as Bailey pointed out a little bone in the foot and then explained the similarity between it and exhibit 13c. That fragment, he said, was part of a small bone of the right foot's fourth toe.

Vincent grunted, and Phalen said, "Boah."

"From the right foot of a very small woman," Bailey added, and Tuthill almost mechanically repeated the words.

"Is this exhibit large or small compared with the average human being?" McEwen asked.

"Smaller, sir."

"How small, comparatively speaking? Would you say, in your judgment, that it is the bone of a small person, or a very small person, or medium-sized person, or what? Can you form any opinion as to the size of the person from whom it came, speaking comparatively?"

"Well, I should say that it was a small person."

McEwen took another small piece of bone from a little pink box. Bailey held the bone up to the light and said, "From the end of the humerus bone."

For what seemed to many like the thousandth time, Vincent slowly stood up and objected, arguing that this evidence should not be introduced. As Tuthill had nearly always done, he overruled Vincent's objection. The bone, which looked like a common pebble, was handed to the defense table, and a half-dozen experts working for Luetgert's lawyers spent several minutes hunched over it.

"Not more the bone of a human than of a dog or another animal," one of the experts said.

"Shhhh," Vincent said. "Not so loud when the reporters are near."

When Bailey returned to the witness stand Monday morning, Vincent asked about the likelihood that the small fragments Bailey had identified as sesamoid bones from feet and hands would be left over after a body had boiled in potash. Although it seemed counterintuitive that these small bones would survive while larger bones dissolved, Bailey said it made perfect sense. He said the sesamoids—nodular masses at joints—would likely fall into the sediment at the bottom of the vat, which would protect them from dissolving.

Vincent cited numerous books on anatomy as he tried to show Bailey had erred in saying the hand could have as many as six sesamoids. The books said the hand contained only two such bones. Bailey insisted the books were out of date. Vincent tried to trip up the witness by presenting him with a sesamoid bone from a dog. He hoped Bailey would call it a human bone, but the professor immediately recognized it as canine. "Ah," Vincent asked, "from the hand or foot of a dog?" Luetgert laughed, causing his chair to shake.

Bailey's testimony was interrupted at 11:30 when one of the jurors, John E. Fowler, was seized with a chill. The judge noticed Fowler turning pale and halted the court proceedings. The bailiffs hurried Fowler over to the Le Grand Hotel, where a doctor examined him. He was so sick that court officials thought he might not be able to return to the jury box, which could result in a mistrial. After a day of rest, however, Fowler had recovered.

In the meantime Bailey had become the subject of some comical stories told around the courthouse. A young man who lived at the same boarding house as Bailey complained to McEwen that the scientist had become so interested in the Luetgert case that he could talk of nothing else. "We don't mind him in the evening on the front steps," the man said, "but when he comes into the dining room and stands a skeleton up on the table and pulls it to pieces between the courses, we think it time something was done."

"That's nothing," McEwen countered. "When Bailey came here Monday, his pockets were full of leg bones in all stages of antiquity, and in his inside coat pocket he had the leg and foot of a sheep, with the skin and flesh still present, and incisions made to show the tendons and sesamoid bones."

Fowler and the rest of the jurors filed back into the courtroom on Wednesday, September 15. Experts flocked through the doors, laden with boxes of bones and bottles of sesamoids. Vincent continued his cross-examination of Bailey, hammering away at the controversy over the number of sesamoid bones in a human hand. Tuthill grew impatient, and whenever the prosecutors objected, he cried out, "'Bjection sustained."

Vincent asked Bailey how he could be so positive that exhibit 13c was one of the phalanges from a human foot.

"I know distinctly that this is a human toe, from the articulation and the tendons," he said. "It is not the toe of a dog, cat or sheep, as can be seen from the attachments of the tendons. Furthermore, the bone shows a compression of such fashion that the toe could have belonged to no animal but one wearing a tight-fitting shoe."

Vincent relinquished the witness, and McEwen got up to ask another question. "Will you explain, Professor, how you are able to identify these bones as human?"

Vincent stood up to object, but before he said anything, Bailey began answering the question in a loud, confident voice, as though he feared he would be interrupted. "Well, I have examined each one," Bailey said. "I have killed and examined dogs and have examined almost every other animal, trying to place them in the animals. I can find bones in the animal kingdom which could coincide almost exactly with any single bone, but I take into consideration that those bones were all found in one place. . . . The only animal that I can place that in, having all those bones of that relative size, is a human being."

Bailey stepped down from the witness stand. With a tired sigh, he told a reporter, "They almost drained me of everything I ever knew."

After the noon recess a smooth-faced young man took the stand. Many spectators were astonished when he gave his name as George A. Dorsey, assistant curator of the Field Museum's department of anthropology. Dorsey was barely thirty, but he was already known nationally as an expert in anthropology. He was the first person to graduate from Harvard with a doctorate in anthropology (and only the second to attain the degree at any U.S. college). He had traveled South America, Alaska, and other parts of the world, gathering specimens for the 1893 Columbian Exposition. In his dissertation Dorsey had acknowledged that his expertise in identifying bones was largely self-taught. "I have never received any instruction in physical anthropology," he wrote. Nevertheless, he had made his reputation by identifying fragments of human and animal bones from the prehistoric mounds of Ohio. The bones had lain in the earth for six hundred years, all jumbled together, but Dorsey had managed to sort them out.

McEwen showed Dorsey a tin box containing yet another bone, one that had never before been mentioned in court. McEwen promised to prove that the police had found this bone in the factory's boiler room. "Open the box," McEwen said.

Dorsey broke its seal and removed a yellow, jagged, rough-looking bone. The box was handed to the defense table, where Luetgert's scientists peered into it. Luetgert looked at the bone, showing little reaction. The box was handed back to the witness. Dorsey told how he had examined this bone with another prosecution expert, Dr. Norval Pierce. They had sawed the bone in half to see its interior structure.

"Have you any opinion regarding the identity of that bone?" McEwen asked.

"I believe it to be a left temporal bone of a man. From its apparently small size, I should judge it to be that of a woman."

"Can you state through what conditions that bone has passed?"

"All I can say is that it has lost its animal matter. It resembles very much bones which I have taken from mounds, which have been long in the ground and consequently have lost their animal matter." Dorsey positively identified it as a section of human skull. He said it contained the internal canals of the human ear and the traces of nerves and blood vessels.

Dorsey testified in a distinct voice, and he was able to explain clearly many technical points. He said he had examined the other bones police found at the factory. Judging from their size, they all appeared to come from the same person—probably a woman, he said. And he identified another bone as part of a left human femur, or thigh bone. He said he had tried, without any success, to find other animals that might have a similar bone.

"I visited the bone room of the Field Museum and examined skeletons," Dorsey said. "I went through them from one end to the other."

"Can you tell anything about the age of that bone?"

"That is the bone of an adult. It has the appearance of having been in a fire."

Questions were raised concerning exactly where and how prosecutors had found some of the bones being used as evidence. Police Sergeant Jacob Spengler testified that he had picked the supposed femur out of a barrel containing various bones near the Luetgert factory's salt house. "I took it because it was the largest one there," he said. But the *Times-Herald* claimed its reporters had watched in May as McEwen, not Spengler, picked the bone out of the barrel, holding it up and saying, "That bone looks as if it might be a human bone. I think I shall have it examined." McEwen called over Sergeant Spengler and handed the bone to him, according to the *Times-Herald*. Another bone that had been found almost by chance was the one identified as a temporal bone fragment. "It was picked up near the furnace by one not connected with the state and was given to Inspector Schaack," the *Times-Herald* reported. "He had to be urged to take it, and reluctantly agreed to see that some expert examined it." The newspaper claimed that police had discounted the usefulness of these two bones until some of the experts took a look at them.

As the experts testified, reporters occasionally left the court to telephone their offices or to look up one of the obscure words the scientists used. The reporters had carefully guarded their seats earlier in the trial, because the chairs were frequently taken by spectators. By now, though, most of them had learned to chain their chairs to the press tables with padlocks.

After calling the bone experts, the prosecution put corset makers on the witness stand. They testified that pieces of burnt and rusty steel the police had found in the ashes at the Luetgert factory were the remnants of a female undergarment. Julian Hawthorne remarked that one of the witnesses was an amiable-looking little man. "One meets a thousand men like the corset maker traversing the city streets on their daily affairs, and never thinks of them again," Hawthorne wrote. "And yet, one day, this unconspicuous person may step into a witness chair and quietly slip a noose over your head. What an awful thing civilization is!"

A dentist named Carl Klein Jr. testified he had made a full upper aluminum denture for Louise Luetgert in July 1893. He examined one of the small bits of matter police had found inside the vat and identified it as a fragment of a false superior lateral incisor. But Klein acknowledged he could not say whether this false tooth was one he had made for Mrs. Luetgert.

After the prosecution's scientific experts had completed their testimony, they found it difficult to put the Luetgert case out of their thoughts. Friends of Bailey said he caught and killed a stray dog and dissected the body, just to be certain the bones he had identified as human were not those of a dog. After being cross-examined by Vincent, Bailey became almost hysterical with worry that he might have made an error, according to the *Chronicle*.

Even after the Field Museum had closed its doors for the day, the night watchman would often see Bailey hunting through the skeletons of hogs, dogs, and heifers to see whether he could find a sesamoid that resembled the one he had identified in court. He bought a great Dane and killed it, because Vincent had intimated that the sesamoid came from one of Luetgert's dogs, which had died in May. Then Bailey bought another three dogs and dissected them, and he went to the stockyards and purchased a heifer. He had the animal slaughtered in one of the shambles of a packing establishment and devoted a night to dissecting the carcass for sesamoids. He also cut up a pig. After all these experiments, he was finally satisfied he had testified correctly.

As McEwen chatted with reporters one day, someone remarked that the scientists were helping the prosecutors prove corpus delicti. Squarely pointing a finger at the man who had made the comment, McEwen said, "You share the popular misapprehension of the nature of the corpus delicti. Those bones are not the body of the crime. . . . The point is to show the jury by the nature of the evidence that a crime has been committed. If a man steals a horse or kills a horse, the horse does not have to appear in court. If a burglar enters a house, there is no necessity for producing the house in court. The circumstances surrounding the killing or the stealing of the horse or the burglary of the house show the jurors that such things transpired."

It may not have been necessary for the prosecutors to produce a corpse in court, but Hawthorne thought they had almost achieved such a trick. Describing one day's scientific testimony, he wrote:

> The main business of the day . . . was the weird process of reconstructing Mrs. Luetgert's dead body from the shreds and scraps of rubbish-heaps, the

scrapings and drainings of the slime of the middle vat, and similar inchoate and unlovely substances. . . . From a witch's caldron of filth and evil-smelling slush we are to see arise the form and lineaments of a human creature, with her rings and her wrapper, her poor false hair and false teeth and her other traits and appurtenances.

The witch by whose enchantments this resurrection is to be accomplished bears the name of Science. . . . So we caught a glimpse of Mrs. Luetgert for a moment. It did not seem a striking likeness; but we are not chemists, and cannot judge. Mrs. Luetgert's husband listened to the evidence in his usual huddled posture, and evinced no signs of interest, except pallor and nervelessness. I don't think he believes that any number of professors can reconstruct his wife.

Hawthorne returned to his theme on the following day:

> Luetgert and his "wife" met today in the stifling courtroom. Two lusty porters brought to the witness stand sundry big boxes containing the mortal remains of the woman; they were packed in jars, cigar boxes, paper boxes, tin pails; there were fragments of dry bones, fibers steeped in gristly solutions; anomalous dung and granules, pieces of rag and cloth; they looked inchoate enough, the mere refuse of dustheaps and ashpiles; but there, all the time, sat grave professors in the witness chair, interpreting and recounting, until, as you listened, the dry bones and dust took on form and life; the rags grew into garments, the garments were fitted on the figure. There stood a woman, in her habit as she lived, and she was the one particular woman who had borne the prisoner's name and given birth to his children. I have seen many strange things, but where shall be seen a thing stranger than this?

25 Autumn

A HEAT WAVE hit Chicago in September, with the temperature climbing into the nineties on several days, setting record highs. A newspaper commented, "There were three men in Chicago who were comfortable during the last week. One was an East Indian, one a Hottentott, and the third a Turkish bath artist who had lost his job, and had been obliged to come up into the outer world for the first time in years. The rest of the population steamed, sizzled, and swore."

It was stifling in court, but big crowds continued showing up for the Luetgert trial. Tuthill had some electric fans placed on his desk to cool off the front of the room.

While the trial went on, the Union Loop, a circle of elevated train tracks in Chicago's downtown, opened for passenger service. The journalist George Ade remarked on the new panoramic views he found by riding an "El" car around the Loop. "Anyone taking a first ride around the Loop will be impressed by the fact that he cannot recognize a locality by looking out at the buildings," Ade wrote. "He sees only the upper stories of the houses. He is brought to a closer inspection of heavy cornices and ornate window caps, which he has never before observed, except in the most casual way. No wonder that he imagines himself in a strange city."

Looking down at the streets, Ade saw weaving crowds of pedestrians, crawling lines of wagons, and cable cars gliding along. He found more entertainment, however, peering into the second-story windows along the El tracks, portals into the interiors of hotels, wholesale houses, retail shops, business offices, warehouses, and factories. In one window he saw three men seated around a table seriously discussing some important business transaction, paying no heed to the staring El passengers a few feet away. In another window Ade saw girls bent over sewing machines or working with needles. And over and over he saw "whole regiments" of typewriter girls.

Meanwhile, the storekeepers and shoppers below were often heard cursing the new Loop. Most merchants had supported the plans for the elevated tracks, but now they complained of the smoke, noise, dirt, darkness, and the hordes of people running to the Loop stairways morning and evening.

Wherever pedestrians crowded, newsboys arrived to sell the latest papers. They boarded the streetcars just when the theater crowds hastened downtown. The boys shouted, "Picture of Mrs. Luetgert with every paper!" Women snatched up the papers and spent some time searching for the picture, only to learn they had been fooled. Some of the newsboys bragged they had deceived the same people several nights in succession by falsely advertising likenesses of the missing woman. The defendant's pictures were also in demand. One of the "morbid visitors" to the trial claimed to have collected more than a hundred newspaper sketches of Luetgert. Bailiffs at the doors of the courtroom had refused to admit several people who were determined to bring in cameras.

Many of those Chicagoans not infected with Luetgert mania that fall appeared to have Klondike fever. At least one Chicago man was believed to have gone insane after obsessively reading newspaper accounts of gold discoveries in the Klondike. When crowds gathered on downtown sidewalks, a colored map of the Klondike country or a Pacific sailing list was often the focus of attention. Chicago stores sold Klondike fur overcoats, Klondike cigars, and Klondike cocktails. A theater put on a musical burlesque called *Klondike*. At least twenty books describing Alaska and the gold fields were published in August alone, and a little four-page newspaper calling itself the *Klondike Morning Times* was exhibited in shop windows, but it turned out to be an advertising sheet published in San Jose, California. People casually mentioned Klondike, Dawson City, and Chilkoot as if they were discussing suburban Evanston or Oak Park.

Another sensation that fall was the case of David Bates, a man from the South Side neighborhood of Englewood facing charges of bigamy. He was married to one woman under the name Bates and another as Gates. He had developed a system of having breakfast at one home and dinner at the other. When he was arrested, police found that he possessed a large bundle of letters from women in various parts of Michigan, Wisconsin, and Illinois. In some of the letters, the women addressed him in loving terms; in others, they reproached him for his inconstancy.

Bates put himself on display at the Clark Street Dime Museum, where he proved to be a popular exhibit. The dime museums were infamous for displaying "freaks" such as Jo Jo the Dog-Faced Boy or Krao the Monkey Girl, as well as stuffed animals, prehistoric skeletons, and notorious criminals.

◆◆◆

In a sermon at the Union Christian Church, the Reverend J. H. O. Smith used the example of the Luetgert case to implore husbands to treat their wives better. "Swiftly the hungry chemicals are supposed to have devoured the face of that helpless wife and mother," he said. "One night did the work. But the slow wife torture of unarrested wife murderers requires long, weary years before the deed is finished. We watch the dreary process, but are powerless to prevent the crime. The young wife does not need to see her husband carousing at his club to know that her home is desolate. She needs not personal evidence to know that her husband's heart is fickle. She reads between the lines of daily conduct the deadly truth. Sometimes she turns and wrecks another home in revenge for her own broken heart. Then it is that sin joins hand with sorrow and drags her faster toward the grave of soul and body—more horrible than the caldron of a Luetgert."

Even Mr. Dooley, a fictional bartender whose wisdom was featured in Finley Peter Dunne's *Chicago Evening Post* column, commented on the Luetgert case. Mr. Dooley once referred to Chicago culture as "th' best Luetgert society." And he summed up the trial as follows: "A large German man is charged with puttin' his wife away into a breakfas'-dish, an' he says he didn't do it. Th' only question, thin, is, Did or did not Alphonse Lootgert stick Mrs. L. into a vat, an' rayjooce her to a quick lunch?"

The Old Salamander Drug House published an advertisement under the banner "Luetgert Confesses." Readers who went on further were bound to be disappointed at the content of Luetgert's supposed confession: "That his knowledge of drugs and chemicals is slight."

◆◆◆

The scent of sizzling sausages suddenly seemed unappetizing to most Chicagoans. A housekeeper in the South Side neighborhood of Hyde Park asked her butcher for a couple of pounds of nice sausage. "Sausage, Madame?" he replied. "Don't keep 'em."

"What!" she said, surprised. "A butcher shop that doesn't keep sausages?"

"Well, I did keep 'em till a short time ago," the butcher said, somewhat embarrassed, "but there hasn't been much call for them since the Luetgert trial began. I kept them for a few days, but there seems to be a suspicion now that sausages are not what they should be and there is a severe prejudice against them."

The woman tried another butcher, who smiled and said, "The Luetgert case hasn't made any difference with you, has it?"

"Certainly it hasn't," she replied. "Has it made any difference with any of your customers?"

"Indeed, it has," the butcher said. "We don't sell a pound of sausage now where we sold ten before this case came up. Our customers seem to have sworn off on all forms of chopped meat, and some of them have declared that they would eat no more sausage till the trial is over."

It didn't matter that Luetgert was never accused of putting his wife into sausage. As his trial went on, the newspapers abounded with reports of a sharp decline in sausage consumption not just in Chicago but in New York, San Francisco, New Orleans, Boston, Seattle, and Washington, D.C. It didn't matter whether it was bologna, frankfurters, wienerwurst, blutwurst, bratwurst, or somerwurst—no one wanted it after hearing the unappetizing stories about the events in Luetgert's factory. Hotels and restaurants stopped serving it, and the street vendors selling "red hots" found themselves on the verge of bankruptcy. The *Chicago Times-Herald* noted that "both 'silk-stockings' and the 'unwashed' show a common aversion for sausage." Even Luetgert's fellow prisoners in the jail seemed to have no stomach for it.

The *DeKalb (Ill.) Chronicle* reported, "One butcher claims that several of his regular customers have asked if he was married, and on being answered in the affirmative, have asked to be presented to her before laying in their stock of sausage."

With fifteen businesses and some six hundred workers, the sausage-manufacturing business was important in Chicago, and its proprietors prayed for a quick end to the Luetgert trial.

26 The Kiss

IN THE MIDST of all the scientific testimony, the prosecutors also put Schaack in the witness chair. He described the discoveries in the factory and his investigation. When Phalen cross-examined the inspector, he accused the police of buying testimony from witnesses. Schaack acknowledged he had given "a little money," five or ten dollars a week, to Frank Bialk, who had been unemployed since Luetgert's arrest. Schaack also said he had paid Frank Odorofsky about one hundred dollars and Nicholas Faber twelve or fifteen dollars.

"Are you paying these witnesses on your own account, or are you paying them for someone else?" Phalen asked. "Do you expect to have it returned to you?"

"There is an appropriation from the county," Schaack said. "I am getting money from Mr. Deneen," adding that he had received $200 since May 15. Explaining why he paid witnesses, Schaack said, "Those witnesses have been kept, and they have been most of the time from court to court and place to place. I had to keep them, and I had to give them money so that their families had something to eat. I kept them in court, they were two weeks here, for the grand jury a couple of days and for two weeks before Judge Gibbons, and since we commenced court here, so all the time they were with us and they had no chance to go to work—"

To Phalen's consternation, Judge Tuthill interrupted, saying, "Now, I'm not going into these details. . . . These witnesses are poor persons, and they have to be kept alive."

Schaack denied feeling any animosity toward Luetgert, and he rejected the defense lawyer's accusations about statements he had supposedly made. Phalen asked him whether he had told Siemering, "Mary, if you don't testify against Luetgert, we will put the rope around your neck with him."

"I never said anything of the kind," Schaack said.

Phalen asked Schaack whether one day at the police station he had told Feld, "Christine, you go home or I will put a rope around your neck, too."

"I did not say anything of the kind," Schaack replied. "I told her to go home and to mind her own business."

Phalen asked him whether the police told Mary Siemering, "You have been intimate with Luetgert, and if you don't acknowledge it, we will have an investigation here at this office."

"Not anything of the kind," Schaack testified. "She said herself she had known Luetgert very intimately."

"Had you not at that time ordered her to be stripped at the station?"

"No, sir," he said. "Prisoners are searched, understand, but there is no one stripped."

The prosecutors were nearing the end of their case, and the defense attorneys looked jubilant as they entered court on Saturday, September 20. "If the case went to the jury right now," Vincent said, "I don't see how there could be conviction. The expert testimony hung in rags by the time the cross-examinations were over. Experts? Sure—experts who could identify a bone as human when it was charred almost to ashes, and couldn't tell what animals a lot of nice, clean, unbroken bones belonged to!" He laughed gleefully.

The day began with testimony from a butcher and grocer named Abraham Seelig, who said he had gone to the Luetgert factory around May 10 to buy up the grocery stock. He said he had purchased thirty-nine bottles of Hunyadi mineral water there. The defense did not cross-examine Seelig, but his quiet testimony seemed to leave an impression on court watchers, who realized that it made no sense for Luetgert to send his night watchman to buy a bottle of Hunyadi water if he had been well stocked with the beverage.

Frank Bialk returned to the courtroom now and sat in the witness chair but didn't say a word. The jury left the room, and the prosecutors argued they should be allowed to present testimony about Luetgert's affections toward women other than his wife. Bialk listened uncomprehendingly with a perplexed expression as the lawyers made their case to the judge.

"Our purpose in offering this testimony is . . . that it affords a motive," McEwen told Tuthill.

"I cannot see that it necessarily does," Tuthill said. "I think it would rather show the opposite. . . . If he was having relations with other women without any interruption from anybody, why should he want to kill his wife?"

Phalen piped in, "He was accomplishing all he seemed to want."

McEwen picked up one hefty law book after another, citing other trials in which judges had allowed similar testimony. Phalen responded that these cases were irrelevant. Vincent finally stood up and addressed the judge. "What possible motive would this man have in killing his wife to obtain possession of a woman who, if the state's claim is correct, was already his mistress—a woman who had no wealth or property?" Vincent asked. The only effect of such testimony, he said, "would be to prejudice puritanical and straitlaced men against the defendant."

Before the court took a recess for the weekend, Tuthill said he was strongly inclined not to allow the testimony. Nevertheless, when the trial resumed three days later, Tuthill let the prosecutors go forward with their new line of questioning. He gave little explanation for his change of heart other than saying a cursory reading of legal precedents showed that the evidence should be permitted. Tuthill's decision drew the trial's biggest crowd in days, including an especially large contingent of well-dressed women armed with opera glasses and lorgnettes. They focused their optical devices on Luetgert's face to gauge his reactions to the testimony about his supposed infidelities.

Bialk went back onto the stand, and this time he was allowed to speak. He said he had seen Mary Siemering in Luetgert's factory-office bedroom many times, as often as three nights a week, ever since she had begun working for the Luetgerts as a domestic servant three or four years earlier. She would usually enter through a window, Bialk said. At least once Luetgert had told Bialk to fetch Mary from the house. Bialk said he would go and tap on the young woman's bedroom window.

Bialk said he had also seen Christine Feld visit Luetgert in the factory. The widow had visited Luetgert there when he was lying ill in bed, Bialk said. And Agatha Tosch had gone into Luetgert's room "many times" as well.

As the watchman testified, women in the audience laughed, leaning forward to catch every word. Some stood up, resuming their seats only when a bailiff threatened to eject them.

McEwen called Odorofsky back to the stand. The former smokehouse employee said he had seen Siemering visit Luetgert in the factory more than twenty times. The last time he had seen her there was one night in January. "Might have been after ten o'clock at night," Odorofsky said. "They walked— Mr. Luetgert walked around together with her through the basement, and then they kept standing against the wall. . . . He stood alongside of Mary against the wall and had his arm around her neck. . . . He kissed her. . . . She stood still against the wall. . . . I was strewing the sawdust on the smokehouse, and I noticed he had his mouth right to hers. How many times he kissed her I didn't count. . . . They put their arms around each other and marched into the office."

On one occasion, Odorofsky said, Mrs. Luetgert had been standing in the shipping room as her husband took Mary into his factory bedroom. "When I observed her standing there, she held a handkerchief to her eyes and was crying," Odorofsky said. "Next morning, when I came to work, I saw Mrs. Luetgert was sitting on a barrel toward that side of the factory. . . . She was sitting and had a white handkerchief and wiping her eyes and crying."

The final prosecution witness was Louise Johnson, a daughter of Mrs. Luetgert's sister, Wilhemina Mueller. Johnson said she had worked for Luetgert about eight years earlier, when he had owned a sausage factory at North Avenue and Sheffield. "Did anything unusual happen there at any time while you were working in the office regarding the relations between Mr. and Mrs. Luetgert?" McEwen asked her.

"Mrs. Luetgert came running down one day and pretty soon Mr. Luetgert followed with a revolver and said he would shoot her." And with that, the state rested its case.

27 Sideshows

DURING A SOJOURN in Europe, a South Side belle named Lizzie Adams had become infatuated with the "new scientific cult" of palmistry. Adams, the daughter of a wealthy merchant at the Union Stockyards, believed hand reading was more than a fad. An experienced palmist told her to study the science by reading the hands of people who'd had extraordinary experiences. Adams read the palms of people prominent in fashion, politics, religion, and learning, but her tutor, an elderly woman, told her she also had to read the palm of a man on trial for murder.

Adams, whom the *Chicago Chronicle* described as "a fair-haired girl, Juno-like in figure and carriage and a member of the most exclusive set of the south side fashionables," came to the jail with her tutor just as the Luetgert trial was getting under way. The jailer Whitman allowed a palm reading to take place in his private office, but the two women had to wait half an hour before Luetgert arrived, with Adams growing more nervous all the while. Luetgert was in a jovial mood as he entered the room. His pleasant appearance and unexpected gentleness left the women momentarily embarrassed.

"I have never believed in fortune telling, and I never shall," Luetgert said.

"But this is palmistry," Adams said. "It is not fortune telling. We came to ask you to let us study the lines in your hands."

"But I am not seeking notoriety."

"Oh, I assure you I am not," Adams protested, turning pale.

"Then I will do it to please you," Luetgert said, throwing away his cigar. He sat down and held out his big right hand. The tutor took the hand and examined it a long time, while Adams's wide blue eyes were riveted on the palm. Then with a sigh of seeming relief, Adams looked up at Luetgert. "You will live to be an old man," she said.

There was an awkward pause, and Adams exchanged a smile with her tutor, but Luetgert remained impassive. "Your line of fate is abruptly broken, and then it begins again as if the flow of your life had been interrupted," Adams said.

"It has been," Luetgert said, grimly.

"It continues and there is a protecting square on the continued line. You will be saved from calamitous happenings. You have made a great financial blunder and you have suffered two money losses."

"Lost my fine business," Luetgert said.

"You have been married twice, but you have been deeply in love three times." A smile flitted over Luetgert's face, and Adams went on. "One wife is dead."

The young woman stopped as she uttered the sentence, realizing what it implied, and looked at her tutor, who quickly added, "You are right, go on. There is the cross line which shows that one wife is dead." A few people watching the scene moved closer to look at Luetgert's hand, but no one said anything.

Adams said, "You have not pursued the same line of business always," and Luetgert nodded. She said, "You will be seriously ill and it may not be a very distant day, but you will not die then. You have a good heart line. You are a practical man of affairs. You are inventive. You do not care what others may do. You follow your own counsels. You are active and energetic. You are more inclined to lead than to follow. You have the faculty of controlling men. You are inclined to be domineering and autocratic. You have a disposition to be exacting with others. You would not keep things in order if you had to do it yourself, but you would compel others to be orderly."

Luetgert interrupted her. "I did have things orderly in my factory. Any one of my workmen could go there in the dark and find any tool he was required to use."

"But you would not pick up a broom and put it in place."

"Well, I didn't care to bother with little things like that."

Adams smiled, continuing, "You are not bigoted. Your character is broad and, and—you are not cruel." She looked timorously at Luetgert, who wore a stern expression. "You assume a brusqueness, which is not a true reflection of your feelings. You act harshly at times to cover up a disposition to shyness."

Luetgert gave an incredulous little laugh.

She asked, "Well, don't you sometimes act more harshly than you feel?"

"Oh, well, that is pretty near to it, I guess," he said.

"Your line of fate is probably the most distinctive. There is a clearly defined square which is the most positive sign of protection. I would like to make an impression of your hand so I might study it with more care and detail."

Adams drew a picture of Luetgert's hand for half an hour, as the prisoner talked of himself and his missing wife. "She was one of the kindest-hearted women I ever knew," he said. "But she was so secretive about her good deeds that very few knew of them. She would give to all who came and never said anything to them except to ask them not to tell about it. I never denied her money, and when she bought things and came to tell me what she paid for them, I would usually tell her not to bother me with such matters, as what she spent was her affair and not mine. She was always loving and kind."

When the palmists had completed their visit, Luetgert arose and shook their hands, saying, "I am sorry I cannot see you to the car."

After Luetgert had gone to his cell, Adams and her tutor compared notes. They agreed that Luetgert had "a strong hand, of which no man might be ashamed," with long and well-shaped fingers and a straight thumb. The tutor asked, "Now you may speak freely. Did anything indicate to you in his hand that he was a murderer?"

"There was no murderous tendency that I could see."

The tutor agreed and asked, "Are you positive that two wives were indicated by the lines and that only one is dead?"

"Oh, yes, that was very plain," Adams said. "There are many traits in his character which I could not admire, but none of them were of a criminal sort."

"Do you believe him innocent of murder?"

"I can only say I observed nothing in his hands which bespoke a criminal tendency. Anyone may interpret what I said of the lines indicating his marriages."

◆◆◆

Inspector Schaack had a bunch of letters with him in court one day. It was rumored that each of the letters contained a threat against his life. "Oh, yes," Schaack laughed, when asked about it. "I have a number of letters threatening my life on account of this case, and I have had them before, at the time of the anarchist riots, for instance. The last series began with the arrest of Luetgert. He was arrested in the afternoon and that evening a misspelled epistle said I would better let the prisoner have his liberty or prepare for death. In a week I had a fine collection and in them I was promised death in about every style, from poison to bullets and the noose. During the week following, I learned new ways of dying from the letters of men who were willing to kill me if I did not liberate Luetgert."

"My!" exclaimed a young lady, who was listening in on the interview. "Aren't you afraid you'll get killed?"

"No. These letters never mean anything. At least, few of them do. If one of the writers should happen to be in earnest about killing me, I think he would get as good as he sent. I continue to get into bed without looking under it."

◆◆◆

The guests in the Auditorium Hotel were startled when they saw a tall man with a mop of kinky, shoulder-length hair that streamed out from his silk hat. For a necktie he wore a long white silken streamer, wrapped five times around his neck and arranged over his shirt with an elaborate display of lace. The man, who had piercing dark blue eyes and wore a long Prince Albert coat, strode into the hotel followed by his secretary. Giving the name of Dr. Alexander McIvor-Tyndall, he checked into room 454 and then gave the clerk instructions that he would see no reporters until three o'clock—not that any reporters had been planning to see him. The hotel employees believed it was a "grand bluff" to attract the attention of newspapermen.

Sure enough, a reporter for the *Chronicle* arrived at three, and the doctor consented to speak with him. He told the reporter he was a hypnosis expert from London. "First, I do not want it said that I came to Chicago seeking money. I will be in the city but a few days and my only reason for coming is that I have taken a great interest in the Luetgert murder trial. In fact, I take delight in mysteries. I hope you will not put me down as a crank. There are cranks among telepathists or clairvoyants, but I want it understood that I do not come under that branch. I have made this subject a study for years—eight years, to be exact. I first studied to become a doctor, following the wishes of my father. Then I took up my present study and I am still studying."

The *Chronicle* reporter noted the doctor's hands were long, though not very thin, and constantly drumming on anything within their reach. "In fact, they do not seem to belong to the doctor's body," the reporter wrote.

Several other reporters visited McIvor-Tyndall's room over the course of the evening. "It is a fair offer that I would make Mr. Luetgert or his attorneys," he told the *Tribune*. "I would place him under hypnotic influence, and it will be impossible for him to tell when in that state anything but the truth. He could certainly have no reasonable objection to the experiment if he is innocent, as he claims. . . . I would really place Mr. Luetgert in a subjective condition, where his unconscious consciousness would predominate. That may sound paradoxical, but it will be understood by those who are familiar with psychical subjects. Of course, what would be said in this condition could not be received as evidence, but it would nevertheless be valuable to the police in giving them clues by which they might ultimately learn the truth."

He sent a written request to Luetgert's attorneys to put the prisoner under hypnosis and even called at the jail to see the prisoner, but Luetgert refused to take part in the experiment. "It's all thinking business," Luetgert said. "I am a hypnotist, too. A hypnotist cannot exercise his power over a man whose mind and will is stronger than his. Why, I am a hypnotist. I told that fellow so, anyhow, and offered to show how I could put him under a spell in a short time."

◆◆◆

A brass-ear phonograph was used to record some of the scientific testimony in the Luetgert trial, but the *New York Journal* speculated it might be used for more sensational purposes. "After Luetgert himself has testified, we shall probably see in the hotels the invitation to drop a nickel in the slot and listen to Luetgert," the newspaper reported.

Courtland Shaw, representing a phonograph company, visited Luetgert in jail with his sound-recording machine. He thought he had worked out an agreement through Luetgert's son Arnold to record Luetgert professing his innocence. Fifty percent of the proceeds from the record would go to Luetgert.

The phonograph began recording, and Shaw spoke into it: "Adolph L. Luetgert's own denial of his guilt, taken in the Cook County Jail October 6, 1897. Now, Mr. Luetgert, just make your statement. Talk ten minutes and get as much in as you can." Luetgert, however, emphatically declared that he would not talk until he saw a contract.

"Oh, that's all right," Arnold said. "I have made all arrangements with these people. Just talk now and it will be all right."

"No, I want a contract now," Luetgert said. "I have been lied to once, lied about, and I will not take any man's word. I have been talking for nothing, but my talk costs money today."

Shaw left the jail, taking his machine with him.

◆◆◆

The Aurora Turner Hall, at Huron Street and Milwaukee Avenue, distributed handbills announcing the opening of a play called *The Sausage Manufacturer of Lake View*. Rumors quickly spread that it was a dramatization of the Luetgert case, even though the author insisted that it was a bucolic love tale. The manager of the theater, L. Schindler, did nothing to discourage the rumors. He told a reporter, "If Luetgert is acquitted, I expect to engage him for the principal part. Don't you think he would make a hit?"

On opening night every aisle, chair, box and beer table in the theater was occupied. The curtain rose to reveal a love story involving the European travels of a Chicago sausage manufacturer's daughter. Audience members kept whispering, "Which one is Luetgert?" Every time a woman came out before the footlights, the spectators thought it must be Mary Siemering or Mrs. Feld, only to be let down. When a big, heavy-shouldered man with a bulbous nose and shaggy wig and mustache came on stage, whistling and shouts came from the galleries: "Dot's him! Look! Look! That's Luetgert!" The character was in fact a sausage maker, but not the infamous one the audience wanted. At one point a boy cried out, "Bring in the sausage man!" Others picked up the cry, and the walls echoed the name of Luetgert. But no Luetgert came.

As grumbling audience members with sheepish expressions filed out of the theater, a boy selling frankfurters at the corner said, "Well, wasn't dere er lot er suckers?" Six of Schaack's detectives were spotted in the audience.

Schindler, the theater manager, denied exploiting the mania surrounding the Luetgert case. "Luetgert? Potash? Vats? Why of course not," he said. "How in the world the sly rumor ever got started that the trial, the disappearance of Mrs. Luetgert and so forth were to be presented I cannot say. Certainly I am not responsible for it. This play is one of the simplest of dramas. It is an old one. I have presented it from time to time for years. Why, only last Sunday night I gave it at Mueller's Hall."

Schindler did acknowledge, though, that he had changed the title of the play from the less sensational *Two Scutcheons*. He said, "The public loves to be humbugged, and I let them humbug themselves."

◆◆◆

While Vincent was busy defending Luetgert in court, thousands of letters, telegrams, and messages were pouring into his offices at the Rookery. People not only from nearby Kankakee but also from Indiana, Iowa, Wisconsin, Minnesota, New York, California, and even Paris and London wrote to him with reports of having seen Mrs. Luetgert. Others offered advice on osteology, paleontology, anthropology, anatomy, chemistry, medicine, surgery, hypnotism, and occultism.

Some letters came from people angry that Vincent was defending a man accused of killing his wife in a such a gruesome manner. One of them warned Vincent, "There is a justice you will haft to meete and you will haft to give an account of ever deede you do let it be good or evil."

Another writer found it impossible to believe a man of German heritage would commit such a despicable crime: "The people who have produced Schiller and Goethe do not commit murder."

Some found religious significance in the trial. One wrote, "I am almost losing my senses, my strong mind biased by the thought of such a benevolent, beneficial and generous man like Mr. Luetgert being persecuted likewise as Jesus Christ, the most benign friend of mankind, was forced in the hands of the enemies by the treachery of Judas to die the most ignominious death."

A woman offered to save Luetgert by entering a hypnotic trance at the risk of her own life. She said she would project her astral body out onto the unknown and fearful astral sea, where she would communicate with the astral body of Mrs. Luetgert to find out where the missing wife had gone.

One writer reported that a "Cuban baby mind reader" had predicted Luetgert's wife would be found in two weeks. The girl with psychic powers had determined that Mrs. Luetgert's brother had taken her away to a big town, but she couldn't say exactly where. The letter went on: "Send me a handkerchief Luetgert has had in his pocket and wiped his face with and also something of hers that she used and I will submit it to the child and get further information. I do not charge anything."

Another writer offered a bit of poetry:

> Suppose a man is innocent,
> Doomed by law to die;
> For circumstances may deceive
> And witnesses will lie.
> When underneath the green turf rests,
> The silent pulseless clay;
> You cannot reproduce the life,
> The gallows took away.

◆◆◆

During the first five months that Adolph Luetgert was held in the Cook County Jail, 2,385 female visitors called on him and 1,202 wrote letters, including 33 marriage proposals, by one count. The visitors left behind 32 parcels containing food, 17 pieces of jewelry, 12 items of clothing, and 101 bouquets of flowers. Luetgert gave the letters to his son Arnold, who tried to send replies but became overwhelmed by the volume of correspondence.

"They come from all over," Arnold said. "Some are from school girls, some are from grass widows,* widows and old maids. They all want to become Mrs. Luetgert. They say they believe father is not guilty and are willing to stand by him. . . . Two prize-winners in the bunch I saw last week—one a little blonde and the other a tall brunette with big, fetching eyes. She was sentimental and wrote an awfully nice letter. The old man laughed at it and turned it over to me with another batch. He gets letters every day from women."

The *New York World* reported, "Several of the letters are evidently the production of female degenerates, if Luetgert has described them correctly."

A woman in Memphis proposed a scheme to rescue Luetgert on a certain day of the trial. He was supposed to wear a white flower on his right lapel. He was to remain perfectly supine and silent no matter what happened, offering no resistance. His unknown rescuer would hypnotize the judge, jury, bailiffs, and spectators, conveying Luetgert through the solid walls to "the free air and liberty and me." Luetgert wore a white flower as the woman had suggested,

---

* The term *grass widow* referred to divorced women, discarded mistresses, or unmarried women with children.

but nothing happened. He spoke of it later as a huge joke, saying he had never put the slightest stock in it. His anger flashed when someone asked him if he intended to accept any of the marriage proposals. Giving Luetgert more of a German accent than usual, the *New York World* reported that his heated reply was: "Vot you tinks I am, hey? I gommit pigamy? Not on your life."

◆◆◆

Judge Tuthill also received some interesting mail while presiding over the Luetgert trial. One letter came from D. Neuman, a mind reader who said he was originally from Russia. The envelope, mailed in New York, contained a circular calling Neuman the greatest mind reader on earth and noting that he traveled with a woman advertised as "the only living Australian Fire Queen." The professor asked to be taken secretly to Luetgert so that he could spend two minutes reading his brain.

"Of course, the letter is foolish," Tuthill said, "but it would be an interesting experiment in a case like this. I confess I would like to see it tried, and I would not be surprised if some of those mind readers could come pretty near to getting at the truth. . . . But I guess the time has not come when courts can engage mind readers to ascertain the guilt or innocence of defendants. If it were possible, it might save a great deal of worry."

◆◆◆

On hearing a rumor that the defense had a secret witness who had seen Mrs. Luetgert leave her home early on the morning of May 2, Vincent scoffed at it as merely the latest in a long line of tall tales.

"Munchausen—Baron Munchausen," Vincent said. "I thought that dreamer was dead."

28 A Game of Tag

A MONTH AFTER the trial had begun, William Vincent finally delivered his opening argument on September 22. "Dripping water will wear away a stone, and for a month now you gentlemen have sat here, and every man who has been jealous of Luetgert's success; every man who hasn't liked the way he cut his hair; every person with whom he has had any family trouble; every person who has been prejudiced against him; and every person with whom he has had any business difficulty has come before you to say what he could to discredit the defendant. . . . Not only is he an innocent man, but he is one of the most infamously wronged men who ever lived in the history of the world.

"If Adolph L. Luetgert is guilty of murdering his wife in the manner that is charged against him . . . , there is but one punishment fitting for him, and that is not sufficient. Gentlemen of the jury, the verdict in this case must be death or not guilty, and I shall not advocate anything else or ask anything less from you."

Vincent spoke for three hours, recounting Luetgert's life story and his success as a businessman. As he closed his speech, the attorney laid out the main reasons he believed Luetgert was innocent: Luetgert had purchased the potash to make soap, which is what he had been doing in the factory the night of May 1. Mrs. Luetgert was alive and had been seen several times since May 1. She had wandered away from home in a state of dementia, and she had often made threats to flee her home if the business failed. The rings found in the vat had never belonged to her. The bones examined by the state's experts were not human, and it would have been impossible to destroy a human body in the manner described by the state. Luetgert had failed to notify police of his wife's disappearance because attorneys had advised him against doing so.

Finally, Vincent said, "Luetgert's anxiety after his wife's disappearance was due to business and domestic troubles and not to the memory of a terrible crime."

And then Vincent set out to prove what he had said. His assistant, Phalen, questioned several witnesses who cast doubt on the credibility of Gottliebe and Emma Schimke, the sisters who claimed to have seen Luetgert and his wife outside the factory the night of May 1. These witnesses said Emma Schimke had gone out with them on May 1 as they walked around the neighborhood and stopped into Diversey Hall, also known as Wetsig's saloon, for a brief dance. Gottliebe hadn't been with them, they maintained, and none of them had seen Mr. and Mrs. Luetgert.

One of the witnesses, seventeen-year-old Rosa Gleich, testified that Emma had told her she had lied during her testimony in the Luetgert trial. According to Rosa, Emma said she had told the story about seeing Luetgert and his wife on May 1 simply to corroborate Gottliebe's tale, so that Gottliebe wouldn't get into trouble for lying. Rosa said Emma had told her to lie, too, if she was ever called to testify.

Court adjourned after Phalen had finished his direct examination of Rosa Gleich. That evening her father was called out of the house at supper time. He was then seen with several of Schaack's policemen in neighboring saloons. When he returned, he was intoxicated. "I am quite certain that Father was induced to drink with them and do all in his power to keep me from testifying," Rosa told the *Chicago Chronicle*. "When he returned, he beat me because I said I would have to go to the court. He told me I was a fool to think of such a thing and should tell the police all I knew."

Later in the evening a messenger boy called at the house and asked whether Rosa Gleich lived there. After being told she did, he ran off without giving any explanation.

The Gleichs retired at 9:30. Loud rapping at the front door awakened them half an hour later. Two men insisted on seeing Rosa. When they were told the girl had gone to bed, they stayed on the steps and refused to leave. The family barricaded the door. William Charles Jr., the son of Luetgert's business associate, was hiding in the front yard at the time. He recognized the men as plainclothes detectives he had seen prowling about the neighborhood.

"They stayed about until we feared that the door would be broken down," Rosa said, adding that the police had been shadowing her ever since her name had been mentioned in connection with Luetgert. "Our house has been watched by police officers for weeks," she said, "and I have feared to go out on account of the boldness of these men." The same day several defense witnesses said they were harassed by Schaack's officers. The *Chronicle* reported Schaack had sent fifty men to scour the neighborhood around the factory.

Officer Charles Griebenow had been watching George Fiedler's saloon, at 618 Diversey. Fiedler's son, Harry, claimed he had been out with Emma Schimke and Rosa Gleich on the night of May 1, and he planned to testify for the defense. On Wednesday Griebenow came into the saloon and took Harry Fiedler into the back room. "That policeman did his best to get me out of testifying," Harry said. "He called me a liar and other names and said that I never told the truth in my life. He shook his fist at me meaningly and declared he would 'fix' me. I thought he was going to thrash me on the spot and was about to shout for assistance. He said the jail was the only fit abode for people like me and predicted I would land there in short order if I testified for Luetgert."

Fiedler's father feared the police might try to withdraw his liquor license because of his son's testimony for the Luetgert defense. "My place is hounded by these agents of Schaack," George Fiedler said. "I do not know what they are going to do with me. My business is going to the dogs in a hurry. I am confident that my former patrons have been told to keep away from my place or they will get into trouble. I have seen men stopped when about to come into my saloon by policemen in citizens' clothes and told to go elsewhere. This is what I am getting for trying to free an innocent man. It's hard on a fellow to see his trade dwindle away. We are being encouraged to assist the ways of justice, I suppose. I can only say that there are forty people in this neighborhood who have been frightened out of declaring themselves just on account of the methods of some of these police officials."

It was reported Schaack's agents had intimidated Amelia Kaiser, who lived in the neighborhood, and offered her money if she would evade answers put to her by Luetgert's lawyers. And Frank Scheve, a defense witness from Kenosha, had been frightened out of coming to Chicago by Officer Michael Harkins.

Griebenow denied all the defense witnesses' stories about police harassment, saying, "They are a pack of liars." Schuettler supported him, saying, "Griebenow would not hold his star ten minutes if such things were true. I would have him reported to Chief Kipley without delay. This talk is entirely without foundation. My men are not guilty of such dirty work."

The *Chronicle* noted that the police offers of money and whisky and the threats of physical chastisement and incarceration were similar to the schemes Schaack's detectives had employed in the Haymarket case and the trial of Alderman O'Malley.

Tuthill said he was inclined to believe the accusations against the police. When Rosa Gleich returned to the witness stand to be cross-examined the next day, Tuthill sent the jurors out of the courtroom and upbraided the police for their conduct. He admonished the police not to interfere with the witnesses and added that the defense team should not do so, either.

As Deneen interrogated Rosa, he suggested that she had been out with Emma on May 2, not on May 1, but the girl insisted she didn't have her dates mixed up. Then he accused Rosa of making up the story about being out with Emma on May 1 so that Rosa's mother wouldn't find out Rosa had been out with some boys until three in the morning. Rosa denied it.

Harry Fiedler, who was also seventeen, took the stand and confirmed Rosa's story of walking around the Luetgert neighborhood on May 1. He also said he had overheard Emma Schimke talking about the Luetgert case September 15 at the Gleich house. He heard Emma say she had been out with Rosa and Harry on May 1 and that her mother had forced her to testify untruthfully so that Gottliebe wouldn't be branded a liar.

Charles Bockelman, who was fifteen, swore he was out with Rosa, Emma, and Harry on the evening of May 1, along with another young man named Joseph Hemple. He said they had played tag that night as they wandered the neighborhood.

Two other teenage girls, Maggie Shaughnessy and Ida Larsen, testified they had been at Diversey Hall from eight until midnight on May 1 for the dance. They had seen Emma and Rosa stop in and dance one quadrille. They also said they had seen Luetgert in the barroom between eight and nine. "He was treating the girls to some drinks of some kind at the bar," Larsen said. "I don't know what it was."

Maud Scherer testified Emma had said to her in July: "My little sister has got me into trouble. I wasn't there, and I did not see Mr. and Mrs. Luetgert the night of May 1. I was with Rosa Gleich that night, and not with my sister Gottliebe."

Maud, who worked at the Deering twine works along with Rosa and Emma, said Emma later told her coworkers, "It is a lie. My damned little sister got me into trouble. I was not there. I did not see Mr. and Mrs. Luetgert on the night of the first of May."

The defense called Emma Schimke back to the witness stand. She insisted that she had told the truth when testifying for the state and that the things she had said outside of court were the lies. As Phalen interrogated her, Emma seemed ready to collapse at any moment. She kept her eyes fixed on the floor. Rosa Gleich, watching the testimony, laughed at her friend's embarrassment.

Asked whether she had told her coworkers at Deering's that she had lied on the witness stand, Emma said, "I don't know whether I did or not. I suppose you take me for a liar? I did see Mr. Luetgert there that night. I don't care what anybody says."

Emma said she told the lies outside court to protect Rosa Gleich from being whipped by her mother, who was angry at her for staying out all night with boys.

The defense also tried to demonstrate that, even if Emma and Gottliebe had seen someone go into the Luetgert factory on May 1, they wouldn't have been able to see who it was. Dr. Charles H. Mills said he had stood in front of the Schimke house at 8:10 P.M. on September 11, when the sky was partly clear and the moon was visible. He said that he had seen some people down the street going into the Luetgert factory but that they had been too far away for him to make out their identity.

Julian Hawthorne thought it was odd that the Luetgert trial was focusing so much on the nighttime exploits of these youngsters. "How queer it is," he wrote, "that the night-larking of these street children should by a freak of fate come to have such importance to a man's life! They are playing tag while murder is being done, but their sole concern is to fabricate a yarn which may save them a spanking when they get home. Whether Luetgert hangs or is acquitted is a side issue. Such is life."

29 Just a Plain Domestic Girl

THE DEFENSE WANTED to show that Mrs. Luetgert had been afflicted with a "peculiar malady" for five or six months before she vanished. The lawyers hoped to question witnesses about Mrs. Luetgert's behavior. They also wanted to bring forward psychologists who would testify Mrs. Luetgert suffered from a form of insanity that would explain why she had run away.

"It is . . . evident that Mrs. Luetgert had an alternating melancholia of degeneracy which had very slowly developed to become accentuated at that period of female life which is so generally critical to neurotic woman—the menopause," wrote J. Sanderson Christison, the criminologist associated with the defense.

Christison claimed Mrs. Luetgert's fascination with the tiny slippers had illustrated "the insanity of her vanity." He further claimed her reaction to the canary to have been another symptom. "Her morbid feelings toward nature were manifested in her declared hatred of such charming objects as flowers and birds."

Mrs. Luetgert was supposed to have had two cousins and a brother who had gone insane. Christison said this showed that mental problems ran in Mrs. Luetgert's family. The shape of her ear was also a bad sign, according to Christison, who believed such things indicated a person's likelihood of going insane or committing crimes. "All of Mrs. Luetgert's closest relatives whom I have seen have that very noticeable type of ear—the projecting," he wrote. Even Elmer and Louis had the "projecting ear" and resembled their mother more than their father, which might explain why Elmer had cried hysterically for three hours that summer about his father's not coming home. "As he is entirely unlike his father, this hysterical exhibition must be explained as a neurotic heritage from his mother," Christison wrote.

But Tuthill wouldn't allow Vincent and Phalen to put any insanity experts on the stand. He limited the testimony about Mrs. Luetgert's behavior to incidents within a week before May 1. "I am not going over the whole life history and let you pick out isolated circumstances," Tuthill said. "You can show anything queer that she did, but that's all."

Several witnesses testified Mrs. Luetgert had said she would leave home if the business went kaput. Amelia Kaiser related how she had visited Mrs. Luetgert on the evening of May 1. Phalen tried to show that Mrs. Luetgert's "strange" reaction to the bowl of cream cheese Kaiser brought her was evidence of her insanity, but Tuthill scoffed, "Oh, that's nothing. She may not have had any *Schmierkäse* for a long time." Tuthill also turned sarcastic when Phalen tried to demonstrate Mrs. Luetgert's insanity with the fact that she had given Kaiser four oranges that evening. "I see nothing queer in that," he said.

The next morning, September 25, a murmur went through the crowd when Phalen called his first witness of the day: "Mary Siemering." As she casually sat down in the witness chair, the spectators were busy whispering about the young lady who had been so much discussed during the trial. She wore a steel-blue shirtwaist and a hat with cloth rosebuds, neither of which matched her complexion or what one reporter called "her irregular features." A reporter suggested the defense had chosen her clothing to dispel any notion that she was beautiful: "Only when she got angry could she have been called even good-looking."

Siemering never looked at Luetgert while she testified, but Luetgert kept his eyes on her the whole time. Siemering described how Mrs. Luetgert had behaved in the last week of April, how she had said over and over that she would run away, and how she had rubbed her hands nervously, put salt into her tea, and spent much time in her room. When Phalen tried to ask Siemering questions about Mrs. Luetgert's behavior in the months leading up to that week, the judge refused to allow it.

Siemering said Luetgert had treated his wife well. She denied ever having seen him strike her or threaten her with violence and said that Luetgert always let his wife have as much money as she needed. Siemering also said Mrs. Luetgert beat her children nearly every day during the six months prior to her disappearance. "Why, she treated them mean. . . . She beat them when they did not do anything wrong, and when they did something wrong, she did not beat any of them."

Siemering told of finding Mrs. Luetgert's room empty the morning of May 2, with the bed all upset. The boys' banks were in the room, too, emptied of all their coins, she said.

Siemering testified about being taken into police custody at six A.M. Saturday, May 15, and placed in a basement cell. As she recounted the way the police had treated her, she grew indignant, her lips making a thin white line. She described Schaack and McEwen asking her repeatedly whether Luetgert had killed his wife. She said she had denied knowing anything about it—and denied having intimate relations with Luetgert. They had called her a liar and threatened her with criminal charges. "Inspector Schaack says, 'If you don't go against the old man'—he called him 'old man'—'if you don't go against him, we will get you and the old man lynched like this.' And he showed me." Siemering demonstrated the gesture Schaack had made to indicate her neck would be put into a noose.

According to Siemering, the police did not release her from custody until Monday, more than forty-eight hours after taking her in for questioning, and they fed her nothing the entire time. She was given a plank to sleep on with one blanket for a pillow, and the police matron had made her strip when she arrived at the station. Officer Walter Dean watched from the door as she stood there naked, she said.

Siemering denied that Luetgert had ever put his arms around her or kissed her or that she had ever gone with him into the basement or the factory office at night. The only time she had gone there, she said, was when she made his bed during the daytime.

When Phalen finished questioning Siemering, McEwen quietly rose, leaning his right elbow on the rail and fixing his eyes on Siemering's face. He questioned her in an agreeable voice. McEwen asked her about the interrogation on May 15, suggesting that he had merely been trying to get the full story when he questioned her. "Didn't I say at that time that all we wanted was to get a full story of just what happened down there and what the situation was at the house?" McEwen asked.

"I do not know," Siemering replied.

Siemering again denied that she had ever made love to Luetgert. McEwen asked her, "Didn't you say that he sometimes said, in a half-joking way or a joking way, that he was going to make you his wife and you would say, well, he not good enough for you, he was too old—didn't you say that?"

"That was while Mrs. Luetgert was present there, while we were joking."

McEwen asked Siemering to recall whether she had told a judge at the courthouse one day that she had been treated well at the police station. She denied saying it.

She further denied having told the police she'd had trouble sleeping for a week after Mrs. Luetgert disappeared. She denied telling the police, "It troubles me all the time. I believe that he done away with her." She denied saying, "About one year ago, I saw him chase her with a revolver." She denied telling the police Mrs. Luetgert had taken the money out of Louis's bank a long time before her disappearance, sometime around Christmas, to keep the money for him. She denied telling William Follbach on May 3 that Mrs. Luetgert was sleeping in the house even though she had known Mrs. Luetgert was missing. She denied admitting to the police that she had told Follbach that story because she feared the disgrace Mrs. Luetgert's disappearance would bring on the family. She denied telling the police she had noticed nothing peculiar about Mrs. Luetgert's behavior. She denied saying, "She was not any more crazy than you are." Finally, she denied telling Schaack that Mrs. Feld was running the house and wanted Siemering to "take a back seat."

Over and over Siemering's sullen answer was "No, sir." McEwen's insistent questioning was taking a toll on Siemering, however. Her face gradually turned paler, her voice lost strength, and she often looked intently at the floor. The women in the audience craned their necks to catch every nuance of her testimony, and they seemed to smile in apparent satisfaction at the servant girl's discomfiture. One reporter thought Siemering looked more frightened of the audience than of the attorneys.

Despite the intense pressure, Siemering refused to be shaken on any important feature of her testimony. It was only at the end of the day that she let her temper get the better of her. She made some extravagant replies, raising laughter in the court. The laughter made her more reckless yet.

"Now," McEwen asked, "you say that she used to beat the children. With her hands or stick or club?"

"With her hands, stick—anything she could get hold of, her slipper."

"She used anything she got hold of?"

"Anything she got hold of."

"Broom?"

"Yes, sir."

"Poker?"

"Yes, sir."

"Anything—pick up a chair?"

"Anything she got hold of."

"Just as apt to use a chair as anything else?"

"Yes, sir."

"Didn't take a stove leg and beat them with it?"

"She would if she could have lifted the stove."

"She would have hit them with the stove leg if she could have lifted it?"

"Yes, sir."

"You know she would have done that?"

"Yes, sir."

"You are not a clairvoyant or mind reader? That is not your business?"

"No, sir."

"Just a plain domestic girl?"

"Yes, sir."

Siemering returned to the witness stand the following morning, but before court began, she sat near Luetgert, chatting with him. She seemed to notice that the women thronging the courtroom were watching her intently. She held her head high and appeared to enjoy being the center of attention.

When McEwen resumed questioning her, he asked about some statements she had made to the grand jury that contradicted the testimony she was giving now. She didn't deny having given the earlier testimony but explained that she had lied before the grand jury because Schaack had forced her to do so. "They made me say it," she said. "Inspector Schaack told me I had to say everything. If I would not, he would punish me for it."

Siemering completed her testimony and sat back down beside Luetgert. He gave her a broad smile.

30 The Many Mrs. Luetgerts

MRS. LUETGERT was everywhere. Since disappearing in Chicago on May 1, she had boarded a train in Fond du Lac, Wisconsin, in a state of intoxication. She had walked into a Decatur saloon with an umbrella and ordered a beer, announcing she had walked 130 miles and was hoping to procure fifteen dollars from someone named Mrs. Mueller. She had asked a lawyer in Nebraska about getting a divorce, explaining she had deserted her husband in Chicago. She was working as a cook on a steam barge that stopped in Tonawanda, New York. She stayed with a Polish family in Ashland, Wisconsin. She had visited an employment agent in Peoria, looking for a job. Mrs. Luetgert, or women supposedly resembling her, had been in many of these places at virtually the same time. She seemed to be criss-crossing the country.

Time and again Luetgert and his lawyers said they believed Mrs. Luetgert would appear in time to save her husband from conviction. "I now have a strong hope of being able to produce Mrs. Luetgert alive before the trial ends," Vincent once said.

Some of the sightings of Mrs. Luetgert were obvious hoaxes. Whiskey and beer bottles containing scribbled notes signed by the missing woman were found floating in Lake Michigan near Chicago, Racine, and Valparaiso, as well as in the Rock River in Rockford. One letter had her saying she wished to die because she couldn't bear to see her husband love another woman. Another had her saying, "I have been imprisoned by some unknown persons, and in an unknown place."

One letter explained Mrs. Luetgert had drowned herself by jumping from the deck of the steamer *Virginia* into Lake Michigan. That letter also included the visiting card of a Chicago woman. When a reporter went to the address on the card, the woman there sheepishly explained she had been traveling on a whaleback vessel in the lake a couple of months earlier. She had given her card to a young man who threw the fake message into the water.

A woman on the North Side found a ring inscribed with the words "Louise Luetgert" and turned it over to police. Schuettler looked at it and discovered it was made of brass. The lettering was crude, apparently scratched with a knife.

According to one story, Mrs. Luetgert was working as a servant in Summit County, Ohio, and being paid a large sum of money by Luetgert's business rivals to stay away from Chicago so that Luetgert would go to the gallows.

In another case a roughly dressed man carrying a bundle with a small sickle traveled through Waukesha, Wisconsin, bringing with him a tale that Mrs. Luetgert was staying with his wife in Helena, Montana. The man, who seemed to have been drinking, said his name was Christ Fathan, but newspapers could find no trace of any such man in Helena. McEwen remarked, "I hardly feel like wasting enough mental energy to express what I think of that story. The season's record of bicycle punctures is not to be compared with the number of these stories that have the wind let out of them as soon as they are sprung."

A man claiming to be an old sweetheart of Louise Bicknese, Alexander Carl W. Grottey of New York, said he had encountered her walking on Broadway in Manhattan on May 7. Grottey added that he had evidence that Mrs. Luetgert had sailed for Europe. He wrote to Luetgert's lawyers and offered to testify.

At first Luetgert said he remembered Grottey. "Why, yes, I know him well," he said. "He is a pretty good fellow, even if I did have to chase him away when he was getting after my girl. But I know he is a faithful man, and I guess he saw my wife there. I feel sure she has gone to Europe."

Captain Schuettler went to New York in August to investigate Grottey's tale, which quickly unraveled. The two men who were with Grottey when he supposedly saw Mrs. Luetgert contradicted his story. No record could be found of Mrs. Luetgert's buying tickets for Europe. Grottey had a history of falsely reporting he had seen people who had been reported missing. Finally, Grottey was a bit young to have wooed Louise—he had been only fifteen when Luetgert married her.

Other sightings of Mrs. Luetgert were cases of mistaken identity. The women mistaken for Mrs. Luetgert were usually insane or alcoholic. On September 15 several farmers walking along a railroad track near Melrose Park, a town just west of Chicago, saw a disheveled woman running through nearby woods. After they chased her, she ran out onto the rails, where she sat down and dug with her hands in the gravel. Her face was tanned, and her hair hung in a tangled bunch down her back. Her fingers were blistered and sore. When she finally spoke, her words were incoherent, and she expressed only a desire to dig in the ground. She said the earth held some great secret that she had to expose at once. The farmers took her to the Melrose Park police station, where some officers thought she looked like Mrs. Luetgert.

On hearing the news, Luetgert said, "Let me get out of here and take me out to Melrose Park in a carriage. I would like to go out and have a look at her. . . . Let me go out and identify her. If it is the woman, we will go back and live together. I want to see her first, though, and make sure that it is she."

It was soon discovered, however, that the woman was Caroline Johnson, who had been admitted into the Dunning asylum in June 1896 and discharged in June 1897. "That woman captured in Melrose Park, I understand, was not my wife," Luetgert said. "The public doubtless think she's turning up pretty frequently, but some of these days she will make an appearance and won't Luetgert roast some people? Oh, no, maybe not."

Local policemen spent a few days in October trailing a crazy or intoxicated woman walking through eastern Indiana in ragged clothing and soleless shoes. "She talks cautiously and does not act like an ordinary crazy person," the *Inter Ocean* reported. Descriptions of the woman vaguely matched those of Mrs. Luetgert, but she turned out to be Lillian English, who had been wandering the area for months.

Women identified as Mrs. Luetgert were seen most frequently in Wisconsin. She was usually said to be hiding as a boarder at a farmhouse, or working as a servant, or being held against her will. The detectives and reporters tracking her down always seemed to come close, saying she was in the vicinity of a particular town, but they never came face to face with the woman.

Luetgert showed Luther Laflin Mills, a prominent attorney supporting his cause, the many letters he had received. Mills was impressed by a letter from a man named Smith who said Mrs. Luetgert was living in a demented condition on a farm outside Bay View, Wisconsin, a small town near Green Bay.

Mills sent for Smith, who told him he had heard about a mysterious woman walking through the farm country and asking for food, shelter, and work. She was travel-stained, worn, and in great mental trouble and would give no name. A farmer had agreed to give the woman a room. Some time later a newspaper with an article about the Luetgert case arrived at the farm. As the family discussed the story, the woman turned pale and almost fainted at the mention of the name Luetgert.

Mills asked Smith to accompany one of his detectives up into Wisconsin to search for the woman. Smith agreed to go but did not arrive at the appointed time the next night. Two days later Mills's detective saw Smith talking with four lumbermen in a saloon on North Clark Street. Early the next morning Smith sailed with the four men on a lumber barge for Green Bay.

After another two days the detective went north. He found the farm where the mysterious woman had been staying, but she was gone by then. The detective discovered that the four lumberjacks he had seen with Smith had visited the area around the farm shortly before the woman vanished. In the coming weeks the detective traveled all over Wisconsin trying to find the woman. He found people who had seen the woman and showed them photographs of Mrs. Luetgert, but the woman was always about two days ahead of him. The *Tribune* reported, "Mr. Mills does not know what to think of the queer goings-on in the Wisconsin woods."

On September 25 three boys from Oshkosh went hickory-nutting south of the town. They saw a clump of trees near a summer watering place on the lake shore but were afraid to trespass on the property. A woman came along the railroad tracks, watching them. At first they believed she was somehow connected with the farm where the hickories grew. They asked her if they could go on her land and gather nuts. She replied that it was not her land and that she was simply visiting. The woman, who said her home was in Chicago, told the boys her name, and they later said it was Luetgert or something similar. She said that her husband was a butcher and that she had fled because he had threatened to cut her up. She added that her husband and his agents were hunting for her, but she had friends to protect her.

A circus equestrian named Daisy Thompson said she had encountered a woman in May sitting alone at the train station in Monmouth, Illinois, where Thompson and her husband were traveling in a private rail car. Thompson said she was "positive" the woman was Mrs. Luetgert. The *Kewanee (Ill.) Star* reported her story:

> I asked her where she was going and she said she thought she might go west, but wanted to find some quiet, out-of-the-way place before starting again. In course of the conversation I said:
> "I expect you will see Ringling's circus—"
> She interrupted my remark, saying she had seen enough of that in Chicago—that her boys were just crazy over shows. She asked me if I lived in that car and said she would like to travel around like that, and asked me if I needed any help. I told her that I was in need of a nurse girl. . . . But as I did not like the woman's looks and actions, I did not give her any encouragement to enter my employ, but told her I would ask Mr. Thompson and see what he said about it. She replied:
> "Do you let him tell you what to do?"
> When I told her that I would have to go, as my husband would wonder where I was staying so long, she replied:
> "My husband will wonder a good long time before he ever sees me again, and when he does, he will be more glad to see me than he ever was before in his life."
> When I told my husband about the strange woman, he said it must be some crank running away. I saw the woman again late in the evening when I was sitting on the car steps. My little boy was sitting beside me, and she commenced to play with him.
> "I left a little boy," said the woman.
> "My, why did you do it?" I asked.
> "He is over five years old," she said, "and besides I had a good servant girl who has been with me for years, who will take care of him."

In Boston Clara Moss said a woman who had stayed across the hall from her in a boarding house for a few days in July may have been Mrs. Luetgert. Moss's story appeared in the *Chicago Record*:

> The woman's room was opposite my room on the same floor, and during the day, as we left our doors open, we could not help seeing one another, and

therefore got acquainted. The woman came to the house on a Monday evening, and was dressed in a black brilliantine dress and black loose cloak and wore a black hat with reddish trimmings. She wore no jewelry except a small chain ring on one finger. During the afternoon of the second day, I think, the woman came into my room and remarked about the pretty pictures I had on the wall. When she learned that my husband and myself were from Chicago she said she, too, was from Chicago, and we discussed various places in that city. She was known at the house as Miss Millie Barker.

Not until the third day of the woman's presence had I any knowledge that her name was other than Millie Barker. One afternoon, upon looking into her room, I found her with a copy of a newspaper in her hand, apparently much distressed. I asked her what the trouble was, whereupon she pointed to an article written by Julian Hawthorne in relation to the trial of Luetgert at Chicago for murdering his wife in a sausage factory. I spoke of how terrible the case was.

The woman appeared to be strangely taken, and suddenly looked up and remarked: "You would be surprised if I told you who I was. I am Mrs. Luetgert." Of course I was astonished at such information, and I made known that my husband, Mr. Moss, had frequently said that he knew the Luetgert factory quite well. He had as a boy resided in the locality.

She said she had left her husband because of his bad actions, and that she did not propose to go back to him. I tried to show the woman that if really she was Mrs. Luetgert it was her duty to return to her husband or at least announce to the world that she was living, and not the victim of the murder as charged against her husband. To all this the woman made answer substantially that she would not return to Mr. Luetgert or make known her existence unless Luetgert was convicted and stood upon the scaffold.

Miss Barker, or Mrs. Luetgert, acted frightened after this conversation and left the house the following day, walking out with an ordinary satchel in her hand.

On September 24 a woman in a dusty dress who appeared tired from traveling stopped into a tavern on North Avenue in Chicago. The saloonkeeper, Arthur Mundwiller, said the woman told him, "They tried to murder me by giving me poison and throwing me into a vat several times." She also said she had gained admittance to the Luetgert factory the day before. As the woman departed, she threw a small gold-plated locket onto the pool table and told Mundwiller to keep it for luck. Luetgert later looked at the jewelry but said it had not belonged to his wife.

Only a few of the people who claimed to have seen Mrs. Luetgert after May 1 were called to testify. A butcher named Jacob Melber thought he had seen her in Wheaton, west of Chicago, on May 6. A woman had asked him the way to Elmhurst, and Melber said she resembled Mrs. Luetgert, whom he had seen once a couple of years earlier when he sought a job at the Luetgert factory. Melber didn't sound overly certain, however, when he was asked, "Was the woman you saw at Wheaton the same woman you saw at Luetgert's sausage factory?"

"Pretty near to it, but I would not swear, but that was pretty near the same-sized woman," he said. "In weight, I cannot tell you it. I cannot tell you by her figures, the color of her hair, or anything like that."

Armadale Opdyke, a fruit peddler, swore he had seen Mrs. Luetgert on June 9. He said he had been driving his horse and wagon toward Janesville, Wisconsin, when he met two women wearing shawls. As he camped beside the road at night, the women came along and asked how to get to Elgin. Opdyke said he had slept outdoors that night, and the two women had slept on the ground about 150 feet from him. Shown a photograph of Mrs. Luetgert, Opdyke said it was one of the two women he had seen.

Several witnesses told the tale of the mysterious woman who visited Kenosha on May 3 and 4, but the prosecutors accused all these witnesses of having previously told Chicago police that the woman in Kenosha did not resemble photographs of Mrs. Luetgert. Now these witnesses claimed the woman they had seen was the same as the one in the photos and tintypes.

Deneen rapidly fired questions at the bartender Matt J. Scholey, and the witness stumbled in his description of the strange woman supposed to be Mrs. Luetgert. "How much did she weigh?"

"Oh, I should judge she would weigh between somewheres around 100—between 135 and 140 pounds."

Deneen smiled, and a disgusted expression appeared on the face of defense attorneys Vincent and Phalen. "One-hundred thirty-five to 140?" asked Deneen.

"No, I should judge she weighed about 115 to 118 pounds. I have got mixed up."

Deneen's smile broadened. He looked at McEwen and Schaack, and all three laughed aloud. Some of the jurors, who had rarely smiled during the trial, joined in the laugh. Phalen was on his feet in an instant. "I don't think it is fair for Inspector Schaack and the state's attorney to laugh and make fun of the testimony of witnesses before the jury."

"I am not making fun," Deneen said.

Judge Tuthill, who seemed to be struggling to suppress a laugh, said, "Well, the witness was smiling himself."

"Anyone would laugh at that answer," Deneen said.

"I made a mistake," Scholey said.

"I don't think it is necessary to become angry about it," Tuthill said.

Deneen added, "I can't help laughing when I look at Mr. Phalen."

Deneen continued his attack on Scholey's story. Scholey denied telling officers, "If you fellows have got any money, I will tell you all about this. My evidence is worth something, and you can get it if you have got the dough. My testimony is worth $1,500, and that is what I am going to get for it."

As for his mistake about the woman's weight, Scholey explained he had been confused because he thought Deneen was asking him how old the woman was. Smiling again, Deneen asked Scholey, "You thought I was inquiring about her age . . . when you said 135 or 140?"

"Yes."

When the defense attorneys showed the policeman Henry Feldshaw a cabinet photograph of Mrs. Luetgert, at first he said it didn't look much like the woman he had seen in Kenosha, but then he changed his mind. Feldshaw denied telling Chicago police that the woman he had seen in Kenosha did not resemble the photo of Mrs. Luetgert. However, he did acknowledge telling the officers the mystery woman "looked like an old sport."

The Kenosha police officer William Smith also told of seeing the woman at the train station. Before testifying, he told a newspaper, "The Chicago 'fly cops' think they know a lot, but we will show them a few things before we get through." But Smith ran into similar problems on cross-examination. He denied having told Chicago police that the woman in Kenosha did not look like Mrs. Luetgert. He also denied demanding fifty dollars from the Chicago cops to disclose the location of the mystery woman.

Frank Scheve, the farm laborer who said he had seen Mrs. Luetgert walking down a country road, faced accusations that a Kenosha attorney had given him five dollars, bought him a suit of clothes and a pair of shoes for his court appearance, and paid for his train ride to Chicago. Scheve denied the lawyer had paid him to lie on the witness stand, and he denied telling the farmer for whom he worked that he was going to testify in the Luetgert case just because he wanted to come down to Chicago and have a good time.

Commenting on the witnesses from Kenosha, Julian Hawthorne wrote, "I can only consider the testimony farcical."

31 Soap and Bones

SPEAKING UNHESITATINGLY in a low but clear voice, William Charles told the court his version of the events at the Luetgert plant in the spring of 1897. In April, he said, he told Luetgert they should clean up the factory. They had ordered potash from Lord, Owen and Company, which shipped them a barrel containing about 375 pounds of the stuff. Sometime during the last week of April, Charles had gone down into the basement and looked into the middle vat, which was about half-full with a potash solution.

According to Charles, at about half past seven on the morning of Saturday, May 1, he and Luetgert put three or four barrels of tallow and grease—rubbish that been lying around for some time—into the vat. Charles said he next saw Luetgert around a quarter to nine that night in Wetsig's saloon, and then they went into the factory. "There is a little fox terrier he has in the basement, and we began turning around for rats, of which he has plenty there. We had thrown and turned around a number of boxes for the dogs to get at the rats. We had quite a hunt there for about three or four minutes pulling boxes away for the dogs to get at the rats."

Charles said he and Luetgert piled up several empty barrels and boxes against the door near the elevator to make room for the terrier to hunt the rodents. They left the boxes and barrels there, blocking the door for the rest of the night, and then went down into the basement. Charles said he watched as Luetgert turned on the steam, so it would run into the vat.

Charles claimed that he next saw Luetgert about half past six on Sunday morning. He said the two of them went into the basement, and Luetgert showed him how his attempt at making soap had turned out. "It was not exactly a success, that's all," he testified. "The grease seemed in one pile; the tallow was lumped in another pile; it was in three distinct masses. I am not much of a soap maker. It wasn't right, anyway. It was not a success in some way. . . . Luetgert put the hose in the vat and turned it on and let the water run in."

Charles said he and Luetgert visited the factory basement again on Monday morning. By that time all that was left in the vat was water: "Mr. Luetgert had left the hose in the vat all that day, and the water had forced out everything on the floor. The floor was all greasy and sticky. It ran right into the sewer and extended about half a foot over the sewer, where it ran over."

The defense attorneys also brought in the chemist and soap manufacturer Louis Gottschalk. They asked what would have happened if Luetgert had tried to create soap under the conditions described by the defense (dissolving 378 pounds of potash in 500 gallons of water, adding 700 to 800 pounds of crude tallow and market trimmings into the vat, and running steam into it at a pressure of 50 to 70 pounds per square inch for 3½ hours).

"With that amount of fat under that heat, for that length of time, well, there would not be, according to my best estimation, true soap," Gottschalk said. "There would be a mixture. The soap at most—there could only be 600, about 630 or 640 pounds actual soap and the balance would be an emulsion. . . . The market trimmings would be partly dissolved and would be made into a kind of gluey substance."

Gottschalk's testimony also showed that it wouldn't have been economical for Luetgert to make his own soap. The soft soap he claimed to have tried making cost him nearly fifty dollars, when he could have purchased ready-made soap at one dollar a barrel.

Luetgert's attorneys brought seven experts into court to dispute the testimony of the state's bone doctors and chemists.

Dr. Bernhart L. Riese described how he had conducted two experiments in the middle vat at the factory, dissolving the bodies of a man and woman. Each of the nude bodies had been placed in a solution containing 378 pounds of potash, along with rags, artificial teeth and plates, corsets, rings, and various other things. The vat had been covered with gunny sacks and doors. Steam had poured into the vat at 68 to 70 pounds of pressure for 3½ hours. Riese was never able to heat the solution to the boiling point with that amount of steam, he said. When he turned off the steam, Riese tried to remove whatever bone fragments remained. He used a shovel and a rake but was able to retrieve only one or two fragments. The liquid in the vat burned his hands, he said.

When the fluid ran from the bunghole into gunny sacks, barely any matter stuck to the sacks, other than "small pieces of bone, all very light pieces, spongy, and a few teeth," he said.

"During the heating at no time was there the slightest offensive odor, nor was I able to detect that odor of ammonia. The odor was such as one would get from a laundry—the potash or lye odor. The same is true on the following day when we removed the plug from the vat. There was not the slightest odor except a light lye odor. The color of that solution and the thickness was like very weak tea."

The defense experts had placed a calico wrapper and half a corset, which they had taken from Mrs. Luetgert's wardrobe, into the vat. Neither dissolved, Riese said.

Riese said all his experiments failed to dissolve the shafts of long bones, although the ends of these bones disappeared or became soft. The bones of the skull were also difficult to dissolve. Artificial teeth remained intact even after being boiled in a potash solution for twenty-four hours. No sesamoids survived his boiling experiments, however.

The defense's main bone expert was Walter H. Allport, a doctor at St. Luke's Hospital and an anatomy instructor at Northwestern University's Medical College. A young, intellectual-looking man, Allport appeared as if he were suffering from a stiff neck as he sat on the stand. Vincent handed him a bone. "Please examine state's exhibit 19. That is alleged to be by the state the fragment of a femur. Can you identify this bone?"

"Yes, sir, I can."

"What is it?"

"It is the femur of a hog."

Allport maintained that it wasn't possible to identify as human any of the bones introduced by the state. In fact, he said, the various bones did not all come from the same animal, and they didn't appear to have been have been boiled in potash. He then launched into a lengthy lecture to explain his findings. The doctor walked up and down before the jury box, bending over to hand a bit of bone to a juror and then stepping back to draw a picture of a part he wished to illustrate. He seemed to lose himself in his speech, forgetting he was a witness in court rather than a professor in class. Tuthill called out, "We are not here to study anatomy," but Allport went on.

"We have now arrived at the lower half of the bone, where it will be noticed that the characteristic of animal bones—"

McEwen interrupted, but still the doctor continued talking.

"It is a rule as invariable as the laws of the Medes and Persians," Allport said.

For the second time, Tuthill said, "We are not here to study anatomy."

Allport bowed and was silent. Vincent rose slowly and said, "But, if Your Honor please, we are here for a more serious matter—that of trying a man for his life."

The judge relented, allowing Allport to continue. The doctor seemed so confident as he testified that Luetgert and his attorneys found themselves smiling, as if they had shown how fallible the state's evidence was. Then McEwen began his cross-examination, bringing large boxes filled with bones into the courtroom to test Allport's bone-identifying abilities. McEwen pulled a leg or arm bone out of a paper sack and handed it to Allport. He asked Allport to find the pisiform bone, the small bone in the wrist that Allport claimed the prosecution witnesses had mistaken for a sesamoid. Allport took out a pocket knife and spent ten minutes poking around, looking for the pisiform. Finally he announced he had been looking for it on the wrong side. He said the skeleton limb had come from a dog.

Professor Dorsey, who was closely watching Allport's testimony, told McEwen it was the arm and hand of a monkey.

"Well, it might be a dog-monkey," Allport retorted. "They look a good deal alike."

Allport made other errors. He thought the thigh bone of a large man was the thigh of a woman. Given another bone, he declared, "This bone, sir, is the femur of a hog."

"Excuse me, Professor," McEwen said. "Dr. Dorsey informs me that bone is the thigh of a musk ox at the Field Columbian Museum."

Several jurors laughed, along with many of the spectators; the bailiffs hushed the courtroom. Allport tried to explain his error by saying the hog and musk ox were in the same family. McEwen asked him if the musk ox was a ruminant and the hog a nonruminant, and Allport acknowledged that was true.

"The musk ox stands four or five feet high, doesn't it?" McEwen asked.

"He is pretty high," Allport said. "I never saw one. I have seen bones, pictures and descriptions of them."

"Whereabouts did you get your information regarding the musk ox?"

"I got the information out of textbooks and by observation. The musk ox belongs to the same family as the sheep and hog."

Anthropologist George Dorsey testifying about the bone fragments found by police. (*Chicago Journal,* Oct. 2, 1897)

Osteologist George Bailey showing how one of the bone fragments would fit into a human arm. (*Chicago Journal,* Sept. 11, 1897)

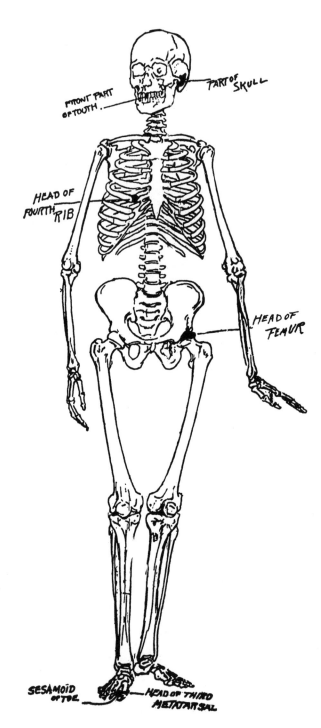

PART OF SKULL

FRONT PART OF TOOTH

HEAD OF FOURTH RIB

HEAD OF FEMUR

SESAMOID OF TOE

HEAD OF THIRD METATARSAL

A newspaper illustration showing which portions of Mrs. Luetgert's skeleton the police claimed to have found. (*Chicago Record*, Sept. 16, 1897)

Assistant State's Attorney Willard McEwen citing a law book. (*Chicago Journal*, Sept. 21, 1897)

A "lively tilt" between the defense lawyer William Vincent (left) and Assistant State's Attorney Willard McEwen (right). (*Chicago Journal*, Sept. 16, 1897)

The watchman Frank Bialk pointing to the diagram of the factory, showing the window where servant Mary Siemering had supposedly entered for a rendezvous with Adolph Luetgert. (*Chicago Journal*, Sept. 21, 1897)

A phonograph recording testimony in the Luetgert trial. (*Chicago Journal*, Oct. 2, 1897)

Mary Siemering, the Luetgert family servant, testifying. (Courtesy of Special Collections, University of Arizona Library, Collection of John Francis Holme, MS 001 no. 9)

A demented woman found near Melrose Park and mistaken for Mrs. Luetgert. (*Chicago Tribune*, Sept. 15, 1897)

Adolph Luetgert reading a newspaper in court. (Courtesy of Special Collections, University of Arizona Library, Collection of John Francis Holme, MS 001 no. 9)

Phalen asking the jurors, "Could you face the Almighty after sending an innocent man to the gallows?" (*Chicago Journal,* Oct. 14, 1897)

The jurors asking Judge Tuthill for information. (*Chicago Tribune,* Oct. 21, 1897)

Juror William Harley, the focus of most press coverage about the jury deliberations in the first Luetgert trial. (*Chicago Tribune,* Oct. 20, 1897)

"The thigh bone of the musk ox is about twice as long as the bone of the hog, is it not?"

"I suppose it is," Allport said, plainly distressed at the way his testimony was going. He became nervous, confused, and angry as the state continued presenting bone after bone, and he struggled to identify an animal for each. After a while, he replied, "I don't know," to almost every question.

Handing Allport another exhibit, McEwen said, "Doctor, I show you what I think I may say, safely state without objection from Judge Vincent, is a human skull."

"Have Inspector Schaack called on to identify that," Vincent called out.

"He will do it," McEwen responded. "He has broken lots of them."

At one point Allport mistook the thigh bone of a gorilla for the thigh of a man. Even the defense attorney Phalen was disgusted with Allport's testimony, saying, "I could have told that it was a gorilla's thigh myself. It was too long and thick for a man's, and then there were the phalanges projecting from it. I don't see how the mistake was made."

Meanwhile the Luetgert family physician, Dr. Clarence Rutherford, told the *Tribune* he had declined to testify for the defense as a bone expert, despite his years of experience as an anatomy professor. He said he believed that one of the bones found by the police was part of a human hand, and he worried that his testimony would hurt Luetgert's chances of being acquitted. Although he said the bone was human, he denied that it had been boiled in potash, as the state claimed. "It has stains on it that look as though they had been acquired in a grave," he remarked.

As the defense's experts continued their testimony over several days, spectators began dozing off. Their answers were filled with references to squamous parts, supracondoloid fossa, tuberosities, and Vaughn's revision of Strangeway. The scientists used almost as much Latin as English. As one of the experts droned on, "Julian Hawthorne . . . suddenly remembered a pressing engagement outside," according to the *Chicago Journal*.

Diedrich Bicknese sat all day in one of the witness rooms, waiting for the bone experts to finish.

"I don't want to get confused and that is why I am staying out of court during the expert evidence," Bicknese said. "I want to be able to form a correct opinion from the evidence as to whether Luetgert is guilty or innocent, so I am just keeping away from the courtroom until this expert stuff is finished."

32 Cigar Talk

SPEAKING BETWEEN PUFFS on his cigar, Luetgert continued granting interviews to reporters at the jail nearly every morning before going to court. He seemed to take special delight in receiving visits from the newspapermen early in the morning, always insisting he receive cigars for the privilege of being interviewed. Sometimes the reporters talked with him as he got his daily shave from the jailhouse barber. Luetgert took care to answer the questions only when the razor was in a safe section of his face. Although he enjoyed joking with the reporters, he didn't always have kind words about the stories they were writing.

"I don't worry me what they print," he said. "They have told a lot of lies. One day they say I am drunk, the next that the jailer sent me a case of champagne, and the next that I am a good-for-nothing loafer. But I don't mind. I read the headlines, take a good smoke, and then have a fine sleep. I'm not nervous. Why should I be?"

After saying how much he despised the papers, Luetgert would often turn back into his cell and begin reading one. "Look here," he told a *Daily News* reporter, "you newspapermen are making loads of money off of me—barrels of it. You sell extras by the thousand. I don't object. I don't want a salary, nor even at spare rates, but if you'd see that some trifling gift be sent up, say a basket of champagne or a dinner from Kinsley's, or some trifling thing like that, it would please me. A box of good domestic cigars once in a while, say two or three times a week, so I could treat the guards, would be a pleasant little thing and I would appreciate it."

In a typical interview Luetgert would sit in his shirtsleeves, his legs crossed and chair tilted back, laughing and chatting about his trial with the levity of a comic actor discussing his latest hit. Whenever he was questioned about the trial evidence, Luetgert insisted he didn't see how any of it would persuade jurors to believe he was guilty. He ridiculed the state's scientific experts.

"Dorsey is a fool," Luetgert said. "He pretends to know more than he does. He made mistakes in his testimony, and you will find there will be more evidence stricken out. I am willing to have the state go on bringing in elephant bones, if they wish. There are lots of other bones out there in the factory yard, if they want them. If you should strike out all the false statements those witnesses have made, you would have very little left."

At other times Luetgert showed flashes of anger and moodiness. The *Abendpost* described him as suddenly flying into rages, cursing the *meineidigen Lügen*—"perjurious lies"—being uttered against him in court. Luetgert struggled to conceal his inner disquiet, and the German newspaper speculated that he had a terrible *Seelenpein*, a "suffering of the soul."

The criminologist Christison said Luetgert's behavior showed his innocence. Despite his temper, Luetgert was able to "completely simulate innocence, from moment to moment, and under every ordeal." Pulling off this feat with a guilty conscience "would require nothing short of a complete reversal of his very nature." Christison said he had "a soft heart and a trusting—yea, an over-trusting—disposition."

Luetgert frequently talked about what he would do when the trial was over, assuming he would be found not guilty. "I can do lots of things," he said. "How would this look for a recommendation: 'Man who has been for months in one of the strongest institutions in the city would like work of some kind'? I could be a bartender. I kept a saloon once and I've had plenty of experience with bars since my arrest. Then, too, I might get a job in a museum, say alongside of Bates, the bigamist." Luetgert laughed heartily and then added in a more serious tone, "I'll build the factory bigger than it is now, that's what I'll do."

Another time Luetgert jokingly proposed creating a business of another sort. "When I get out of this," he said, "I am going to start up a factory to manufacture witnesses. I guess, judging by developments in my trial, that there is good money to be made in such a business. The state could get as many as it wanted, and I would see to it that veracity would be the quality which would sell them."

Luetgert offered some ominous words for Mrs. Feld, saying, "I will go straight to the house of my dear, darling Christine and settle things with her. She owes me $4,000 in good money, and because I was locked up in this place she thought she would never have to pay me. But I will fix that, . . . darling Christine, dear she-devil."

Another prisoner, the self-proclaimed inventor John G. Dame, had some plans of his own regarding what Luetgert would do after the trial. Dame, who was serving a sentence for horse theft, occupied his time by drawing plans for a steam snowplow that gold hunters could used to traverse the Klondike.

"Adolph Louis Luetgert, the sausage maker, will be half-owner in this invention, and perhaps will be one of the party," Dame said. "Myself and Luetgert hold daily conversations regarding the invention, and when we both get our freedom will at once set to work to carry out our ideas."

Luetgert enjoying joshing the guards in the jail, and he treated Kelly as a pal. He insisted that people calling out for the guard should call him "Mr. Kelly" rather than use the more common gruff, "Ho, Kelly!"

"My attachment for Kelly is something lovely," he said. "I really don't feel as though I could leave him. Sometimes I think I'll go, but there is some vague, restraining influence sways me, and I stay. Perhaps three bars have something to do with it," Luetgert said, catching hold of a bar with his tight grip.

The newspapers claimed that Luetgert was getting special treatment at the jail, being allowed to roam the corridors after midnight. In addition, they reported that other prisoners were serving Luetgert as private secretaries. Whitman, the jailer, said, "The story is all nonsense."

Luetgert's activities in the jail remained a source of interest for the newspapers, as when he had a badly ulcerated tooth pulled in mid-September. When the dentist appeared with his "instruments of torture" a general murmur of excitement came from the guards, many of whom took breaks from their regular duties to escort the forceps-wielding dentist to Luetgert's cell. "Here's where you howl," one of the guards cheerfully told Luetgert.

Luetgert looked at him scornfully. "Me holler? Nit!" he responded, opening his capacious mouth. The dentist pulled mightily and brought into the air an unusually large upper back tooth with long clinching roots. "That's better," said Luetgert. "Give me some water." He put the tooth into his vest pocket, retreated to his cell, and refused to see visitors for the next eighteen hours.

Luetgert soon was suffering from another malady. He began to use crutches when he walked into the courtroom, a pained expression showing on his face. It was initially reported that the damp weather had brought on an attack of rheumatism or that he had sprained his leg while exercising. It was later learned, however, that Luetgert had been injured in a fight with a prisoner named William Young. The incident had begun as good-natured sparring and escalated into a rough-and-tumble fight when Luetgert lost his temper. Luetgert saw that Young—a tall, slender man, all bone and muscle—was getting the better of him. Luetgert rushed at Young like a mad bull. Young dodged, caught Luetgert low around the waist, and hurled him backward, almost twenty feet, against the tile pavement and a steel door. Luetgert was unable to get up and had to be helped to his cell.

When the *Chronicle* reporter Katharine came to visit Luetgert a few days later, he quietly related how Louise had left him once before, going away for a week and then returning without explaining where she had gone. Luetgert praised Louise for her housekeeping skills, the way she had made sure that not a speck of dust could ever be found from the cellar to the attic. "In his wife Luetgert found a housewife in the old German fashion, not a comrade to whom all trials and joys should be told," Katharine wrote.

When Luetgert recounted how bitterly disappointed his wife had been when Davey disappeared, along with Luetgert's deal to sell the sausage business, he began to weep. Luetgert "wiped tears from his eyes . . . as he talked of his wife," Katharine wrote. "I rather think he did not want me to see them fall, for he turned away once or twice as though to hide them, but they fell upon the cheeks which are pale from long confinement."

Luetgert said his wife had insisted on knowing the bad news about his business, and after he had told her, "She was never right after that."

"How is it that you have been able under such awful conditions to keep your nerve?" Katharine asked.

"It is not nerve," he replied, as he placed his crutch to one side, "nor is it my wonderful constitution that you people lay it to. It is simply a clear conscience. That is what keeps me up. Anyone would be able to endure anything with a clear conscience, and this is what I have."

"Then you feel perfectly sure of an acquittal?"

"Of course. Don't you? I am sure that the verdict will be for me. Why, the worst that the jurors can do is disagree, and I don't think they will do that. They are too intelligent."

"But how are you going to get around Mrs. Feld?"

"I will fix that. Why, that woman hasn't one particle of honor. I will prove that, and, what is more, I will prove that she would profit by my death, and that is what she is after."

"Weren't the letters pretty sweet, if she is the kind of a woman you say, Mr. Luetgert?"

"Why, they had to be," he said, smiling. "You know one can catch more flies by sugar than you can by vinegar, and I did it, didn't I?"

Luetgert said he was sure he would become rich by writing a book about his life. "Every time a sensation is added to this case it will make me richer in the end," he said. "Every time the state brings in an elephant's tooth or the lip of a mosquito, it will help sell the book of my life and I will yet have money. The book is all ready to go to the publisher and will be printed in English as well as German, and I will make money by it, and then the time I have spent here in jail will not be in vain."

In interview after interview Luetgert insisted he would testify in his own defense. "I have fully made up my mind to go on the witness stand and defend myself," he said. "I don't intend to sit idly here and permit that jury to render a verdict until they have heard me tell my side of the story."

Luetgert had persuaded one of his attorneys, Phalen, to let him testify, but Vincent was against it. Vincent expected the state to be merciless in its cross-examination, and he feared that Luetgert would lose his temper in front of the jury. On October 5, while Vincent and Phalen were wrapping up their case, Luetgert came into court determined to be the last defense witness. As the opening of court neared, Luetgert's fingers twitched nervously. Phalen suddenly stood up and beckoned to Luetgert, who was combing back his hair with his fingers. "Come in the jury room, Mr. Luetgert," he said.

Luetgert and Phalen cast withering looks at Vincent, who remained in his seat as they got up to leave the courtroom. The jurors began whispering. As a deputy sheriff closed the door of the jury room and stood on the outside, Vincent suddenly stood up and hurried for the jury room, his face flushed. Deneen and McEwen laughed and pored over an armful of typewritten questions they were ready to ask Luetgert.

When Vincent went into the jury room, he said, "Well, Luetgert, you know what my opinion is about your going on the stand. I wash my skirts of the whole matter." Vincent said he would leave the case if his client didn't follow his advice against testifying.

Phalen told Luetgert he would not stand in the way of his testifying. At the last minute, however, Luetgert changed his mind. He paused a moment and then said he guessed he had "better keep out of it." A few moments later the two attorneys and Luetgert returned to the courtroom. Vincent whispered to Tuthill that Luetgert had decided not to testify. About thirty minutes later the large crowd that had gathered to see Luetgert defend himself was disappointed to hear the words: "The defense rests."

33 Oratory

OVER THREE DAYS the prosecutors presented a string of witnesses to undermine Luetgert's defense. The prosecutors cast doubt on the claim that Luetgert and Charles had thrown scraps of meat and fat into the middle vat on the morning of May 1. Albert Dreinke testified he carted bones and tallow away from the Luetgert factory on May 1, just as he had every week since the time the factory closed in February. Anton Schuster, a butcher employed by Luetgert, and his helper, Herman Frank, testified it had been their habit to throw refuse into barrels, where it was picked up by Dreinke. Schuster said the barrels had been emptied on May 1. Ham Frank and Smokehouse Frank said they had seen no barrels of tallow in the basement on May 1.

Nine witnesses testified that they'd had business dealings with William Charles and that they wouldn't believe him under oath. They said he didn't pay his debts and couldn't be relied on to keep his word. Feld testified that William Charles and his wife had tried to influence her to testify that the rings found in the vat did not belong to Mrs. Luetgert.

The prosecutors questioned why Luetgert would have tried to make soap. Frank Moan, the sheriff's employee who had served the writ that closed the Luetgert grocery store on May 4, said he had inspected the grocery and noticed that Luetgert had at least fifty boxes of soap. Abraham Seelig testified he purchased 159 boxes of soap when he bought out the Luetgert grocery store in May.

The prosecutors also questioned why Luetgert had sent Bialk out for two bottles of mineral water on the night of May 1. Corydon Clark, a salesman for Lord, Owen and Company, said he had sold Luetgert fifty bottles of mineral water on March 17. As for the suggestion that the first bottle Bialk purchased was the wrong brand, Clark said the bottling company had simply changed its label. He said that he had explained that to Luetgert nearly a year earlier and that Luetgert knew both kinds of bottle contained the same water.

The prosecutors also attempted to puncture the story of Mrs. Luetgert's supposed visit to Kenosha. Nine people familiar with the bartender Matthew Scholey testified that they wouldn't trust him to tell the truth. The defense attorneys asked them whether Scholey owed them money, and they all said he did.

The prosecutors called eight witnesses who said that between May 3 and 5 they had seen a strange woman near Kenosha matching the description of the woman seen by Scholey and the others. However, all these state witnesses said the woman did not resemble Mrs. Luetgert in the least. One of them even said he had met Mrs. Luetgert in the past, which made him all the more certain that the mystery woman was someone else.

The prosecutors tried to shake the reliability of Mary Siemering's testimony. Five members of the grand jury came to the witness stand and said Siemering had told a much different story when she had testified in front of them. They said Siemering had admitted having an affair with Luetgert. Schaack and Schuettler denied threatening Siemering when they first questioned her at the station. Two police matrons testified Siemering was not subjected to any indignities while under arrest. Two newspaper reporters said they had watched as Schaack met Siemering in the anteroom outside the grand jury chambers. They said Schaack never threatened her there, as Siemering now claimed. And Judge Arthur Chetlain testified about a talk he'd had with Siemering in his chambers at a pretrial hearing. He said that she wasn't nervous and that she had made no complaints against the police.

Half a dozen boys who played tag with Emma Schimke testified they had seen her out with Rosa Gleich and the other boys on May 2, not May 1. Emma herself was called back to the stand again, to repeat her story about seeing Luetgert and his wife on May 1. As she stepped down, she stuck her tongue out at Phalen and smiled at McEwen, prompting a roar of laughter in the court. The bailiffs angrily pounded their gavels, but even Judge Tuthill laughed. The girl sat down in the courtroom and found herself surrounded by women who wanted to ask her about the case. Over and over, she said, "I'm the girl that saw Mr. and Mrs. Luetgert enter the factory that night."

Finally, seven friends and relatives of Mrs. Luetgert testified she had always been a kind mother to her children.

After the prosecutors had finished their rebuttal case, the defense lawyers spent just one morning on surrebuttal, their chance to offer rebuttals to the state's rebuttals. William and Edward Lister, brothers in the glue business, testified they had seen about eight hundred pounds of butcher's trimmings and tallow in Luetgert's meat market between May 1 and 11. In addition, five men testified William Charles was a man of integrity.

All the evidence was in now, and the lawyers began their closing arguments. The four speeches would last six days in all.

McEwen went first, telling the jurors in a matter-of-fact tone that a strong set of evidence proved Luetgert was guilty of killing his wife. "It has been said that this is a circumstantial case, and some slight has been put upon it. . . . All cases are more or less circumstantial," he said. "Direct evidence of crime at all points is rarely secured. I venture to say that nine-tenths of all the cases tried in the Criminal Court of Cook County are cases where circumstances must be relied upon to a greater or less extent in order to secure a conviction of the crime."

McEwen rejected the idea that police could have fabricated the evidence. "Is there a police officer who could have gone to that vat in the factory—could have known the chemical composition of that liquid which remained in the vat? Could he have known regarding the rings, the fact of the marking of the rings, Mrs. Luetgert's rings? Could he have known the effect of caustic potash? Could he have known Luetgert had bought the potash? Could he have known all of those circumstances—those scientific facts—so that he could have gone out and created this case? I submit to you that one of the strongest points in this case is the absolute harmony running between and among all of the circumstances. . . . They are founded on truth."

Phalen came next, delivering a speech reporters described as earnest but inelegant. His voice rose into falsetto until it broke, forcing him to take a lozenge. He made almost grotesque gestures with his arms, mixed metaphors, and occasionally mangled his grammar. But he held the jury's attention.

"Adolph L. Luetgert has sat in this courtroom," Phalen said. "He has been calm, deliberate, quiet and gentlemanly. But they may say that is indicative of crime; those are the things that a criminal possesses. . . . Now, gentlemen, if he had wept before you, if he had wrung his hands and pulled his hair before you, they would say it was the strong arrows of remorse piercing his guilty heart."

As far as the spectators were concerned, the main act was the third speech, which came from Vincent. He began his oratory on Thursday, October 14.

"Gentlemen of the jury," he said, "is Mrs. Luetgert alive or is she dead? Was she alive on the second of May this year, or was she dead? Is Luetgert guilty or is Luetgert innocent? Gentlemen, you can do nothing but acquit A. L. Luetgert, and acquit him promptly. Why? Because there is a doubt in your minds. . . . The state must show that she is dead. They must show what became of her remains."

While insisting Luetgert was innocent, Vincent conceded that the man would be a "demon" if he had committed the acts of which the state accused him. But it wasn't simply a case of the state against Luetgert, he said: "Upon the indictment, it reads, 'The People of Illinois vs. Adolph L. Luetgert.' But this is not the case of the people of Illinois against Adolph L. Luetgert. It is the case of Michael J. Schaack, seeking to hold a job, against Adolph L. Luetgert."

As he spoke Vincent shook his hand in the direction of Luetgert and raised his voice. A stir went through the audience. "Now, I don't say that Inspector Schaack, poor an opinion as I have of him—I don't say that Inspector Schaack deliberately started out to manufacture evidence to hang an innocent man. It is pretty cold-blooded to do that and pretty bloodthirsty. I believe, however, that he would feel that the end justified the means, and that he would manufacture evidence to see that justice was done according to his ideas of justice. . . . I believe that he has done that very thing."

Vincent continued his speech on Friday. He recounted the story young Louis Luetgert had told the court. He turned toward the boy and raised his hand, trembling with emotion. "My God, gentlemen!" Vincent said. "What a terrible thing it is to put a child in the witness stand to swear against his own father. I may be too, too sympathetic. I might not be a good prosecuting lawyer, but I would never secure a conviction if I had to put a child on the stand and ask him to give testimony which might condemn his father to death—which would send him through life with a noose before his eyes— which, in each waking, yea, each sleeping hour, would make him fearful lest he had slipped the noose down over his own father's head."

The spectators seemed to be deeply moved by Vincent's strong words. Luetgert started up in his seat, showing a flash of anger. "Louie Luetgert, state's witness," Vincent said, "tells you that at about two o'clock he heard a rustling of a dress, and when he asked who it was, his mother's voice replied. The rustling was made by Louise Luetgert. The poor, deluded woman was preparing to leave home. She was wrapping up a few worldly belongings and was preparing to creep out at the front door into the darkness of the early morning. But the state charges that its own witness committed perjury."

The lawyer again pointed at the boy. "Look," he said, "at the handsome, honest, manly face of that boy and judge if he is a liar!" Just then, as the spectators rose in their seats to get a better look at the boy, a window shade slipped out of a bailiff's hand and snapped up to the top of the big window case. Sunshine burst into the room, falling on the face of young Louis. The light seemed to be directed straight at his blond hair and rosy face. The spectators were astounded at the sudden flash of light, and one reporter thought its timing seemed supernatural.

The courtroom was oppressively hot during Vincent's speech, although the windows were open and electric fans whirred away. The heat wave had not let up, even though October was half gone. In the midst of his argument Vincent paused. He wiped the perspiration from his forehead and then turned to Tuthill and said, "Your Honor, the warm weather has exhausted me. After eight weeks of constant work in court, I do not feel able to continue without rest."

The judge allowed him to finish his speech on Saturday. On the third day of his address, after mocking several of the state's witnesses, Vincent focused again on his client. "It is hard for any poor devil to be obliged to sit with sealed lips while the pitiless lawyers for the prosecution weave a net of guilty circumstances around him and inflame the minds of his judges with fiery denunciations. Then his own lawyers have a chance to make a few feeble pleas. After that his persecutors have the last word, and the last word is a dangerous one."

Dropping his voice down to a soft, pleading tone, Vincent continued, "Think of Luetgert's condition. He has lost his liberty. He has lost his name. He has lost his property. He has lost his wife. Gentlemen of the jury, will you deprive him of his life?"

Without another word Vincent turned and bowed to Judge Tuthill. Luetgert sat stolid and motionless as his son Arnold wept and Louis sobbed. A clatter of applause rose from the benches at the back of the courtroom. The clapping spread, until men, women, and children in every corner were making noise. The judge yelled for quiet and the bailiff banged his gavel. The crowd fell silent almost instantly, and many of the spectators looked fearfully toward Tuthill.

"It is outrageous," he said. "Bailiffs, clear the court of those who have so far forgotten the gravity of this case and the dignity of the court."

The bailiffs marched down the rows of seats and asked those who had clapped their hands to leave. Nobody stirred. The judge leaned over the bench and pointed straight at a young woman. "Put out that woman with the feather in her hat! I took particular pains and went out of my way to get her a seat, and I saw her violate the rule of this court."

As the bailiffs struggled to determine who should be ejected from the courtroom, Tuthill gave up and adjourned court for the day. A dense throng of women rushed toward Luetgert and Vincent. Spectators clasped Vincent's hands to congratulate him. Luetgert grabbed one of Vincent's hands, as if to apologize for their earlier difference over whether Luetgert should testify. Vincent's face turned red under the battery of resounding praise and admiring eyes. He patted Luetgert's children, gave a few words of good cheer to Luetgert, and then waited quietly until the crowd thinned enough for him to leave the court.

34 Twelve Men

FOLLOWING EACH DAY's adjournment the bailiffs escorted the twelve jurors back to their quarters at the Le Grand Hotel, at Kinzie and Wells Streets. The three bailiffs looking after them had served in the Army of the Potomac during the Civil War, and the old veterans straightened up whenever they marched the jurors to the hotel, as though they were once more with their comrades in blue.

The jurors were not allowed to receive visits from friends and family members or to receive or answer letters. The only newspapers they were permitted to read had been mutilated by the scissors of sheriff's employees, who had removed any references to the Luetgert case. On some days that meant barely any part of the news section survived the censoring.

"We used to regard his [Luetgert's] privileges with longing," said one juror, James Heichhold.

The jurors stayed on the Le Grand's third floor, taking up the entire south side and part of its east side. The large and airy corner room contained three beds, where Heichhold, James Hosmer, and Robert Bibby slept, but the room also became the "parlor" where all twelve men gathered at evening.

As they sat around the room's large table, the juror designated "master for the night" had power to call on anyone for entertainment. Story telling was one of the most popular diversions. Joseph Boyd said he told his "fish" stories to relieve stress. He had lived in every state east of the Mississippi and one or two west of the river, and he labeled his stories by state or city. "This is my Maine story," he would say as a preamble to a hunting tale. "This is my New Orleans story," was how he introduced a fairy story dealing with African American children—"pickaninnies," as he called them. Another juror later remarked, "I don't think Boyd's well of stories ever once ran dry."

The men also frequently played cards to pass the time, trying out almost every game with the "pasteboards" except for "sixty-six," which none of the Germans on the jury wanted to play. They most often played poker and whist, although euchre sometimes held sway. Backgammon was also popular.

Another juror, Henry Franzen, had an antiquated fiddle. At first his modesty kept him from making any attempts to play it, but one evening, when no one could think of any other entertainment, they induced him to draw the bow. They withstood the torture for ten minutes and then fled. At the end of a week, however, they realized that bad music was better than none at all and allowed him to play a little each day. His playing seemed to improve with practice.

The men arose each day at 6:30 and had breakfast at 7:15, followed by an hour of leisure, usually spent reading whatever remained of the newspapers.

When a juror found a bone in his meat at dinner, he would invariably hold it up and ask gravely for opinions on its classification. Because he was a butcher, John Behmiller was appointed the unofficial bone authority among the jurors.

One day they were served a dish of crisp-looking wienerwurst for breakfast, but none of them would touch the sausage. Finally John E. Fowler Jr. said, "Take 'em away," turning his head sideways from the table.

"I don't fancy 'wienies' either," Behmiller said.

"I'd as soon eat soap," added Franzen.

The jurors' confinement felt like torture during the hot weeks of September. Fowler, the youngest juror, came down with fever and chills twice during the trial. The lack of exercise proved one of the hardest things for the jurors to bear. The bailiffs occasionally took them on a Sunday walk around the block or through Lincoln Park.

A few days after being allowed to play a game of baseball on a vacant lot in late September, the jurors were taken in a carryall wagon to the National League Park on the West Side, where the Chicago Colts* played. The jurors chased one another over the grounds like schoolboys for ten minutes. With a couple of deputy sheriffs rounding out their lineups, the jurors then divided into two teams and played baseball for an hour. No one passing by outside appeared to realize who was playing in the park. "The game was not played strictly according to '97 rules, and between . . . innings the jurors ran races and went through other gymnastics exercises," the *Tribune* reported.

The court planned to send the jurors back to the ballpark for more games, although some people worried they might injure themselves, particularly considering how miserably the Colts had played that summer. "This fear rests largely on the stories of the Colts' awful slaughter . . . , and they fear the league park is a 'hoodoo,'" the *Tribune* reported.

After Deneen had finished his closing argument and Judge Tuthill had read his instructions, the twelve men filed into the narrow, brown-walled jury room, which they were not permitted to leave without reaching a verdict. It was 4:45 P.M. on Monday, October 18. As the reporters for the *Journal* listened through the vent (the *Tribune* reporters eavesdropped as well, through means the paper never divulged), the jurors began discussing the evidence.

They laid aside their coats and hats and elected Heichhold foreman. At 5 P.M. Heichhold took a poll. Each man wrote his vote—guilty or not guilty—on a small slip of paper and dropped it into a hat being passed around the table. Heichhold counted the ballots: seven to five in favor of conviction. Although it was ostensibly a secret ballot, it wasn't long before the jurors had figured out who had voted which way. T. J. Mahoney, Boyd, Franzen, Bibby, Hosmer, Fowler, and Joseph Shaw had voted guilty; Heichhold, Behmiller, William Harley, Samuel Barber, and Louis Holabird had voted not guilty.

They decided to go over it point by point. They talked about the Schim-

---

* Now known as the Cubs.

ke girls and whether they could be believed. Bibby said he thought they had told the truth about seeing Mr. and Mrs. Luetgert on May 1. He said the only reason the girls had contradicted themselves was that they were intimidated by Phalen's cross-examination.

The jurors paused for supper in an adjoining room and then spent a long time looking over exhibits. Mahoney, whom the jurors had elected as their secretary, read the judge's instructions aloud. They especially pondered the definition of reasonable doubt. Mahoney accused Harlev, who was emerging as the most ardent advocate for acquittal, of ignoring the evidence. When Mahoney finished his reading at 8:45, they again looked at the exhibits.

"Bones, bones, bones," one of them sighed, picking up some of the relics piled on the table. "Did somebody say bones? This is the femur of a gorilla. This is the femur of a hog."

Instead of delving deeper into the subject of bones, the jurors began an animated discussion on the rings. Soon everyone was talking at once, and Heichhold had to bang a gavel to bring the room to order. Each juror was given a chance to say what he thought about the rings.

"I believe they are Mrs. Luetgert's rings, and I would like to have some one of the gentlemen explain how they got into the vat," Fowler said.

"Those rings were certainly worn by some woman," Franzen said. "I know something about how women wear rings, and I know these were worn on the same finger."

Heichhold doubted the identity of the gold bands, but Bibby put absolute faith in them. Harlev called attention to a photograph of Anna Greiser wearing rings that she had borrowed from Mrs. Luetgert. Harlev said this was absolute proof that the rings of the missing woman were both the same size, unlike the two rings found in the vat.

Boyd, who had been regarded as the most conservative man on the jury, jumped to his feet. "Harlev, don't you remember that Luetgert's own son said she wore a guard ring like that? He said one was a guard ring and the other a plain wedding ring."

One juror with a German accent said he believed "the rings came in the vat by the police."

Around ten o'clock the discussion became heated when three jurors said that, before the case had gone to the jury, Harlev "had made injudicious remarks concerning the proper way to dispose of the evidence." Insults and charges of ungentlemanly conduct flew back and forth, until the men agreed to drop all such recriminations.

Franzen later recounted a confrontation with Harley. "Harley and I had rather a hot time of it Monday night," he said. "We talked loud and possibly a bit threateningly. We were both angry, I perhaps particularly so, but you'll believe me the provocation was great. I sat on the table swinging my legs, thinking. My hand dropped to my side and fell on a bundle of papers. They were the letters of Luetgert to 'Dear Christine.' I had heard them in court. I picked them up and read them as I sat on the table. They struck me then for the first time in their full force. They were enough to make a strong man sick at his stomach. They did not affect me that way, but they did make me mad, and I turned on Harley, who was sticking out for acquittal, somewhat savagely. He gave me as good as I sent, and I suppose our altercation, for it was that as much as an argument, was heard outside and gave rise to the report that we had come to blows. We argued and argued until we were exhausted, then we'd rest awhile and go at it again, hammer and tongs. Perhaps if the truth be told, those of us who were for conviction had something of an advantage, for we outnumbered the others, and could go at them in relays, one squad relieving the other."

They took another vote, and this time the result was seven to four for conviction. The only difference from the first vote was that Behmiller was undecided this time. After the votes had been tallied, Harley sat in a corner, folded his arms, and refused to argue any longer. Shaw, the oldest man on the panel, shook his fist at Harley, denouncing him. Harley threatened to "wipe the floor" with Shaw, and some other jurors stepped between them.

"I have doubt about the case," Harley said. "I tell you I won't argue it. I have my doubts, and the judge said there was to be no conviction if we had any doubts."

"Well," another man said, "if there are points which you cannot understand, let us argue them. Perhaps we may convince you we are right, perhaps you can convince us."

But Harley and the three men backing him remained quiet for a time. And then, after a long break, they began talking about the vat and its contents. Was it possible to destroy a body in the manner described by the police? Some of the jurors pointed out that it had been proven that the solution in the vat couldn't be raised to a boiling point.

"Well," shouted Shaw, who was a retired locomotive engineer, "I want to impress upon the minds of you gentlemen the important fact that the defense disintegrated the bodies of two human beings in that same vat and in the same manner as described by the state. Therefore the boiling point has nothing to do with the matter. Why not discuss points which have some weight?"

They talked about the witnesses from Kenosha. Heichhold and the seven men who had voted guilty said they didn't believe Scholey, Scheve, and the other people who claimed to have seen Mrs. Luetgert. The other four jurors disagreed.

The jurors looked at the judge's instructions again and sought a way of compromising. Some suggested finding Luetgert guilty but not sentencing him to death. Several of them said they were worried that Mrs. Luetgert might return after they found her husband guilty of murder; others broached the idea merely in an attempt to win over the jurors favoring acquittal. As Franzen later recounted, "Many of us hated to do this, for we thoroughly believed Luetgert should be hanged, but better a 'lifer' than a miscarriage of justice." Harlev, however, insisted the penalty should not be part of their considerations about Luetgert's guilt. If he was guilty, he deserved death; if he was innocent, he deserved freedom.

Holabird and Boyd almost came to blows as they swapped insults, and Heichhold intervened and tried to calm them. They took another vote at midnight, and this time Behmiller voted guilty. It was eight to four. By 1:45 A.M. the men were growing drowsy, but the discussion went on. Fowler impetuously exclaimed, "We would have thought a good deal more of Luetgert if he had taken the stand."

Harlev was ready with a retort: "The court instructs . . . that this fact shall not be considered a circumstance against him."

The other men sensed another argument was brewing. One of them suggested, in a despairing tone, "Let's all go to sleep."

"Let's take another ballot," Shaw said.

They put their slips into the hat. Once again, the result was eight to four.

"We're just where we were before," Fowler said impatiently.

"Let's go to sleep," someone else said, but Fowler was vexed. He said, "Well, how do you people get around those rings? That's what I want to know. The evidence shows they were found in the vat. You must admit they were Mrs. Luetgert's."

"Well, I don't—not in a hundred!" Harlev said.

The jurors shrugged their shoulders in despair and paced the floor. "We'll stay here until Thursday at nine o'clock, I guess," one of them said, laughing.

"It's too bad we can't have a Sunday intervene, so as to have a carriage ride," another man said, remembering the few pleasant breaks the jurors had been allowed during the trial.

Some of the more tired men said they should take a recess, but Fowler remarked, "There is no rest for the wicked." They talked about the bones, and several said they were more impressed by the state's experts than the defense's. They all expressed satisfaction with Dorsey's testimony, although not everyone believed his identification of the bones as human. Some of them sharply criticized Dr. Allport, saying he had tried to confuse them with his anatomy lectures. The youngest members of the jury, Fowler and Franzen, firmly believed the bones were human.

The silences became longer as some of the jurors nodded off. They sat in chairs and lounged on the table, occasionally making comments like, "Boyd, get your feet over," and "Let me get my chair over there." A few of them asked about breakfast.

"I wonder if they will give us anything to eat," one man said, sounding somewhat alarmed.

"The waiter won't come in here and say, 'What'll ye have, boys?' That's a cinch," another juror responded sleepily.

Most of the jurors seemed to fall asleep around 4:30. The room became quiet.

35 Queer Reports

AT 2 A.M., as the jury went through its first long night of deliberations, three men showed up at the East Chicago Avenue police station and insisted on seeing Schaack, saying they had important information. Schaack wasn't there, but they telephoned him at home and later visited him there, telling him they had knowledge of a plot to bribe some jurors to vote not guilty.

Court officials intercepted a letter addressed to the jury foreman and read its contents, which may have been related to the rumored plot: "Mr. Foreman—Dear Sir: A powerful influence is at work to save Adolph L. Luetgert. Money is scarce and in these hard times a $100 bill comes handy. I have $1,600 to divide among you twelve men. If you want it, have two good men, smooth-faced, that are discreet, at the southeast corner of Randolph and Dearborn streets tomorrow at 1 P.M. Let them wear white linen neckties, or if they prefer it, red bow ties. Everything will be all right. The money is secure in a State Street bank. GEORGE ATTRILL."

The supposed Mr. Attrill wrote another letter, asking why the men in white linen ties hadn't shown up for their appointment. Tuthill and Deneen believed the letters were just another hoax, but Schaack investigated nevertheless. Schaack had assigned men to keep a watch on the jurors throughout the trial.

"The detectives have watched the jurors during the time they were in the hotel with more than usual care, and some things have come to my notice which are very queer, to say the least," Schaack told a reporter. "I am satisfied that attempts have been made to tamper with the jury, and I believe that is the real reason why the verdict is not in by this time. I am beginning to think that the verdict will not be what it ought to be, but I hope it may turn out that my suspicions are wrong and that the men I suspect are not guilty of being influenced unlawfully."

Schuettler said he suspected one juror was holding out against conviction. "We have been suspicious of him since we knew all about him," he said. "I have been looking up the jury systems of the European countries lately, and I say the only thing for the legislature to do is to change the law making a two-thirds vote sufficient to convict or acquit in criminal cases."

Although neither Schaack or Schuettler named Harlev as the object of their suspicions, the newspapers made it clear he was the man they were watching. It was reported that Harlev, a construction contractor, had been indicted in 1887 on charges of conspiring to defraud the Cook County government of $20,000. He was charged with bribing a county official to get the building contract for a wing on the insane asylum at Dunning. Several county board members and other contractors were indicted in the "boodling" case along with Harlev, and some were convicted and sentenced to prison. The charges against Harlev were dropped, however, and the man who had been the prosecutor at the time could no longer remember why. Harlev, who also dabbled in politics, had always insisted he had been charged unfairly.

When the lawyers in the Luetgert case had questioned potential jurors, they didn't know about Harlev's background and did not bring up the boodling case. They did ask him, though, whether he was acquainted with Luetgert's lawyers. He said he had used the services of attorney Adams Goodrich, who represented Luetgert on business matters. "I don't believe I ever met Judge Vincent," he said. "I may though." Harlev's previous indictment and his acquaintance with one of Luetgert's lawyers now cast suspicion on his motives for voting not guilty.

A large crowd again gathered in the streets outside the court-jail complex, awaiting a verdict. The *Tribune* described the curiosity-seekers as "unwashed, uncombed and ragged men." The *Abendpost* called them a *Volksmenge,* or "mob." The Germans in the mob were often heard asking, "*Was wird das Verdikt der Geschworenen sein?*" ("What will the jurors' verdict be?") As the spectators gazed up at the jail's grated windows, their presence seemed to excite the inmates. Yells and hoots greeted the crowd, and the jail corridor rang with shouts. One of the cries that could be heard among the chaotic noise was, "Hang up Schaack!" The jailer, Whitman, told the corridor guards to inform the prisoners they would all be punished and confined to their cells the entire day unless the demonstration ceased. It was still some time before the prisoners quieted.

Luetgert's children visited him at the jail, and Elmer again asked the question he had been asking ever since May 1: "Where is Mama?" When a reporter paid a call, Luetgert ridiculed the notion that he was behind any attempts to bribe the jury.

"This fake story of bribery of the jury makes me laugh," he said. "Luetgert has no money to do that if it could be done. . . . This delay—this long wait to know what is coming—it is hard, but I said tonight, 'Luetgert, you go to sleep and hope for good news tomorrow,' and in a little while I go to bed."

At five o'clock "Big Jack" Schaffer, the jail doorkeeper, handed Luetgert the afternoon newspapers and a basket containing a steaming supper cooked by Mary Siemering. The papers unanimously agreed that eight jurors had voted for conviction. Luetgert was furious, and he stormed and swore when one of the prisoners asked him about it. He called a reporter who tried to interview him a "barefaced hypocrite" and accused the newspapers of lying. Luetgert was cross the rest of the evening. He retired early and covered himself with a blanket but tossed restlessly and continued grumbling in an irritable manner.

"The trouble with Luetgert," a jail attendant said, "is that he confidently expected to be at liberty by this time. He had made the frequent boast that he would be acquitted, and the attitude of the jury is a keen disappointment to him. He can't help showing it and he will talk to no one."

Two bailiffs guarding the narrow doorway leading into the jury room were alarmed at the *Journal*'s almost verbatim reports of the deliberations. Policemen were now stationed around the building to catch snoopers. Details of the jurors' discussions continued to make it into the newspapers, however. The *Journal* bragged that its report was the talk of the court building, with everyone asking how the information was secured. For the time being, however, the newspaper refused to explain its methods, saying only, "The story was a clean scoop on every paper in Chicago." The *Tribune* printed its own account of the deliberations the morning after the *Journal*'s report.

◆◆◆

Even in Des Moines, Iowa, much of the population was caught up in the suspense over the Luetgert verdict. It was the topic of discussion on the streets and in the cafes. In one establishment a small man with an air of omniscience about him said he had just talked to somebody who had read an evening paper.

"Well, I see Luetgert's acquitted," he observed.

"Yes?" everyone said in chorus.

"Why, of course he's acquitted. I knew they couldn't convict him. How could they? When I was down in Chicago, before the trial, I told them they could never convict that man. You see, one of the very first things necessary in a case of that kind is to prove the corpus delicti. That's just what they couldn't prove, just exactly what they couldn't prove, and I knew it from the start and I told 'em so."

On hearing the news, and thinking he had inside information on the verdict, one man bet some people who hadn't heard the story $18.50 that Luetgert would be acquitted. He proceeded to get drunk on the strength of his good fortune, but then came the news that the jury was still out. He was stunned to learn of his "hard luck."

The telephones at the offices of the *Des Moines Leader* rang all night, as caller after caller asked, "Anything about the Luetgert verdict?" The newspaper tallied the calls it received about the Luetgert case in a single day at 3,147.

Most callers said they believed Luetgert should be hanged, but they predicted an acquittal or a hung jury.

◆◆◆

On the third day of deliberations, a loud pounding on the jury room door was heard around ten in the morning, and a bailiff named Freeman Connor came running. The door opened and the disheveled hair and sallow face of Heichhold appeared. "Send for Judge Tuthill and tell him we want to get some instructions," he said in a low tone.

Almost at the same instant Tuthill stepped out of the elevator. The corridor was packed with spectators, and the deputies plowed through the crowd to make a path for the judge. The crowd ran into the court, but after a whisper from Tuthill, a deputy shouted, "This courtroom must be cleared at once by the court's order. Everybody get out." A groan went up from the audience, and spectators dragged their feet from the room.

The jurors began filing in. First came Franzen, staggering in coatless, bedraggled, and unshaven. Barber, with a thick growth of stiff beard bristles, looked as if he had aged ten years. He was collarless and resembled a tramp thrown from a boxcar. Harlev's beard was tousled, and his hair, uncombed. Bibby's mustache was ragged, and his eyes were bloodshot. Fowler looked as though he had not slept for three nights. His hands shook when he took hold of his chair, and his eyes were wild and sunken. Shaw and Boyd, the two oldest men on the jury, appeared to have withstood the ordeal better than any of their younger counterparts. Tuthill surveyed the jurors curiously as they came in. Several of the men cast angry glances in Harlev's direction.

Luetgert, who seemed to be expecting a verdict of not guilty, entered with his mouth stretched into a grin. As he sat down, the jurors did not even look at him. The attorneys walked in, and a sound of scuffling came from the doors as some members of the mob tried to break past the bailiffs. Luetgert looked toward the noise.

"Gentlemen, I am ready to hear you," Tuthill told the jurors. "What questions did you wish to ask me?"

"We would rather not ask them before these people," Shaw said, pointing at Luetgert and the lawyers.

"Well, I cannot send them away. The accused has a right to be present and to be represented by his counsel at all times during the trial."

"Well, we want to ask for a little information."

"Very well. Tell me what it is you wish light upon."

Heichhold stood up and said, "It is not about the law. We all understand your instructions as to the law. But we cannot come to an agreement about some of the evidence. Some of us believe one way and some the other. What we want to know, first, is if we cannot leave out of consideration the evidence of the Schimke sisters and Nick Faber and bring in a verdict based on the rest of the evidence."

"Gentlemen of the jury, you alone can decide upon that matter. It would be unlawful for me to answer that question, and it is entirely in your hands, and you must decide that among yourselves. Your instructions are plain. . . . The court cannot possibly advise you what weight you may attach to any part of the evidence. The court can only refer you to the instructions. You have to make up your minds, unaided, as to the facts of the case."

"Your Honor," Heichhold said, "the other point is that we wish further instructions regarding the penalty. Several of the jurors desire to know, should a majority decide on a life sentence or a penitentiary sentence—say for fourteen years—and the rest want acquittal, if those standing out for acquittal cannot be compelled to compromise."

The judge, with his glasses in his hand, replied, "Gentlemen of the jury, in answer to that question, I will inform you that all must agree on a penalty."

Heichhold sat down, disappointment written on his face. Holabird sprang to his feet and cried, "I am tired of this and I want you to discharge us, for the reason that we cannot come to an agreement." Harlev, struggling to his feet, said he agreed.

The other jurors who had voted for a guilty verdict shook their fists at Harlev and shouted, "You are the one holding us here!" "If it were not for you, we would have been through last night!"

Tuthill banged his gavel. "Mr. Holabird," he said, as the jurors sat back down, "this trial has been tedious and has cost the state and defense a considerable amount. I know full well, gentlemen, that this is a great task. I will request you, before I retire you into the jury room, to come to an agreement, and when you call me again I hope such will be the case."

"Your Honor," asked one of the jurors favoring conviction, "is there much use of our deliberating much longer if one man says he won't change his mind in a thousand years?"

"Oh, yes," Tuthill said, "you had better try it again. A man often says something in the heat of argument he may not mean in serious earnest. He may take a stand from which he will afterwards recede. I think you had better go back to your room and talk the matter over together."

Heichhold said the jury's vote stood exactly as it had the night before. Tuthill leaned toward the jury box and said, mildly, "Well, gentlemen, I think you had better retire again." Silently the twelve men filed out.

Just as the last of them had disappeared into the jury room, Luetgert surprised his lawyers by walking over to Deneen and giving the prosecutor's hand a hard squeeze. Grinning, he said, "That was a hot roast you gave me on Monday, but I have no kick coming. You didn't go outside the evidence, and you treated me fair. I'm much obliged to you."

"Oh, that's all right," Deneen said, smiling. "I tried to be fair, that was all."

"Well, you were," Luetgert replied, and then he turned to his own attorneys and shook their hands as well. "I guess it's about ended," he said, and walked back to the jail.

36 Telescopic Views

AS THE JURORS returned to deliberations for a third day, Mary Charles again took Luetgert's children to the jail for a visit, and Luetgert cried as he stretched his hands through the bars toward them. "Louis and Elmer, you will have to treat Mrs. Charles with the greatest consideration," he said. "She must be regarded by you as both father and mother. Since your own parents are unable to look after you, you will have to mind Mrs. Charles whenever she asks you. Papa will soon be liberated and then he will try to make up for his seeming neglect of you. When I get out of debt, I will buy a pony for each of you."

Elmer was visibly disturbed to see his father in the jail. The boy wept as he asked, "What are these bars for, Father?"

"Do not mind them, my dear," Luetgert said. "We will be playmates together before Sunday and they won't have to take your father back to this place."

Elmer seemed appeased when Luetgert promised to buy him a pony. The boy dried his tears and sat on Mrs. Charles's knee. With both hands he clutched his father's large index finger. "Pa, my rabbits have got little ones," he said.

"How many?" Luetgert asked.

"I did not count them, Pa, because we were so anxious to see you."

"What color are they?"

"Oh, some are white and some are white and black. They have great big ears too and little bits of tails. Their eyes are just open and they will be able to jump about soon."

"Who are you going to give the baby rabbits to?"

"You will get two, Pa. Arnold will get half a one and Louie another half, and I am going to give all the rest to Mrs. Charles."

Promises of ponies weren't enough to mollify Louis, however. He was inconsolable for many minutes. "Won't you come home with us, Father?" he implored.

"I'll ask Jailer Whitman," Luetgert said. "Maybe he will be kinder to me than the twelve men who are talking about it across the alley."

When Mrs. Charles took the boys away, Luetgert watched them through the iron bars, throwing kisses toward them until they had disappeared around the turn in the corridor.

Reporters for the various newspapers were perched four hundred feet away on the roofs of buildings on Illinois Street, peering toward the court with binoculars and spyglasses. Yellow curtains, drawn halfway up on the jury room's four windows, blocked their view of the deliberations, but now and again the reporters would catch a glimpse of a juror's hand raised aloft. Occasionally the curtains bulged outward when a juror, tired of sitting in his chair, perched on a window sill.

At 11:10 A.M. Mahoney appeared at the open window of the toilet room adjacent to the main jury chamber. He saw scouts for the *Chicago Chronicle* on the roof of the Garden City Billiard Table Company's building; the men had a powerful telescope and a pair of field glasses. They motioned for him to roll up the curtains in the main jury room, but he pantomimed "No" and quickly withdrew from the anteroom.

A few minutes later the *Chronicle* reporters set up a twelve-foot stepladder on the billiard table company's roof. One scrambled to the top, attracting the attention of five laughing jurors, who thronged the anteroom window. Bibby grabbed a plan of the Luetgert factory and, rolling it into a cylinder, mimicked the spyglass man on the ladder. Gazing out some of the courthouse's other windows, policemen and bailiffs scowled.

Throughout the day jurors would appear in the anteroom window, holding their hands under a stream of water falling into the sink and occasionally peering out at the reporters. At times two or three jurors would hold a side conference in the toilet room, as the reporters looked on and wondered what they were discussing. Harlev peeped out for a moment but drew back hastily when he saw the battery of lenses trained on him.

Behmiller grinned broadly and waved his hand across the courtyard and the top of the old jail to the reporters. Looking through a field glass, one of the correspondents got a close view of Behmiller. He had thrown off his collar, and his open vest showed the smudged linen beneath it, but he seemed cheerful enough. Behmiller's shoulders shook with laughter as the reporters used their fingers to telegraph questions across the housetops to him: "Eleven to one?" "Ten to two?" "Nine to three?" "Eight to four?" Behmiller never offered a sign, either affirmative or negative, about the jury vote.

The reporters witnessed Heichhold and Barber corner Harlev as they tried to convince him of something. Then Harlev, Holabird, and Bibby used a jeweler's glass to examine the rings, which glittered through the window. At other times the jurors stood with their hands in their pockets, looking haggard and worn out. Shaw pulled out a timepiece and wearily shook his head. They paused for drinks of water. They examined the bones. They walked back and forth. They looked over the map of the factory for the fiftieth time. They shrugged their shoulders. One of them ate an apple. Others smoked cigars and corncob pipes. They drank from tin cups. One looked at his reflection in a hand glass.

Down in the streets curb orators took sides, some of them condemning the police department for persecuting Luetgert. As if to buttress the argument, officers would invariably appear to clear the sidewalk and break up the crowds forming around the speakers. One man, with great wads of greenbacks in his hands, shouted, "Ten to one on a clear acquittal." He must have had two or three hundred dollars, and he waved the bills defiantly in the faces of all comers but found no takers.

As night fell the *Journal* reporters continued listening through the jury-room vent. The jurors seemed to be in good humor, telling stories, laughing, chatting, posing riddles, and proposing conundrums. They demonstrated mathematical tricks and discussed the definition of ruminating animals and the dimensions of the jury-room table. At nine o'clock some of them suggested going to bed, but Fowler said, "Oh, there's no hurry. Let's wait till half-past anyhow."

Speaking in a low tone, Franzen said something about a remark Harlev had made back at the hotel one day, referring to some of the testimony. Harlev jumped from his chair and shouted, "No man can call me a liar in a jury room or anywhere else." The two men almost broke out into fisticuffs, but Heichhold and others came between them and broke up the fight.

After a few minutes of silence, Franzen said, "Harlev, you've called me names here right along, and I'm going to remember it after we get out of here."

Harlev denied he had called anybody any names. "As it is," he said, "all you fellows have got it in for me."

After another spell of silence, someone said, "What should happen if someone should overhear this business? They might have a phonograph around here somewhere. You can't tell."

The jurors began talking about holes in the wall, wires, and phonographs. Harlev said, "I wish I had a phonograph in here. I could make all kinds of money after the case is over." Several of the jurors said they were sleepy, and within ten minutes, all that could be heard from the room was snoring.

On the morning of Thursday, October 21, Tuthill received a message from the jury and told Connor to get the jurors ready. He told another bailiff to open the outer doors. A hundred reporters, lawyers, and spectators who had been waiting in the hall rushed into the room, jostling the bailiffs out of the way.

As the gray light of a cold autumn morning came through the large windows, Tuthill smiled, sphinxlike. The lawyers took their places. "Bring in the jury," Tuthill said, motioning toward the low door in the wall behind the jury box. The jurors filed in, each man moving stiffly to his accustomed seat. Their brows were lined and the pallor of their cheeks was ashen. Some of them had shaved, half of them were collarless, and all were unkempt.

The room was hushed and tense as everyone waited for Luetgert to appear. Several messenger boys came running up through the mosaic-floored entrance to the courtroom, their footsteps echoing. Up from the basement came the soft whine of the dynamos. The clink of jostling gas pipes over on Clark Street seemed almost a din. The door of the elevator between the jury rooms clanged back into its groove, a sharp footfall crossed the hall, and

Luetgert appeared, his broad face shaded by a black derby. He snatched the felt hat from his head and walked swiftly past the jury box, inside the bar. He took the chair reserved for him beside his attorneys and shook Phalen's hand.

Luetgert looked haggard. The creases from his nose to the corners of his mouth were deeper than before. His long, coarse hair was brushed straight up over his forehead in a scraggly manner, and the small white patches where his hair had thinned in recent months were more conspicuous than ever. He kept fingering his hat. Although his son Arnold was beside him, the two didn't say a word to each other. Luetgert glanced across the faces of the twelve jurors and swallowed hard when he saw the white paper rolled up in Heichhold's hand. At least one reporter noticed a smile flicker across Luetgert's face. Vincent's face was drawn tense; Phalen's was pale. Only Deneen failed to betray signs of tension or nervousness.

A stirring came from the back of the room as some spectators tried to push forward, but then the bailiffs restored order. The hands of the clock on the west wall of the courtroom showed 11:45. A full minute of quiet passed, with no one in the room uttering a word. Tuthill adjusted his glasses and eyed the twelve men in the jury box. Each man's expression seemed to proclaim a dogged determination. Harlev, under a rainfall of glances, looked calm and tranquil, as if nothing of any moment was on his mind.

Judge Tuthill's first words cut through the silence like a sharp knife, although he said them in the most matter-of-fact of tones. "Mr. Foreman, have you agreed upon a verdict?" Luetgert's muscles stiffened as he saw Heichhold rise, the folded paper in his hand. One reporter wrote that Luetgert's face turned the color of a corpse.

"We have not," Heichhold said. The reply brought the blood back to Luetgert's face, and his quavering arms relaxed.

"Do you think there is any prospect of your agreeing?" asked Tuthill.

"I think not," Heichhold said. "In fact, I am almost positive—"

The rest of what he said was inaudible because of the sudden noise from the crowd. A moment later quiet was restored, and Heichhold continued.

"I am positive, I should say, that we cannot agree upon a verdict. The ballot has been the same now for upward—exactly thirty-eight hours, since the fifteen minutes of eight o'clock day before yesterday."

"It has been the same?"

Heichhold made a weak attempt at smiling and said, "It has been the same, and I have put the question to each member of the jury, and they say they will positively hold to their opinions and will not change their minds. No influence and no argument will cause them to change their minds."

The judge asked each of the jurors whether he believed it was possible to reach a unanimous verdict, and every man said it could not be done. And then Tuthill asked, "What is the disposition of the defendant and his lawyers?"

Vincent said, "It seems to me there is only one thing to do, and that is to discharge the jury. After listening to this case for eight weeks, I think they have served faithfully and well."

Tuthill asked, "Mr. Luetgert, how are you impressed?" Luetgert rose awkwardly, his elbows thrust out, and said, with a stronger German accent than usual, "I agree with my attorneys." Some detected a note of delight in his voice. As he sunk back into his chair, he smiled at his son Arnold.

Deneen agreed that the jury should be dismissed, and then Tuthill said, "So it seems to the court. The court has kept you here an exceptionally long time, because the evidence was so voluminous and so much detail that I wished to give you full time to discuss it in all its aspects and to give you time to discuss the matter among yourselves to see if there could be any possibility of harmonizing your views. It is very much to be regretted that you are unable to agree. The case has been very long and protracted. It is the most important case, one of the most important cases, that has ever been tried in this country, and I was anxious that the jury might come to some conclusion, but I am bound to accept . . . that it is useless to keep you longer confined in this matter. I, therefore, enter an order for the discharge of this jury. The defendant will be remanded. You will apply to the clerk for your certificates."

The jurors asked to retire to the jury room for a few minutes before being dismissed. The court became quiet again as everyone waited for the jurors to come back out. Tuthill, whose red and swollen eyes were half-closed, sat with his head bowed on his hand, his hair ruffled. When the jurors returned, they presented a statement signed by all twelve, thanking the judge and all the attorneys for the "very kind treatment" they had received during the trial.

"As to the Trial," the clumsily spelled statement read, "we wish to state, while the Evidence were such that we were unabel to agree on a Verdict, one Thing we did agree about, and that is that the Circumstances were such that the Police had ampel reason to prosecute on the showing, without hearing the Defence, and we commend them for having done their duty in the case."

37 Aftermath

THE SPECTATORS pressed forward to offer congratulations to the various attorneys, swarming around Vincent and Phalen. Meanwhile Schaack was hiding from the crowd in Deneen's office. In a laconic voice he said, "All right. I expected it from the time the jury was out." He stared blankly out the window at a brick wall, looking away only when Deneen came into the room.

Tuthill spoke to reporters about the case for the first time, saying the trial had been fair. He said the hung jury had not surprised him. Asked whether he believed Luetgert would be tried again, he said he didn't know, adding, "I fancy that he will never be tried again in a Cook County court. . . . From the wide publicity . . . which the newspapers have given the evidence in the case, the marked attention which it has attracted in all parts of the country and the frenzied interest which the people of Chicago have taken in the outcome of the trial since the case went to the jury, I hardly think that the prosecution can find twelve men who have not already tried the accused in their own minds and either acquitted or convicted him. That is the problem confronting the state's attorney now, and unless he solves it by producing the men, of course Luetgert will go free."

A reporter asked Arnold Luetgert whether his father would be released on bail, and a reporter for the *Chronicle*, which had staunchly defended Luetgert, yelled out, "He can get $2 million if required. The bonds are ready for any possible amount."

Some reporters dragged one of the jurors, Boyd, into the state's attorney's office. He looked ready to faint from exhaustion and sank into a chair. "For goodness' sake, don't bother me," he cried. "I'm nearly dead and there is so much worrying me. I will not talk." He left the building surrounded by a hundred people who begged him to tell something of the last three days' events inside the jury room.

"There they go!" a stout man shouted as two forlorn-looking jurors left the county comptroller's office. Everyone within range of the man's voice stopped, turned, and watched the two jurors walk to the elevators. "Those are two of the Luetgert jurors," the man called out. "They have just been in to draw their pay."

Questioned by a reporter as he walked from the courthouse, Behmiller said, "It was awful. . . . There were wrangles almost every hour and we got little sleep. . . . No blows were struck, although I won't say that some of them didn't come near to it at times."

Behmiller rubbed his face and suggested to Holabird that they get a shave, but the questions kept coming. Like many of the other jurors, Behmiller said they had barely even considered the scientific evidence. "The bones did not cut any figure at all, hardly, though they were piled on the table at times," he said. "We did not give much credence to the allegation that the police had been manufacturing evidence and intimidating witnesses. We agreed that the officers had simply done as it was their duty to do—sift what looked like suspicious circumstances to the bottom. It is no indication that because an officer does everything possible to get at the facts in a case instead of sitting quietly down and waiting for somebody to come and commit a murder in front of them that they are persecuting someone. We took it that way and Schaack, Schuettler, and the officers stand higher today in our estimation than any officers we knew before. Most of us had an idea that the police of Chicago didn't like to work, and that idea was shattered." And with that, Behmiller hooked arms with Holabird, and they made their way to a barber.

The jurors were astonished to learn the *Journal* and *Tribune* had reported what they had been saying in the jury room. After seeing the articles, the jurors verified their accuracy.

As Bibby tried to escape the crowd of interviewers, he said, "That man was guilty. I know it. I would have stayed there forever and voted guilty every time a ballot was taken rather than change my vote and set free a man who was capable of killing his wife in a way that it would seem should take all the devilish ingenuity in a dozen devilish natures to conceive."

Like many of the jurors, Franzen and Fowler said the rings were the strongest evidence of Luetgert's guilt. "I can't see how any sane man would vote for acquittal in the face of those rings," Fowler said. "There they were in that vat, stuck together with cartilage, too. The police throw them there? That's all bosh. They wouldn't have stuck together if they had been even dropped in. I argued with those fellows till I was hoarse, but they sat there with their arms folded and muttered a few words now and then. It made me mad."

Franzen called the defense's soap-making story implausible. "It was absolutely ridiculous, and anyone with a practical knowledge of soap manufacture would agree with me," he said. "Bones could be of no use at all in soap making, and if bones had been put in the vat with the grease they would certainly have all been found there later. Had Luetgert been placed on the witness stand, I would have asked him if he had ever attempted to make soap in the factory before."

Harlev, clad in a gray spring overcoat with his black derby hat pulled down over his ears, hastened out of the alley that ran from the old jail out to Clark Street, followed by a big crowd. When approached by a *Journal* reporter, he said, "I hear that I have no character left. Everybody will be pointing his finger at me and shouting 'Give me half.'"

"Have you heard the charges of bribery?"

"Of course. . . . They called me names even in the jury room."

Harlev was shown one of the *Journal*'s extra editions from the second day of the jury's deliberations. "Hello!" he said. "Here is a head: 'Charges of Bribery against One Juror.' That means me, I suppose. Well, I can stand it."

"Have you anything to say about your action on the jury?"

"Nothing but this: I swore to be guided by the law and the evidence. I don't say Luetgert is an innocent man, but I do say no evidence has been presented to me that convinces me he is guilty. Therefore, I should have been false to my oath and guilty of that man's blood if I had voted contrary to my convictions."

When Harlev reached Clark Street, someone in the mob cried out, "Three cheers for Harlev!" The crowd shouted for half a minute and Harlev's face reddened.

Harlev later said he wouldn't have signed the jury's statement if he had known it would be seen as an endorsement of everything the police had done. He also offered the newspapers some harsh words about the other jurors, reserving his greatest contempt for Fowler. "This man Fowler no doubt meant well enough, but he seemed to be a sort of spoiled child, and was sick nearly all of the time and petulant," Harlev told the *Record*. "There were a good many remarks made in the jury room which seemed to me a long way from what a man should say when deliberating on a verdict that might have hanged a man. For instance, I heard it said: 'Oh, let's hang him and get home.' Again I heard it said: 'Come on boys, let's get together in some way so we can get out of here; I'm getting tired.' Now it didn't seem to me that the fact that I was tired—and I guess I suffered as much as some of the younger men—would justify me in giving a verdict that I didn't think was right simply because I wanted to go home."

As Holabird left the courthouse, he said, "The talk in some of the papers about bribery is the worst bosh I ever read. It would have been an impossibility for anyone to have even reached us. I know the bailiffs watched me like hawks. My own wife couldn't talk to me without a bailiff being there to hear."

T. J. Mahoney, interviewed later in the day as he sat in the parlor of his home, surrounded by his smiling wife and prattling children, said, "I have no reason to believe Harley was not as conscientious as any of us. There was some talk about him, but any suspicion was furthest from my thoughts. The insinuations reflecting on his honor are based on supposition and surmise, so far as I know. Everyone was sincere in what he thought. Of course, there were some very forcible expressions of opinion, but no juror was abusive or indulged in personalities."

Reporters went to the jail and interviewed Luetgert, who was pacing back and forth behind the screen of the visitors' cage. A crowd of other prisoners stood behind him, separated from him by the iron doors. They offered him congratulations. Other than saying he wanted a new trial right away, Luetgert spent most of the interviews joking around.

"Eh, boys," he said, poking a rolled up newspaper through the bars and chucking one of the prisoners in the side with it. "Luetgert's all right, ain't he?"

"You bet. You're the whole thing," responded an inmate (whom the *Daily News* described as a "sharp-featured little darky"). The prisoners called out a dozen responses. One said Luetgert was "half right at least," and another said he was "the only one of the kind in the jail."

"You see," Luetgert said. "They like Luetgert, and if he should go away, they would get homesick."

When asked if he would seek bail, Luetgert cried out, "No, sir!" slapping his paper against the bars of the cage. "What for? I want to stay right here. A new trial is what I want. What could I do if I got outside?"

One of the newspapermen reminded him he had said a few days earlier he could make $5,000 a month if he were exhibited in a museum. Luetgert then proceeded to conduct a mock auction, laughing as he offered to sell off the various witnesses who had testified against him. Then he walked back to his cell and took an afternoon nap.

Whitman, the jailer, commented, "He is the most remarkable character that has ever come under my observation. I cannot believe that his actions are natural, and I have been moved to think that he is one of the greatest living actors. Even if he is innocent, as he claims to be, he ought to show some signs of fear. But he does not. Nothing seems to worry him. He eats regularly and sleeps like a child. I can't fathom him."

38 Editorials

NEWSPAPERS AROUND the country weighed in with their opinions on the Luetgert trial. Several said the evidence against Luetgert was strong and that the jury's inability to reach a verdict only proved the folly of using a jury system.

The *Hartford (Conn.) Times* editorialized, "No stronger case of circumstantial evidence is recalled, in all the history of criminal trials, than the case against Adolph Luetgert."

"While there was plenty of proof that Luetgert dissolved some body in the vats," the *Buffalo Enquirer* wrote, "there was lack of absolute proof that some body was Mrs. Luetgert and on that rock the jury split. Yet the circumstantial evidence was unusually strong. . . . There is a prevalent prejudice against conviction on circumstantial evidence. It is unaccountable but undeniable."

The *Los Angeles Times* described trial by a jury as "nonsense" and a "worn-out relic of antiquity" and called for a better method of determining guilt, although it didn't say what that system would be. The *Times* said it didn't understand why a single "stubborn or corrupt man" who refused to listen to common sense should be allowed to thwart the punishment of a criminal.

The *Milwaukee News* said the men who held out for a not-guilty verdict should not be blamed for having reasonable doubt. Nevertheless, the newspaper proposed letting a three-fourths majority of the jury suffice to determine a verdict. The paper added, however, that if the courts allowed defendants to be convicted by less-than-unanimous verdicts, they would also have to abolish the death penalty, since the minority voting not guilty might later prove to have been correct.

The *Newport News (Va.) Press* acknowledged that hung juries waste time and money but called them "a necessary evil," noting, "To provide against hung juries would be to tamper with one of the bulwarks of liberty."

The *Sacramento Record Union* questioned why a majority of jurors should be allowed to bully a minority into changing their minds about the verdict. "There is just as much likelihood of a minority being right, and being persuaded or wearied into error."

The *Washington (Del.) Post* called the hung jury in the Luetgert case a "triumph for justice." The *Post* editorialized, "What strikes us is the fact that the proof of Mrs. Luetgert's death has never yet been produced. We desire justice, but we shrink from the idea of pursuit and persecution."

The *Des Moines News* compared Schaack to Inspector Javert of *Les Miserables,* adding that whereas Javert was motivated by duty, Schaack's motive was pride. The newspaper said Schaack "cared nothing for the man's guilt or innocence, provided he might convict him and add to the reputation of Schaack as a sleuth."

The *Bloomington (Ill.) Pantagraph* said the case was not strong enough to convict, and the *Chicago Chronicle* asserted there wasn't an iota of proof that Mrs. Luetgert was even dead. "Hundreds of people have disappeared without any cause to suppose they had been murdered," the *Chronicle* editorialized. "This was no exceptional case." The paper said it would be a waste of money to try Luetgert again.

The *Chicago Tribune* called for a retrial. "The second trial should be stripped of all extraneous matters, of all merely technical points, of all time-killing expedients, of all expert rubbish, and of all the devices of cunning lawyers which make for delay," the *Tribune* wrote, asserting Luetgert would have quickly been found guilty if he had been tried in Britain or Canada.

"The recent trial was a shocking illustration of time-killing," the *Tribune* wrote. "All sorts of frivolous questions addressed to witnesses were allowed.

All sorts of indecorous and undignified performances were allowed. It was at times hard to tell whether Luetgert was on trial or the police officers who made the arrest. . . . Is it any wonder that busy and intelligent men in this city dislike to serve on juries when they see a case like this Luetgert one spun out by all sorts of quips and technicalities and cunning devices, so as to last through a whole summer and half of an autumn?"

The *Chicago Daily News* also believed another trial should be held but expressed doubt that an impartial jury could be found. "About the first question, 'Have you ever read the newspaper accounts of this case?' would prove the disqualification of every man in Cook County who knows his alphabet. And the man who cannot read should not be allowed to pass judgment on the guilt of another, particularly when that other's guilt, if he be guilty, is surrounded by such a labyrinth of complexities as developed in the Luetgert trial," the *Daily News* wrote. "Few men can have read the newspaper reports of the Luetgert trial without forming an opinion. This is evidenced by the discussion heard on the streets, in bars and at home."

Several papers criticized the expert testimony. The *Minneapolis Journal* said it was unwise to rely on the speculations of scientists who contradicted one another. The *Streator (Ill.) Free Press* declared, "Purchased expert testimony is a farce." The *Philadelphia Press* called for the creation of a permanent commission of independent experts, appointed by the government, who would issue objective reports on the scientific evidence used in court cases.

The press coverage of the trial and the public's hysterical response also came in for criticism. "There is nothing stranger in all the course of the sensational Luetgert trial than the way the Chicago papers tell all the secrets of the jury room," the *Buffalo News* wrote. "They do queer things in the Windy City."

The *Chicago Journal,* the newspaper responsible for reporting those jury secrets, reported its circulation in October had been more than 3 million, with a daily average of 119,755. The newspaper noted, "The Luetgert trial furnished a rare opportunity for clever handling, and that the efforts of the *Journal* staff elicited the plaudits of the appreciative public is evidenced by the greatly increased circulation during what might be appropriately characterized as 'Luetgert month.'"

The average daily circulation for the *Daily News* had been 219,557 in September and 229,763 in October, setting an all-time high for the newspaper up until that time.

The editorials after the Luetgert trial saved some of their venom for the women who had attended the trial. The *New York Journal* editorialized, "It seems as if the sympathy of the morbid Chicago woman is governed entirely by the enormity of the crime with which a prisoner is charged. To kill a wife in the Eastern style, say, with a pistol, is conventional. To boil her in a vat strikes the emotional woman as worthy of tears of condolence. So Luetgert, ever since his trial began, has been a sort of lion among these women, who would have carried him out of the courtroom in their hysterical arms if it were not for the unemotional policemen."

The *Peoria Journal* criticized the "hysterical and morbidly curious women" for desiring to marry Luetgert. "It is bad enough that he has been compelled to become the object of so much curiosity, and that he has been compelled to repel the advances of hypnotists, photograph men and sensational journalist schemes. It may be well to inquire of the public what our human nature is coming to? Are there no limits to the work of cranks and the conceptions of the cranky? Will nothing short of the walls of the insane asylum cut off the emanations of this sort which now rise up to conflict the public?"

The *Syracuse (N.Y.) Courier* suggested that crowds should be kept out of future murder trials. Only people directly connected with the cases should be allowed in court, the newspaper said. This would prevent the "demoralizing effects upon the general public," the *Courier* wrote.

During the trial H. Gilson Gardner of the *Chicago Journal* had wondered exactly what it was about the Luetgert case that inspired such frenzied responses. "Is it because the late deceased was robbed of her funeral services that the public takes a special interest in her taking off?" he wrote. "Is it, then, the aesthetics of society that have been outraged by this butcher, and does the public mind resent an innovation on its old-time murder methods? . . .

"But after all the mind involuntarily returns to the subject of the vat . . . the slimy, steaming wooden trough. Its top is covered with a wooden door laid over pieces of rough burlap. By its side, with spade in hand, ready to stir the contents, is Adolph Luetgert, and within—but the mind, though fascinated with the revolting subject, here stops short."

After the first trial had ended, the *Chicago Daily News* noted how true tales of crime hold a morbid fascination for the public. The newspaper editorialized, "Rarely in the whole annals of criminal law has there been a case which had in it materials better adapted to grewsome romance than in the now celebrated Luetgert trial."

39 Between Trials

OFFERS OF MARRIAGE and reports of Mrs. Luetgert sightings continued pouring into the jail. What Luetgert really needed, however, was money to pay his lawyers for a second trial. William Charles began collecting donations from Luetgert's supporters. A museum manager offered to post $25,000 in bonds for his release and to pay him a salary of $500 a week to put himself on exhibition. Luetgert turned down the proposal, believing he could get better. Another entrepreneur offered $1,000 a week, an eastern publishing house guaranteed $2,000 and generous royalties for a book, and a newspaper paid him $500 to write a short article.

It isn't certain which newspaper had made that offer, but on October 24 the *St. Louis Republic* published an article written by Luetgert in which he bemoaned the manner in which the authorities had railroaded him. "I have learned that in this boasted land of liberty a man charged with a crime is treated as I have read they are treated in Russia," he wrote. "I have realized that the presumption that a man is innocent until he is proven guilty is bosh and nonsense. I realize that something is wrong with society and a system of court procedure which causes a man to be confined in a cell, inaccessible to his friends, except in the presence of others, so that it is impossible for him to go out and hunt up testimony and prepare for trial, while an unprincipled wolfish police force strives with all its might and main to terrorize and intimidate those who might have testified for me, and who bring about . . . a state of terror."

Luetgert condemned Chicago's newspapers for treating him unfairly. "If I was pale, they said it was a sign of guilt; if I retained my usual complexion and countenance, they said it was brazen; if I smiled, they said I was hysterical; if I seemed despondent, they said I was breaking down. They have published pictures of my eyes, my nose, my ears, my mouth, my teeth and my hair, all so horribly distorted that those who have not seen me, and who do not know me, must have suspected sometimes that I was a monster in appearance. In fact, everything that a man says or does when he is charged with crime is said to be an evidence of guilt."

Luetgert explained the apparent indifference he had shown when handling the bones and other pieces of evidence, which some reporters had taken as a sign of his monstrousness. He said he saw no reason to treat the bones with any deference because he knew they were not those of his wife or any human being. "I knew those bones were hog and sheep bones," he wrote. "Why should I not examine them with indifference and with considerable amusement?"

◆◆◆

After months of trepidation Chicago police officers finally found out on October 26 which of them would keep their jobs. Claiming he was merely following the new civil-service law, Superintendent Kipley discharged 405 patrolmen and officers and forced another 24 to retire. They were replaced by members of the Star League, the Democrats who had been fired from the police force during the previous Republican administration.

On seeing their names on the list of discharged officers, some men quit on the spot, turning in their badges and letting the tide of traffic take care of itself. Scores of men thronged City Hall, denouncing Kipley and demanding their jobs back.

The newspapers immediately took note of the fact that, other than Schaack and Schuettler, most of the officers connected with the Luetgert and O'Malley cases were being fired. Eleven officers who had worked on the Luetgert investigation were on the discharge list, including George Hutchinson, Walter Dean, Charles Griebenow, and Frederick De Celle. A *Tribune* reporter asked Kipley, "Why did you discharge almost all of the policemen connected with the Luetgert case on the eve of the second trial?"

Kipley looked blankly at the reporter for a moment and then said, "What men?" He claimed to know nothing about it, saying he was simply following civil-service procedures. The *Tribune*, however, documented that many of the discharged officers had excellent records, including those on the Luetgert case.

When a *Dispatch* reporter showed Deneen the list of Luetgert-case officers who had been discharged, he exclaimed, "What! Not all of them? . . . Can it be possible? This is a surprise. They were all good men, and have done good work. These men are invaluable to the state in the approaching trial of Luetgert, and this part of the chief's order should have been held back till after the trial. I am very sorry for this action. It will cripple our case."

A couple of days later Kipley announced that the officers connected with the Luetgert case would remain on the force at least until Luetgert's second trial had ended. Dean said he would help the prosecution whether or not he kept his job with the police department. "I believe Luetgert is guilty, and I have thought so since I found the rings in the case," he said. "I feel it my duty to serve the state as far as I am able."

◆◆◆

Luetgert's attorneys announced they had found some trace of Mrs. Luetgert's long-lost brother, who had disappeared in Colorado years before (and who was alternately referred to as Henry, Herman, and Fred in newspaper accounts). An attorney in Colorado wrote Phalen, saying the brother had once been committed to an asylum. "I know where he is at the present time. For years past he has been partially insane and addicted to roaming from one place to another," the lawyer wrote. The defense lawyers hoped the story would show Mrs. Luetgert had also been insane and prone to wandering off, but McEwen mocked the theory.

◆◆◆

A palmist, Bernhard Cola, called on Luetgert at the jail and asked to read his hands, but Luetgert asked, "What will you give me if I let you examine my hands?" When the palmist refused to pay money, Luetgert refused to show his hands. Cola pulled his white fedora over his black, curly hair and left.

"This is another scheme to create a newspaper sensation," Luetgert said loudly on the way back to his cell. "Luetgert will not furnish sensations of this kind in the future unless he is paid. My hands were read once and the results published. I don't see why they should want the same thing again."

◆◆◆

Before Luetgert went on trial again, he faced a change in attorneys. Vincent told his client that the time he had spent on the case had hurt his practice. Vincent's decision to quit prompted an angry outburst from Luetgert.

Phalen chose Max Riese, the brother of one of the defense's bone experts from the first trial, as his assistant counsel. But Luetgert wanted to bring in another lawyer, Lawrence Harmon. Phalen went to the jail on November 28 and demanded he be given complete control of the case. Luetgert, his son Arnold, and William Charles were angry at Phalen's "nerve." According to newspaper accounts, the three of them said Harmon should take charge of the case. After arguing for an hour, Phalen jumped up and said, "Well, you can't put any splint on my nose." He walked out of the jail and the Luetgert case.

Nevertheless, Phalen told the *Tribune* Luetgert had begged him to stay on and had offered to let him be the lead attorney. Phalen said he quit because he anticipated disagreeing with Luetgert over the best way to run the trial and the "character" of some of the evidence. "I have been looking around for weeks for an excuse to get out, and the conference this afternoon offered me a loophole," he said. "I feel as though I ought to be congratulated."

Harmon, a fifty-two-year-old Irish immigrant who had lived much of his life in Peoria, took over the case. The *Daily News* described him as resolute, keen-eyed, and physically strong, a man who spoke with emphasis and decision. Harmon bragged of his strong record. He said he had defended many accused criminals, but none of them had ever been sentenced to death. He acknowledged the great challenge he faced in defending Luetgert, however, particularly since he hadn't closely followed the first trial. "Nevertheless, I enter the case with a firm belief in his innocence—a feeling of confidence which counts much for a lawyer."

◆◆◆

A night cabman was drinking beer in a saloon at Michigan and Clark Streets at fifteen minutes after midnight one night in late November. Five men, all "hard-looking customers," entered the place and hurriedly demanded drinks, swallowed them, and left. Three of the men had no coats or hats, and their faces were pale, as if from long confinement.

The cabman told his story to some policemen he encountered a short time later, and they soon discovered that three men had escaped from the jail by sawing through the iron bars on a window in the jail's old section. They had used sheets to lower themselves into the alley.

After the escape the *Tribune* noted that the jail had been lenient with visiting privileges, making it easier for contraband items to be smuggled in. The paper cited a typical scene in which Mary Siemering chatted with Luetgert during exercise hour. "Luetgert was all smiles. He tilted back and forth on his feet and talked rapidly to the girl for whom he is said to have grown tired of his wife. Mary answered in quiet tones, but turned her face away when she saw that she was observed. It would have been a simple matter for her to have passed to him a steel saw or a package of poison, but Luetgert is not interested in trying to escape his confinement by either of these means."

In the wake of the escape, jail officials made a thorough search of the facility. While some of the prisoners were surly whenever they were searched, Luetgert would throw up his hands with a smile and say, "That is your business. Go ahead."

The search turned up a curious billy club constructed from a piece of leather, tinfoil from packages of smoking tobacco, and a roll of hard paper. A couple of prisoners had fashioned knives out of tin-cup fragments and steel shoe insteps. The guards also found a bunch of grapes intertwined with opium-laced strings and a sardine box containing an "outfit" for injecting morphine.

Just as preparations for the second Luetgert trial got under way, the news came that the case had become the object of obsession for an insane man in Denver. Threatening to burn his wife and children in an old garbage crematory near his home, John H. Dame* announced, "I will follow in the footsteps of the great Luetgert. I will vindicate his name. You and the children may prepare for death at once." Later he sharpened an ax and told his wife

---

* Not to be confused with the Cook County Jail inmate John G. Dame, who is mentioned in chapter 32.

he would use it to chop her and the children into sausage meat. After being arrested, Dame raved about Luetgert all night in his jail cell, protesting that the sausage maker was innocent.

When a woman passed by in the corridor outside Dame's cell, he exclaimed, "There's Mrs. Luetgert. I knew she was not dead. Give me that knife and I'll make sausage of her. To hell with women anyway. They all ought to be killed. There she goes. Don't let her hide from me until I can show that Luetgert did not do his duty. Let me out of here." The next day Dame was sent to the county hospital.

40 Turbulence

BEFORE LUETGERT'S second trial could begin, a new judge had to be chosen. Luetgert said he was pleased when the case went to Judge Joseph E. Gary, who was best known for presiding over the 1887 trial of the anarchists accused in the Haymarket Square bombing. Born and raised in New York State, Gary studied law in St. Louis and went west with the California gold rush. A reporter, Francis A. Eastman, later noted that Gary had spent three years in San Francisco during the 1850s, a time of "lawless terrors" when the city was "in the grasp of thieves and cutthroats." Eastman believed that experience profoundly affected Gary, steeling him to "bravely meet and firmly resolve questions relating to the mob and its dastardly works." During the anarchist trial Gary "doubtless remembered the corruption and cowardice of the judges and other officials in San Francisco and in so doing gained added strength to discharge that duty in a manly and exemplary manner." Although many admired Gary's tough attitude toward criminals, the Haymarket trial showed his unrelenting bias against the defendants. He had allowed men to sit on the jury even though it was clear they were prejudiced against the alleged bombers, he had given the prosecutors free rein to say almost anything they wanted in closing arguments, and he had skewed his instructions to the jury so that it was almost impossible to find the men not guilty. Despite these flagrant injustices, no newspapers of the time criticized Gary. It was only later, after passions about the Haymarket case had cooled, that some people realized what a travesty it had been. When Governor Altgeld pardoned the surviving Haymarket defendants, he said Gary had conducted the trial with "malicious ferocity." Others noted how Gary had added to the trial's circus atmosphere by permitting a parade of female visitors to sit next to him during testimony.

Despite these criticisms, many people still respected Gary. When he was assigned the second Luetgert trial, the *Chicago Journal* called Gary "the most venerable jurist in the county." He had marked his thirty-fourth anniversary as a Cook County circuit judge a week before. He was moving to the Superior Court and had not tried criminal cases for ten years.

His gray-whiskered face was not as familiar around the criminal courts as it once had been. During the first Luetgert trial, Gary was stopped in the building by some guards who thought he was a curiosity seeker trying to sneak into Judge Tuthill's court. A guard had told him, "You're pretty smooth, old man, but you can't fool me," only to become embarrassed on learning Gary's identity.

Now that Gary had been named to preside over Luetgert's second trial, Luetgert said, "I think Judge Gary will be all right. He is an upright judge and has an excellent general knowledge of law, thus insuring me a fair trial and even chance. Yes, I am satisfied—no kick coming at all."

Luetgert also offered predictions: "My trial will not be more than half as long as the first one. I think the expert testimony will be shelved. Any old nigger cook could tell the jury what those bones are. What is the use of a lot of testimony about bones? The question before the court, boiled down, is this: Mrs. Luetgert is missing. Is she dead or alive? If dead, was she murdered? No one knows today beyond a reasonable doubt where my wife is, or whether she is dead or alive."

Despite the warnings of Judge Tuthill, the *Daily News,* and others that it would be almost impossible to find an impartial jury in Chicago, the trial was not moved to another venue. Jury selection began on November 30, 1897. The court questioned more than two hundred men, all of whom had read about the Luetgert case. Nevertheless, as in the Haymarket trial, Gary held that it didn't matter whether jurors had read about the case in question as long as they swore they had an open mind about it.

One potential juror was disqualified when it was learned he had talked with Agatha Tosch about the case. Another man said he was prejudiced against police testimony. He explained, "I believe a policeman's testimony is his bread and butter. If he doesn't testify right, he is discharged." One man was chosen for the jury and then dismissed when it was rumored that he had once said, "Luetgert is guilty and ought to be hanged."

On December 14 the last of twelve men was chosen. A reporter studying their faces thought they seemed to be a mild-looking bunch, not likely to vote for hanging a man. The jury for the second trial comprised an insurance solicitor, a furniture dealer, a restaurant proprietor, a student in applied mechanics, a clerk, an unemployed machinist, an electrician, a salesman, a blast-furnace worker, a collector, a musician, and a pressman.

Gary reorganized the courtroom for the new Luetgert trial, setting up the furniture in the same unusual arrangement he had used in the Haymarket case. Rather than sitting in the customary jury box, the twelve jurors sat in two rows of chairs directly in front of the judge's bench, facing away from the judge. An old chair—the same seat that had been used in the Haymarket trial a decade earlier—was set up a few feet in front of the jurors, facing toward the jury and the judge. The newspapermen were given seats in the area normally used as the jury box.

The trial began with McEwen's opening argument, and then the jurors took a tour of the Luetgert factory. Before the case could get any further, however, Luetgert's lawyers learned one of the jurors, Henry Boasberg, had made statements showing prejudice against Luetgert. One of Boasberg's coworkers, Albert I. Mallory, swore in an affidavit that, one day at lunch, he had heard Boasberg say, "I believe Luetgert is guilty. The law ought to be here like it is in the old country, where a majority can hang a man, and if I was on the jury, I would be for convicting him, and if they let me, I would be the one to put the rope around his neck."

Another coworker, O. F. Armstrong, said he often saw Boasberg stop in front of newsstands and excitedly read stories about Luetgert. "On one occasion I heard . . . Boasberg say that he was positive Luetgert had killed his wife and cooked her up into sausage and that we were eating the sausage," Armstrong said.

Boasberg was dismissed. Luetgert angrily denounced Boasberg's presence on the jury as a police plot, telling a bystander in court, "If I could have that man five minutes, I would sweep the floor with him. If I never committed murder before, I would do it now. It's just another conspiracy, like the first trial. The state knew all the time that Juror Shaw was against me, and that he had expressed his opinion, but they allowed him to stay on the jury. We got reports about it, but it was too late to act."

Attorneys observing the second Luetgert trial were surprised that Gary allowed the other eleven jurors to remain in the courtroom as Boasberg's alleged prejudice against Luetgert was being discussed. "Many lawyers who examined the facts offhand expressed the belief that already there existed excellent ground for taking the case to the Supreme Court, did future events make this desirable," the *Daily News* reported.

A new juror, a shoemaker named Robert Anners, was selected, and the case began all over on December 17. The court was still crowded, but it wasn't thronged as it had been in the fall; female interest seemed to wane. The press continued covering the trial, but most days the stories were buried in the back of the papers instead of plastered across the front page. Julian Hawthorne didn't bother showing up. The same witnesses everyone had heard before came back to the stand and told their stories again.

Harmon, the new lead defense attorney, seemed to be working around the clock, driving himself to the point of exhaustion. His assistants, John Kehoe and Max Riese, complained that Harmon was handling everything himself, giving them no opportunity to cross-examine the state's witnesses or determine the defense strategy. It was rumored once that Harmon was planning to leave in the middle of the trial to defend another accused wife murderer then in the headlines, Christopher Merry, but he stayed with Luetgert.

Like Luetgert's last set of lawyers, Harmon attempted to show that Mrs. Luetgert's family had a history of insanity and disappearances. Once again, however, the court refused to allow any evidence about that, saying it was irrelevant. Harmon made repeated promises that he would prove that Mrs. Luetgert was still alive, but no solid evidence ever surfaced.

Luetgert's attorneys had little hope of getting any money out of him; the only material gain they would receive from the trial would be the publicity. Luetgert was unable to profit from his notoriety. A court-appointed receiver who was trying to raise money to pay Luetgert's creditors announced plans to sell the infamous vat to a museum, but prosecutors objected and Gary threatened the man with contempt, so the sale never happened. During the trial newspapers reported that Luetgert's son, Arnold, had paid William Vincent with three forged checks, bearing a total value of $4,750, which had supposedly been endorsed by a friend of Luetgert's named Paul H. Jaeschke. At first Arnold denied the allegation, but then he told the *Journal* he had forged the notes to save his father from the gallows. The end had justified the means, he said.

Luetgert's financial troubles were mounting. He owed $76,900 on various mortgages and debts. People who had bought property from him learned that Luetgert had already mortgaged the land to others. Several people went public with information about money that Luetgert owed them.

Luetgert issued a plea for donations. Although he did not want to beg, he said he had no choice but to ask for "loans" to pay his legal bills. "The spirit of American law is supposed to give every man a fair trial for his life, but it is plain that without money for [necessities], such as bringing witnesses from long distances, paying stenographers, and compensating the experts whose pay must necessarily be large, I can barely hope to wage a successful battle for my vindication," he said.

Harmon ran out of money to pay his stenographers, whom the defense needed to keep a record of the testimony, since the defense and prosecution paid for their own transcripts. Harmon wanted the prosecutors to provide him with a copy of their transcript, but Judge Gary refused to order it.

"We will have to go back to the old-fashioned method of taking the record in longhand," Harmon said. After that he and his assistants laboriously wrote out a record of the trial. He raised objections more often than ever, possibly to stretch out the pauses in the testimony so that he would have time to write down what was being said.

Harmon indulged Luetgert's apparent pleasure in watching the prosecution witnesses squirm under embarrassing questions. When Agatha Tosch testified, Luetgert prompted Harmon to ask her about the relationship she'd had with Luetgert. Harmon posed the questions his client suggested, even though they were of questionable value to Luetgert's defense. Harmon asked Tosch whether Luetgert had kissed her when she came back from a trip to Germany. She denied it indignantly. Luetgert leaned over and told Harmon that Tosch had been drunk at the time of the alleged kiss. Harmon asked her whether this was true. The question brought an angry flush to her cheek. She glared at Luetgert and muttered in German, "You're crazy, you brute." Luetgert, who was wearing a flower in his buttonhole, chuckled. The *Daily News* reported, "He has acted like a man at a vaudeville show ever since the second trial began, jesting and joking with all who came his way, and laughing incessantly over every bit of testimony."

As Harmon cross-examined Sophia Tews, who had identified the two rings police found in the vat as Mrs. Luetgert's, he placed the two rings on the table in front of him and then covered them with a sheet of paper. Gary ordered him to uncover the rings, but he refused to do so.

"Leave the paper off," Gary repeated.

"I have the same right to examine the rings without any reflections from the court as the prosecution has, and I protest against these remarks," Harmon said.

"It is very necessary," Gary said. "The clerk—"

"The clerk has the marks upon the rings and no man is interfering with them," Harmon said. "It is simply a reflection on counsel to make such remarks as that."

"If there would be no covering on the rings," Gary said, "if they were left open and exposed on the table all the time, there would be no need for the clerk to be cautious."

Harmon was getting more and more excited. He insisted on his right to cover up the rings. "It is my privilege to do that and I deny the right of the court to deprive me of it," he said.

McEwen interrupted, saying, "When I handled them, I always put them where everyone could see them."

Captain William Knoch, the clerk of the court, stood up at his desk and looked at Harmon. "The other day," he said, "I gave counsel the rings with a rubber band to go around the box they were in, and as I was very busy or something, I overlooked them for a minute. I went to look for them and found that they had made their way into his pocket."

"Didn't I bring them back to you?" Harmon retorted.

"You did," the clerk said. "The box and all found their way into your pocket."

Harmon lost all control, shouting at Knoch, "Do you mean to intimate any reflection on me? I deny your right or the court's or anybody's else's to reflect on me."

Harmon finally uncovered the rings and continued his cross-examination. He tried to ask Tews about her sister, Louise Law, who had died in the insane asylum at Kankakee. Harmon said he expected to show that the so-called wedding ring found by the police had never belonged to Mrs. Luetgert. Harmon said the ring had in fact belonged to Louise Law, which explained why "L. L." was engraved on it. Gary refused to let Harmon follow this line of questioning, however.

"We shall be glad to meet Mr. Harmon on the evidence of Louise Law," McEwen said. "He knows he will never produce anything of the kind."

"No, I won't produce Louise Law's ring. *You* produce it. There it is!" Harmon shouted, holding out one of the rings that prosecutors had entered into evidence. Harmon waved it aloft in front of the jury. McEwen excitedly rose to his feet to object. Gary dryly said, "That's all buncombe."

And then, as Harmon asked Tews another question, McEwen objected, claiming Tews had already answered it. Turning toward McEwen and gesticulating fiercely, Harmon yelled out, "She has not answered any such thing! This question was objected to. This witness has not stated. Counsel has stated."

Gary said, "Mr. Harmon, I don't know but it may be to your advantage to endeavor to create so much turbulence before this jury."

"I am not creating any turbulence at all," Harmon said.

"To charge another man with telling an untruth is not a very decorous mode of conducting an examination," Gary said. "It is equally indecorous to tell us what you did."

"The gentleman does not know the truth when he sees it," McEwen said.

"I won't have that," Gary said.

"I have to protect myself when he passes a criticism on me," McEwen said.

"Mr. Harmon is here, as we know, from the proceedings, under very embarrassing circumstances, and you must make some allowance for him if he is carried too far," Gary said.

"Don't make any allowance for me," Harmon said. "I ask no indulgence or favor of the court or counsel or jury. I am here to do my duty and fight this case fairly and win it if I can. I ask no favor of anyone."

"Now that you have made that little speech, let us go on," Gary said.

"I want my legal right and no more," Harmon said.

Gary threatened to fine Harmon for contempt of court, and even Luetgert and the other defense attorneys could not conceal their disgust over Harmon's behavior. The *Inter Ocean* observed that Harmon was "extremely nervous."

While questioning Edward Cady, an expert on corsets, Harmon brought out the fact that Cady had never worn a corset himself. "Never mind that sort of a thing," Gary interrupted. "We don't care whether this man wears corsets, bloomers, divided skirts or socks. Let him proceed with his testimony."

Christine Feld returned to the witness stand wearing a sealskin and large spectacles that resembled miniature opera glasses, which prompted Harmon to remark, "So this is 'My Beloved Christine.' What was your costume at the last charity ball?"

The letters she had received from Luetgert were again introduced into evidence. As Gary looked over the letters, he said, "Well, they are pretty. Luetgert was an ardent lover if he wrote these things. Some great bard has said that love is blind, and after this I should not be surprised if the bard was right." As the letters were read aloud, Luetgert shifted nervously in his chair. He said to William Charles, "All I'm afraid of is that these men might think I am crazy to rave over this woman. I wrote those letters just to jolly her up and get back the money I had loaned her."

Afterward, however, Luetgert enjoyed himself as his lawyers cross-examined Feld, again posing questions he suggested. She had difficulty following the interrogation because of her unfamiliarity with English.

"What did you call Mr. Luetgert?"

"I never called him in my life. He spoke to me first," she said.

"In what manner did you address him?" Judge Gary explained.

"He wrote me a whole lot of letters, and I only sent him one. Do you want me to read it?"

The judge was exasperated, and Harmon said, "Did you ever call Mr. Luetgert 'my tootsey-wootsey,' 'my only Louis,' 'joy of my heart,' 'deary,' 'chickie,' 'sugar plum' or 'gallant cavalier'?"

"He was only 'Luetgert' to me; that was all."

When Feld and the young female stenographer began giggling at the questions, Gary sternly said, "If you cannot be quiet . . . , I shall take measure to stop that unseemly exhibition."

Speaking with a dignified air, Feld replied, "It is a shame that they ask me so many things that are not so. He is such a foolish man, anyhow." She pointed to Harmon.

Harmon then asked her, "Did you ever kiss Mr. Luetgert?"

Feld looked at Gary, hoping he wouldn't make her answer the question, but he declined to interfere. Finally, she said, "No, I wouldn't do that."

"Did he ever kiss you?"

The only answer she gave was a toss of the head. Feld grew angry as the questioning went on. She asked several times for a German interpreter. At one point, she said, "I can't understand that question; I wish I got a man here," apparently meaning an interpreter.

"Want another man, no doubt," Harmon said.

Feld jumped up in her chair and shouted, "Take that word back! Don't insult me here!"

The judge ordered Harmon to stop insulting the witness and threatened to turn the examination over to one of Harmon's assistants. But Harmon kept up his sharp questions, prompting Feld to call him and Luetgert liars. She denied that Inspector Schaack had ever used terms of affection for her, that Schaack had used her as a spy during the Haymarket case, or that Schaack had asked her to go on a trip to Colorado with him.

The prosecutors called a new witness, Frank Hangel, who said he had talked with Luetgert in the Tosch saloon in January 1897. "I was reading in a newspaper a story about a woman who committed suicide because she was jealous of her husband," Hangel said. "He asked me what I thought I would do if I were a married man and could not live happily with the woman. I said I would get a divorce, or, if I could not do that, I would simply pack up and get out. He said they [women] were all beasts, and if he had a woman like that, he would take and throw her where there would not be enough left for the sun to shine on, and he kind of shook his fist, so." Hangel demonstrated the gesture Luetgert had made, pretending to strangle a person with both hands. Hangel continued: "He said, 'I have the same troubles, but I will soon get rid of them. It will not last much longer.' I could not tell what he meant."

Hangel said Luetgert left the saloon but returned some time later, sat down at his table, and said, "Frank, I always like you, and I know you are a close-mouthed fellow. You know how to keep it to yourself when you hear something."

According to Hangel, in February 1897 Luetgert offered to pay him a large sum of money for an unspecified job. He said Luetgert had told him, "You are a bright young fellow, and I cannot see why you want to be working always in a factory. A man like you ought to be able to make more on the outside."

Hangel said he had responded that he had never had a chance for a better job. He testified that Luetgert came closer and nudged him, saying, "How would you like to make a thousand or a couple of thousand dollars and go abroad until things had blown over and then come back and get a nice job?" Hangel said he broke away from Luetgert without answering his offer, using the excuse that he had to go eat supper. He left Chicago soon afterward, fearing he would get mixed up in some trouble with Luetgert.

When Harmon cross-examined Hangel, he focused much of his questioning on an illustration of the emperor of Germany that had appeared in the newspaper Hangel was reading at the time of his conversation with Luetgert in the Tosch saloon. Harmon asked whether the emperor had been shown wearing boots, spurs, a helmet, a full fighting rig, and epaulets and whether he had been mounted on a horse or standing alongside his steed.

Harmon had originally agreed to let Riese question scientific witnesses, but Harmon now insisted he should have that duty. When Riese protested, Harmon threatened to withdraw from the case. Riese retorted, "You know as much about cross-examining an expert as a blacksmith. It is a cruel and discreditable thing to desert a client because you cannot have your own way. I am not a quitter. I shall leave the matter to Mr. Luetgert."

Accompanied by Luetgert and his son Arnold, the attorneys stormed off into the judge's private room to work out their differences. "I am managing this case and if I don't have my way I'll get out," Harmon said.

"But it was understood that I was to have charge of the experts," Riese said. "I would not have entered the case had not this concession been made by Mr. Luetgert."

"That is no matter," Harmon said. "You cannot frighten me in that way. I will not permit this important phase of the case to go into your hands."

"He examined [the anatomist Robert A.] Howe yesterday," Luetgert interjected, "and I think he did admirably."

"I have declared myself in this matter," Harmon said. "Either I have my way or I go."

"Well, then, if you are so made up about it, you had better go," Arnold Luetgert said. Harmon then rushed off into the dressing room next to the judge's chambers and put on his overcoat. Grabbing his hat, he made to leave.

"That's a nice way to leave a man with the shadows of the gallows about him," Riese said. "No matter in what straits my client was, I would not abandon him to satisfy my own selfish designs." Tears began to well up in Luetgert's eyes, and then Riese said, "Harmon, I waive a point. What Luetgert says should be final. If he wants you to go ahead with the cross-examination in spite of the promises made me, why, I will not desert him." Luetgert told Harmon he could handle the questioning if he wanted, and then they all went back into the courtroom.

After that, Riese was allowed to question some witnesses, but Harmon still handled most of the cross-examination. At one point Gary complained impatiently that Harmon was wasting time with his questions. Harmon said he took exception to "the court's unfriendly criticism."

"Go on, go on," Gary cried. "Every interruption only leads to a waste of time."

"I am compelled to put Your Honor's words down," Harmon said, bringing the proceedings to a halt so he could write down in longhand what Gary had said.

A short time later Gary interrupted another one of Harmon's questions, saying, "That question is not competent."

"I'd like to know why?" Harmon shouted, jumping up and flourishing his pad.

The judge quietly replied, "Go and read the books."

The scientific testimony from the first trial was repeated, with one key difference: the prosecutors were now using only four tiny bone fragments. The three largest bones from the first trial were out of the picture. It was reported that officials may have lost those bones, but Deneen said he had decided against using them because they were the most hotly disputed exhibits during the first trial. According to another report, a jawbone that police found in the factory had been one of the most promising pieces of evidence. The chemistry teacher Delafontaine had lost it even before the first trial, however. "The famous expert . . . like many deep students has an ingredient of absent-mindedness mixed with his genius," the *Chicago Journal* remarked.

Dorsey came back to court and testified in even stronger terms than before that the fragments found in the Luetgert vat were human bones. Harmon took the four tiny pieces and placed them on a quarter. "Dr. Dorsey, here you see these four small bones within the periphery of this twenty-five-cent piece, American money. Tell me what characteristics you find in them that enable you to pronounce them the bones of a small woman?"

McEwen objected to the question, calling it "display and claptrap."

"What are you doing there?" Gary asked, ordering Harmon to put the evidence back into its receptacles.

The word around the courthouse was that the jurors were growing impatient with Harmon's antics.

41 The Ghouls

DUNNING, Cook County's insane asylum and poorhouse, was often the site of scandals. Cadavers were periodically stolen from its morgue building, which housed the dead before they were buried in the potter's field or claimed by relatives. In 1898 the Chicago newspapers linked the latest Dunning scandal to the Luetgert case.

In December two men—a drayman, John Ludes, and a night watchman, Henry Ulrich—confessed that the previous October they had stolen four corpses from Dunning, which stood on Chicago's far northwestern edge. Ulrich said two doctors had paid him for the cadavers, and he had hired Ludes to drive the bodies out of Dunning under the dark of night. Ulrich and Ludes had then looked on, pale-faced, as the doctors emptied jugs of embalming fluid into the arteries of the bodies at a remote cabin.

The Chicago Police Department fired Officer William Stine on the charge that he had helped to organize the body-snatching scheme, an accusation Stine denied. Authorities also called for the extradition of Dr. William Smith, the professor who had taken possession of the bodies, who was back in his home state of Missouri with the stolen goods.

In mid-December an inmate of the Dunning infirmary named Adolph Dinkledge wrote a letter to Lawrence Harmon, saying he had important information related to the Luetgert case. Harmon sent Andrew McGarry, a detective working for the defense, to see Dinkledge, who claimed to be a former detective and newspaperman. McGarry came back with a startling tale: Dinkledge and two other Dunning inmates said they had seen Ulrich and a Chicago police officer dissolving a corpse in the Dunning laundry building and fishing out some bone fragments back in May 1897, just a couple of days before police had arrested Luetgert. Dinkledge speculated that these bones might have been planted at the Luetgert factory as false evidence.

On New Year's Day 1898 reporters for the *Chronicle* and *Inter Ocean* got wind of the story and interviewed Dinkledge and Adolph Boelsteff, an old baker who had been in the Dunning infirmary since a bread-kneading machine had crushed his hand two years before. The *Chronicle* reported that the two men were reluctant to talk to the press, fearing retribution from both Ulrich and the county authorities who operated Dunning. "Don't let this be printed," Dinkledge said. "Ulrich might do me harm. Then I believe we would be thrown out of the poorhouse in the dead of winter if the authorities knew we dared to tell secrets, even if we are weak invalids. . . . Our terror is real."

The men did agree to tell their tale, however, sitting with the reporter in a small room distant from the institution's main building. They were nervous as they spoke, and when Superintendent Albert Lange passed by outside at one point, Dinkledge drew back from the window in fright.

Boelsteff's job was to watch the laundry building, which was isolated, standing a couple of hundred feet from the morgue and not far from the potter's field. He said he was in a small side room of the building on May 14. The next room contained two metal tanks, five feet high, six feet long, and four feet wide, where clothes were boiled. Authorities also occasionally used the vats for making soft soap.

"I was taking a rest in one of the rooms of the laundry about nine or ten o'clock in the evening some time after the middle of last May," he said. "Hank Ulrich came into the laundry and began working around the tubs used for boiling the washing. . . . He was the kind of a man I didn't care to have any trouble with. He stood up on the step in front of the boiler and stirred the stuff he was boiling with a rake. I watched him for a while and then went out of the building."

The next day Boelsteff talked with John Knauss, a patient in the infirmary, who said he had seen Ulrich walking into the laundry around nine o'clock the night before with something resembling a human body. They also recalled seeing Ulrich and another person drive up in a wagon and enter the laundry with a barrel that Boelsteff believed was full of concentrated lye.

"The next night I was in the same place in the laundry and saw Ulrich working around the boiler again," Boelsteff said. "There was another man with him. He was rather tall and slender and wore a drooping mustache. They took their coats off, as it was rather warm standing over the vat. I saw a large star on the man's vest, such as the police wear. They fished around in the vat with a rake and took out what looked to me to be pieces of bones. These they put in a small box and the other man took them away with him.

"Knauss and I wondered what Ulrich was doing this for, and to make sure that he had boiled up a body, we went over to the potter's field and found that a grave had been opened in a two-week-old trench. We then felt confident that he had taken the body out of there to boil it in the vat. We thought a good deal about the matter because there was so much in the papers about the Luetgert case. We knew that Ulrich would make it hot for us if we said anything about it, so we kept the matter secret.

"After Ulrich was arrested for robbing the morgue, we decided to tell what we knew. We talked to Dinkledge about the matter and he finally wrote to Luetgert's lawyers. We don't know who the officer was who got the pieces of bones from Ulrich or what he did with them. We have been expecting to go to the trial and see if we would recognize the man there."

Dinkledge conceded the only evidence linking Ulrich with the bones used in the Luetgert trial was circumstantial. "It may be the silly notion of an old man, but I could not help figuring out—we read the newspapers here, most of us—that perhaps no human bones were to be found in the sausage factory and that some zealous detective got Ulrich to do this job. The police formed a determined theory that Mrs. Luetgert was killed and her body dissolved. Maybe the officer who got the bones and planted them in the factory thought he was helping justice."

After interviewing Dinkledge and Boelsteff, the *Chronicle* paid a visit to Ulrich, who had been released from jail on bond, at his home in the Irving Park neighborhood on Chicago's Northwest Side. Initially he wouldn't speak without being paid, but he was in a talkative mood, bragging how his politically connected friends had "fixed" it so he wouldn't be convicted. Then he added, "However, it may be I am just being jollied along lest I should tell more and implicate some of the active politicians who are selling corpses every day and shipping them away in coffee sacks."

"But what do you know about the bones found in the Luetgert vat?" the reporter asked.

"Oh, that is a long story. I have known Luetgert and Inspector Schaack

Lawrence Harmon, who took over as the defense attorney for Luetgert's second trial. (*Chicago Tribune,* Nov. 29, 1897)

Judge Joseph E. Gary, who presided over the second Luetgert trial. (Chicago Historical Society, ICHi-18750; photo by Mosher's Historical National Photographic Art Gallery)

Luetgert testifying at his second trial. (*Chicago Tribune*, Jan. 22, 1898)

Smiles at Judge Garys Joke.

He Chews a Pencil to Clear Away Mental Cobwebs

Henry Ulrich, who was charged in the Dunning body-snatching scheme, which some newspapers connected to the Luetgert case. (*Chicago Chronicle,* Jan. 1, 1898)

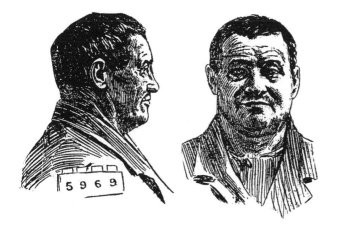

A newspaper drawing based on the mug shot taken of Luetgert during his last year in prison. (*Chicago Inter Ocean*, July 28, 1899)

A crowd surrounding the burial plot of Adolph Louis Luetgert at Waldheim Cemetery. (*Chicago Record*, July 31, 1899)

for many years. If Mrs. Luetgert was boiled in that vat in the manner charged, her hair ought to have been found there. It seems to have been taken for granted that the rings could not be got off Mrs. Luetgert's finger, though about the only testimony on that point is the babble of her little son. We all know that our mothers' stock excuse for refusing to give up their rings to us for playthings in our babyhood days was that the golden circlets could not be got off the finger—just what Mrs. Luetgert told her little son . . .

"While over in the jail, I saw Luetgert one morning in the little room that is used for church purposes," Ulrich continued. "I felt sorry he was in such a hole. I make no pretensions to religion. But I felt ashamed in that instant. I would have liked to put a bee in his ear. But it was impossible. All the conversation I was able to have with him was a 'howdy' from a distance. I don't know that he knew why I was locked up. But knowing as I did that I am myself the victim of conspirators who are trying to make me a scapegoat for the purpose of saving big men, I was able to readily realize the position of Luetgert—a victim of a still darker and deeper conspiracy."

"Do you know how the bones came to be in the vat?"

"Perhaps I do."

"Are they Mrs. Luetgert's bones?"

"Well, I have said I am not talking on that matter."

"You believe they are not her bones?"

"Believe! I know it," Ulrich said, acting as if he had accidentally allowed the answer to slip out. "Just think for a minute of the chances for planting those bones and rings in that vat. A stretch of two weeks between the date of Mrs. Luetgert's disappearance and the finding of the rings! And most of that time the police had Luetgert under suspicion. For the three or four days after the night of May 1—the time of Mrs. Luetgert's disappearance—Inspector Schaack's detectives were unaware that there was a disappearance. Still, this smart man Luetgert, then unmolested, did not remove those bits of evidence from the vat. Why? Because the evidence was not yet there. One would think that's the common-sense view, as Luetgert is no fool."

"Did any bones come into the hands of the police from you?"

"Now, I am not looking for any more trouble with grand juries," Ulrich replied sullenly.

"Did you have anything to do with the work of boiling a body or bodies at Dunning or elsewhere last May?"

After thinking of a few seconds, Ulrich said, "What is there in it for me if I tell?"

The reporter said there was "nothing in it" and then asked, "Did you supply Inspector Schaack's police or the inspector himself or any of his agents or go-betweens with any human bones at any time?"

"I am not talking on that matter," Ulrich said. After a long pause, he continued, "Inspector Schaack's men are going about here making threats of trouble. Now, I don't want any more trouble of any kind. But I will not be bullied or frightened. While some of the gang are making those threats, others are scurrying around getting lawyers for me and preparing my defense. But I would rather pay my own lawyer. Though my friends say I cannot be convicted, as I know nothing of the plans to break down the morgue doors and steal the sheets with the four bodies, still I am suspicious, for I believe the gang would rather see me in Joliet than at liberty. They are afraid of me. That's the truth, and they know why they are afraid."

"Who can throw any light on the connection between the bones found in the Luetgert vat and those taken from Dunning—if any such connection exists?"

"Go to ex-Patrol Sergeant Stine of the Irving Park police. He knows," Ulrich said, turning on his heel.

When approached by an *Inter Ocean* reporter on the same day, Ulrich at first denied any connection with the supposed laundry-vat plot but then he blurted out, "It's true, but I can't tell you anything more about it. Stine was in on the deal."

Stine told the *Inter Ocean* he had nothing to do with the plot. "I wasn't in on *that* job with Ulrich," he said, with a strong and suggestive emphasis.

When the *Chronicle* interviewed Stine, he wouldn't positively deny that such a plot had taken place. "Well, I don't know anything about that deal of Ulrich's," he said.

"Then there was such a deal?"

"Oh, I don't know that there was."

"Ulrich intimates you aided in procuring bones from Dunning for Inspector Schaack."

"I have worked under Inspector Schaack but have seldom spoken to him," Stine said.

"Did you have anything to do with any plans for getting bones or a body from Dunning last May for Inspector Schaack, or others?"

"You cannot get me to answer such questions," Stine said. But then he went on to say he was puzzled by his firing and why his name had been connected to the Luetgert case. "However, I am glad that those so-called Dunning scandals are being agitated afresh. . . . By and by perhaps some real culprits will be uncovered. I am convinced there are cleverer heads than Ulrich's plotting those so-called disclosures."

The *Chronicle* and *Inter Ocean* ran their stories about the alleged Dunning-Luetgert connection on January 2, under banner headlines such as "Luetgert May Be a Plot Victim." Harmon said the evidence was strong, but he feared the premature publication of the story would ruin his chances of getting the real facts, because some of the witnesses would be reluctant to talk.

Police, prosecutors, and county officials called the story ridiculous and silly. "Dramatically interesting and absolutely false," Deneen said. "I regard the story as a piece of fiction and I can hardly believe it was concocted with the serious intention of bringing it into the trial. These men are either romancers or they have been coached by some friend of Luetgert to tell this stuff."

Dunning officials said hogs unfit for human consumption were sometimes thrown into the laundry vat, bones and all, to make soft soap. The bones would be raked out afterward. Dunning's assistant superintendent, M. T. Campbell, said the steam heat for the laundry was shut off each day at 4 P.M. and the building was locked up at night, so Boelsteff's tale about Ulrich and the police officer raking out bones was highly unlikely.

"A lot of these paupers have a habit of writing letters on all kinds of subjects to all sorts of people," Campbell said. "They are cranks, and many are really harmless, insane patients. . . . The story is a baseless fabrication."

Dr. J. T. Johnson, the Dunning physician, said, "The inmates of the poorhouse are just as thoroughly in touch with the events of the day as persons who live outside of these walls. They have the daily papers, and, as many are men of weakened mentality, all sorts of vagaries are built upon a slender basis of fact."

After the stories were published, Ulrich told authorities there was no truth in them. He also threatened to sue the papers for libel. Dinkledge and Boelsteff denied what they had previously said, claiming they had thought they were speaking with agents for Luetgert's defense team rather than newspaper reporters.

Nevertheless, McGarry, Luetgert's detective, insisted that the story was true and that even more evidence would come to light connecting the laundry vat and the bones in the Luetgert trial. He said Dinkledge and Boelsteff had stopped talking only because they had been scared by the publication of the news stories.

"Dinkledge is not a fool by any means, and the fact that he and Boelsteff have been forced to take refuge in the poorhouse is no reason why their testimony should be disregarded," he said.

Harmon said he planned to call the Dunning witnesses to testify, but he accused county authorities of intimidating them. "Ulrich was out there today," he said one day at the courthouse, "and was accompanied by several commissioners, who saw the people we have thought of using as witnesses and warned them that their positions depended on their silence. I am afraid our plans may be seriously interfered with."

The Luetgert defense never called the Dunning witnesses into court, but when Inspector Schaack testified, Harmon threw out a series of suggestions that the police had used false evidence. Schaack was amused as he rejected Harmon's accusation that the police had dug up the body of a great Dane on the factory grounds and sent the bones first to a police station and then to the Rush Medical College for examination.

"Do you remember going to a Milwaukee Avenue dentist with a woman and waiting while she had a tooth pulled, sometime in May?" Harmon asked.

"There ain't such a thing true," Schaack said excitedly, lapsing into his German accent.

"Do you remember going there with a lady and following her into the operating room?"

"No," he thundered.

Harmon then asked Schaack if he knew Bernard Cigrand, the dentist at the office on Milwaukee Avenue.

"No, but I know the fake you are working on," Schaack replied, and even the jurors laughed. Schaack opened his mouth wide and defied anyone to find evidences of a dentist's work there.

"I do not mean your own teeth were doctored," Harmon said, "but did you not last summer at a dentist's office procure some false teeth for use in this case?"

"No."

Harmon asked Schaack if he knew that reporters had placed bones in the South Side rooming house of the infamous serial killer Herman Mudgett, known as Dr. Henry Holmes, for the purpose of creating sensations. Schaack said he didn't know anything about it. Judge Gary ordered that the question and answer be stricken from the record.

After Harmon had finished his interrogation, McEwen mockingly told a reporter, "Schaack had an awful hard time to get bones and went about it in a very peculiar way. He needed bones to put in the vat and had to go all the way to Dunning to get them and then came away with a few little pieces. He needed a false tooth and made the mistake of having a natural tooth drawn from a woman."

After Schaack testified, his doctor suggested he should take a couple of days off from attending the trial. "I'm afraid I will go nutty if I have to stick this out from day to day," Schaack said when he returned from his respite. "If I feel so tough, those jurors must be in a terrible condition. They ought to have a vaudeville performance at the hotel."

On January 9 the *Chicago Times-Herald* published Dr. Smith's own account of the body thefts at Dunning. He admitted taking the bodies in much the manner Ulrich and Ludes had described, but he claimed he hadn't realized Ulrich lacked the authority to sell him the corpses.

Smith said Ulrich had offered to procure a living patient. "It is a man or a woman—blamed if I know what to call it—which has been on exhibition in the city museums as the 'bear man,'" Ulrich had said, according to Smith. "It went daffy over a Circassian beauty or a snake charmer, I forget which, is a real fancy freak, with six fingers on each hand, and can walk on all fours. If you'll take it you can have it for $50."

Smith said he had replied that he wanted cadavers, not living inmates. Ulrich supposedly responded, "That's all right, doc. . . . He's in the 'killer ward' and they'd just think he'd wandered off—they're always doing that, you know."

After the *Times-Herald* printed Smith's account, Cook County Board president Daniel Healy and Dunning superintendent Lange denied the existence of a "killer ward," saying they had never heard the phrase used even jokingly.

County officials never got the chance to bring Smith into court. Missouri's governor refused to extradite him, saying the charge of stealing sheets was trivial. Ulrich and Ludes were found guilty on that charge and sent to jail.

Meanwhile Healy posted a notice at several places in Dunning, warning inmates and employees to stop talking to the press. He said their gossip to reporters had created scandals that later proved groundless. "Hereafter press bureaus disbursing of kitchen gossip and below-stairs politics will not be tolerated," the notice read. "Discipline must be maintained."

Nothing further came of the story that the police had used bones from Dunning as Luetgert evidence. The county told one of the men behind that tale, Adolph Dinkledge, that he was no longer welcome at the poorhouse.

"When a man is being fed, clothed and housed by the county, he has no business to spread . . . scandalous things that can result from nothing but a diseased imagination," Healy said.

42 Denials

ON JANUARY 21, 1898, as the defense was presenting its case, the courtroom was more crowded than usual. The rumor was that Luetgert might finally testify. At about 11:30 Luetgert's lawyers asked Judge Gary for a recess until the afternoon. Kehoe explained that several witnesses the defense had subpoenaed could not make it court before then.

"Your Honor, had we not better take an adjournment until two o'clock?" he said, with some nervousness in his voice.

"No, I guess not," Gary replied laconically, looking up at the big dial over the door and reading the time. "No, go on with something else."

A rustle ran through the court. Luetgert straightened himself in his chair and looked defiantly at Deneen and McEwen. McEwen smiled sardonically under his drooping mustache. The two prosecutors said a few words to each other. The *Tribune* reporter wrote that they "regarded Luetgert much as the hound does his prey just before he seizes it." Harmon bent over some papers and then, without lifting his head, called out in his most resonant voice, "Adolph Louis Luetgert! Take the stand."

Spectators stood and craned their necks, and the sketch artists began drawing rapidly. The *Tribune*, always quick to add a sardonic comment to its trial coverage, noted: "The unidentified riffraff in the rear of the room, unkempt and unwashed, leaned forward and gaped, open-mouthed. Surveying them, it was hard to believe in the survival of the fittest." The news that Luetgert was testifying spread to the outer corridor, and the courtroom, which had begun to empty, quickly filled with eager faces.

"This bustle must cease," Gary said sternly. "There must be absolute silence. There must be no one standing and no moving about. The bailiffs will see that the room is cleared of all persons not seated, and that no one not directly connected with the case is allowed to enter the room."

Luetgert sprang to his feet and walked jauntily to the witness stand. His son Louis, who had testified earlier in the day, came back into the room. He got up, as if to follow his father, but William Charles sat the boy down on his knee. Unlike the other witnesses, Luetgert did not take the oath at the base of the witness stand. Instead he climbed on the platform and raised his right hand so high that it came close to touching the incandescent bulbs of the chandelier overhead. Knoch, the court clerk, recited the words of the oath slowly. Luetgert bowed his head solemnly and let his "I do" ring out loudly, and then he sat down in the capacious armchair. He surveyed all twelve faces in the jury box and then calmly looked at Gary. Luetgert inhaled deeply and unbuttoned his vest. A big batch of papers stuck out of the upper side coat pocket of his short gray cutaway suit. Sticking his thumbs under his suspenders, he stated his name. Those who had never heard him speak before were surprised to find his voice less deep than they had expected; it was more of a high tenor.

Responding to questions from Harmon, Luetgert told his life story, from his schooling in Westphalia to his rise in the sausage industry. The jury leaned forward to catch every word. Luetgert weighed each question carefully before answering, often in a grave and impressive manner. He frequently gestured as he spoke. Luetgert remained calm until Harmon asked him about his first wife's death. The *Tribune* noted that Harmon's quavering voice sunk into the "minor chords," as if he were attempting to provoke an emotional response. Luetgert sat silent for a moment, looking down. Then he reached back into his coattail pocket for his handkerchief. He wiped his right eye and then his left. Tears were glistening in his eyes and gathering on his cheeks. He dabbed the moisture from the corners of his mouth, where it had collected in his bristly mustache. "Take your time, Mr. Luetgert," Harmon said, almost whispering. Another minute passed while Luetgert continued to wipe his eyes. Many spectators seemed amazed at Luetgert's sudden outburst of convulsive sobbing. Deneen stopped rocking his chair gently back and forth and an expression described by the *Tribune* as a "semi-saturnine smile" came over his face. McEwen smiled as well, looking coldly cynical. Luetgert, his shoulders shaking, covered his face with his hands.

"Your Honor, will you not adjourn now?" Harmon asked Gary in a pleading tone.

Gary bluntly replied, "No, go on."

Some of the reporters covering the trial believed Luetgert had faked his tears. The *Tribune* speculated that his sobs were prompted not just by his first wife's death but also by all the troubles that had been piling up in his life for the past year. Although Luetgert put on a firm front, inside "there was seething the inward volcano of these pent-up emotions," the newspaper wrote.

Luetgert finally recovered sufficiently to continue, and Harmon asked him more questions about his life and his methods of manufacturing sausage. After some time Harmon began prompting Luetgert to respond to the allegations witnesses had made about his behavior toward Louise. He denied ever waving a gun at her. "Never in my life have I made a threat against my wife or any soul on earth with a revolver, nobody on earth," he said.

Luetgert described how his business had declined and how he had been tricked by Davey. Harmon asked him how his wife had responded to the news of his financial difficulties. Luetgert first looked down and then glanced up, bit his lip, and swallowed. He leaned back in his seat, and drummed audibly with his pencil. Finally he reached back for his pocket handkerchief and began crying. Gary, who had been watching Luetgert closely, adjourned court for the day. Luetgert looked relieved.

The following day Luetgert returned to the stand and spent the first hour describing his wife's illness and her strange behavior in the months leading up to her disappearance. "Her body health was all right, but her mind health was not all right," he said. "Her general condition was not good. . . . She had all kinds of medicine in the house. After the failure of the Davey plan, she became worse and worried more than ever. I quieted her down and told her things would come out all right."

The *Chronicle* noted Luetgert spoke of Louise without the same tenderness he had shown when telling of his first wife's death. "He seemed to regard her as a party to the conspiracy to place him on the gallows," the newspaper reported.

Luetgert described his own health problems, which resulted from over-work. He explained that his business had required him to get up as many as four times a night to check on the meat stored in the icehouses or to see whether his night employees had fallen asleep on the job or gotten drunk. That was why it became necessary for him to sleep in the office, he said.

He said he was a victim of dyspepsia and overwork and he required the frequent attendance of a physician. In the last few years, he said, he had been "broke down" from working too much. He said he had originally fallen sick during 1894. The family physician had ordered him to stay in his factory office while he recovered, Luetgert said. Since then, he had been taking herbal tea and Hunyadi water each night. Luetgert said the doctor had told him, "I couldn't help you. Any physician couldn't help you, on account of your work is so unregular, therefore your health cannot be restored except you go out of business entirely."

When he was lying sick in the office, his wife, Mrs. Feld, and Mary Siemering would come out to check on him, he testified. But he insisted his wife was the only one who had ever stayed there by his bedside for an entire night.

Luetgert said he had purchased a barrel of potash in March so he could make some soft soap. He said he had learned to make soap while working in a tannery years before. "It was my intention to get the factory scrubbed from top to bottom, so I could sell it," he said. "It was at the suggestion of Wil-liam Charles that I decided to make the soap, because he told me I could make better soft soap than I could buy."

Luetgert largely corroborated his employees' accounts of breaking up the potash in the vat.

Finally, Harmon began asking Luetgert about the events of May 1, 1897. Luetgert said he had taken breakfast alone before going out to the stable and telling a teamster to move four barrels—filled with tallow, grease, discarded mutton stew, and hams—from the icehouse to the factory basement.

Luetgert said he had gone downtown in his buggy that afternoon to con-sult with his attorney, Adams Goodrich, about settling debts. He returned home in the afternoon, spent some time in his office, and then went home for supper with his wife, his children, and Mary Siemering.

"Louis was anxious to go to the circus and asked for ten cents," he said. "Mama declared we did not have any more money and Louis would have to stay in the house. I felt in my pocket and got the coin. I thought the little fellow ought not to be denied an evening's entertainment, though our circumstances were not encouraging."

Harmon asked Luetgert what he and his wife had talked about after Louis had skipped down the front steps and off toward the circus. "That is a matter I don't care to discuss," Luetgert said, "unless the court commands me to do so."

"You are testifying for yourself," Harmon said, "and the court is not going to force you to tell anything that you do not volunteer to tell as a witness. I tell you as your counsel, openly, candidly and above-board, that I wish you to state what was said at that meal, every word of it."

Luetgert went on with his story, explaining that Louise had asked him about their financial troubles. She was convinced they were going to lose everything, despite Luetgert's reassurances. He testified she had said, "Is this then what you get for all your hard work since in this country?"

"I told her that I could do any kind of work, no matter how it would be, thick or thin, and dirty or clean," Luetgert said, but Louise had expressed fear that people would laugh at her if he were forced to take a lowly job. "I told her, 'Let them laugh. After I get to work, no matter what it is, they cannot take anything away from me by laughing. It is not necessary to stay in Chicago. We can go somewheres.'

"Well, she says, 'I wouldn't care at all, no matter where it is, but I wouldn't stay in Chicago and have people pointing fingers at me.'

"'Nonsense,' I says, 'let them laugh.'

"She says, 'I won't stand that no matter how it comes, if it should come.' She says, 'I won't be with it.'

"I told her, 'You stay right with me. I have been pulling the wagon so far, and I will pull it further, don't you bother yourself.'

"She says, 'The way it stands you have been working now for thirty years in this country, working like a slave day and night.' . . . Louise said she was sorry little Elmer was not laid below the grass at Waldheim Cemetery, where other of her children had been placed," Luetgert testified.

The jurors looked horrified at the statement. Luetgert, almost overcome with emotion, paused and looked out the wide windows of the court at the fast-falling snow outside. For a moment he seemed buried in deep reflection.

Luetgert continued his story, explaining that after supper on May 1 he had gone to the saloon across the street for a cigar and a glass of ice punch. He saw William Charles there, and they discussed Luetgert's plans to make the soap and clean up the factory for a prospective buyer. The two of them went over to the factory and Luetgert turned on the steam to begin the vat boiling, he said. After that, Bialk had come to him with the keys for the storefront portion of the factory, which he had just closed for the night. Luetgert sent Bialk to the drugstore to buy some celery cola. While he waited for Bialk to return, Luetgert and Charles went to Wetsig's saloon. When Luetgert returned to the factory office alone a short time later, he found the bottle that Bialk had purchased at the drugstore. "He brought that bottle during the time I was with Mr. Charles across the street," Luetgert said.

Luetgert said he took the medicine but could not find any tea. Mary usually brought some to his office, but he recalled that she had strained her leg and probably had been unable to deliver the tea. He went back to the house.

"My wife was sitting in the kitchen," he said. "She was sitting with her back against the east wall. On the east wall there was in one corner a sink, and right next to the sink . . . there was a gaslight. . . . She was reading a paper . . . under the gaslight near the stove."

Luetgert said he went into the basement pantry and got some tea, and then went back upstairs and into the bathroom. As he returned to the kitchen, he saw his son Louis.

"My wife was sitting there in the same place and Louis came from the circus," Luetgert testified. "He started talking about the circus and of this and that and I told him, 'You talk circus tomorrow. You go up to bed. You have to go to Sunday school tomorrow and get up in time.' Louis said, 'Good night,' and I went downstairs."

"As you started to go down the stairs, where was your wife, Louise Luetgert?"

"She was sitting in the kitchen."

"As you turned so you could see her no more, was she still there as long as you could tell?"

"She was there as long as I could see, reading the newspaper."

"Have you ever seen her since?"

"No, sir."

Luetgert said he left the house by a side door and returned to the factory. "After I had prepared my tea, I tried to drink it, and took the Hunyadi water bottle and found there was only about a thimbleful in it," he said. "I took the bottle then and went to the boiler room and gave it to the watchman and told him, 'Frank, you get me a bottle like this here. It seems kind of late, but if you hurry you will find the store open.' He says to me, 'It is kind of late. I lose my steam if I go.' I said, 'Never mind the steam. I take care of the steam, and so you hurry up and you will find the store open.' And he went away. I gave him a dollar and I took care of the steam during the time he was gone. It didn't take very long. I asked him if the store was open. He said, 'Just ready to close up.' And so he give me the bottle and I went to the office and he went with his fires."

Luetgert said Bialk had brought him the wrong brand of mineral water; he already had plenty of that sort inside his own store. It wasn't the kind with diamond on the bottle, which is what Luetgert had wanted.

"I had my tea, and after I had my tea, I went in the basement and set the valve so that the soap would just keep on bubbling," Luetgert said.

"Were you the only person down in that basement at that time of this occasion?"

"Yes, sir."

"The only human being there that you know of?"

"Yes, sir."

"Dead or alive?"

"Dead or alive."

Luetgert said he had gone to sleep in his office after setting the valve. On waking up the next morning, he had returned to the basement and checked on the soap. It wasn't boiling any longer, he said, and the steam pipes were cold and full of water. Luetgert opened a valve and let the water run out of the pipe.

"After the water was out, I turned on the steam again and I seen that it made a kind of noise and I shut it off again, examined the contents in the vat, and to my judgment I thought everything was to my satisfaction, so I stirred up the soap with the shovel," Luetgert said. "There was a stick there about, say, four or five feet long. Not a stick, but a fenceboard we had been using to stir up the liquid. I took this board and I found the matter, to my judgment, that it was rather rich, so I left it that way and went upstairs, and it didn't take very long until Mr. Charles, he rapped at the window and I let him into the office and I told him, 'Say, Charles, the soap is done now.'

"He says, 'How well?'

"'To my judgment it is all right,' I says. 'I want to show it to you.'

"So I showed him it and he kind of laughed at it and he said, 'That is not soap. You don't know anything about soap.' He said, 'It wants more water.'

"I said, 'Yes, I think so myself, but it is rather rich. The richer it is, the more water it can use.' So I turned on the water and we went upstairs."

Charles left, and Luetgert went over to his house at six o'clock to have breakfast, he said. Mary was the only other one at the breakfast table that morning. He said he asked Mary where his wife was, and she replied that she didn't know.

When Luetgert had dinner around noon that day with Mary and his two boys, he told Mary that Louise was nowhere in the house or the factory.

"Had you and your wife ever had any cross or angry words during the two or three years or more, or for nine or ten years preceding May 1, 1897?" Harmon asked.

"Once in a while we had some," Luetgert replied. "Sometimes there was matters she would say that I didn't like, but we changed our minds and spoke it over and then we were through with it, and then we didn't have it."

Luetgert said he had ordered his employees to clean up the basement on May 3, but he denied telling Smokehouse Frank to throw the slime and debris out into yard or offering him a lifetime job if he promised not to say anything.

Harmon finally got around to asking Luetgert about the charges against him in the indictment. Gradually raising his voice, Harmon began to enumerate all the various ways in which the grand jury had accused Luetgert of killing his wife.

Judge Gary interrupted, "Don't answer that question. I'll have no more of this nonsensical method of conducting a case. If he didn't kill her at all, that's the end of it. You may frame your question that way or not at all." Harmon took exception to the ruling and demanded that Gary repeat his words, so that Harmon could get them down in longhand. Gary said the words again with emphasis.

Harmon then asked Luetgert, "I will ask you to state to the jury whether or not in any way or manner you killed your wife, Louise Luetgert, on the first day of May or any other time."

"I did not," Luetgert said in a clear, calm voice.

"I will ask you to tell this jury whether or not you ever in your life had any intention or purpose in your mind to kill your wife."

"No, sir. Never."

"I will ask you to state to the jury whether or not you have ever had any intention or purpose to harm your wife in any way by any kind of physical violence?"

"Never in my life."

Harmon repeated the question in several different ways, becoming more melodramatic as he went on. Gary interrupted, saying, "You have been over that. A sonorous voice don't cut any figure as to the evidence in the case."

"I object to the 'sonorous voice,' and I except to the language," Harmon retorted. "I am sorry other gentlemen have not an equally sonorous voice, but I can't help it."

A short time later court adjourned. After a Sunday respite, Luetgert came back for a third day of questioning. He asked the judge to add something to his earlier testimony about the conversation he'd had with Louise the night of May 1. He said he now remembered that Louise had said she wanted to visit her oldest brother, Henry, the one who had disappeared years earlier.

"She mentioned that she intended to go to her brother, and I replied that she didn't know where her brother was," Luetgert said. "So she said she would find him all right."

Luetgert maintained that he still believed Louise was alive. "When do I expect to see my wife?" he said. "Every minute, I hope, today."

Luetgert finished his direct testimony with a string of denials. He denied taking part in either of the conversations that Frank Hangel had recounted. He said he had scarcely said more than five words to Hangel in his entire life. He denied having any of the discussions described by Agatha Tosch, explaining she was drunk most of the time: "She was as full as a fiddle."

Luetgert, who said he had always provided well for his wife and given her whatever money she wanted, said he never had any interest in marrying Christine Feld or Mary Siemering. He also denied having kissed Mary. "I never kissed her or never had any intention of kissing her," he said. "I did all the kissing I wanted at home."

Luetgert claimed that the knife that he gave to Feld on his arrest was one that he used for cutting samples from sausage strings. "It is the sort of knife we need in the sausage business, and I had always had one like it. My salesmen also had knives just like it, as other sausage salesmen and manufacturers had."

Luetgert said Feld visited him in jail following his arrest, bringing him apples. She had told him Schaack was trying to get her to testify falsely against him. "She told me—she gave me a warning to be very careful. 'You don't know how Inspector Schaack does,' she said." He added that she had warned him that Schaack said he had manufactured evidence in other cases, including the O'Malley trial, and he would do it again in Luetgert's case if he had to.

Luetgert recounted the conversation he'd had with Bialk, when Officer Klinger had been hiding under the bed. He acknowledged asking Bialk what the police had been looking for in the factory but denied saying anything incriminating. He claimed to have concluded his talk with Bialk by saying, "Don't you worry at all. We will start [the factory] again in a week or two and you go to work with your son."

Luetgert testified he had spoken with Officer Griebenow in the bowling alley at Tosch's saloon the night before he was arrested. Luetgert said Griebenow had told him the police were after him because of the widespread belief that he was wealthy. According to Luetgert, Griebenow had said, "It seems to me this is a kind of a money scheme. . . . The people, they all think you have lots of money. I seen it myself in the papers you sold your factory for $300,000, and so, therefore, you must have money." Luetgert said Griebenow had told him the police were up to "some tricks," but the officer had declined to be specific for fear of being fired—although he had suggested he would give Luetgert information if he were paid for it.

As Harmon completed his questioning, he asked the defendant about his wife's rings. Luetgert said Louise's wedding ring was a little bit larger than the one the police claimed to have found in the vat. He had been able to put his wife's ring onto his little finger as far down as the first joint, he said, but the wedding ring that prosecutors had entered into evidence wouldn't go onto his finger at all.

◆◆◆

Throughout almost all Luetgert's testimony, Deneen and McEwen had sat silently, only rarely raising an objection. Now Deneen stood up to begin his cross-examination. Luetgert gripped the arms of the witness chair, as if bracing for a shock. He had been told to expect the prosecutors to level sensational accusations at him within the first five minutes of questioning, so he looked relieved when Deneen asked him in an offhand way who first suggested cleaning up the factory. He hesitated a moment and then said, "Why, Mr. Charles, of course." Deneen rapidly asked Luetgert a seemingly endless string of questions about soap making. Luetgert responded calmly, never wavering from the story he had told under questioning by his own attorney.

Deneen asked him what he had cleaned his factory with on other occasions, when he didn't have any homemade soft soap. Luetgert said he had used soda and hot water.

"In place of scrubbing with soap, you threw the soda on the floor and poured hot water on it?" Deneen asked.

"No, sir."

"Or with a bucket of water?"

"Oh, no. You are seven miles behind the moon," Luetgert said, prompting a burst of laughter. As Gary tried to quiet down the audience, he knocked the cornice off his desk.

Luetgert acknowledged that the grocery store in his factory had about 150 boxes of soap or scrubbing soda in stock at the time that he decided to make some of his own soap. He said he didn't remember telling Carl Voelcker that buying soap was cheaper than making it, as Voelcker had testified.

Deneen repeatedly asked Luetgert to describe the stuff he had found in the vat on the morning of May 2. Again and again Luetgert insisted the only words he could find to describe it were "a soapy substance." He said that there had been no solid lumps in it and that he hadn't noticed any bones or grease around the vat that morning. "It may be there were some bones mixed in the slime," Luetgert said. "I didn't make any special search." This answer contradicted the testimony of William Charles, who had said the vat contained tallow, unassimilated grease, lye, and some soap.

As Deneen kept on asking about the slime and Luetgert kept on saying it had been "soapy," Gary interrupted.

"You don't understand what he is getting at," Gary said to Luetgert.

"Oh, yes, I do," Luetgert replied. "What he's getting at, Your Honor, is to catch me." The jurors exchanged curious glances at Luetgert's remark.

Deneen retorted, "And when you can't answer, you say, 'soapy substance.'"

Luetgert said he had gone into the basement four times on the night of May 1. On one of his trips downstairs, he had brought along his fox terrier, Fanny, and another pet named Tige.

"They called my attention to some noise and I listened, and I heard either young mice or young rats squeaking," Luetgert said. "I stopped for a moment. I thought there must be rats or mice. I went in the butcher shop and took the hook, put a piece of candle on it, and took a chair out of the office, and went downstairs and stepped on the chair so I could see between the joists. As I moved that hook with the candle, I saw there a big nest, but I couldn't see what was in the nest. I put the candle back and took the hook and moved the whole nest forward. There I found some young rats. I started and pulled the thing out. I didn't have—"

"That is sufficient," Deneen interrupted. "That is how you happened to get the chair in the basement."

"Yes, sir."

A minute later Deneen asked, "You didn't boil those rats in the vat?"

"I didn't say I boiled the rats," Luetgert replied.

As Luetgert's third day of testimony concluded, Deneen asked, "When did you first know that you were suspected of the crime of murdering your wife?"

"It was published by a brass band and in the newspapers," Luetgert said.

On the fourth day Deneen questioned Luetgert about the allegations that his company had forged its books and falsified its inventory. Luetgert denied the charges or claimed to have forgotten the incidents. Although his memory had seemed fine during direct testimony, Luetgert now repeated the phrase, "I don't recollect," dozens of times. He grew testy but showed only one flash of anger. Answering one of the allegations that he had committed fraud, Luetgert turned square around in his chair till his blazing eyes rested on Fred Mueller, his wife's nephew and a former clerk at the factory. Luetgert shot out his arm to its full length and pointed a quivering finger at Mueller. "It's a lie—an absolute lie, I say—a fabrication by that man Mueller!" The courtroom was silent, so still that hailstones could be heard pattering against the windows.

Deneen then asked Luetgert about his claim that he had called up hospitals on May 2 in an effort to find Louise. "How many hospitals did you call up?"

"All I could find in the business directory and whose telephone numbers I could find in the telephone book."

"How many did you call up?"

"I don't know."

"How many as near as you can recollect?"

"I don't know."

"Can you name any of them?"

"Give me the business directory and the telephone book and I will give you the whole list of them."

"Did you call up the County Hospital?"

"I guess I did."

"What did you say over the telephone to the County Hospital authorities?"

"I asked them if a lady arrived there and gave my wife's description."

"Give the description."

"Well, a little over five feet high, blond hair, kind of stout build, with square shoulders, I guess."

"Anything else?"

"It may be I have said something else. I don't recollect."

"Did you give your name to the hospital authorities?"

"I did not."

"Did you give her name to the hospital authorities?"

"I did not."

"Did you leave a message to be called if such a woman was brought in?"

"No, sir."

"Did you do that at any hospital to which you telephoned?"

"No, sir. I didn't want to have it published."

"Did you call up any police station on the telephone?"

"No, sir."

"Did you call up any morgue in the city?"

"No, sir, not to my recollection."

"Did you make any search of the clay holes about your residence when the police were there searching for your wife?"

"I did not."

"Did you assist in making a search of the river near your premise?"

"I did not."

A short time later Deneen suddenly said, "Very well, I am through with him," and sat down. Luetgert, who had expected the cross-examination to continue for at least another day, looked surprised. "Did you say, 'That's all'?" he asked, rising from the chair. Harmon stopped him from getting up, but after a few more questions from Harmon, Luetgert stepped down from the witness stand. He had testified 18½ hours in all, answering 1,771 questions from Harmon and 1,238 from Deneen. He had responded "I don't recollect" 116 times and "I don't know" 54 times.

The *Chicago Record* was impressed with Luetgert's testimony, saying the prosecutors were unable to shake his story. "Taken all in all his testimony was more favorable than hurtful to his cause," the newspaper stated.

His testimony prompted the *Tribune* to offer a detailed analysis of Luetgert's personality, concluding he was a "partial emotional type." He was cunning but intellectually limited and far from subtle. He was a vain and self-centered man, for whom Adolph Luetgert was "the whole thing." The *Tribune* said Luetgert's insistence on repeating the same answers might not have had the effect on the jury that Luetgert had intended. Luetgert recited some of his replies like a parrot. The *Tribune* claimed this indicated that he was a bald-faced liar—that he was "ding plain and fancy lying on purpose," as the newspaper put it. "A man who has nothing to conceal does not fear to alter the manner of his reply."

43 Winter

CHRISTINE FELD told Captain Schuettler she had seen two ghostly apparitions as she walked home one evening from the trial. An astral body resembling Adolph Luetgert appeared in front of her, and she called out, "*Adolph, bist das Du?*" (Is that you?). The tall figure did not reply. She cried, "*Geh weg, geh weg!*" (Go away) and ran, but before she had gone half a block, another vision confronted her: the face of a woman. "Louise!" she shouted.

Schuettler believed Feld had been hallucinating, but he assigned two officers to escort her home each night. One remained on call near her home during the night. Feld bolted and barred the doors of her home to keep out ghostly visitors.

◆◆◆

After fifteen years of experiments, Frank Waber of Chicago announced he had discovered a process to create gold. Waber, a bronze-skinned, athletic man then about thirty-five years old, told the *Daily News,* "Gold is what might be called the oil of metals. The problem, then, is to extract this oil. Roll a piece of copper into a very thin sheet and expose it to the elements. After years of exposure to the chemical action of the elements, a piece of gold about the size of the head of a lead pencil will remain. That is the principle on which I work, using chemicals and fire for the dissolution of the metals instead of waiting for the action of nature." Waber said he was forming a small gold-manufacturing company with capital from three Chicago investors.

◆◆◆

Harry Morris, a comedian, called on Schaack and asked permission to wear one of his uniforms in a new play. Schaack was beaming with smiles when he emerged from his meeting with Morris. He called the East Chicago Avenue station and instructed the officers there to accommodate Morris. The inspector and the actor had the same measurements, so it was not necessary to change the uniform. One day in court Schaack took Deneen and McEwen aside and told them Morris was going to portray him in a theatrical production. He seemed excited that his fame was growing. He told a *Chronicle* reporter, "When it is all over, I will tell about it. Who knows but what Dr. Harper will have me fill the seat of osteochronipoly in the University of Chicago."

◆◆◆

Six and a half inches of snow fell on Chicago one Saturday night the same week Luetgert was testifying. By Sunday morning the city's snow-encased trees looked as if they were made of marble. The air was still and frosty as cutters and bobsleds of all types filled the streets. The city's horses seemed invigorated by the cold air and the spring of well-packed snow under their hooves. As sleigh drivers raced each other, crowds along the boulevards would call out, "Here they come!" The spectators would lean forward and hold their breath. An unusually fast or close contest would bring forth a hearty cheer. Some of the Chicagoans who had ventured out with cameras to capture the scenes of winter beauty noticed the Luetgert jurors racing about the North Side in a big white sleigh drawn by four horses. As the twelve men enjoyed their Sunday recreation, they became a popular target for the photographers.

◆◆◆

While Luetgert's second trial went on, a scientific debate about the causes of criminal behavior raged in the press. Professor Elmer Gates of the Smithsonian Institution in Washington declared that science would soon put an end to all crime. "The irascible, the depressing, the malignant and the fearful emotions create poisons in every cell of the body, while the good emotions augment the nutritive changes in every cell of the body," Gates explained. He said the "disease of immorality" could be cured by building up "chemical formations" in the brain that would keep out all wicked influences.

Those comments prompted a letter to the editor from John A. Benson, a professor at the College of Physicians and Surgeons of Chicago and the Chicago School of Law, who said Gates's theories were "scientific absurdities." "The kidneys, skin, intestines, and lungs of the most virtuous man on earth are engaged in just the same works as in the most determined criminal," Benson wrote.

In an essay inspired by Benson's remarks, the *Tribune* held the city of Chicago at fault for Christopher Merry's murder of his wife. The newspaper blamed the killer's behavior on the environment of saloons and filthy tenements where he had grown up. "There is unavoidable contact with the low, the base, the brutish, and the wicked," the *Tribune* observed.

The *Tribune* contrasted Benson's outlook on crime with that of the philosophers who believed the sources of evil behavior lie in physical and mental abnormalities or heredity. "They would explain Merry by the measurements of his head and the weaknesses that had been transmitted to him through his father, and then throw up their hands and go their ways, as if that were the end of the question," the newspaper remarked. "Heredity has been a fad of late, and an excuse for a silly sort of fatalism."

44 The Verdict

AFTER LUETGERT had finished testifying, the defense brought forth a parade of witnesses who claimed to have seen Mrs. Luetgert since her disappearance. The men from Kenosha and other witnesses from the first trial made return performances.

It had been rumored the state would prove the woman seen in Kenosha to be someone other than Mrs. Luetgert. This woman had supposedly sat in the audience at the Luetgert trial on several occasions. According to one theory, the defense had hired a woman to travel the countryside, dropping just enough hints everywhere she went that she might be mistaken for Mrs. Luetgert. The defense attorneys responded with their own theory: the state had hired a Mrs. Luetgert impersonator to appear at scattered locations, hoping the defense would waste its time and money investigating. None of the rumored Mrs. Luetgert impersonators ever materialized on the witness stand, however.

Other stories said the defense lawyers were bribing people to say they had seen Mrs. Luetgert. Diedrich Bicknese investigated one of these tales and spoke with William Marquardt, who owned the old Luetgert farm near Elgin. Marquardt told Bicknese that Luetgert's brother, Arnold, had offered Marquardt's mother $200 to say she had seen Mrs. Luetgert near the farm around May 6. The mother denied that anyone had tried to bribe her, however. According to another rumor, Luetgert's agents offered the constable of the western suburb Bloomingdale $200 to testify he had seen Mrs. Luetgert. William Charles laughed off the charges, saying, "We haven't any money to even investigate such a matter, much less pay a man to fix up an alibi for Mrs. Luetgert."

The defense offered several witnesses from Monmouth, Illinois, who testified they had seen a woman resembling Mrs. Luetgert in their town on August 25, 1897. All six—four police officers, a real-estate man, and a newspaper reporter—described the woman as fashionably dressed, graceful of carriage, and speaking excellent English. The jurors seemed to regard their story as a joke.

A bookbinder named Otto Klatt said he had passed the Luetgert home in his buggy a few minutes after eleven P.M. on May 1. He heard a gate slam and a few seconds later his horse's nose touched the shoulder of a woman hurrying across the street through the fog. "Look out, or I'll run over you," he cried, reining his horse. The woman, who was carrying a small bundle, hurried east, he said. Klatt drove home and thought no more of the incident until October, when he drove along the same route again. He said it then occurred to him that the woman might have been Mrs. Luetgert.

For half an hour McEwen peppered Klatt with questions about the streets in Lake View, hoping to show that he might be confused about the place he had seen the woman, but the witness proved himself something of a local geographer.

"Was it freezing that night?" McEwen asked.

"Nit," Klatt said.

"Was it foggy?"

"I should snicker to snort—worse'n wash day and dark," Klatt responded, causing a titter in the courtroom.

Another witness, Theodore Arndt, said he had taken a ride on the Metropolitan El line with Mrs. Luetgert on July 14. Everyone in the courtroom was incredulous when Arndt claimed he had never heard about the first Luetgert trial. This statement prompted the *Journal* to run the headline, "Here's a Man Who is Certainly Queer."

Gary refused to let the defense air testimony about the supposed threats Mrs. Luetgert had made to run away. In addition, Harmon was reprimanded for putting on the stand three doctors who were supposed to be bone experts but turned out to be physicians for some of the jurors. McEwen called it a "cheap trick."

After the defense rested its case, the prosecutors put their rebuttal witnesses on the stand, including Joe Detloff, who testified he had seen Luetgert and Frank Hangel drinking, bowling, and playing cards together often, contrary to Luetgert's testimony that he had rarely spoken with Hangel.

During his cross-examination Harmon seldom gave Detloff a chance to answer one question before he posed another. Harmon laughed as Detloff stumbled over the answers, and Luetgert was enjoying the spectacle as well. Their smiles vanished when a voice came from the jury, surprising the lawyers and spectators.

"Give the witness a chance to answer before you break in on him with another question," Charles Snow said in a loud, aggressive voice, the juror leaning forward and looking directly at Harmon. The lawyer drew back as if he had been struck. He asked the witness another question but looked angrily at Snow: "What answer was it you could not finish? What was it you said that the jury could not hear?"

"That is not a proper question to ask," Gary said.

"Well, I wanted to find out what answer it was the jury could not hear," Harmon said.

A murmur of protest came from the jury box. Another juror, Thomas Gardner, leaned forward in the front row and exclaimed, "We cannot hear anything. It's all mixed up. We cannot tell which is question and which answer. . . . We can't hear any of his answers because you break in so much."

"There is no necessity for that sort of thing," another juror said.

In an irritable tone, Harmon asked the jurors, "Well, what do you want?"

"The testimony," one of the men responded. Luetgert looked disturbed by the way the jurors had addressed his attorney, and the other defense lawyers wore grave expressions. Harmon went on with his questions, asking them in an angry tone but allowing Detloff to complete his answers.

Two newspaper reporters, Frederick A. Stowe and Frank Hassler, testified they had interviewed Luetgert in jail on August 7. When they asked him about an experiment to dissolve a human body with caustic potash at Rush Medical College, Luetgert had told them it was a farce. He had said he would allow a body to boil twice as long in one of his vats. The reporters said he had demonstrated a detailed knowledge of anatomy during the interview.

As the trial drew to a close, Gary grew tired of Harmon's erratic behavior and his constant statements taking exception to Gary's rulings. Gary finally blurted out, "I don't care for you to say that what I do or say is right or wrong. I have got tired of your continuous sanction, at times when I do something which you think calls for your approval. I never saw a man try a case as you do. I never heard such a thing. I never saw a man before come into the court and comb his hair before a jury and wash his face with his wet fingers from his mouth."

Harmon was astonished at Gary's admonishment. "We except to the language of the court as a characterization unbecoming a court and unbecoming gentlemanly conduct of a trial," he said.

"Save his point for him," Gary quietly said to the stenographer.

"I want to get it all down—every word, every word," Harmon said.

"Certainly. Get it all in. Put down all the remarks of the court," Gary said.

On February 1 it was time again for closing arguments. McEwen's speech lasted an entire day, as he attacked Luetgert's testimony, especially his failure to remember important events related to his sausage business. "Taking into consideration his intelligence and his experience and his situation, when he says, 'I don't remember,' you can put him down as a falsifier and reject his testimony on all points, except where he is corroborated," McEwen said.

John Kehoe then spent the next day and a half speaking for the defense, concluding with a prediction that Mrs. Luetgert would return some day. Luetgert's other lawyer, Max Riese, spoke for half a day, and then it was Harmon's turn. He launched into a tirade against the police, claiming Luetgert had faced worse persecution than had anyone else in the entirety of human history. "He stands the best-abused man that ever lived or died," Harmon said, striding up and down and swinging his arms as he spoke in his most dramatic voice. "Is that an exaggeration? Within your knowledge, within the realm of all your reading, tell me where is a man who has lived in the centuries that have rolled in the dead and mighty past, where lives or has lived a man that has been abused like Adolph L. Luetgert."

Harmon's speech went on and on, stretching out over four days and setting what was believed to be a new record for the longest speech in a Cook County trial. He quoted poetry, told stories, and read from law books. He likened himself to a man in a lifeboat, bent on saving a fellow human from death. He asked the jurors to lend a hand at the oars so that Luetgert might be restored to his family in time to eat dinner at home that Sunday. But the jurors did not seem to be paying much attention to his oratory. They looked exhausted.

On February 9 Deneen delivered his closing argument, the final speech of the second trial, which had now gone on as long as the first trial. He spoke for several hours, standing before the jurors and making few gestures. As he neared the end of his oration, Deneen told the jurors that the law itself was on trial. "As was said by Mr. Harmon in his speech, this is an extraordinary case," Deneen observed. "It is the most remarkable case in the annals of the world. Nothing like it has gone before. No man has noticed a case like it in its fiendish atrocity, in the calm study of its execution, in the length of time the malice was nursed in his mind before he tried to strike the fatal blow.

"The law is on trial in this case. The civilized world knows of this case. The civilized world knows of the evidence in this case, and the civilized world is watching Illinois to see whether a jury in her state is strong enough or intelligent enough or law-abiding enough or courageous enough to fit the punishment to the deed, to see that the law here is vindicated. The world shall notice whether there shall be a premium placed upon murder that conceals the corpse. You are to decide whether the law is strong enough, whether you are strong enough, whether you have the courage when guilt is shown to stand up and announce a fit penalty for this atrocious murder. I believe you have.

"This great state can only act and speak through you. I am sure after all the evidence here, when this whole case is considered, you will be inclined, not compelled, to acquit yourselves in such a way that the people—not only of this county, or this city, or this state, of this country, but people everywhere who know about this case—will feel that the law has been vindicated and a new security placed about human life."

Gary gave the jurors his instructions, telling them the prosecutors did not need to produce a corpse to prove that Mrs. Luetgert had been murdered. Finally, after hearing testimony from 146 witnesses—and 866 objections by the defense lawyers—the twelve men retired to the jury room at 3:50. This time the jury deliberations remained secret.

That night, at about a quarter to eleven, word came from the jurors that they wanted to come back into court. A carriage went to Gary's home and brought him back to court. The lawyers and reporters took their places. Harmon, who hadn't expected the jury to finish deliberating so soon, appeared anxious and distraught. Kehoe and Riese avoided Harmon, showing their bitter feelings toward the man who had controlled the defense team. Deneen was tired, his voice husky from his address to the jury.

At 11:30 Gary ordered the jurors be brought into the courtroom. They took their seats and Gary asked, "Gentlemen of the jury, have you agreed upon a verdict?"

"We have, your honor," said Thomas H. Bacheler, the foreman. He handed a paper to the clerk. Luetgert, who had just arrived in court under the escort of four deputy sheriffs, took his place at Harmon's side and listened to the clerk reading the words on the paper: "We, the jury, find the defendant, Adolph L. Luetgert, guilty of murder in manner and form as charged in the indictment, and we fix his punishment at imprisonment in the penitentiary for the term of his natural life."

As he heard the word *guilty,* Luetgert scarcely moved a muscle in his face. When the clerk announced the punishment, Luetgert closed his eyes. One observer believed he saw Luetgert laugh. Harmon looked blankly around him. Dazed, he clutched at Luetgert's hand for support. His grasp was only feebly returned.

45 Lines of Destiny

THE DAY AFTER THE VERDICT, a *Chicago Journal* reporter visited Luetgert at the jail. Between puffs of a cigar, Luetgert raised his voice almost to a shout. "I say to you that I am as innocent of this crime as you are," he said. "I would say the same thing if I was facing a hundred scaffolds. But if the men on that jury believed I am guilty, they should have hanged me. I say that plainly. When they gave me neither death nor liberty, they proved they were cowards. . . .

"I suppose . . . that Judge Gary's criticism of Harmon had some effect on the jury. But Mr. Harmon was working in his own way and I think he was right. But the whole thing seems ridiculous to me. I laughed at the verdict last night and said it was foolishness, and that is what I say this morning. I believe one of those jurors must have been fixed . . . and that explains the conviction. I am innocent of the crime, and the Supreme Court will give me my liberty in the end."

Although most of the newspaper editorial writers around the country didn't believe Luetgert's proclamations of innocence, many of them agreed with his opinion that the jury's combination of a guilty verdict and a life sentence had been cowardly. The *Washington Star* remarked, "Luetgert is either guilty or innocent. He should be hanged or liberated. Such verdicts bring discredit upon the jury system." The *Buffalo Enquirer* said, "The big, blubbering coward undoubtedly killed his wife. He has been sentenced to prison for life. . . . He should have been hanged." The *Brooklyn Eagle* called the jury's decision "illogical" but said it was understandable, given the absence of direct evidence against Luetgert. And the *Baltimore Herald* worried: "The leniency shown . . . will diminish the dread for the terrors of the law which malefactors might feel if justice were more exacting."*

Other newspapers were satisfied with the verdict and sentence. The *Buffalo Times* said, "The verdict will be viewed with satisfaction by most people conversant with this case." The *Chicago Journal* called the outcome "The best possible solution," explaining, "The jury doubted Luetgert's guilt too much to hang him and not enough to let him go. Its imposition of the life imprisonment penalty is a solution of the problem that does credit to the prudence of the jurors. . . . Should Mrs. Luetgert be found alive, her husband can be restored to liberty. Hanged, he could not be restored to life." And the *Green Bay Advocate* declared, "Occasionally justice finds its way, even to wicked Chicago."

In an interview the jury foreman, Bacheler, said he was surprised the verdict was being viewed as a compromise. "I think that every one of the twelve men is satisfied with the verdict. Without saying more on this point I ask you one question. Which would be worse: For a man convicted of murder, for which he must suffer, to expiate his crime by his death? Or to be doomed to live where he will have nothing to think about except his crime, and where the chances are not one in a million for escape?"

Bacheler denied the jury had decided on a guilty verdict based on the behavior of Harmon or anyone other than Luetgert. He questioned the accuracy of news stories describing the ballots taken in the jury room, noting he had burned all the ballots and memoranda from the deliberations. He denied a story that the jurors had quickly decided on the verdict then waited in the room for some time before announcing it. "We felt that we had seen quite enough stage play, and that this would have been outrageous," he said.

Harmon was threatening to investigate some of the jurors to see whether they been corrupted, but Jacob A. Loeb, another juror, said, "It is absurd for a man like Harmon, who has blustered and talked all through the case, to

---

* Given the outrage in some quarters over Luetgert's supposedly lenient sentence, one might think it was unusual for murder convicts of the time to receive anything less than the death penalty. In fact, it happened often. Exactly 600 murder convicts were sent to the Illinois State Penitentiary in Joliet from 1875 to 1900. Of those, 233 had life sentences; sentences for the other 367 averaged twenty years.

come out now and ascribe motives of any nature to our action." As for Luetgert's testimony, Loeb said, "Luetgert told a good story, but our verdict indicates how we regarded it as far as veracity is concerned."

While Luetgert remained in Cook County Jail, awaiting either a successful appeal by his attorneys or a trip to the state penitentiary in Joliet, the jail's other prisoner recently convicted of wife murder, Christopher Merry, awaited death by hanging. Merry's attorney, Frank Fay Pratt, came to jail one day with an X-ray expert hoping to take pictures of Merry's head, thinking they might show something about his brain that would persuade state officials to commute his sentence. But Merry said he had a headache and asked for the experiment to be postponed.

Pratt also happened to be a palmist, and he examined Merry's hands for an explanation of his criminal tendencies. Pratt published the results in an article he cowrote with Dr. O. Clifton Hall. They described palm reading as a scientific study of character traits.

They said Merry's unusually thick hand—with its poorly developed "mounts," the elevated areas of the palm below each finger—spelled out his combative, stubborn, and brutish personality. By viewing Merry's "line of destiny," Pratt and Hall were able to discern a record of his troubled childhood. "In many respects Merry is more sinned against than sinning," they wrote. "Fate with him was an ill-favored goddess. She did not raise him as others have been raised. She surrounded him with baneful influences. . . . Merry's hand shows none of the finer influences which have been brought to bear upon the lives of the majority of people. Such a hand deserves charity, sympathy, different environment, more friends, hope, a better destiny, and not a hangman's rope."

A week after Luetgert was convicted, a young woman sauntered into the state's attorney's office. With her arms akimbo, she demanded to see Merry and Luetgert. Told they were at the jail, she responded, "Well, I'll go there. I want to tell the men who kill their wives what I think of them."

The woman went to the jail, where she told the guards, "Men are back numbers nowadays. Women know it all, and if women were on the jury, those murderers and thieves would all get what they deserved. . . . I want to see those men to tell them that hanging is too good for them." The sheriff's deputies refused to let her into the jail, calling her a lunatic as she stormed off.

◆◆◆

At 4 P.M. on Saturday, March 5, the assistant jailer came to Luetgert's cell and told him to be ready in five minutes to leave for prison. Luetgert hadn't expected to go this soon, so none of his friends or relatives were there to bid him farewell as the jailer Whitman, the jail clerk Davies, and a couple of guards walked him out of the building and into a waiting cab. Luetgert wore a shabby, ill-fitting suit; he had decided to leave behind his better clothes as a legacy to any friend who might need them.

Luetgert and his jailers arrived at Union Station fifteen minutes before the 5 P.M. Joliet-bound train left on the Chicago and Alton Railroad. They sat near the front of the smoking car. Whitman sat next to Luetgert, who was not handcuffed or otherwise restrained. Luetgert chatted with his guards and the reporters who surrounded him.

The news spread that Luetgert was on the train, and although the smoking car was cloudy and hot, well-dressed women and men trooped forward from the rear coaches to catch a glimpse of him. Soon every seat in the car was filled. Looking out the window, the prisoner noticed a crowd on the platform gazing at him. Frequently one person in the crowd would nudge another and point at Luetgert. He made no attempt to avoid their stares; the attention seemed to amuse him. With a smile he raised his hand and saluted the crowd, remarking, "Yes, that's him. He's the one. Take a good look at him."

As the train pulled out, no one in the jail party uttered a word. Luetgert sat still and puffed at his cigar. When the conductor came around for tickets, Luetgert assumed his old air of jocularity. The conductor told him that he had asked Whitman to bring Luetgert down on this train, because he would consider it an honor to transport him. "There, boys, you hear him," replied Luetgert. "You make a note now that it was an honor for me to ride on this train."

Luetgert joked about the fact that he was riding the train for free, on a ticket bought by the sheriff. He spoke of himself in the third person, joyously declaring Luetgert was a privileged character, about as big a man as President McKinley. He said would get a new trial some day, and then Chicago would hear again from Luetgert. "Luetgert goes to the penitentiary proud," he said, addressing the conductor. "If ever an innocent man went there, it's Luetgert."

As the train ran through a desolate section of Bridgeport, someone asked Luetgert what he expected to do in the prison. "I can work as hard as anybody and I'm not afraid of it," he said. "Yes, I can cook to please anybody, but I don't care where they put me at. I will like it better and I will be better off there than in the jail. I will be better all around. I was never in better health in my life than I am now. All the trouble I have is rheumatism and they will cure me of that at the prison."

Luetgert evinced no interest in the huge banks of rock and mud on the right side of the track near Willow Springs, which showed the proximity of the sanitary channel. When someone mentioned it, Luetgert made no comment in reply, but noticing how the air was free from smoke and dirt, he turned to the reporters and said, "You see I get the best of you fellows anyhow. The air at Joliet is pure—much better than it is in Chicago."

Someone asked Luetgert if he would like to take charge of the sausage mill at the prison. He said he would as soon do that work as anything else. "If I do that work," he said, "I will save all the sesamoids and femurs that I get hold of and send them to the French exposition in 1900 or to the experts in Chicago."

Luetgert told yarns about life in the old country, and then the train stopped for a moment in Lemont. As the train stood at the platform, a crowd gathered and peered in the window at him. Luetgert amused himself by pointing at Davies, indicating to the crowd that the clerk was the man they wanted to see. As the train began to pull out, Luetgert waved his hand to the crowd and smiled good-naturedly. He yelled through he window, "Yes, that's him—that's the one—that's Luetgert." He indicated himself now by crooking his index finger. Then he turned to the jailer and newspapermen and dryly remarked, "Rubber necks!"

Luetgert had plenty of cigars with him, and he distributed them with a liberal hand. He puffed away as he reminisced about the trial, told jokes, and even sang a tune—"Ach, Du Liebe Augustin!"—for the entertainment of everyone in the car.

Before the train reached Joliet, five women entered the car, and Luetgert turned about in his seat, raising his hat to them. They stood gazing at him several minutes but did not approach. Luetgert drew forth a silver watch from his pocket and asked Whitman to deliver it to William Charles.

"Joliet! State Penitentiary!" the conductor called out. Luetgert, who had not removed his worn brown overcoat during the entire trip, got up and waited for the train to come to a standstill. No crowd waited for him at the last stop.

The prison, stretching nearly a thousand feet wide, stood like a castle in the center of a plain. The building and the massive walls around it, twenty-five to forty feet tall, were made of what was called Joliet limestone, a dark grayish rock that added to the place's somber mood. Blue-coated men with Winchester rifles under their arms patrolled the platforms surrounding the building's rough-hewn towers. Luetgert remarked on the neat appearance of the prison grounds as he walked with a rapid, firm step toward the massive front gate, with a guard on either side. The *Tribune* reported that Luetgert "wept freely in the jail and the tears dimmed his vision," but the *Chronicle* wrote, "He exhibited no nervousness."

Luetgert passed into the prison and took a seat in the waiting room until Warden Robert Wilson McClaughry issued an order to take Luetgert to the prison's "court solitary" area for new arrivals. They walked through the kitchen to the office of the night keeper, Holcomb, who searched Luetgert. He found only a few small articles, including $15.85. "Give Mr. Whitman one dollar out of that," Luetgert said. "I owe it to him for the cab hire."

Illuminating their route with a lantern, the night keeper led Luetgert and the Cook County Jail officials up two flights of stairs to the upper tier of the court solitary. The door of the last cell on the right side stood open. Luetgert stepped in and the guard slammed the door behind him. Luetgert turned about and took a last look at his friends from the jail. "Good-bye," he said, his voice a trifle husky. He then walked away into the dark shadows of his cell, and the officials lost sight of him.

Luetgert spent the next day in solitary confinement. He heard barely a sound all day, except when a convict came from the kitchen with "rude tin service containing the prison fare," the *Tribune* reported. The following day a prison trusty awakened Luetgert at daybreak and led him to the office of Assistant Warden Moses Luke. It was time for the prison's latest batch of "fresh fish," as new arrivals were known, to be "salted." Officials took Luetgert's civilian clothes and handed him a bluish-gray suit consisting of a blouse, trousers, coarse underclothes, a striped shirt, and a cap. Luetgert donned his new garb without a word, and then a trusty sewed a little tag on his right shoulder bearing the figures "5969," his new identity.

Luetgert was taken next to the barber shop, where his hair was cut and his mustache shaved off. He and a gang of other new prisoners were marched in lockstep to the Bertillon gallery. For twenty years prison officials had been using the Bertillon system to identify prisoners, although they were considering a change to the newer technology of thumbprints. The prison took precise measurements of each prisoner's height and numerous skeletal dimensions, which would remain unchanged even if the prisoner gained or lost weight. Luetgert weighed in at 220 pounds. The officials photographed him in profile and full-face view and then asked him a number of questions. When they asked whether his wife was living, a queer expression flashed over his face and his eyes seemed to tear up. After the words "Wife Living," an official wrote "Yes?" The form also noted, "Profanity: Yes. Drink: Yes. Smoke: Yes. Chew: Yes. . . . Condition of Heart: Normal." At fifty-three Leutgert was among the older prisoners at Joliet; about 50 percent were in their twenties.

Luetgert was given a tin cup of steaming coffee and a half-loaf of bread for breakfast, which he ate without enthusiasm. After he had eaten, he was called from the file of marching prisoners by the receiving officer, a man named Green. Knowing that Luetgert had experience in the tanning business, Green assigned him to work as "the selector" of the prison's harness and leather department. At noon Luetgert was taken to the office of Warden McClaughry, who gave him the usual advice about good conduct and obedience. At promptly 6:30 P.M. a trusty led Luetgert to cell 31 in the east wing, his new home.

When a prisoner was taken to his cell at night, he stepped inside, closed the door after him, and stood close to the door, clutching the bars. He remained in this position until the guard had passed along, locking the doors and counting the prisoners. The guard then walked along the gallery again, glancing sharply into each cell to make sure he had made no mistake in his count. He wrote the number on a slip of paper and handed it to the deputy warden, who entered it in the daily count book. After that the convicts were left alone for the night.

Like all the other cells at Joliet, Luetgert's was seven feet deep, four feet wide, and seven feet high. It was arranged to hold two men, with a double iron bunk on one side of the cell. The beds were provided with husk mattresses, straw pillows, sheets, and heavy woolen blankets. In the typical cell, a shelf at the rear contained a few books and papers, bottles of vinegar, and small tin boxes containing salt and pepper—for meals to be eaten in the cells.

A Bible sat on the shelf in each cell. The other furnishings included two stools, a small mirror on the wall, and a wide-mouthed granite-ware crock that held drinking water. Wooden washbuckets were stored under the bed. An electric lamp brightly illuminated Luetgert's new surroundings, burning every day from daybreak until nine at night. Even the commissioners who oversaw the prison believed the cramped conditions were inhumane. "It must be very repellant, and at times almost impossible, for a prisoner to eat in a cell where lingering odors, and all the unpleasant associations of dreary hours and abhorrent necessities, combine to depress and discourage him," they reported. The human stink of the crowded cells was not the only odor enveloping Luetgert and his fellow prisoners. Smoke, dust, and gases from a neighboring steel mill filled the air. Around twenty prisoners died each year, about half of them from tuberculosis.

◆◆◆

Around the time Luetgert went to Joliet, Schaack took some time off from his police work. His health was poor, and some blamed it on the incessant effort he had put into prosecuting Luetgert. One newspaper later reported Schaack had seen a premonition of his own death. He turned over all his files to a subordinate and went home, where he remained bedridden for the next two months. Schaack, who was suffering from diabetes and inflammatory rheumatism, died in his sleep on May 18, 1898.

46 Prisoner 5969

DURING LUETGERT'S first year in prison, he was seldom seen except with a happy, smiling face. He always insisted on his innocence and steadfastly claimed he would get another trial. After the prison closed its harness shop, officials assigned Luetgert to the chair-caning shop. Later he was put in charge of the meats in the cold-storage warehouse. Officials described him as a model prisoner.

In 1899 Luetgert began to smile less, wearing a morose and sullen look.

He became rough-spoken and quarreled with the convicts working near him. The Fourth of July was the only day all year long when the inmates were free to roam in the prison yard, playing sports, listening to music, and dancing. A year earlier on the same occasion, Luetgert had been the happiest man in the prison, but this year he just wanted to ignore everyone. Many of the prisoners who had exchanged pleasantries with him on the previous Fourth of July came up to him again, but he answered their greetings with a scowl. The only person he would talk with was Nic Marzen, his former cellmate from the Cook County Jail, who had been found guilty of murder again but sentenced this time to thirty years rather than execution. Luetgert and Marzen went off into a corner of the yard and conversed together in low tones for two hours.

On July 20 Luetgert got into a heated argument with an agent of Armour and Company about the quality of meat the firm was shipping to the prison. Luetgert was placed in solitary confinement for two hours for "disobedience and quarreling." He was transferred back to his old job in the cane shop on July 25.

Some people said the real thing bothering Luetgert was a legal proceeding under way in Cook County. Diedrich Bicknese was seeking the guardianship of Luetgert's young children, Louis and Elmer, who were being cared for by William and Mary Charles. Luetgert had said of the Bicknese family, "They have deprived me of everything on earth, and now they want my boys. They can't even support themselves, without thinking of taking additional cares. I do not want such people to bring up my children." He was particularly disturbed when he heard that Louis had signed a court document stating he had no father and that his mother was dead.

Every morning at half past five the day keepers of the prison assembled in the great guard hall. All was quiet in the cell house, except for an occasional cough echoing through the corridors. A few electric lights illuminated the corridors, casting long shadows. The night watch captain twice rang the shrill bells in each cell-house. The convicts then got up from bed, slipped into their uniforms, and washed.

The wall guards took their repeating rifles from the armory, buttoned up their greatcoats, and marched to their places in the towers and the sentry boxes along the top of the wall. Some fifty guards took up their heavy canes—the only weapons of defense allowed inside the prison—and entered the cell houses. They hurried along the galleries, unlocking cells. On a signal fifteen hundred convicts swarmed into the corridors. When they reached the stone floor below, the guards quickly formed them into lines and shouted, "Forward march!"

On July 27, as on every morning, Luetgert and the other prisoners marched in lockstep into the yard. They stopped near the west wall, emptied their waste buckets into the sewers, and hung the buckets on racks. They marched back to the cell houses. As they passed the ration tables, each convict helped himself to a quart cup of coffee, as many slices of bread as he desired, and a pan containing a breakfast ration of hash. This day the breakfast was a tin plate of Irish stew.

Luetgert took his ration and went back to his cell—which was now no. 152, on the second tier of the east wing—and sat down to eat. Walking by in the corridor, a guard named Peter Blone noticed that the door to Luetgert's cell wasn't shut. He asked Luetgert why he had failed to close the door. "I didn't know it was open," Luetgert said. "I must be a little slow this morning."

Blone fastened the door and passed on. He passed by the cell again a few minutes later and noticed that Luetgert had risen from his stool and was sitting on the edge of his bed, bent over. Luetgert soon looked up, however, and resumed eating.

As the 6:45 signal for work sounded, Luetgert was not among the men pouring into the corridors. The stories about the next events differ. One newspaper said a convict told the guards, "Sir, there is something the matter with the big fellow, as I heard him grunting in his cell." Another paper said the guards heard a groan coming from Luetgert's cell. Another said the guards merely passed by his cell and saw that something was wrong.

Blone and another guard, George Geissler, went into the cell, where Luetgert was stretched out on his cot, his arms and legs convulsing violently, his face turning purple, and his breathing coming in great gasps. Luetgert wore his hat and coat, as if he had been preparing to march to his daily work. With help from six stalwart convicts, the guards carried Luetgert out into the corridor, hoping the fresh air would revive him.

"What is the matter, Luetgert?" Blone asked. Luetgert made no reply. His eyes half opened and the muscles of his face twitched nervously, as if he was trying to speak. After an instant the eyelids closed, the muscles relaxed, a faint gurgling sound escaped his lips, and the life passed out of him.

The guards laid Luetgert's body on a blanket and carried it to the prison infirmary. The prison physician, Dr. Thomas J. O'Malley, and the coroner conducted an autopsy later in the day, determining that the fifty-three-year-old Luetgert had probably died from heart trouble, angina pectoris. The autopsy also showed that Luetgert's liver was greatly enlarged and in such a condition of degeneration that "mental strain would have caused his death at any time." "The marvel to me," Dr. O'Malley said, "is how he lived so long with that heart. I don't understand how he got through the two trials. The heart was like a sponge, and was enlarged out of all proportion."

One hour after Luetgert died, a letter from Lawrence Harmon reached the prison; it contained the news that an earlier court order giving Diedrich Bicknese guardianship over Louis and Elmer had been set aside. Louis testified he hadn't seen the wording of the petition that he had signed earlier and that he never would have signed it if he had realized it stated that his mother was dead. Louis's new statement persuaded the court to change its course, allowing the children to stay in the home of William Charles. Elmer, who was seven years old, was attending school, but Louis could not bear the constant taunts from his classmates about his father, so he had left school and gone to work as a cashboy at Carson, Pirie, Scott and Company.

Harmon said he had wanted Luetgert to hear the news about the latest court decision right away, "in order that he might feel gratified to know that his children would remain with the friends in whose charge he had left them, and that they would not be placed in the custody of the most vindictive of his enemies. His children have always believed in their father's innocence, and were devoutly attached to him, and, whenever they could, visited him in prison and cheered and comforted him."

If Luetgert had lived another day, he would have heard another piece of good news. The day before, thanks to a donation of $1,500, his son Arnold had finally paid for a copy of the 4,620-page trial transcript, and Harmon was more hopeful than ever that the Supreme Court would hear the case. "But at the very moment when matters were shaping themselves most favorably for this last effort to secure justice for Luetgert, death suddenly called him away," Harmon said.

In downtown Chicago people going out for lunch were greeted by the cries of newsboys. The German newspapers declared, *"Luetgert ist todt!"* (Luetgert is dead). His death was the main topic of discussion in restaurants and hotels. A reporter brought the news to Mary Siemering, who had recently married a saloonkeeper named Lambert Schurz. "What—the old man dead?" she said. "Well, it was better so—better for him and all concerned. I for one will weep no tears."

"You can send for the body and help with the funeral, Mary, if you wish," her husband said good-naturedly.

"No, Lambert, no. Let them bury him down there, or let someone else attend to his funeral. Luetgert was dead to me long ago, and I can do nothing for him now," she replied.

Otto Tosch said he couldn't believe Luetgert was dead. "It's a put-up job," he said, "to smuggle him out of the penitentiary and set him free." His wife, Agatha, laughed and said she had no reason to doubt that Luetgert was really dead.

The first member of Luetgert's family to arrive at the prison was his brother Arnold. He went to see the body in the prison morgue, where it lay on a slab shrouded in a winding sheet, with a prisoner standing sentinel nearby. Luetgert's lips were composed into a peaceful smile, and his face looked calm.

"He looks perfectly natural," Arnold said, looking at the cold, white face. He stood gazing at the body for some minutes. "Well, well, his case is ended now," he said, turning away.

47 Confessions and Eulogies

AS SOON AS Luetgert died, new stories about his trial came to light. Frank Fay Pratt, the lawyer for Christopher Merry with a penchant for palmistry, told the *Chicago Journal* that Luetgert had sent for him to come to his jail cell around the time of his second trial. Luetgert had extended his hand through the bars of his cell and asked Pratt to interpret the lines on his palm. Pratt recalled saying, "Mr. Luetgert, you need not tell me you did not kill your wife. I know you did. Predestination and fatalism combined, as shown by the lines nature has left in your hand, tell me that. You were led on by influences you could not resist. I do not want you to make a confession to me. I am acting in a professional capacity and what I have learned from the study of your hands I will not repeat."

He went on to tell Luetgert the characteristics of his life. "You have loved but once," Pratt told Luetgert, and Luetgert bowed his head as if giving an affirmative answer. Luetgert then spoke of the affection he had for his first wife and his strong feelings for his son Louis.

Pratt continued examining Luetgert's hand, pointing out things that indicated the impulses that caused him to commit crime. Luetgert said, "At one time I was engaged in the saloon business and I attribute a great deal of my brutal instincts to my connection with it. I have always liked the smell of blood and the sight of raw meat."

"I know you killed your wife, but you will not be hanged—you will die suddenly," Pratt said.

Pratt claimed Luetgert told him, in a wailing tone, "I did—I did do it, and yet God knows I did not know what I was doing." Luetgert became agitated, walking about the cell and muttering incoherently. He wouldn't tell Pratt anything about the way he had committed the murder other than to say, "The ———— dogs growled." Turning to Pratt, Luetgert had said, "I can't understand why I told it to you. No one could get it out of me—priests, lawyers or anyone. Why did I tell it to you?"

According to Pratt, his palm reading led him to believed that Luetgert was a degenerate who had made it through the ordeal of the trials through sheer brutal strength. "So far as palmistry teaches, his life was marked by great stress on the multiples of three, five, and nine, with a special influence regarding nine," the *Journal* reported. "Mr. Pratt calls attention to the fact that he was born in 1845 and on the 27th day of the month—both figures representing multiples of nine, and that he died on the 27th in 1899, which dates are likewise multiples of the same number."

Harmon called Pratt's story "ridiculous," and Luetgert's son Arnold said, "It is simply a fake, and I can see no other reason for his saying it than that he wants some cheap advertising for his palmistry business. My father did not make a confession to anybody, and he would not have picked out such a man as that if he intended doing so. He could not have confessed he was guilty, for that would not have been true."

Clarence Darrow, who had once worked in the same law firm as William Vincent and Adams Goodrich, also dismissed Pratt's tale. Darrow said, "It is the height of foolishness to assume that a man who had gone through the trials which Luetgert survived would have confessed to Pratt or any other hand reader when he steadfastly declared his innocence to his lawyers and closest friends. . . . The palmist may have thought that Luetgert confessed to him, but you can attribute that to a vivid imagination."

John Whitman, the Cook Couty jailer, also refuted Pratt, saying, "Luetgert never made a confession to my knowledge. I was present at an interview that Pratt, who claimed to be a palmist, had with the big sausage maker. Pratt examined Luetgert's hands and spoke about the lines on the palms, but not a word was said that resembled a confession in any way."

Pratt responded, "Jailer Whitman, who says he was present at the time of the interview but heard no confession, is mistaken. He was not there. I will stand to the end on what I have said."

Deneen disclosed some of the evidence that prosecutors had not used during the trial. He let a *Tribune* reporter see an affidavit, dated September 10, 1897, that the state's attorney's office had taken from a man who was in jail at the time of Luetgert's arrest. In the affidavit, the inmate, whose name was not revealed by the *Tribune,* recounted a conversation he'd had with Luetgert on a Saturday that spring:

> He asked me the different kinds of murder, and said: "What is the word they use upstairs when they claim I had thought a long time about it?"
>
> I told him that was what they called premeditated, and I then explained to him as well as I could what manslaughter was, where one kills in the heat of passion, without thinking beforehand. He said:
>
> "McEwen tells the judge all the time I planned this for weeks and weeks, and he makes it the hanging kind."
>
> Then he said: "Supposing I come out and find my little boy with my woman, and send him to bed, and I ask her to go with me to the office, and she refuses. Then I kick her (showing me how he kicked her in the side). I think she will come back and everybody will know we had trouble. I took her to the office, and I think she will come back, and I got out and come back, and then I think—"
>
> I then stopped him and said: "Don't tell me any more, but tell your lawyers the whole truth." . . .
>
> He came to my cell often to talk with me and to ask questions, and one time—I think it was on the Sunday following the Saturday conversation—he said: "I made one damn mistake—them bloody rings." . . . Whenever

he spoke about the rings he showed by gestures and by words that he had made a mistake as to the rings and that he worried more about them than anything else.

When he began to tell me about the case he started by saying: "Suppose I did," so and so, but before he got through he put it more in the form of a statement and said: "I kick her in the side," showing how he did it, and then he said, "I think she will come back," et cetera, meaning, as I understand it, "I think she will come to."

Deneen said the affidavit amounted to a "moral confession" by Luetgert, even if he hadn't directly admitted to murdering his wife. "I have not the shadow of a doubt that the conversation took place just as it is sworn to here," he said. "The man who made it served a short term in Joliet afterwards, but his word is beyond reproach, in my mind. I have talked with his attorney, and we both consider it best not to disclose the man's name. He is living an honorable life in a town not far from Chicago, and I don't wish to handicap him by letting people know he has been in the penitentiary. I don't think it would raise his reputation to have people know that he and Luetgert were on friendly terms."

Deneen said he had other, similar affidavits locked away inside the steel vault in his office, including one that was even more damning. Without explaining why, he claimed that trial rules had prevented him from using these statements as evidence. Although Deneen and McEwen insisted this additional evidence had been solid and credible, McEwen said it had been "so hampered and so undefined . . . that we dared not introduce it."

After the *Tribune* published the anonymous affidavit, the palmist Pratt elaborated a bit more on his supposed conversation with Luetgert, telling the *Record,* "He told me that he had not intentionally killed his wife, but that she had died from a kick in the side he gave her when angry. It was a professional secret with me, and I promised him I would keep it as long as he lived. This he asked me to do."

◆◆◆

At nine in the morning on Sunday, July 30, an undertaker delivered Luetgert's coffin to the Northwest Turner Hall at the corner of Southport and Clybourn, not far from the Luetgert factory. The hall was already surrounded by several hundred people, but three policemen kept the crowd back until the body had been carried inside.

The black cloth-covered casket was ornamented with silver handles. A silver plate was inscribed with Luetgert's name and the dates of his birth and death. The casket was placed on a draped stand in the room's center. A window on the casket revealed Luetgert's face. The only floral offering was a pillow-shaped arrangement of red roses and pink and white carnations at the head of the casket. The crimson blossoms on its face spelled out "OUR FATHER'S WORDS: 'I AM INNOCENT.'"

The doors of the hall were thrown open, and for two and a half hours anyone who cared to enter was allowed to view Luetgert's body. An unbroken chain of thousands of people filed past the bier, each glancing at Luetgert's smoothly shaven face, which bore a half-smile. Most of them seemed to be drawn by curiosity; only a few cried.

Elderly German matrons came in twos and threes, standing close together to stare at Luetgert's face and then discussing the crime as they moved on. Young girls in the daintiest of summer costumes bent over the casket and shuddered. Women with children dragging at their gowns moved along with the line and lifted their little boys and girls to gratify their teasing appeals of "Let me see." When the neighborhood's Sunday schools let out, droves of small boys and girls carrying prayer books hastened into the hall and passed by the body. Several bicycle clubs riding through the area saw the multitude and stopped in to see the spectacle.

Not satisfied with one glimpse of the pallid face, some women in the crowd returned to the line and passed again and again before the casket. One woman attracted considerable attention when it was noticed that she had walked past the casket about fifteen times, scrutinizing the features each time with a pained look of anxiety. It was learned afterward she was a prominent psychologist from the South Side who was using the occasion to study the facial characteristics of a noted criminal.

Large groups of middle-aged Germans adjourned to an adjacent saloon to discuss the crime over their beer glasses. The saloon did a thriving business on the warm morning, and for a time a line of men extended from the hall to the bar.

Many in the crowd whispered that Louise Luetgert was likely to appear, now that punishment had been fully meted out to her husband. Something like a faint murmur of applause came from the crowd when a white-haired German woman standing in front of the casket recited a couplet from Friedrich Schiller's *William Tell* in a low voice: "Bereitet oder nicht, zu gehen / Er muß vor seinen Richter stehen" (Ready or not to go / He must stand before his judge).

Luetgert's relatives and friends arrived for a service around 11:30. A crowd rushed to pack the hall, but no chairs were provided other than those reserved for the pallbearers and the relatives, which were arranged in a circle about the casket. The police stopped the curiosity seekers from entering when the room was comfortably filled. Men who could not force their way into the hall stood in groups outside and debated the Luetgert mystery. One man insisted the body in the casket might not be Luetgert's. "They might have worked a trick to get him free because he was rich," he said.

"How could they do it?" someone asked.

"By putting him in a coffin alive and then changing him for a dead man when he got out."

"No, that was him in the coffin in there."

"Did you know him?"

"Sure. Of course I knew him," the man said proudly.

"So did I," the first man said, "but they wouldn't let me in, and I thought something was wrong."

All the members of Luetgert's immediate family were at the service, but none of Louise's relatives attended. Although the funeral arrangements had called for the attorneys Kehoe and Phalen to be among the honorary pallbearers, the only lawyer to show up was Harmon. When Mary Charles walked in, wearing a black veil, some by-standers thought it might be Mrs. Luetgert.

Harmon arose, placed his hand on the casket, and read from a typewritten speech. As he spoke of Luetgert's genial character, Louis and Elmer sobbed. At times Harmon was almost overcome with emotion. The *Inter Ocean* noted, "The majority of those present, however, appeared to regard the speech as an interesting incident to an entertaining function."

Harmon dramatically cried out, "I call upon Louise Luetgert, the missing woman, for whom he suffered without ever uttering an unkind word regarding her, to come forth and remove the unmerited stain from the name of the father of her innocent children." He paused, and the hundreds of people in the room looked around, as if expecting to see Mrs. Luetgert appear. Nothing happened.

Harmon concluded, "This man, with all his human frailties and all his good qualities, has passed before the great tribunal, where justice is eternally enthroned. Farewell, old friend and client! You have found in that heavenly court that perfect justice that was denied you on earth. May you forever rest in peace."

After Harmon sat down, the pastor of St. Paul's German Evangelical Church delivered a speech in German, appealing for charity toward Luetgert's children. And then the casket was taken in a long funeral procession to Waldheim Cemetery, west of the city. Few of the people who had attended the service at the Northwest Turner Hall followed the procession of a half-dozen carriages to the cemetery, but the news of Luetgert's burial drew another big audience at Waldheim. Newspapers estimated it was one of the largest crowds ever assembled there, rivaling the size of the groups that had gathered at the cemetery during memorial services for the anarchists executed in the Haymarket trial.

The big bell over the cemetery gate tolled fifteen minutes before and after the arrival of the carriages. The procession moved down the main drive in the midst of a large meadow of trees and shrubs, with two artificial lakes reflecting the sky above. Six thousand people lined the driveway within the cemetery grounds and followed the procession to an open grave in the Luetgert family plot. As the coffin was finally lowered into the ground, the spectators craned their necks. A hush fell as everyone waited to hear the sound of dirt being dropped onto the lid. Luetgert's son Arnold threw in the first handful of earth. Soon the grave was filled and Luetgert's sons placed the floral arrangement with the words "I AM INNOCENT" on top of the mound.

The funeral party left the cemetery, and most of the curiosity-seekers dispersed, but hundreds lingered in the graveyard. They pushed and struggled to reach the inner circle of spectators standing around the patch of bare earth and staring at it silently with half-fearful expressions. The coming of night finally drove them away. The last of the morbid men and women passed out through the cemetery gates, leaving Adolph Louis Luetgert's grave behind them in the darkness.

 EPILOGUE

IN DECEMBER 1898 George Dorsey offered physicians and other scientists tips on identifying bones in a court of law. Speaking to the Medico-Legal Society of Chicago, he used the same sort of thick anatomical jargon—basilar synchondrosis, promiment glabella, superciliary eminences—that had confounded reporters during the Luetgert trials. Laymen might have found it a dry lecture, but after Dorsey finished, two doctors who had testified for Luetgert's defense team, Walter H. Allport and William T. Eckley, responded with harsh words. "The world is full of those who, in the name of science, would claim to circumvent the impossible," Allport said. Without insulting Dorsey by name, he alluded to him as a "recently created scientist" who had ventured outside his realm of expertise in search of "novelty."

Allport compared Dorsey's testimony in the Luetgert trial to the evidence in the famous 1850 trial of Dr. Webster at Harvard, Dorsey's alma mater. "It is to be noted that the papers of the day congratulated the Harvard faculty on their skill in identifying, placing and restoring Dr. Parkman's skeleton, some 156 bones being present. The advance made in teaching at this institution is remarkable, for a recent graduate of the same school now identifies a woman from four fragments of bone the size of peas." If Dorsey said anything to defend himself, it is not reflected in the society's minutes.

Dorsey continued serving as the curator of the Field Museum's anthropology department, but he shifted his focus away from identifying skeletal remains to other pursuits, such as collecting the folktales of Native Americans. In 1915 he left his position at the Field Museum—and his wife, Ida—receiving a commission as a lieutenant commander in the U.S. Navy. After leaving the navy he moved to New York's Greenwich Village. One of the anthropologist's old colleagues from the Luetgert case, Willard McEwen, represented Ida Dorsey in divorce court in 1922. "We are not asking alimony," McEwen said. "The doctor has no means; he is living in New York a life of—I don't know—I suppose you would call it that of a bohemian. He writes incessantly and has a notion that some day he will strike a 'popular chord.'"

Dorsey did in fact achieve some popular success with a 1925 book titled *Why We Behave Like Human Beings.* But Dorsey, who died in 1931, never testified in another criminal case. It would be decades before forensic anthropology became established as a way for criminal investigators to identify bone fragments and other human remains.

In 1978 T. Dale Stewart, a pioneer in the field, reviewed the old press accounts of the Luetgert trials and decided they showed that "Dorsey acquitted himself credibly on the stand." Stewart added a less encouraging note, however: "Besides, his identification of the small bits of bone seems not to have influenced the outcome of the trial." In 1999 the anthropologists Eugene Giles and Linda L. Klepinger also looked back at the Luetgert trials, concluding, "America's first expert forensic testimony by a professional anthropologist was an inauspicious beginning, and by contemporary standards would probably not pass muster." Indeed, even with all the scientific advances that occurred in the eight decades following the Luetgert case, Clyde Snow wrote in 1982 that it wouldn't be easy to determine a person's sex from small bone fragments.

By testifying in a criminal case, Dorsey had placed himself in a position many scientists find uncomfortable, wrote Snow, the world's foremost forensic anthropologist. "It disturbs some physical anthropologists to find that the law perceives the truth in black and white instead of the infinite spectrum of greys observed by scientists," he wrote. "They feel the law, by ignoring the scientific method, is somehow 'not playing the game.' The search for truth in the laboratory and the search for truth in the courtroom are games that are played by different rules."

In the Luetgert case the judges placed few restrictions concerning which experts they allowed to testify. Courts around the United States began taking a closer look at that question in 1923, after a local appellate court in Washington, D.C., ruled on the murder conviction of James Alphonso Frye. Frye wanted to show he had passed a kind of lie detector called the "systolic blood pressure deception test." The appeals court ruled out the evidence because its scientific basis had not "gained general acceptance in the particular field in which it belongs." That decision became known as the "Frye rule," widely quoted by judges and lawyers. In 1993 the U.S. Supreme Court ruled further that scientific testimony needs more than "general acceptance." Rather, courts must determine whether it is based on sound scientific methodology.

A century after the Luetgert case jurors still sometimes puzzle over contradictory and confusing testimony from battling teams of scientific experts. Jurors can be misled by scientific testimony, especially if they put too much credence in a statement simply because it was uttered by someone labeled "an expert." "A similar error is encouraged by pasting a doctor's picture on a bottle of medicine," Kenneth R. Foster and Peter W. Huber write in their book *Judging Science.* "The medicine may or may not work, but the picture of the doctor suggests not merely the individual endorsement of one physician but the approval of the medical community."

Some commentators have called for judges to appoint fact-finding experts who would determine the validity of scientific evidence, a system used in certain European nations. Others question whether it would be wise to take this power away from jurors. "While this might make complicated subjects easier to fathom for the judge and jury, it ignores the fact that the practice of science is as porous as a sponge," write Christopher Joyce and Eric Stover in their book *Witnesses from the Grave.* "It is honeycombed with dispute. Over time even the surest of theories is replaced. The Anglo-Saxon approach at least ensures that both sides get a hearing, fair or otherwise."

◆◆◆

Shortly after Luetgert's conviction, some observers who had watched the trials published their analyses. Dr. J. Sanderson Christison, who was supposedly employed by Luetgert's defense team, wrote about the case in 1899 when he revised his book *Crime and Criminals.* Christison took the defense's side on virtually every argument, wholly buying into the notion that Mrs. Luetgert was insane and had run away from home. Christison was still predicting Mrs. Luetgert would eventually appear: "Her secretiveness is not likely to last long after public interest has ceased."

Christison persuasively raised doubts about the prosecution's bone evidence, but he seemed almost obsessed with the physical characteristics of witnesses. Clearly a follower of Cesare Lombroso's theories, Christison dismissed much of the prosecution's case by pointing out "the marked degenerate or defective character of the majority of the chief witnesses for the State." He implied that many witnesses could not be believed, for some were "defective" and one was "an unemployed laborer."

In the 1898 book *Murder in All Ages* Matthew Worth Pinkerton held steadfastly to his belief that Luetgert was guilty. "Luetgert must have long meditated this crime, having purchased the potash nearly two months before he carried the plan into execution," Pinkerton wrote. "The annals of crime contain few instances where preparations for a murder were made so long in advance, and the depravity of the wretch's heart may fairly be deduced from the circumstance."*

The most thorough dissection of the Luetgert case came from the Northwestern University law professor John Henry Wigmore, who would write an important law text in 1904, the monumental *Treatise on Evidence.* In an 1898 *American Law Review* article, Wigmore put little credence in the theory that Mrs. Luetgert had voluntarily left home. Wigmore mistakenly asserted that the defense witnesses who bolstered this theory didn't come forward with their tales until the trial had begun. "Their recollection . . . had the suspicious appearance of being forced or manufactured for the occasion," he wrote. Newspaper reports from the time of Luetgert's arrest, however, did quote people describing how Mrs. Luetgert had threatened to leave home.

Wigmore also thought Luetgert's story about making soap seemed like a lie concocted long after the fact. The testimony that the factory had no barrels of grease on May 1 made the soap-making tale "not merely an improbability, but an impossibility," Wigmore wrote. In addition, he viewed Luetgert's behavior after his wife's disappearance as strong proof of "guilty suppression of evidence." The bone experts on both sides were "reputable and competent," Wigmore found, but even if the state didn't conclusively prove the bones were human, the defense couldn't prove they weren't. Wigmore also said it was "abundantly shown" that the rings were Mrs. Luetgert's.

Wigmore found too many inconsistencies and contradictions to believe the testimony of the Schimke sisters and other witnesses who reported seeing Mr. and Mrs. Luetgert the night of May 1. Even without that testimony, however, Wigmore believed the state's case against Luetgert was "a thorough array of significant circumstances."

The defense's main achievement, he said, was its constant attack on the

---

* This author was not related to the famous Pinkerton detectives. According to the detective Allan Pinkerton's son, William A. Pinkerton, "The book . . . was written by some Methodist preacher for Matthew Pinkerton and was a fraud, the name Pinkerton merely being used for the purpose of selling the same."

prosecution case, resulting in "a noise and smoke of general conflict." None-theless, Wigmore thought that once the smoke had cleared, it was obvious that Luetgert was guilty.

Not everyone was convinced that Luetgert was a murdering monster, however. In 1913 the *Chicago Tribune* reported that "men learned in crimi-nal lore" who had studied the case believed Luetgert had been innocent. According to these observers, he was "one of the great army of martyrs who suffer penal servitude purely because of perverted circumstantial evidence." The newspaper added that Luetgert's conviction had not solidly established his guilt in "the public mind."

Looking at the Luetgert trials from today's perspective, it's hard not to imagine how much easier it would have been to solve the case with the aid of DNA testing—or even fingerprint, hair, fiber, and blood-type identifi-cation techniques. Unfortunately, officials at the offices of the Cook County state's attorney, the clerk of the Circuit Court, and the Chicago Police say they have no idea what became of the physical evidence in the Luetgert case—the rings, the bone fragments, photographs, or anything else—so unless these clues turn up unexpectedly, it will be impossible to resolve the Luetgert mys-tery with today's forensic science. If current DNA technology had existed in the 1890s, scientists might have been able to determine whether the bone frag-ments were those of Louise Luetgert, although it's far from certain that the small fragments would have contained enough usable DNA. It's likely that all the nuclear DNA was destroyed if the body was dissolved in potash, but the bones still might have contained maternally inherited mitochondrial DNA, which is less likely to deteriorate than the DNA found in the nuclei of cells. If the bones from the Luetgert trial could be located today—and posi-tively identified as those used in the trial—it might still be possible to see whether they belonged to Louise Luetgert by comparing their mitochondrial DNA with that from a descendant of her sister or the bones of Louise's daugh-ters. Scientists used this technique in 1993 to identify the bones of Russian czar Nicholas II, his wife, Alexandra, and their children. Like Louise Luetgert's bones, the Romanov family's bones were disintegrated pieces. Their bodies reportedly were burned with gasoline and doused with sulfuric acid, but enough mitochondrial DNA remained in the fragments to make their identification possible seventy-five years after the Romanovs' deaths.

If the scientific testimony in the Luetgert trials is too questionable to accept (as even Wigmore suggests), is the remaining circumstantial evidence enough to prove Luetgert's guilt? Other than the prosecution's explanation, no credible theory explains what might have happened to Louise Luetgert on the night of May 1, 1897, or what Adolph Luetgert was doing. That may not be enough to persuade everyone of his guilt, however, leaving some people with a reasonable doubt.

Even if Luetgert did kill his wife, whether he received a fair trial is another matter. It is easy to imagine an appeals court overturning his conviction for any number of reasons. To name a few:

- the effect of newspaper publicity, which made it all but impossible to find an impartial jury in Chicago;
- incompetent defense by at least one attorney, Lawrence Harmon, whose erratic behavior ruined Luetgert's chance of winning any sympathy from the jury;
- the careless handling of evidence, including bones that were handed from one person to another without much caution or documentation;
- the police intimidation of defense witnesses (although some of the witnesses who were harassed, such as Harry Fiedler and Rosa Gleich, may not have had much to contribute to the case); and
- police payment of prosecution witnesses, a practice that has echoes in today's courts, when prosecutors cut deals with jail inmates and criminals in exchange for testimony.

If Luetgert had lived long enough to appeal his conviction to the Illinois Supreme Court, he conceivably might have won a new trial for any one of these reasons. If he had succeeded in such an appeal, however, it's likely that many people would have viewed him as a murderer who was set free on a "technicality."

Luetgert's accusations that the police planted or concocted evidence against him were a typical defense ploy and were sometimes hard to believe. Would the police really have known what sort of rings to place in the vat if they wanted to frame Luetgert? Given the history of the Chicago police, however, including Schaack's tactics in the Haymarket case, it's not out of the question that the police tampered with or planted at least some of the evidence against Luetgert. The tale of a policeman getting bones at Dunning may sound far-fetched, but it never got a full hearing because Cook County officials intimidated the poorhouse inmates who came forward with the story. If any of these allegations about police misconduct in the Luetgert case contained a grain of truth, it's unlikely that Luetgert would have received a fair opportunity to show it in court, given the atmosphere at his trials.

Clarence Darrow, talking at the time of Luetgert's death, may have summed up the case better than anyone: "I really believe that he was guilty but that he was convicted on insufficient evidence."

◆◆◆

As the Luetgert case faded from the headlines and entered Chicago's lore, many of the witnesses, police officers, jurors, and assorted characters whose names had become familiar to the entire city in 1897 and 1898 faded into obscurity.

The swindler Robert Davey's further adventures are unknown. Diedrich Bicknese died in 1901. Smokehouse Frank Odorofsky found work in a butcher shop, Ham Frank Lavandowski got a job in the Deering factory, and Frank Bialk was employed in a brickyard. His son, John Bialk, became a detective sergeant for the Chicago police and was killed in the line of duty in 1916.

After Luetgert's conviction, Christine Feld sued to recover some of the money Luetgert owed her, while other creditors sued her. According to a court document submitted by Feld's attorneys, the trust she had once placed in Luetgert had been transformed into "a source of constant expense, annoyance, loss, and litigation, and [had] been paraded before the public as a reproach; insinuations and slurs have been cast upon her . . . ; her good name tarnished; and her means, left by a kind, thoughtful and provident husband, have been wasted and scattered." It was not long before Feld made a new start, however, marrying Albert Link and moving to Indiana.

Judge Gary remained stubbornly proud of his record, denying he had ever shown bias. In a speech at his eightieth birthday party in 1901, he said, "I have been diligent, no one will deny; that I have not been partial, I will stoutly maintain." Gary died at the age of eighty-five on October 31, 1906. He served as a judge until the day of his death, spending forty-three years on the bench. His obituary in the *Tribune* was filled with adulatory praise and gave little hint of the controversies over his record. Today he is largely remembered as the judge who allowed the hanging and imprisonment of innocent men in the Haymarket trial.

Judge Tuthill achieved his greatest claim to fame in 1899 by presiding over the Cook County Juvenile Court, the first court in the nation specifically designed to handle juvenile cases. Tuthill made headlines again in 1916 when he handled a lawsuit between a producer filming Shakespeare's plays and a man questioning the original authorship of those plays. Tuthill ruled that Francis Bacon was the author of Shakespeare's plays. Asked about the decision, a Northwestern University English professor remarked, "Judge Tuthill may be a pretty good judge, but he doesn't know much about Shakespeare." In August 1919 Tuthill nearly drowned while swimming in Lake Michigan. An anonymous girl rescued him, dragging him onto the beach and then disappearing. Tuthill underwent surgery and fell ill with a "throat affection." He never fully recovered, dying on April 10, 1920.

At the time that Charles S. Deneen was prosecuting Luetgert, the *Times-Herald* had remarked, "He is modest in speaking of his aspirations, and it is doubtful if at the present time he thinks of ever being more than state's attorney." But after serving two terms as state's attorney, Deneen was elected the governor of Illinois, a position he held for eight years. He later served one term as U.S. senator. Throughout all that time he maintained his reputation for integrity, an unusual accomplishment in Illinois politics. Deneen kept clippings of just about every newspaper article written about him, ending up with 213 thick scrapbooks, including six on the Luetgert case, which are now kept at the Illinois State Historical Library in Springfield. Deneen was practicing law in Chicago when he died in 1940.

Outraged by the politically motivated hiring and firing in the Chicago Police Department, the Republican-controlled Illinois Senate set up a committee to investigate in early 1898. As a result, a grand jury indicted members of the city's Civil Service Commission. They were acquitted, however, and politics remained an important qualification for job applicants at Chicago City Hall.

Herman Schuettler remained one of Chicago's best-known policemen for two decades after the Luetgert case. When a trio of young men known as the Car Barn Bandits terrorized Chicago for five months in 1903, killing eight people, Schuettler received much of the credit for solving the case. He also led many raids on gambling establishments, a tactic not always popular with the city's corrupt politicians. Schuettler served as the police department's second-ranking officer from 1904 to 1917, when he was appointed superintendent. Later the same year he suffered an illness the press described as a "nervous breakdown," and he took a leave of absence, hoping to recover. Schuettler—whom police officers affectionately called "Old Herman" or "The Big Fellow"—died on August 22, 1918.

After the Luetgert case, Dr. J. Sanderson Christison continued to weigh in with his opinions on criminal cases. In one trial he proposed the theory that a defendant had confessed because he was under the "hypnotic influence" of Schuettler's eyes. In 1908 Christison was working on a book about the differences between suicidal and murderous wounds when he died, a possible suicide himself. Two men found him lying on a curb one night, seemingly under the influence of some drug. They took him to his apartment, where he died the next morning of asphyxiation from illuminating gas. Reporting his death, the *Tribune* noted, "One of Christison's favorite theories was that all persons are slightly insane." An inquest on his death was inconclusive.

Another expert involved in the Luetgert case, the prosecution's witness George Vincent Bailey, later fell on hard times and dropped out of the sciences altogether. Starting around 1916, the osteologist and paleontologist worked for fifteen years as a foreman for a road construction company in Orchard Park, New York. He died in 1936.

In early 1898, around the time Luetgert was convicted, Julian Hawthorne received his most famous assignment as a newspaper reporter when William Randolph Hearst sent him to Cuba. Hearst's biographer Ben Proctor notes, "To Cuba he sent his most 'creative' journalists, those who had few if any qualms about reporting unfounded rumors or uncorroborated stories as factual." Proctor calls the Hearst journalists "apostles of venom and make-believe," although Hawthorne's reporting in the Luetgert trial had shown him to be more of a purple-prose artist than an outright fabulist. Hawthorne reported from Cuba about the dreadful conditions suffered by the population in the colonial Spanish government's "reconcentration camps." His articles aroused widespread sympathy in the United States, building the public sentiment for war against Spain, which broke out that spring.

After writing mystery novels and reporting on criminal trials, Hawthorne found himself the target of prosecution in 1912. The author wrote hundreds of letters on light yellow stationery to friends and acquaintances, urging them to invest in some Canadian mines. The mines were a scam, and Hawthorne was found guilty of mail fraud. One observer remarked, "How much better it would have been if Julian Hawthorne had written one Scarlet Letter instead of all those yellow ones!" Hawthorne served six months in a federal penitentiary in Atlanta in 1913, an experience that inspired him to call for the abolishment of the "wicked" practice of penal imprisonment. "It breeds and multiplies the evils it pretends to heal or diminish," he wrote. Following the disgrace of the "yellow letters," Hawthorne continued writing essays, journalism, and other nonfiction works for the remaining twenty years of his life. Although he won some critical praise during his career, his writings are now largely forgotten. Hawthorne, who never escaped the shadow of his father's towering reputation, died in 1934.

Louise Luetgert was never seen again, although a creditor suing the Luetgert family published a notice in the *Chicago Daily Law Bulletin* demanding her presence in court. The same man also served the Foreman Brothers bank with papers, saying, "We command you that you summon Louise Luetgert." Despite these efforts, she "came not but herein made default," the court dryly noted.

For years children in Lake View sang a gruesome tune: "He ground her up into sau-ha-sage meat, and Luetgert was his name." The Luetgert house was an object of fear, the yard overgrown with ragweed. From time to time a tenant stayed in the home, but never for long. The factory was also empty for a few years, standing over the neighborhood like a grim specter. Its windows became a frequent target for rocks thrown from the railway embankment. The building occasionally attracted the curious and the insane.

Only a month after Luetgert's death, the factory custodian came on a man inside the office, searching the safe and inspecting the books. He tried to eject the stranger, later identified as Albert Boyer, but Boyer seized a hatchet and chased the guard into the street. A police officer came to the scene and arrested Boyer. The patrolman asked him to explain his behavior. "I am looking for Mrs. Luetgert," he replied, "and I can find her if you let me alone. She is in this building somewhere and I think she is still alive." A court ruled Boyer was insane and sent him to Dunning.

The tangle of litigation involving the failure of Luetgert's business came to a conclusion on August 1, 1900, when the Superior Court of Cook County held a public auction for the factory and its grounds. The estate of Ellen

Tuohy, one of Luetgert's creditors, offered the highest bid for the lot containing the factory, $41,297.57, and Lina Fischer bought the large lot south of the factory for $20,000. The properties formally transferred to their ownership in 1901 and 1902, respectively. The Library Bureau Company, founded by the Dewey Decimal System creator Melvil Dewey, began leasing the building in 1903, using it as a workshop and storehouse for its line of library furniture and office supplies. During renovations the firm discarded the notorious vats from the basement.

Charles Westerholm was alone in the building shortly after 1 P.M. on Sunday, June 26, 1904. After starting the building's boilers, the assistant engineer went up to the fourth floor. He smelled something burning and returned downstairs, discovering the entire first floor to be filled with smoke. Flames were bursting from the basement. After trying in vain to extinguish the fire himself, Westerholm turned in an alarm. By the time the first of the horse-drawn fire engines arrived, the flames had spread up the grease-soaked floors to the top of the factory. As firefighters manning the fourteen engines equipped with steam-powered pumps battled the four-alarm fire, people around the city heard that the old Luetgert factory was ablaze. The *Tribune* and *Journal* both estimated that 10,000 people rushed to the scene. The fire department blocked the railroad line next to the building for an hour, and passengers got off the trains and joined the crowd. Police officers held back the spectators, who were pressing dangerously close to the walls. Thick black smoke enveloped the factory, pierced in places by bursts of flame. Fearing that the fire would spread, neighbors fled their homes, carting out prized possessions.

After about three hours the firemen put out the blaze. The factory was still standing, but almost everything inside had been obliterated. Investigators said they weren't sure what had caused the fire, which had begun at almost the exact spot where Luetgert's middle vat once stood. Although newspapers reported that Westerholm had started fires in the boiler room, A. J. Mount, an officer of the Library Bureau Company, said, "There were no fires, no electrical current, no gasoline or other explosive or highly inflammable matter in the building, and we are at a loss to account for it." The *Chronicle* reported, "The source of the fire is a mystery and none has been able to offer any better explanation than the superstitious folk who . . . have an idea that some supernatural intervention against any commercial enterprise operating at the scene of the murder has been invoked." The most likely cause, officials said, was spontaneous combustion of mill dust and wood shavings from the furniture built inside the factory. The headline in the next day's *Abendpost* was "*Mordhaus in Asche*"—murder house in ashes.

Despite the destruction of the factory's interior, the Library Bureau reopened its facilities in the Luetgert building; the factory was expanded and changed hands several times over the decades. In 1907 a contracting mason bought the Luetgert house and moved it from behind the factory to another lot in the neighborhood. The part of Hermitage Avenue that intersected with Diversey was later vacated. By the 1990s the factory stood empty in a scrubby landscape, facing a row of vacant lots interrupted only by a couple of decrepit-looking frame houses. In 1999, however, the hundredth anniversary of Luetgert's death, the former sausage warehouse was converted into loft condominiums.* A new sign for Hermitage was erected in 2002, although the street's latest incarnation is little more than a driveway leading back to a parking lot occupying the land that once belonged to the Luetgerts. An entirely new neighborhood of fashionable brick homes has sprung up all around the factory, with a Starbucks coffee shop taking the place of the old saloons.

The courthouse where Luetgert was tried is now an office building, anchoring a trendy area of restaurants. The jail that stood adjacent to the court is gone, replaced by a fire station.

When Joliet's second prison, known as Stateville, opened in 1925, some people began to call for the closing of the antiquated Joliet Correctional Center, where Luetgert had spent the last fifteen months of his life. The old prison continued housing Illinois convicts, however, until the state finally shut it down in 2002.

The Luetgert family plot in Waldheim Cemetery—currently known as Forest Home, the English translation of its old name—is now an inconspicuous patch of grass. Although the ground holds the remains of Adolph Luet-

---

* Other recent accounts of the Luetgert story incorrectly assert that the factory burned down. Adolph Luetgert's descendants insist the building currently on the site is the same one that was there in 1897. A comparison of the architectural details in depictions of the Luetgert factory with those of the current building leaves no doubt that they are the same, although the turret and south-wing building are now gone. Chicago's building-permit index cards include a clerical error stating that the current building was constructed in 1899. This error, which was repeated in the Commission on Chicago Historical and Architectural Landmarks survey of historic buildings, stems from a confusion of the factory with a neighboring structure that was built in 1899. The correct building permit is the one issued to "A. L. Luetzer" on June 20, 1892.

gert, his first wife, and the three Luetgert children who died young, only the faded headstone of Luetgert's daughter Elsa is still there.

When Luetgert died in prison, his family had not yet seen the end of its tragedies. In 1908 Luetgert's brother Arnold went to a house in Elgin where he had once lived and told the current occupants that he wanted to see the room where his son had been born. Later in the day he visited Lord's Park, also in Elgin, and went out to one of the islands in the lagoon. He drew the attention of some bystanders by firing a gun into the air three times and then shot himself in the head. A woman watching the scene shrieked and fell to the ground, unconscious. She later said, "The man had such a terrible look in his face when he was taking his life that I will never forget it. It was a face of another world."

Most of the Luetgerts, though, went on to lead normal and even successful lives, untainted by the sensational stories from the turn of the century. Adolph Luetgert's eldest son, Arnold, moved to Portland, Oregon. Although Louis and Elmer Luetgert were living with William Charles at the time of their father's death, they lived with other family members in the coming years. Louis assumed most of the responsibility for watching over his younger brother. It is said that they both accepted the fact that their mother had died.

Elmer, who came to be known by the nickname "Slim," worked as a milkman for the Borden Milk Company. He had one son, who died before he was a month old, and one adopted daughter. Elmer moved to Michigan and died in 1976.

Louis spent most of his life working as a postal clerk, eventually rising to become the postmaster and a respected citizen of Elmhurst, a suburb west of Chicago. He had four sons, one of whom died young.

In the 1920s one of Louis's sons, Howard, received an offer from Deneen, who was then a U.S. senator, for an appointment to West Point. Howard Luetgert declined the chance because he was not interested in a military career. He was suspicious for years that Deneen had extended the offer because he felt guilty over the duress his prosecution had caused the Luetgert family.

Neither Louis nor Elmer would say much about the trials they had witnessed as boys. Louis may have talked about it with his children, because his son Howard would later express the strong belief that Adolph Luetgert had been innocent. But Louis, who died in 1960, never even mentioned the case to his grandchildren. They noticed the family had a glass paperweight containing a quaint picture of horse-drawn carts coming and going from a red-brick "sausage works" building as a steam locomotive chugged along a nearby track. They looked inside the paperweight and saw the factory their family had once owned, but their grandfather never told them what had happened there.

ACKNOWLEDGMENTS

MY IDEA for this book came out of a visit to the Palatine Historical Society, where Marilyn Pedersen is always a source of friendly advice. I did most of my research at the Chicago Historical Society, Chicago's Harold Washington Library, and the Illinois State Historical Library, in Springfield, which holds one of the most valuable sources of information on the Luetgert case, the scrapbooks of Charles Deneen.

Other sources of information included the Cook County Recorder of Deeds Office; Chicago's Sulzer Regional Library; the University of Illinois at Chicago library; the Illinois Regional Archives Depository, at Northeastern Illinois University; the Center for Research Libraries; the Newberry Library; the Illinois Department of Corrections; the New-York Historical Society; the Arlington Heights Memorial Library; the Palatine Public Library; and various Web sites, including www.ancestry.com.

Two of Adolph and Louise Luetgert's great-grandchildren, Jim and M. J. Luetgert, were kind enough to talk to me about their family and provide photos for use in this book. Deborah Tegtmeier, the great-great-granddaughter of Diedrich Bicknese, also tracked down some family history for me.

Phil Costello and the rest of the staff at the archives of the Office of the Clerk of the Circuit Court of Cook County assisted me with court records on the Luetgert trials and other cases.

From across the Atlantic Ocean, the city archivist Stephan Grimm and the family historian Detlev Lütgert sent me historical information on Gütersloh, Germany, and the Lütgert genealogy. My German teacher at Harper College, Renate von Keudell, checked my translations for accuracy.

Fred Dahlinger Jr. at Circus World Museum in Baraboo, Wisconsin, provided background on the circus Louis Luetgert attended the night of his mother's disappearance.

Eugene Giles, an anthropology professor at the University of Illinois at Urbana-Champaign, gave me copies of several articles he had collected on the anthropological testimony in the Luetgert case.

After a seemingly endless search to pinpoint the date of the fire at the Luetgert factory, I talked to the journalist Patrick Butler, who suggested calling Kenneth Little, an unofficial historian of the Chicago Fire Department. With a quick check of his records, Little solved a mystery I had been trying to answer for years.

My friends Eric and Susan Parker and Kevin Kieffer read an early draft of this book and offered helpful feedback. As I was revising my manuscript, I received invaluable critiques from Richard Wentworth at the University of Illinois Press; Perry Duis, a history professor at the University of Illinois at Chicago who has written several books on the city's history, including the insightful *Challenging Chicago;* and John E. Hallwas, an English professor at Western Illinois University who wrote the fascinating historical true-crime book *The Bootlegger.*

Over the years many other friends, family members, and teachers have given me their encouragement, which is something every aspiring writer needs. Finally, I want to acknowledge my parents. My father, Robert, who died in 1992, loved to tell a good story and was enthusiastic about my early work as a journalist. My mother, Virginia, says she knew I would be a writer from the time I was born. She may or may not have a gift for seeing the future, but she taught me to love reading and writing. It's something for which I will always be grateful.

NOTES

TO AVOID CONFUSION, I have standardized the spellings of people's names, which often appeared in two or more variants. I have consulted court documents, property records, and the Lakeside City Directory of Chicago to determine the spelling of some names. In most cases I have chosen the most frequent spelling. Although most stories about the Luetgert case spell Christine Feld's name as Feldt, her name is spelled without the *t* in court documents and other official sources.

When using quotations from courtroom testimony and newspaper interviews, I have changed some punctuation and capitalization to improve readability. I corrected spelling errors but retained some of the era's archaic spellings and idioms.

All the newspapers cited here are Chicago publications unless otherwise noted. The year has been omitted when it is the same as that in the previous citation. All the *New York Journal* articles by Julian Hawthorne cited here were reprinted in the *Chicago Tribune,* and I relied on those reprints. For all articles from newspapers based in cities other than Chicago, as well as *Chicago Dispatch* articles and all *Chicago Chronicle* articles from 1897, I used the copies in the Deneen scrapbooks at the Illinois State Historical Library.

INTRODUCTION

Fred A. Smith: *Palatine Independent,* Oct. 23, 1897.

"Major courtroom trials": Lawrence M. Friedman, *Crime and Punishment in American History* (New York: Basic Books, 1993), 254.

Reputation of Chicago police: Richard C. Lindberg, *To Serve and Collect: Chicago Politics and Police Corruption from the Lager Beer Riot to the Summerdale Scandal, 1855–1960* (New York: Praeger, 1991; repr., Carbondale: Southern Illinois University Press, 1998), xi.

Chicago reporters' shenanigans: John J. McPhaul, *Deadlines and Monkeyshines: The Fabled World of Chicago Journalism* (Englewood Cliffs, N.J.: Prentice-Hall, 1962), 8–12, 70.

Role of women in the 1890s: Lauren Rabinovitz, *For the Love of Pleasure: Women, Movies, and Culture in Turn-of-the-Century Chicago* (New Brunswick, N.J.: Rutgers University Press, 1998), 5–11.

Lombroso: Christopher Joyce and Eric Stover, *Witnesses from the Grave: The Stories Bones Tell* (Boston: Little, Brown, 1991), 55–58.

Mudgett case: Harold Schechter, *Depraved: The Shocking True Story of America's First Serial Killer* (New York: Pocket Books, 1994).

"The Corpus Delicti": Melville Davisson Post, *The Strange Schemes of Randolph Mason* (New York: G. P. Putnam's Sons, 1896; repr., Philadelphia: Oswald Train, 1973), 19–76.

"A large mahogany chest": Oscar Wilde, *The Picture of Dorian Gray* (London: Ward, Lock, 1891; repr., Toronto and London: Dover, 1993), 126.

Parkman murder: Joyce and Stover, 45–53.

"Until the Parkman case, legal authorities": Robert Sullivan, *The Disappearance of Dr. Parkman* (Boston: Little, Brown, 1971), 144–45.

Lemuel Shaw's jury instructions: Helen Thomsen, *Murder at Harvard* (Boston: Houghton Mifflin, 1971), 220–21.

Rufus Choate's remark: ibid., 224.

"Member of the Legal Profession": Sullivan, 145.

"Virtually every student": ibid., vii.

CHAPTER 1: OMENS

Story of the sparrow and Luetgert's comments in jail: *Tribune*, Oct. 18, 1897.

Scenes from the first day of jury deliberations: *Journal*, Oct. 18; *Tribune* and *Record*, Oct. 19.

The account of the *Journal* reporters listening in on the jury: *Journal* and *Palatine Independent*, Oct. 23.

Report by Katharine: *Chronicle*, Oct. 19.

CHAPTER 2: LEGENDS

Descriptions of Chicago: Paul Borget, *Outre-Mer, Impressions of America* (New York: Charles Scribner's Sons, 1895); William Archer, *America To-Day: Observations and Reflections* (New York: Charles Scribner's Sons, 1899); George Warrington Steevens, *The Land of the Dollar* (New York: Dodd, Mead, 1897); Bessie Louise Pierce with Joe L. Norris, *As Others See Chicago: Impressions of Visitors, 1673–1933* (Chicago: University of Chicago Press, 1933); William Stead, *If Christ Came to Chicago* (Chicago: Laird and Lee, 1894); Arnold Lewis, *An Early Encounter with Tomorrow: Europeans, Chicago's Loop, and the World's Columbian Exposition* (Urbana: University of Illinois Press, 1997); Susan E. Hirsch and Robert I. Goler, *A City Comes of Age: Chicago in the 1890s* (Chicago: Chicago Historical Society, 1990); George Ade, *Chicago Stories* (Chicago: Caxton Club, 1941; repr., Chicago: Henry Regnery, 1963).

"The smoke of Chicago": Archer, 106.

Descriptions of Lake View: Helen Zattenberg, *An Historical Sketch of Ravenswood and Lake View* (Chicago: Ravenswood–Lake View Historical Association, 1941); Chicago Historical Society, *History of the Lakeview Community, Chicago*; Stephen Bedell Clark, *The Lake View Saga* (Chicago: Lake View Trust and Savings Bank, Lerner Newspapers, 1985); *Tribune*, Sept. 1, 1957; Sharon H. Galitz, "Memories, 1880–1893, by Robert E. Haskin," *Chicago Genealogist* (Spring 1992): 71.

"A different class of people": oral history of Winfred P. Dunn, Chicago Historical Society.

Descriptions of Luetgert factory and home: *News*, May 17, 1897; *Tribune*, May 17–18; *Illinois Staats-Zeitung*, May 18.

Opening argument of Willard McEwen: *Record*, Aug. 31.

Germans and Poles: *Tribune*, Oct. 19.

Arson, poison rumors: *Illinois Staats-Zeitung*, May 18, 1897.

Death of Luetgert's first wife: *Tribune*, May 18; Waldheim Cemetery interment records.

Stories handed down in Bicknese family: Michelle Y. Moeller, *My German Heritage: A History of Max Moeller and Emma Bicknese* (privately printed, 1986).

Rumors about Luetgert's father and grandfather: *Abendpost*, May 19, 1897.

Luetgert's reminiscences about his life: transcripts of testimony in second trial and articles about his testimony in *Tribune*, *Chronicle*, *News*, and *Record*, Jan. 21–22, 1898; article by Luetgert, "Adolph L. Luetgert Tells of His Life in America before He Was Charged with Killing His Wife," *St. Louis Republic*, Oct. 24, 1897.

Genealogical information on Luetgert's ancestors courtesy of Jim and M. J. Luetgert and Detlev Lütgert.

History and descriptions of Gütersloh: Hans Hilbk, *Gütersloh und Preussen: Eine Wahlverwandtschaft, 1818–1888* (Gütersloh and Prussia: an elective affinity) (Gütersloh: Flöttmann Verlag, n.d.); Hermann Eickhoff, *Zur Geschichte der Stadt Gütersloh und der Nachbarstädte des Kreises Wiedenbrück* (On the history of the city of Gütersloh and the neighboring cities of the Wiedenbrück district) (Gütersloh: City of Gütersloh, 1925).

Accounts of Chicago's history: Donald L. Miller, *City of the Century: The Epic of Chicago and the Making of America* (New York: Simon and Schuster, 1996); Herbert Asbury, *Gem of the Prairie: An Informal History of the Chicago Underworld* (New York: Knopf, 1940; repr., Dekalb: Northern Illinois University Press, 1986); Finis Farr, *Chicago: A Personal History of America's Most American City* (New Rochelle, N.Y.: Arlington House, 1973).

Death of Hugh McGowan: *Times*, Sept. 12, 1879; *Tribune*, Sept. 13; Cook County Coroner's inquest no. 575, Sept. 11–12, 1879; *Daily Sun*, *Tribune*, and *News*, May 18, 1897.

Children's deaths: Waldheim Cemetery interment records.

Luetgert's saloon profitable: *Tribune*, Oct. 19, 1897.

Dyspepsia: J. Sanderson Christison, *Crime and Criminals*, 2d ed. (Chicago: S. T. Hurst, 1899), 165.

Hunyadi water advertisement: *Tribune*, Mar. 4, 1902.

Description of first Luetgert sausage factory: *A Business Tour of Chicago* (Chicago: E. E. Barton), 136.

Louise did not care: Christison, 159.

"My head is always so full . . .": interview, *News*, Sept. 6, 1897.

"'Imported' frankfurters": *Chronicle*, Oct. 10.

Louise never ceased to chide him: *Tribune*, Oct. 19.

Luetgert's comment on the sketch of Davey: *Inter Ocean*, May 19, 1897.

CHAPTER 3: THE ENGLISHMAN

Predictions of criminals coming to Chicago for the fair: Edwin Wilson, *Inter Ocean,* Feb. 19, 1893.

Stories of Davey in Chicago: *Inter Ocean,* Feb. 3–9.

Story of Davey in England: *London Truth,* Jan. 19, reprinted in *Inter Ocean,* Feb. 3; *London Truth,* Jan. 26, reprinted in *Inter Ocean,* Feb. 11.

Davey's travels and return to Chicago: *Inter Ocean,* May 19, 1897.

Luetgert's remarks about Davey and deal between Luetgert and Charles: Luetgert testimony, *Tribune,* Jan. 22, 1898.

Thatcher quote: *Inter Ocean,* May 19, 1897.

Conversation between Davey and Luetgert about bank failure: Luetgert testimony, *Tribune* and *Record,* Jan. 22, 1898.

Bank failures: *News,* Dec. 21, 1896; F. Cyril James, *The Growth of Chicago Banks,* vol. 2: *The Modern Age, 1897–1938* (London: Harper and Brothers, 1938) 673–77.

CHAPTER 4: EVERYTHING IS GONE

Incorporation of Luetgert company, loans, and mortgages: Office of Cook County Recorder of Deeds.

Luetgert's comments about the events of early 1897: Luetgert's testimony, *Tribune, Record, Journal,* and *Chronicle,* Jan. 22–26, 1898. Luetgert's account of his conversation with Oscar Foreman is largely corroborated by Foreman's own testimony, reported in the *Record,* Sept. 9, 1897, although the wording differs.

Foreman's relation to Nathan Leopold Jr.: Hal Higdon, *The Crime of the Century: The Leopold and Loeb Case* (New York: G. P. Putnam's Sons, 1975), 66.

"Family jars": *Tribune,* Oct. 19, 1897.

Descriptions of Feld: *Inter Ocean,* May 19; *News,* Sept. 4.

Diedrich Bicknese quote: *Journal,* Aug. 24.

Clarendon Rutherford comments: Christison, 158.

Satin slippers, canary: ibid., 156–57.

Quotes from Mary Siemering, Fred Mueller, Mary Charles: *Record,* Oct. 5, 1897.

Louis Balgamann quote: *Record,* Oct. 7.

Adolph Elandt quote: *Tribune,* Sept. 23.

Quotes from Charles Bahanke and Frank Dettler: *Tribune,* Sept. 28.

Marcus Heineman quote: *Tribune,* Sept. 29.

CHAPTER 5: MOVING DAY

Events of May 1, 1897: *Tribune, Inter Ocean, News,* and *Record,* May 1 and May 2, 1897; *Tribune,* Apr. 25; testimony of Henry J. Cox, official forecaster of the United States Weather Bureau, *Record,* Oct. 5.

Luetgert purchased two tickets: Christine Feld's testimony, *Tribune,* Sept. 5.

Remarks by Siemering, William Follbach, Anton Schuster, Amelia Kaiser, and Mary Charles: *Record,* Oct. 5.

Howe's London Circus: *New York Clipper,* June 6, 1896; *New York Clipper,* Mar. 27, 1897; John D. Draper, "The History of the Howes and the London Titles," *Bandwagon* (Jan.–Feb. 1978): 23–24; *Tribune,* Aug. 29 and 30, 1896.

Louis Luetgert quotes: *News,* May 24, 1897.

CHAPTER 6: MISSING

Mary Siemering's account: *Record,* Sept. 25, 1897.

Agatha Tosch quote: *News,* Aug. 31.

Conversation with Adams Goodrich: Goodrich testimony, *Tribune,* Sept. 23.

Follbach quote: *Dispatch,* Oct. 7.

Ralph Bradley quotes: *Tribune,* Sept. 23.

Frank Moan: Moan's testimony, *Tribune,* Oct. 7.

Diedrich Bicknese's account: *Tribune* and *Record,* Aug. 31; *Tribune,* Jan. 29, 1898.

Sophia Tews's account: *News,* Sept. 3, 1897.

Schuettler's account of questioning Luetgert: *News, Record,* and *Tribune,* Sept. 3.

Schuettler's comment on missing dog: *Tribune,* Nov. 2, 1913.

CHAPTER 7: CASE HISTORIES

Descriptions of Schaack: *News,* Aug. 31, 1897; *Chronicle,* May 18, 1898; Paul Avrich, *The Haymarket Tragedy* (Princeton, N.J.: Princeton University Press, 1984), 236, 273–74; Julian Hawthorne, *New York Journal,* Sept. 12, 1897.

Schaack's early life and police career: *Chronicle,* May 18, 1898; John J. Flinn, *History of the Chicago Police* (Chicago, 1887), 364–68; Lindberg, 63.

Incompetence at police department: Michael J. Schaack, *Anarchy and Anarchists* (Chicago: F. J. Schulte, 1889), 183–85.

Anonymous tip: Schaack, 187–88.

Raids on suspected anarchists: Avrich, 221, 222–24; Lindberg, 68; *Chronicle,* May 18, 1898.

Threats against Schaack: Schaack, 199, 201, 216.

Descriptions of anarchists: ibid., 207–8.

Schaack's comments on the state of panic: ibid., 183, 206.

Schaack made the panic worse: Avrich, 223.

Ebersold quote: Rudolf A. Hofmeister, *The Germans of Chicago* (Champaign, Ill.: Stipes, 1976), 148–49.

Quote on "delusions": Charles Edward Russell, "The Haymarket and Afterwards: Some Personal Recollections," *Appleton's Magazine,* Oct. 1907, 405.

Schuettler's arrest of Lingg: Avrich, 232; Flinn, 378.

Neebe quote: *The Famous Speeches of the Eight Chicago Anarchists in Court,* rev. ed. (Chicago: Lucy E. Parsons, 1910), 34.

Hubbard quote: *Tribune*, June 12, 1889.

Cronin case: Henry M. Hunt, *The Crime of the Century; or, The Assassination of Dr. Patrick Henry Cronin* (H. L. and D. H. Kochersperger, 1889); Lindberg, 82–88.

Chief Hubbard's remark: *Tribune*, June 12, 1889.

Schaack dismissed: Lindberg, 98.

O'Malley case: *News*, Dec. 30, 1896, and Feb. 6, 12, and 13, 1897.

Catholic enemies: *Chronicle*, May 18, 1898.

Demands for Schaack's dismissal: *News*, Apr. 28 and 30, 1897.

CHAPTER 8: THE SEARCH

Description of North Branch of the Chicago River: *Times-Herald*, Nov. 14, 1897.

Descriptions of police search: *News*, Sept. 8 and 15, 1897.

Description of factory interior: *Tribune*, May 17 and 18; *News*, May 17; *Inter Ocean*, May 18.

Mix that included saltpeter: *News*, Sept. 3, 1897.

Feld's story: *News*, Sept. 4.

Articles on Mrs. Luetgert's disappearance: *Tribune*, May 9 and 10.

Luetgert visits Schuettler: *Tribune*, Sept. 3.

Luetgert sends men to *Tribune* offices: *Tribune*, May 18.

Dean and Qualey encounter Bialk: *News*, Sept. 3.

CHAPTER 9: STRONG STUFF

Bialk's story: *Record*, Aug. 31, 1897; *News*, Sept. 9.

Odorofsky and Lavandowski's stories: *News* and *Record*, Sept. 1 and 2.

Pökelhaus Frank: *Abendpost*, Sept. 2.

Schinkenfranz: *Illinois Staats-Zeitung*, Sept. 2.

Celery compound advertisement: *Tribune*, July 5, 1902.

Timing of Bialk's second errand: John H. Wigmore, "The Luetgert Case," *American Law Review* 32 (Mar.–Apr. 1898): 194.

CHAPTER 10: GREWSOME CLEWS

Agatha Tosch's story: *News*, Aug. 31, 1897.

John Bialk's story: *Tribune*, Sept. 9, 1897.

Police visit factory: *News*, Sept. 2 and 3; *Record*, Sept. 2, 3, and 16.

Description of rings: Wigmore, 190.

Article on "sensational developments": *Tribune*, May 16, 1897.

Luetgert's conversation with Frank Bialk: Klinger and Bialk's testimony, *News*, Sept. 2; *Record*, Sept. 3.

Fred Mueller: *Tribune*, May 17.

Luetgert's arrest: *News* and *Journal*, May 17; *Tribune*, May 18.

Note on crude potash: David Wilburn, Thomas Goonan, and Donald Bleiwas, *Technological Advancement—A Factor in Increasing Resource Use,* U.S. Geological Survey, Open-File Report 01-197, appendix 4 (online document posted 2001 at <http://pubs.usgs.gov/openfile/of01-197/html/app4.htm>).

CHAPTER 11: THE SWEATING

Arrest statistics: *Report of the General Superintendent of Police, to the City of Chicago for the Fiscal Year Ending Dec. 31, 1897.*
Luetgert's initial confinement: *News,* May 17, 1897; *Tribune* and *Inter Ocean,* May 18.
Reporters visit factory: *Inter Ocean,* May 18 and 20; *News,* Sept. 8.

CHAPTER 12: THE WOMAN IN BLACK

Statements by Kenosha witnesses: *Record,* Sept. 23, 1897; *Tribune,* Sept. 24 and 25.
Vincent and Charles investigate: *Tribune,* May 20 and 21.
Vincent and Tripp's statement: *Inter Ocean,* May 20.
Kipley's comments: *Inter Ocean,* May 21 and 22.
Schaack's comments: *Tribune,* May 20.
Anonymous detective's comments: *News,* May 20.

CHAPTER 13: CELL 21

Arrest statistics: *Report of the General Superintendent, 1897.*
Descriptions of Luetgert and his son: *Tribune,* Aug. 24 and 31, 1897; *New York World,* Sept. 4.
Arnold Luetgert visits jail: *News* and *Abendpost,* May 20.
Court hearings: *News,* May 22, 24, and 26.
Feld's comments: *Abendpost,* June 4; *Tribune,* June 5.
Indictment: Office of the Clerk of the Cook County Circuit Court, archives.
Interview with Luetgert: *Abendpost,* June 5.

CHAPTER 14: SPRING AND SUMMER

Alchemy experiments: *News,* May 26, 1897.
Economic recovery: *Tribune,* Jan. 1, 1898.
Kipley: *Tribune,* Apr. 26, June 10, and July 12, 1897.
New jail: *News* and *Tribune,* July 11.
Nic Marzen's history: Office of the Clerk of the Cook County Circuit Court, archives; *Tribune,* Feb. 20, 1896.
Luetgert and Marzen cook in jail cell: *Journal,* Oct. 11, 1897.
Marzen's comment: *Journal,* Aug. 25.
Luetgert's comment: *Journal,* Sept. 23.

CHAPTER 15: FIXED OPINIONS

Interviews with Luetgert: *Tribune,* Aug. 22 and 23, 1897; *News,* Aug. 23.

First days of trial: *Journal, News,* and *Tribune,* Aug. 23 and 24.

Background of Tuthill: *The Bench and Bar of Chicago, Biographical Sketches* (Chicago: American Biographical, 1890), 140–44; *Memorials of Deceased Companions of the Commandery of the State of Illinois Military Order of the Loyal Legion of the United States,* vol. 3, Jan. 1, 1912–Dec. 31, 1922 (Chicago: Commandery of the State of Illinois, 1923), 582; *Journal,* Sept. 22, 1897.

Description of Deneen: Robert P. Howard, *Mostly Good and Competent Men: Illinois Governors, 1818–1988* (Springfield, Ill.: Illinois Issues, Sangamon State University and Illinois State Historical Society, 1988), 211–18; *Times-Herald,* Jan. 2, 1898.

McEwen: *News,* Sept. 15, 1897; *Chronicle,* Nov. 7, 1900.

Vincent: *Herringshaw's Encyclopedia of American Biography of the Nineteenth Century* (Chicago: American Publishers' Association, 1902), 964; Norman Anderson, *Ferris Wheel: An Illustrated History* (Bowling Green, Ohio: Bowling Green State University Popular Press, 1992), 55, 62; *News,* Sept. 17, 1897.

Bicknese confronts Luetgert: *Journal,* Aug. 24.

Jury selection: *News,* Aug. 24, 25, and 27; *Tribune,* Aug. 28; *Record,* Oct. 19.

CHAPTER 16: THE RUSTLING NOISE

McEwen's opening argument: *News,* Aug. 30, 1897; *Record,* Aug. 31.

Bicknese's testimony: *News,* Aug. 30; *Tribune* and *Record,* Aug. 31.

Note on "Low Dutch": Hofmeister, 54.

Louis Luetgert's testimony: *News,* Aug. 30; *Tribune, Record,* and *Inter Ocean,* Aug. 31.

Christison "connected with the defense": *Inter Ocean,* Sept. 1.

Christison talks with Elmer: Christison, 154–55.

CHAPTER 17: THE MORBID WOMEN

Crowd scenes: *News,* Sept. 1, 3, and 7, 1897; *Record,* Sept. 3 and 25; *Journal,* Sept. 3 and 4; *Inter Ocean,* Sept. 15.

Newspaper reporters: *News,* Aug. 26 and Sept. 10; *Times-Herald,* Sept. 19; Charles Deneen scrapbooks.

Descriptions of women: *Inter Ocean,* Sept. 1; Katharine, *Chronicle,* Sept. 3; *New York World,* Sept. 4; H. Gilson Gardner, *Journal,* Sept. 11; Hawthorne, *New York Journal,* Sept. 3.

Julian Hawthorne's background: Maurice Bassan, *Hawthorne's Son: The Life and Literary Career of Julian Hawthorne* (Columbus: Ohio State University Press, 1970), ix–xi, 202–3; Ben Proctor, *William Randolph Hearst: The Early Years, 1863–1910* (Oxford: Oxford University Press, 1998), 81, 90.

Letter from "A WOMAN": *Tribune,* Sept. 4.

CHAPTER 18: TRAINED BEASTS

Tosch's testimony: *News*, Aug. 31, 1897; *Record*, Sept. 1. (In Tosch's testimony the names *Mary* and *Mrs. Luetgert* have sometimes been substituted for pronouns to clarify the meaning.)

Bialk's testimony: *News*, Aug. 31; *Record*, Sept. 1.

Luetgert's reaction to testimony: *Inter Ocean*, Sept. 1.

Luetgert's appearance, comments on witnesses: *News*, Sept. 1.

Bialk's cross-examination: *News*, Sept. 1; *Record*, Sept. 2.

Odorofsky's testimony: *Record*, *Inter Ocean*, and *News*, Sept. 2; *Tribune*, Sept. 3.

Lavandowski's testimony: *News*, Sept. 2.

"These men are as simple": Hawthorne, *New York Journal*, Sept. 3.

Anonymous lawyer's comment: *News*, Sept. 1.

John P. Clark's testimony: *Record*, Sept. 3.

CHAPTER 19: TRIAL BY NEWSPAPER

Descriptions of Luetgert: *News*, Sept. 3, 1897; Katharine, *Chronicle*, Sept. 3; H. Gilson Gardner, *Journal*, Sept. 14; Hawthorne, *New York Journal*, Sept. 3; *Tribune*, Sept. 3 and 4 (Hawthorne's allusion to Ralph Waldo Emerson is a quotation from the 1846 poem "Hamatreya").

Critique of sketch artists: *Inter Ocean*, Sept. 20.

Comment on pictures of women: *St. Paul Dispatch*, Oct. 1.

Schuettler testifies about ring: *Record*, Sept. 3; Hawthorne, *New York Journal*, Sept. 3 (Hawthorne quotes Horatio from Shakespeare's *Hamlet*).

Critiques of press coverage: *News*, Sept. 3; *Inter Ocean*, Sept. 12; *Waukegan Gazette*, Sept. 11; *Tribune*, Sept. 4; *Kansas City Times*, Sept. 12; *Rochester Port and Express*, Sept. 14.

Jacob Kern's anecdote: *Record*, Oct. 22.

CHAPTER 20: THE THROWING MANIA

Divorce court: *News*, May 1, 1897.

Stanger's testimony: *News*, Sept. 3.

Pancake editorial: *Chronicle*, Sept. 5.

Voelcker's testimony: *News* and *Journal*, Sept. 3; *Abendpost*, Sept. 4.

Grieser's testimony: *News*, Sept. 4.

Schultz's testimony: *Tribune* and *News*, Sept. 8.

Debate over the rings: *Times-Herald*, Sept. 21.

Testimony of Harris, Tews, and Mueller: *News*, Sept. 3 and 4.

Description of Luetgert: *News*, Sept. 4.

CHAPTER 21: THE WIDOW

Rumor of Feld fleeing country: *Record*, Aug. 25, 1897.
Descriptions of Feld: *News*, Sept. 4; *Tribune*, Sept. 5; *Inter Ocean*, Sept. 5; Hawthorne, *New York Journal*, Sept. 5.
Feld's testimony: *News*, Sept. 4; *Tribune*, Sept. 5.
Luetgert's letters to Feld: *News*, Sept. 4; *Tribune*, Sept. 5; *Abendpost*, Sept. 6.
Comment on Luetgert's writing: *News*, Sept. 7.
Feld's testimony continues: *News*, Sept. 7.
Luetgert's comment about knife: *News*, Sept. 9.

CHAPTER 22: THE EXPERIMENTS

Reporter approaches factory: *Inter Ocean*, Aug. 29, 1897.
Experiments: *Tribune*, Aug. 31; *Journal*, Sept. 20.
Sausage Society: *Chronicle*, Oct. 10.
Curiosity seekers: *News* and *Chronicle*, Sept. 6.

CHAPTER 23: CRIES AND WHISPERS

Hengst's testimony: *News*, Sept. 8, 1897.
Faber's testimony: *News*, Sept. 7; *Tribune*, Sept. 8; Hawthorne, *New York Journal*, Sept. 8.
Gottliebe Schimke's testimony: *News*, Sept. 4; *Tribune*, Sept. 5.
Emma Schimke's testimony: *News*, Sept. 8.

CHAPTER 24: THE EXPERTS

Delafontaine's testimony: *News*, Sept. 9 and 10, 1897; Hawthorne, *New York Journal*, Sept. 10 and 11; *Inter Ocean*, Sept. 10; *Tribune*, Sept. 11.
Description of evidence in the courtroom and Luetgert's reaction: *Journal*, Sept. 9; *Tribune*, Sept. 10.
Haines's testimony: *Record*, Sept. 10.
Bailey's testimony: *Tribune*, Sept. 11; *News*, Sept. 11, 13, and 15.
Fowler's illness: *News*, Sept. 13 and 15.
Comical stories about Bailey: *News*, Sept. 14.
Dorsey's background: Eugene Giles and Linda L. Klepinger, "The Butcher Who Rendered His Wife? Chicago's Luetgert Case and the Beginning of American Forensic Anthropology," *Proceedings of the American Academy of Forensic Sciences* 5 (1999): 295.
Dorsey's testimony: *Journal*, Sept. 15, 1897; *Tribune*, Sept. 16; Hawthorne, *New York Journal*, Sept. 17.
Spengler's testimony: *Times-Herald*, Sept. 18.
Corset makers: Hawthorne, *New York Journal*, Sept. 9.

Klein's testimony: *News,* Sept. 8.
Experts' obsession with Luetgert case: *Chronicle,* Sept. 26.
McEwen's comment on corpus delicti: *News,* Sept. 16.
Hawthorne's commentary: Hawthorne, *New York Journal,* Sept. 9 and 10.

CHAPTER 25: AUTUMN

Heat wave: *Tribune,* Sept. 19, 1897; *News,* Sept. 10.
The Loop: *Tribune,* Oct. 3, 1897; George Ade, "Stories of the Street and of the Town," *Record,* Oct. 22; *Tribune,* Jan. 2, 1898.
Newsboys: *Chronicle,* Sept. 30, 1897.
Klondike fever: Ade, *Record,* Aug. 30 and 31, Sept. 2.
Bates's story: *Tribune,* Aug. 5.
Dime museums: Perry Duis, *Challenging Chicago: Coping with Everyday Life, 1837–1920* (Urbana: University of Illinois Press, 1998), 206–7.
J. H. O. Smith's sermon: *Tribune,* Sept. 29, 1897.
Mr. Dooley: Barbara Schaaf, *Mr. Dooley's Chicago* (Garden City, N.Y.: Anchor Press/Doubleday, 1977), 99.
Drug advertisement: *Journal,* Sept. 24, 1897.
Sausage sales: *DeKalb (Ill.) Chronicle,* Aug. 25; *Bloomington (Ill.) Eye,* Sept. 12; *Times-Herald,* Sept. 26 and Oct. 10.
Number of sausage manufacturers: *Tribune,* Jan. 1, 1898.

CHAPTER 26: THE KISS

Schaack's testimony: *News,* Sept. 15, 1897; Hawthorne, *New York Journal,* Sept. 16.
Vincent's comment: *News,* Sept. 18.
Seelig's testimony: *News,* Sept. 18; Hawthorne, *New York Journal,* Sept. 19.
Argument over allowing testimony: *News,* Sept. 18; Hawthorne, *New York Journal,* Sept. 19.
Tuthill's decision: *Times-Herald,* Sept. 22.
Testimony of Bialk, Odorofsky, and Johnson: *Record,* Sept. 22; *Tribune,* Sept. 23.

CHAPTER 27: SIDESHOWS

Story of Lizzie Adams: *Chronicle,* Aug. 27, 1897.
Threats against Schaack: *News,* Sept. 13.
Story of Alexander McIvor-Tyndall: *Journal,* Oct. 2; *Chronicle,* Oct. 3; *Times-Herald,* Oct. 4; *Tribune,* Oct. 3 and 5; *Dispatch,* Oct. 7.
Phonograph in courtroom: *New York Journal,* Oct. 4.
Phonograph at jail: *Chicago Journal,* Oct. 6.
Play at Aurora Turner Hall: *Chronicle* and *Tribune,* Oct. 9; *Times-Herald* and *Record,* Oct. 11.

Letters received by Vincent: *Chronicle,* Oct. 10.

Letters from women to Luetgert: *News,* Oct. 22; *Record,* Oct. 23; *New York World,* Oct. 31; *St. Paul Dispatch,* Oct. 1.

Letter to Tuthill: *Times-Herald,* Sept. 22, 1897.

"Munchausen": *News,* Sept. 15.

CHAPTER 28: A GAME OF TAG

Vincent's speech and Gleich's testimony: *Record,* Sept. 22, 1897; Hawthorne, *New York Journal,* Sept. 23.

Police following witnesses: *Chronicle,* Sept. 24.

Tuthill's reaction to allegations about police, Gleich's second day of testimony: *Record,* Sept. 23.

Fiedler's testimony: *Tribune,* Sept. 25.

Testimony of Bockelman, Shaughnessy, and Larsen: *Record,* Sept. 28; *Tribune,* Sept. 29.

Scherer's testimony: *Record,* Sept. 24; *Tribune,* Sept. 25.

Emma Schimke's testimony: *Record,* Sept. 23; *Tribune,* Sept. 24.

Mills's testimony: *Record,* Oct. 5.

Hawthorne's commentary: Hawthorne, *New York Journal,* Sept. 25.

CHAPTER 29: JUST A PLAIN DOMESTIC GIRL

Mrs. Luetgert's "peculiar malady": Christison, 156–60.

Tuthill's ruling on evidence, Kaiser's testimony: *Tribune,* Sept. 25, 1897; Hawthorne, *New York Journal,* Sept. 25.

Siemering's testimony: *Record,* Sept. 25; *Tribune,* Sept. 26 and 28; Hawthorne, *New York Journal,* Sept. 26.

CHAPTER 30: THE MANY MRS. LUETGERTS

Decatur: *Tribune,* May 22, 1897.

Tekamah, Neb.: *Tribune,* Oct. 5.

Tonawanda, N.Y.: *Record,* Sept. 3.

Ashland, Wis.: *Tribune,* Dec. 11.

Peoria: *Record,* Sept. 30.

Remarks by Vincent: *Boston Herald,* Sept. 21.

"I have been imprisoned": *Green Bay (Wis.) Advocate,* Aug. 13.

Letter thrown from steamer: *News,* Oct. 16.

Ring inscribed with knife: *News,* Sept. 7.

Summit County, Ohio: *Cleveland World,* Dec. 29.

Helena, Mont.: *Tribune,* Sept. 16.

McEwen comment: *News,* Sept. 16.

New York: *Tribune,* July 20 and Aug. 10; *Journal,* Aug. 19; *Record,* Sept. 3.

Melrose Park: *Dispatch* and *Journal,* Sept. 14; *News* and *Tribune,* Sept. 15.
Washington Park: *Tribune,* Sept. 26.
Morris, Ill.: *Tribune,* Sept. 29.
Indiana: *Record,* Oct. 6, 7, and 9; *Inter Ocean,* Oct. 8 and 9.
Mills's Wisconsin investigation: *Tribune,* Sept. 1.
Oshkosh, Wis.: *Tribune,* Sept. 26.
Daisy Thompson: *Kewanee (Ill.) Star,* Nov. 20.
Boston: *Record,* Dec. 10.
Arthur Mundwiller: *Record,* Sept. 24.
Jacob Melber: *Tribune,* Sept. 28.
Armadale Opdyke: *Record,* Sept. 28; *Tribune,* Sept. 29.
Testimony of Kenosha witnesses: *Journal,* Sept. 23; *Tribune,* Sept. 24–25; *Record,* Sept. 24; Hawthorne, *New York Journal,* Sept. 24.

CHAPTER 31: SOAP AND BONES

Charles's testimony: *Record,* Sept. 27, 1897; *Tribune,* Sept. 28.
Gottschalk's testimony: *Record,* Oct. 4; *Tribune,* Oct. 5.
Riese's testimony: *Record,* Sept. 28; *Tribune,* Sept. 29.
Allport's testimony: Hawthorne, *New York Journal,* Sept. 30 and Oct. 1; *Record,* Sept. 30 and Oct. 1; *Tribune,* Oct. 1 and 2.
Rutherford's comments: *Tribune,* Oct. 2.
Spectators doze: *Tribune,* Oct. 3; *Journal,* Oct. 2.
Bicknese's comments: *Journal,* Oct. 2.

CHAPTER 32: CIGAR TALK

Interviews with Luetgert: *News,* Sept. 2, 9, and 11, 1897; *Journal,* Aug. 25 and 27, Sept. 18; *Abendpost,* Sept. 6; *Dispatch,* Sept. 9.
Christison's comments: Christison, 163–64.
John G. Dame: *Dispatch,* Oct. 11, 1897.
Luetgert and Kelly: *News,* Sept. 2.
Special treatment: *Journal, Dispatch,* and *Record,* Sept. 9.
Tooth pulling: *News,* Sept. 14.
Walking with crutches: *Journal,* Sept. 16; *Inter Ocean,* Sept. 17; *Tribune,* Sept. 20.
Interview with Katharine: *Chronicle,* Sept. 19.
Luetgert's insistence on testifying: *News,* Sept. 2 and 15.
Luetgert's lawyers persuade him not to testify: *Record,* Oct. 5; *Tribune,* Oct. 5 and 6.

CHAPTER 33: ORATORY

Prosecution rebuttal and defense surrebuttal testimony: *Record,* Oct. 6, 7, 8, and 12, 1897; *Tribune,* Oct. 7, 8, and 9.
McEwen's speech: *Record,* Oct. 12.

Phalen's speech: *Record*, Oct. 14.

Vincent's speech: *Record*, Oct. 15; *Journal*, Oct. 14, 15, and 16.

Crowd's reaction to Vincent's speech: *News*, Oct. 16.

CHAPTER 34: TWELVE MEN

Bailiffs escorting jurors: *News*, Oct. 16, 1897.

The daily life of the jurors: *Chronicle*, Oct. 25.

Baseball game: *Tribune*, Sept. 29.

Deliberations: *Journal*, Oct. 19, *Tribune*, Oct. 20.

CHAPTER 35: QUEER REPORTS

Bribery letter and police comments: *Record*, Oct. 20, 1897.

Harlev's history: *Inter Ocean* and *Record*, Oct. 21; *Times*, Sept. 25, 1888.

Crowd waits outside courthouse: *Tribune*, Oct. 20, 1897; *Abendpost* and *Journal*, Oct. 19.

Luetgert's children visit jail: *Abendpost*, Oct. 19.

Luetgert talks to reporter: *Record*, Oct. 20.

Luetgert gets angry: *Tribune*, Oct. 20.

Journal reports jury deliberations: *Journal*, Oct. 20.

Reaction in Des Moines: *Des Moines Leader* and *Des Moines Register*, Oct. 20.

Jurors question Tuthill, and Luetgert speaks to Deneen: *Tribune* and *Record*, Oct. 21.

CHAPTER 36: TELESCOPIC VIEWS

Luetgert's children visit jail: *Chronicle*, Oct. 21, 1897.

Reporters watch from roofs: *Chronicle* and *Record*, Oct. 21.

Orators in the street: *Tribune* and *Chronicle*, Oct. 21.

Jury deliberations: *Journal*, Oct. 21.

Jury announces deadlock: *Chronicle*, *Journal*, and *News*, Oct. 21; *Record* and *Tribune*, Oct. 22; *Georgetown (Del.) Journal*, Oct. 23.

Jury's statement: Office of the Clerk of the Circuit Court of Cook County, archives.

CHAPTER 37: AFTERMATH

Schaack: *News*, Oct. 21, 1897.

Tuthill: *News*, Oct. 21; *Record*, Oct. 22.

Arnold Luetgert: *Journal*, Oct. 21.

Boyd: *News*, Oct. 21; *Tribune*, Oct. 22.

Crowd follows jurors: *Journal*, Oct. 21.

Behmiller: *News*, Oct. 21.

Jurors astonished: *Journal*, Oct. 21.

Bibby: *Tribune*, Oct. 22.

Franzen and Fowler: *Tribune* and *Record*, Oct. 22.

Harlev: *Journal* and *News*, Oct. 21; *Chronicle*, Oct. 24; *Record*, Oct. 23.

Holabird: *Tribune*, Oct. 22.

Mahoney: *Record*, Oct. 22.

Luetgert interviewed at jail: *News*, Oct. 21; *Record*, Oct. 22.

Whitman: *St. Louis Star Sayings*, Oct. 21.

CHAPTER 38: EDITORIALS

The editorials quoted in this chapter are from the *Hartford (Conn.) Times*, Oct. 21, 1897; *Buffalo Enquirer*, Oct. 21; *Los Angeles Times*, Oct. 21; *Milwaukee News*, Oct. 21; *Newport News (Va.) Press*, Oct. 22; *Sacramento Record Union*, Oct. 21; *Washington (Del.) Post*, Oct. 22; *Des Moines News*, Oct. 25; *Bloomington (Ill.) Pantagraph*, Oct. 22; *Chronicle*, Oct. 22; *Tribune*, Oct. 24; *News*, Oct. 22 and Oct. 23; *Minneapolis Journal*, Oct. 1; *Streator (Ill.) Free Press*, Oct. 1; *Philadelphia Press*, repr. in the *Trenton (N.J.) Advertiser*, Oct. 31; *Buffalo News*, Oct. 22; *New York Journal*, Oct. 21; *Peoria Journal*, Nov. 27; *Syracuse (N.Y.) Courier*, Oct. 12.

Circulation figures: *Journal*, Nov. 3; *Chicago Daily News Almanac, 1898*, 423.

H. Gilson Gardner column: *Journal*, Sept. 21, 1897.

CHAPTER 39: BETWEEN TRIALS

Luetgert comment on bail: *News*, Oct. 27, 1897.

Charles raising funds: *Tribune*, Oct. 23.

Luetgert on museum offer: *New York Times*, Oct. 23.

Book offer: *Record*, Oct. 23.

Article by Luetgert: *St. Louis Republic*, Oct. 24.

Police dismissals: *Tribune* and *Dispatch*, Oct. 27; *Journal*, Oct. 28.

Letter from Colorado: *Chronicle*, Oct. 31; *News*, Nov. 1.

Vincent withdraws from case: *Dispatch* and *News*, Nov. 10; *Journal*, Nov. 10, 13, and 17.

Palmist Bernhard Cola: *Journal* and *Post*, Nov. 18.

Harmon and Reise hired: *News*, Nov. 25, 29, and 30; *Tribune*, Nov. 29.

Jailbreak and subsequent crackdown: *Tribune*, Nov. 21 and 28.

Story of John H. Dame: *Denver Times*, Nov. 29; *Denver Post*, Nov. 30; *Denver Republican*, Nov. 30.

CHAPTER 40: TURBULENCE

Background of Gary: Avrich, 252–53, 262–66, 281, 303, 423; Henry David, *The History of the Haymarket Affair: A Study in the American Social-Revolutionary and La-*

bor Movements (New York: Russell and Russell, 1936), 240–41, 245, 249–50, 309–10, 495; *Journal,* Nov. 23, 1897; *Chronicle,* Nov. 21, 1903.

Guard fails to recognize Gary: *Journal,* Oct. 12.

Luetgert's comments: *News,* Nov. 23 and 24.

Jury selection: *News,* Dec. 2, 4, 8, 10, and 14; *Journal,* Nov. 30 and Dec. 2.

Arrangement of courtroom: *Journal,* Dec. 8.

Affidavits on Boasberg: Office of the Clerk of the Cook County Circuit Court.

Luetgert's comment on Boasberg: *Journal,* Dec. 16, 1897.

Comments from lawyers: *News,* Dec. 16.

Friction between attorneys: *Inter Ocean* and *Journal,* Dec. 23.

Harmon questioning Schuettler: *Journal,* Dec. 20.

Arnold Luetgert on forged checks: *Journal,* Dec. 21.

Adolph Luetgert's plea for funds: *Inter Ocean,* Dec. 7.

Tosch: *News,* Dec. 27; *Inter Ocean,* Dec. 28.

Stenographers quit: *News* and *Inter Ocean,* Dec. 29.

Argument over rings: *Inter Ocean,* Dec. 30.

Edward Cady: *Chronicle,* Jan. 8, 1898.

Feld: *Chronicle,* Jan. 8 and 9; *Tribune* and *Inter Ocean,* Jan. 9.

Frank Hangel: *Tribune,* Jan. 12; *Inter Ocean,* Jan. 13.

Arguments between attorneys and questioning of scientists: *Tribune,* Jan. 12 and 15; *News* and *Inter Ocean,* Jan. 13; *Chronicle,* Jan. 14.

Change in bone exhibits: *Record,* Jan. 5; *Chronicle,* Jan. 15.

Delafontaine loses bones: *Journal,* Jan. 4.

CHAPTER 41: THE GHOULS

Frequent scandals: Duis, 335.

Morgue thefts and arrest of Ulrich and Ludes: *Journal,* Oct. 25 and 28 and Dec. 19 and 22, 1897; *Tribune,* Oct. 25; *Inter Ocean,* Oct. 26, Dec. 6.

Supposed police plot to remove bones: *Chronicle,* Jan. 2; *Inter Ocean,* Jan. 2 and 4; *News* and *Journal,* Jan. 3; *Tribune,* Jan. 4.

Authorities intimidate Ulrich: *Chronicle,* Jan. 6.

Schaack testifies: *Tribune* and *Inter Ocean,* Jan. 4.

Schaack takes time off: *Chronicle,* Jan. 13.

Dr. Smith's statement and the reactions to it: *Times-Herald,* Jan. 9 and 10; *Tribune,* Jan. 10 and 11.

Missouri refuses to extradite: *Journal,* Jan. 12.

Healy's edicts against gossip: *Inter Ocean,* Jan. 14; *Tribune,* Jan. 15.

CHAPTER 42: DENIALS

Description of court as Luetgert is called to testify: *Chronicle,* Jan. 22, 1897; *Tribune,* Jan. 22 and 31.

Luetgert's testimony: *Chronicle*, Jan. 22, 23, and 25; *Tribune*, Jan. 22, 23, 25, and 31; *Record*, Jan. 25 and 26; *News*, Jan. 21 and 25; *Journal*, Jan. 21.

Statistics on Luetgert's testimony: *Record*, Feb. 10.

Commentary on Luetgert's testimony: *Record*, Jan. 26; *Tribune*, Jan. 31.

CHAPTER 43: WINTER

Feld sees apparitions: *Chronicle*, Dec. 22.

Waber's alchemy business: *News*, Dec. 13.

Schaack and Harry Morris: *Chronicle*, Jan. 7.

Snowstorm and sleighing: *Tribune*, Jan. 24, 30, and 31; *Record*, Jan. 24.

Elmer Gates: *Tribune*, Jan. 2.

John Benson: *Tribune*, Jan. 3.

Comments on Merry: *Tribune*, Jan. 2.

CHAPTER 44: THE VERDICT

Rumors about Mrs. Luetgert impersonators: *Journal*, Dec. 22, 1897; *News*, Dec. 27; *Chronicle*, Jan. 1, 1898.

Bribery rumors: *Inter Ocean*, Dec. 11, 1897.

Monmouth witnesses, Otto Klatt, and Theodore Arndt: *Record*, Jan. 26 and 27, 1898; *News* and *Journal*, Jan. 26; *Tribune*, Jan. 27.

McEwen and "cheap trick": *Tribune*, Jan. 20.

Joe Detloff: *Tribune* and *Record*, Jan. 29.

Reporters testify: *Post*, Jan. 28.

Gary admonishes Harmon: *Tribune*, Jan. 30.

Closing arguments: *Record*, Feb. 2 and 10; *Tribune*, Feb. 10.

Verdict: *Record* and *Tribune*, Feb. 10.

CHAPTER 45: LINES OF DESTINY

Interview with Luetgert: *Journal*, Feb. 10, 1898.

Editorials: *Washington Star*, Feb. 10; *Buffalo Enquirer*, Feb. 10; *Brooklyn Eagle*, Feb. 10; *Baltimore Herald*, Feb. 11; *Buffalo Times*, Feb. 10; *Journal*, Feb. 10; *Green Bay Advocate*, Feb. 10.

Average sentence at Joliet for murder: *Report of the Commissioners of the Illinois State Penitentiary at Joliet for the Two Years Ending September 30, 1900* (Springfield: Phillips Bros., State Printers, 1901), 75.

Bacheler's and Loeb's comments: *Journal*, Feb. 10.

Christopher Merry: *Tribune* and *Journal*, Feb. 14.

Pratt's explanation of palmistry: *Journal*, Feb. 12.

Angry woman visits jail: *Dispatch*, Feb. 17.

Luetgert's train ride and arrival in Joliet: *Chronicle*, Mar. 6; *Tribune*, Mar. 6–8.

Description of prison: S. W. Wetmore, *Behind the Bars at Joliet: A Peep at a Prison, Its History, and Its Mysteries* (Joliet: J. O. Gorman, 1892), 20, 22, 25, 34, 210–14; S. W. Wetmore, *New York Illustrated American,* Mar. 8, 1890.

Luetgert's prison form: Illinois Department of Corrections files.

Prison conditions: *Report of the Commissioners,* 10–12, 25–32.

Ages of inmates: ibid., 71.

Schaack's death: *Tribune,* May 19, 1898.

CHAPTER 46: PRISONER 5969

Luetgert's life in prison: *Record* and *Times-Herald,* July 28, 1899.

Luetgert's comment on Bicknese: *Dispatch,* Feb. 26, 1898.

July 20 incident: *Record* and *Times-Herald,* July 28; Illinois Department of Corrections files.

Description of a typical morning in the prison: Wetmore, *Behind the Bars* 20–33.

Death of Luetgert and reactions to it: *News* and *Journal,* July 27, 1899; *Tribune, Record, Times-Herald,* and *Inter Ocean,* July 28.

Custody battle over Luetgert's children: Office of the Clerk of the Cook County Circuit Court, probate court archives.

CHAPTER 47: CONFESSIONS AND EULOGIES

Pratt's story: *Journal,* July 28, 1899; *Record,* July 31.

Harmon and Arnold Luetgert's reaction: *Tribune,* July 29.

Clarence Darrow: *Inter Ocean,* July 30.

Whitman: *Tribune,* July 30.

Deneen's additional evidence: *Tribune,* July 28 and 30.

Luetgert's funeral and burial: *Tribune, Inter Ocean, Times-Herald* and *Record,* July 31.

Description of Waldheim Cemetery: Andreas Simon, ed., *Chicago: The Garden City: Its Magnificent Parks, Boulevards, and Cemeteries* (Chicago: Franz Gindele, 1893), 167.

EPILOGUE

Medico-Legal Society meeting: *Chicago Medical Recorder* 16:172–79.

Dorsey divorce: *Tribune,* July 4, 1922.

T. D. Stewart, "George A. Dorsey's Role in the Luetgert Case: A Significant Episode in the History of Forensic Anthropology," *Journal of Forensic Sciences* 23, no. 4 (1978): 790.

Quote from Giles and Klepinger: Giles and Klepinger, 295.

Quote from Snow: Clyde Collins Snow, "Forensic Anthropology," *Annual Review of Anthropology* 11 (1982): 100–102.

Frye case: Kenneth R. Foster and Peter W. Huber, *Judging Science: Scientific Knowledge and the Federal Courts* (Cambridge, Mass.: MIT Press, 1997), 11, 225.

Changes in Frye rule: ibid., 11, 13, 226, 229.

Supreme Court ruling: U.S. Supreme Court, no. 92–102, William Daubert *v.* Merrell Dow Pharmaceuticals, Inc., June 28, 1993.

Jurors can be misled: Foster and Huber, 215, 250.

European system: Joyce and Stover, 75–76.

Christison's comments: Christison, 138–77.

Pinkerton's comments: Matthew Worth Pinkerton, *Murder in All Ages* (1898), 492–508.

Footnote on Pinkerton: William A. Pinkerton, letter dated Feb. 19, 1918, to the Chicago Historical Society.

Wigmore's comments: Wigmore, 187–207.

"Men learned in criminal lore": *Tribune*, Nov. 2, 1913.

DNA: e-mail correspondence with Jack Ballantyne, a forensic geneticist at National Center for Forensic Science, and the University of Illinois anthropology professor Eugene Giles; *New York Times*, July 10, 1993.

Clarence Darrow: *Inter Ocean*, July 30, 1899.

Diedrich Bicknese's death: correspondence from Jim Luetgert.

Odorofsky, Lavandowski, Bialk, and Feld: *News*, July 27, 1899.

Feld's court document: Office of the Clerk of Cook County Circuit Court archives, Circuit Court case 182789, Ernst Reuback *v.* Christine Feld, filed Mar. 29, 1898.

John Bialk: *Tribune*, Sept. 25, 1916.

Gary's birthday speech: Alexander F. Stevenson, *Memorial of Joseph E. Gary* (speech booklet in Chicago Historical Society collection, 1906), 20.

Gary's death: *Tribune*, Nov. 1, 1906.

Tuthill's Shakespeare ruling: *Tribune*, Apr. 22, 1916.

Tuthill's death: *News*, Apr. 10, 1920; *Tribune*, Apr. 11.

Deneen: *Times-Herald*, Jan. 2, 1898; Howard, 211–18.

Chicago Police: Office of the Clerk of Cook County Circuit Court, archives; *Tribune*, Jan. 7, 9, 14, and 30, Feb. 24, Mar. 6 and 11, 1898; *Inter Ocean*, Jan. 12, 14, and 27, 1898; *Chronicle*, Jan. 24 and Feb. 13, 1898.

Schuettler and Car Barn Bandits: Asbury, 223–31.

Schuettler's gambling raids: Lindberg, 102–4.

Schuettler's death: *Tribune*, Aug. 23, 1918; *News*, Aug. 23.

Christison: *Tribune*, May 9 and 10, 1908; Cook County Coroner's inquest no. 45049.

Bailey's later life: correspondence with Thelma M. Bailey.

Hawthorne in Cuba: Proctor, 117–18.

Hawthorne's fraud case and later years: Bassan, 212–24.

Louise Luetgert summoned to court: Office of the Clerk of Cook County Circuit Court, archives, Superior Court case 190071, William Eckhardt *v.* Adolph L. Luetgert et al., filed Aug. 5, 1898.

Children's song: *Herald-American*, Mar. 17, 1949.

Albert Boyer visits factory: *Journal*, Aug. 31, 1899.

Sale of Luetgert property: Office of the Cook County Recorder of Deeds.

Fire: *Tribune, Chronicle, Journal, Inter Ocean*, and *Abendpost*, June 27, 1904.

Luetgert house moved: *Evening Post*, Sept. 18, 1907; *Record-Herald* and *American*, Sept. 19.

Arnold Luetgert's suicide: *News*, Oct. 17, 1908.

Later story of Luetgert family: correspondence and interviews with Jim and M. J. Luetgert.

Index

ROBERT LOERZEL, a graduate of the University of Illinois at Urbana-Champaign with a degree in journalism, writes and edits arts and entertainment coverage for Pioneer Press newspapers in the suburbs of Chicago. He has received numerous awards from the Illinois Press Association, the Chicago Headline Club, and other press organizations for investigative reporting, feature stories, and the editing of newspaper sections. He runs the Web sites alchemyofbones.com, which includes special features on many of the topics covered in this book, and robertloerzel.com.

The University of Illinois Press
is a founding member of the
Association of American University Presses.

Composed in 10.5/14 Minion
with Modula Tall display
by Jim Proefrock
at the University of Illinois Press
Designed by Paula Newcomb
Manufactured by Cushing-Malloy, Inc.

University of Illinois Press
1325 South Oak Street
Champaign, IL 61820-6903
www.press.uillinois.edu